PATERNOSTER BIBLICAL AND THEOLOGICAL MONOGRAPHS

Attributes and Atonement:
The Holy Love of God
in the Theology of P.T. Forsyth

Titles in this Series

Daniel J-S Chae
Paul as Apostle to the Gentiles
His Apostolic Self-Awareness and its Influence on the Soteriological Argument in Romans

Stephen M Dunning
The Crisis and the Quest
A Kierkegaardian Reading of Charles Williams

Keith Ferdinando
The Triumph of Christ in African Perspective
A Study of Demonology and Redemption in the African Context

R T Kendall
Calvin and English Calvinism to 1649

Leslie McCurdy
Attributes and Atonement
The Holy Love of God in the Theology of P T Forsyth

Stephen Motyer
Your Father the Devil?
A New Approach to John and 'the Jews'

David Powys
'Hell': A Hard Look at a Hard Question
The Fate of the Unrighteous in N T Thought

Ian M Randall
Evangelical Experiences
A Study in the Spirituality of English Evangelicalism 1918-1939

G M Thomas
The Extent of the Atonement
A Dilemma for Reformed Theology from Calvin to the Consensus

Graham Tomlin
The Power of the Cross
Theology and the Death of Christ in Paul, Luther and Pascal

Peter Taylor Forsyth (Photo: Copyright © Dr Williams's Library)

PATERNOSTER BIBLICAL AND THEOLOGICAL MONOGRAPHS

Attributes and Atonement:
The Holy Love of God
in the Theology of P. T. Forsyth

Leslie McCurdy

paternoster

Copyright © Leslie McCurdy 1999

Published by Paternoster Press,
P. O. Box 300, Carlisle, Cumbria CA3 0QS United Kingdom

03 02 01 00 99 98   7 6 5 4 3 2 1

The right of Leslie McCurdy to be identified as the author of this work has been asserted by him in accordance with the Copyright, Designs and Patents Act 1988.

All rights reserved. No part of this publication may be reproduced, stored in a retrieval system, or transmitted in any form or by any means, electronic, mechanical, photocopying, recording, or otherwise, without the prior permission of the publisher or a license permitting restricted copying. In the U.K. such licenses are issued by the Copyright Licensing Agency, 90 Tottenham Court Road, London W1P 9HE.

British Library Cataloguing in Publication Data

A record for this title is available
from the British Library

ISBN 0-85364-833-6

Typeset by the author
Printed and bound in Great Britain
for Paternoster Publishing
by Nottingham Alpha Graphics

In 1912, P.T. Forsyth presented his wife with a copy of his most recent book, *Marriage: Its Ethic and Religion,* and inscribed it with words that I adapt by way of dedication.

To Katharina

"true yokefellow" and therefore co–author

Contents

Contents vii
Preface and Acknowledgments ix
Abbreviations xii
1 – P. T. Forsyth and God's Holy Love 1
   1. SAMPLING THE SIMPLICITY, EXPLORING THE GRAMMAR 2
   2. 'HOLY LOVE': AN EXPRESSION WITH A HISTORY 5
   3. THE INTRODUCTION OF HOLY LOVE IN FORSYTH'S THEOLOGY 14
   4. THE EXPERIENCE OF HOLY LOVE 23
2 – Literature Survey 39
   1. FORSYTH'S VIEW OF ATONEMENT AND ATTRIBUTES IN ACADEMIC CONTEXT 40
   2. EARLY RESPONSE TO FORSYTH'S THEOLOGY 42
   3. THE POST-WAR RENAISSANCE IN FORSYTH STUDY 45
   4. HOLINESS, LOVE, AND HOLY LOVE: THE DEBATE ILLUSTRATED ... 54
3 – The Knowledge of God 56
   1. THE POSSIBILITY OF A NATURAL THEOLOGY 58
   2. CONSCIENCE AND CHRIST 60
   3. CONSCIENCE AND CORRELATION 64
   4. CONSCIENCE AS A POINT OF CONTACT 69
   5. THE POWER OF SIN, AND THE LIMITED VALUE OF GENERAL REVELATION 73
   6. THE GOSPEL RECONSTRUCTS OUR VIEW OF CONSCIENCE 78
   7. IMPLICATIONS FOR THE PRESENT STUDY 80
   8. A CHRISTOLOGICAL STARTING-POINT 83
   9. A QUESTION OF ONTOLOGY 85
   10. THE INCARNATION AND THE ATONEMENT 88
   11. THE CENTRALITY OF THE CROSS 93

4 – The Attributes of God 94
   1. PROCEDURAL DIFFICULTIES AND POSSIBILITIES 94
   2. REVEALED RATHER THAN DISCOVERED 97
   3. TWO REPRESENTATIVE ATTRIBUTES 100
   4. THE FATHERHOOD OF GOD 107
   5. EXPRESSIONS OF THE DYNAMIC GOD 112
   6. GOD IS PERSONAL – AND FREE 114
   7. MORAL UNITY AND FUNCTIONAL DISTINCTIONS 117

5 – The Prominence of Love 123
   1. THE PROMINENT PLACE OF GOD'S LOVE IN FORSYTH'S WRITINGS 124
   2. THE CHARACTERISTICS OF GOD'S LOVE 130
   3. AN ASSESSMENT OF GOD'S LOVE IN FORSYTH'S THEOLOGY .. 134
   4. THE INADEQUACY OF LOVE ALONE AS A DESCRIPTION OF GOD 136
   5. THE NECESSITY OF A WIDER CONCEPTION OF GOD'S NATURE .. 145

6 – The Importance of Holiness 149
   1. AN ACCENT ON HOLINESS 150
   2. "THE OFFERING": AN ATONING SACRIFICE 162
   3. "A HOLY SELF": THE SINLESSNESS AND OBEDIENCE OF JESUS 172
   4. "TO A HOLY GOD": THE ACKNOWLEDGMENT OF THE FATHER'S HOLINESS 175
   5. "FROM SIN'S SIDE": THE HUMAN CONTEXT 182

7 – The Centrality of Holy Love 189
   1. A STRIFE OF ATTRIBUTES? 191
   2. THE NOTE OF JUDGMENT 193
   3. GODFORSAKENNESS: THE TASTE OF SPIRITUAL DEATH 195
   4. THE GRAMMAR OF HOLY LOVE 200
   5. THE HARMONY OF GOD'S ATTRIBUTES 204
   6. TRINITARIAN HOLY LOVE 222
   7. THE VICTORY OF HOLY LOVE 235

8 – The Future of Holy Love 239
   1. THE TWENTIETH-CENTURY PROGRESS OF AN IDEA 239
   2. A THEOLOGICAL FUTURE 265

Conclusion 273

Bibliography 283

Preface and Acknowledgments

Among all themes of Christian teaching, none is more capable of eliciting aesthetic theological pleasure than the study of the divine perfections. It is a joyful act to study eternal joy. It is merciful that God has allowed us to study God's mercy. It is the delight of theological reflection to see in their proper light the unity, harmony, balance, and proportion of the characteristics of the divine life.

Thomas Oden

We analyse God, we map out His nature, we display His psychology, we chase His goings, we chart the currents of His process, and we think we can keep Him by that near us, or look thus into His veritable face. But nay. Not so do we behold the face of any God that will stay with us and be our peace. Not by the lamp of seeing, but by the heart's vision of trust do we win and hold our soul's lord.

P. T. Forsyth

About twenty years ago, when the name of Peter Taylor Forsyth was first drawn to my attention by a fellow student, I had no reason to expect that the consequences would lead to a full-scale investigation of his theological writing. Then, Forsyth's books proved their usefulness in other ways: in reminding me that there is a Higher Critic than the higher critics,[1] in reviving my spirit when preaching became a wearisome task, and in spurring my interest in systematic theology. Now, after four years of studying his convictions, I am more convinced than ever of the importance of Forsyth's contribution. If this study may contribute to the continuing influence of his thought, I will be pleased.

An important aspect of the present work has been the compilation of a bibliography relating to Forsyth, comprising both

---

[1] Although this comment sounds decidedly Forsythian, I have been unable to confirm its provenance.

primary and secondary material. The recent discovery of papers left by his daughter, Jessie Forsyth Andrews, will add measurably to our understanding of Forsyth. These papers, which include letters, manuscript sermons, poems, and a notebook, are held at Dr Williams's Library, London. Research for the bibliography has also resulted in the unearthing of a considerable number of Forsyth's journal articles and published letters, not known previously.

Although the argument of this thesis is fully introduced in its first chapter, two words of explanation may be in order. First, as much as possible, I have allowed P. T. Forsyth to express his ideas in his own words; for that I offer no apology except A. M. Hunter's contention that "no theologian is more quotable."[2] Secondly, the reader is forewarned that (as J. K. Mozley said) "any sort of organized treatment purporting to represent Dr. Forsyth's positions as so many points in a dogmatic system is almost sure to introduce an impression of logical coherence and orderly advance more formal than the writings themselves warrant."[3] Forsyth's passionate and predominantly unsystematic style, and his deep engagement with the issues and especially with the God he writes about, provide some explanation of the continuing interest and abiding value of his work. Nevertheless, his writing is not infrequently the cause of scholarly frustration.

In the way of acknowledgements, my sense of dependence on others is deep, and my gratefulness profound. Above all, I am thankful for the sacrificial love and faithful prayer of my wife Katharina, whose encouragement and persistent support in our life together has never faltered. I gladly thank her for her effort on another front: in her capacity as InterLibrary Loans librarian at the Queen Mother Library, University of Aberdeen, she has been of invaluable help both for the main argument and for the appended bibliography.

Although I am pleased to say that our children have not had to bear the absence or inattention of their father throughout this project, they have bravely endured all the Forsyth stories, and the frustration of not being able to play computer games because their father was 'working on the thesis.' I thank them for their patience and encouragement during our years in Scotland. Paul's and Micah's

---

[2] A. M. Hunter, *P. T. Forsyth: Per Crucem ad Lucem,* SCM Book Club, no. 217 (London: SCM Press, 1974), p. 13.
[3] J. K. Mozley, *The Heart of the Gospel* (London: SPCK, 1925), p. 72.

willingness to help in unusual ways, and Sarah's time and interest in bibliographical detail and errant italicization are all appreciated.

I am grateful, too, to my parents, Jessie and Charles McCurdy, whose support during our time in Scotland was only the latest example of their commitment to me, and to us. Among much else, they instilled in me the confidence that difficult tasks (like this one) were possible.

At the University of Aberdeen, for which this thesis was prepared, my chief debt of thankfulness is to the Rev Dr Trevor Hart, now Professor of Systematic Theology at St Mary's College within the University of St Andrew's, from whose thoughtful supervision I have profited greatly. His initiative and effort in presenting a colloquium on Forsyth's life and work in June 1993, was a significant event for Forsyth studies, and a timely encouragement to my own work.[4]

The staff of the University of Aberdeen's Queen Mother Library, including the Department of Special Collections and Archives, have been gracious and helpful. For their consistent and practical service I am very thankful. Other libraries deserve thanks for their assistance with the bibliography: Dr Williams's Library in London, the National Library of Scotland, the Edinburgh Public Library, the university libraries in Oxford and Cambridge, and the British Library at Boston Spa, Bloomsbury, and Colindale. I readily acknowledge grants from the Coward Trust toward travel costs relating to the bibliography.

The support of colleagues and friends has been of invaluable help. I am particularly grateful to Alan Lamb for his friendship in things Forsythian, and to Davor Peterlin, Dan MacDougall, Chris Partridge, and Kwang-shin Cha for their camaraderie in the academic cause and beyond. Just as importantly, at Deeside Christian Fellowship in Milltimber, Aberdeen, we experienced the unique support of friends who pray, and then act on their prayers.

Leslie McCurdy

---

[4] The papers presented at the colloquium are published as *Justice the True and Only Mercy: Essays on the Life and Theology of Peter Taylor Forsyth,* ed. Trevor Hart (Edinburgh: T&T Clark, 1995). They appeared after the completion of this thesis.

Abbreviations

Full details about Forsyth's books are included in the bibliography, Section 1. Within the text, citations to his works are given in two forms. The first time a book is mentioned in each chapter, a longer citation is given, comprising the main title, the edition if pagination differs between editions, and the date of publication. Subsequent citations are in a short form, comprising either the main title, or for the more commonly cited volumes, the abbreviated form below:

Authority	*The Principle of Authority in Relation to Certainty, Sanctity and Society: An Essay in the Philosophy of Experimental Religion*
Cruciality	*The Cruciality of the Cross*
Father	*God the Holy Father*
Freedom	*Faith, Freedom and the Future*
Justification	*The Justification of God: Lectures for War-Time on a Christian Theodicy*
Missions	*Missions in State and Church: Sermons and Addresses*
Person	*The Person and Place of Jesus Christ*
Positive Preaching	*Positive Preaching and [the] Modern Mind*
Preaching of Jesus	*The Preaching of Jesus and the Gospel of Christ*
Work	*The Work of Christ*

Forsyth's name is omitted from citations to his works, unless it is necessary to include it in order to avoid confusion.

Chapter One

P. T. Forsyth and God's Holy Love

God in the revelation that he has made of himself to the world by Jesus Christ, has taken care to give a proportionable manifestation of two kinds of excellencies or perfections of his nature, viz. those that especially tend to possess us with awe and reverence, and to search and humble us, and those that tend to win and draw and encourage us. By the one he appears as an infinitely great, pure, holy and heart-searching Judge; by the other, as a gentle and gracious Father and a loving Friend: by the one he is a pure, searching and burning flame; by the other a sweet, refreshing light. These two kinds of attributes are as it were admirably tempered together in the revelation of the Gospel: there is a proportionable manifestation of justice and mercy, holiness and grace, majesty and gentleness, authority and condescension.

Jonathan Edwards

The theologian Peter Taylor Forsyth was noted for his care with words. His daughter Jessie Forsyth Andrews says that "every word was written by his own hand, and corrected and re-corrected,"[1] a fact vouched for by his editors, one of whom complained that when Forsyth returned a corrected proof, it was usually less expensive to have the type entirely reset.[2] Readers who have savoured Forsyth's epigrams, smiled at his alliterations, or marveled at his powerful rhetoric, can attest the truth of his daughter's further observation

---

[1] Jessie Forsyth Andrews, "Memoir," in P. T. Forsyth, *The Work of Christ* (1938; orig. pub. 1910), p. xxvi. Forsyth's name is omitted from footnotes, unless required to avoid confusion.

[2] Arthur Porritt, *The Best I Remember* (London: Cassell, 1922), p. 129.

that "he loved words for themselves, having that Sprachgefühl – that deep sense of word-values – which is born in every Celt; and like every faculty of his, it was pressed into the service of the truth."³

Two words which constantly recur in Forsyth's careful writing were combined in a distinctive formulation: 'holy love.' Used almost exclusively to refer to the nature of God, these words are a trademark of Forsyth's style, and appear so often that one writer feels compelled to answer "those who object to his repetitious use of the term."⁴ The word combination depends on the attributes of love and holiness which are always prominent in any discussion of the divine perfections, and although Forsyth spoke of both individually, Stephen Sykes is nonetheless correct to say that Forsyth employed "the notion of holiness in every use of the idea of divine love."⁵ The two went together in his mind, and often they literally went together on the printed page as "holy love." Forsyth's correspondent and interpreter J. K. Mozley calls it "the expression that meant so much to him."⁶ But of course they were more than words – Forsyth filled this expression with content of the most crucial kind.

In this chapter, our purpose is to introduce this distinctive phrase, first by a brief sampling of Forsyth's usage, secondly by an exploration into the background of the term in earlier writers who may have influenced him to speak of God's holy love, and then thirdly by an examination of Forsyth's introduction of the term against a background of his own theological development.

1. SAMPLING THE SIMPLICITY, EXPLORING THE GRAMMAR

P. T. Forsyth, judged by a prominent public figure of his day to be "one of the most brilliant minds in Europe,"⁷ spoke about God's

---

³ Andrews, "Memoir," in Forsyth, *Work*, 2nd ed., p. xxvi. For a list of abbreviations of Forsyth's major works, see above, page xiii.
⁴ W. L. Bradley, *P. T. Forsyth: The Man and His Work* (London: Independent Press, 1952), p. 143; these (hypothetical?) objectors are not identified.
⁵ S. W. Sykes, "Theology through History," in *The Modern Theologians: An Introduction to Christian Theology in the Twentieth Century*, ed. David F. Ford (Oxford: Basil Blackwell, 1989), vol. 2, p. 9.
⁶ J. K. Mozley, *The Heart of the Gospel* (London: Society for Promoting Christian Knowledge, 1925), p. 51.
⁷ John Morley (1838–1923), later Lord Morley, British writer and statesman, in conversation with D. R. Davies, as reported in the Foreword to Forsyth, *The Justification of God*, 2nd ed. (1948; orig. pub. 1916), p. 5.

holy love often, and in a large variety of ways. The frequency of its usage can be seen in all Forsyth's distinctly theological books.[8] Perhaps the quotation of one passage will suffice as an example at this point, given that we will be investigating his use of the expression at length in the chapters that follow. In his last book, *This Life and the Next,* Forsyth devotes a brief chapter[9] to a consideration of the following proposition:

> The Church in preaching a holy God, a jealous God, a sole God, is charged with preaching an egoist God; and the Christian course, it is said, must be to discard Him for a God whose holiness is only purity, and whose being as pure love is spent in bestowing Himself on His creation without a thought of His own self or dignity.

To this, Forsyth replies with the words that will be our focus for much of this thesis: "The Christian revelation is a God of *holy* love and not of hearty love only." The theological stance that would elevate love above holiness is met here with the same moderating influence that Forsyth at other times would proffer to "an orthodoxy that made everything of God's justice and nothing of His love." It is a question of balance, of holding two apparently contradictory attributes of God as equally worthy of full consideration.

This is not an unimportant issue, urges Forsyth: "If we cannot hold both sides of a paradox we are not fit for the kingdom of heaven," and "the God of holy love is a paradox." He continues: "[This God] combines two things which, as thoughts, we can adjust in no theology; but we can grasp them by a faith of their reconcilement in a person with whom we have to do – a moral reconcilement, and not one worked out by the process of an idea." In this short explanation, Forsyth accents several ideas that had occupied his best thought for the last three decades of his life: the revelation of God's nature in Christ, the combination of love and holiness in his person and work, and the fact that at the cross of Jesus, the holy love of God is seen as reconciled and harmonious. In

---

[8] To take only one representative passage from several of these books, see *Positive Preaching and [the] Modern Mind,* 1st ed. (1907), pp. 253–255; *The Cruciality of the Cross,* 1st ed. (1909), pp. 199–210; *The Person and Place of Jesus Christ* (1909), pp. 224–229; *Work,* pp. 131–137; *Faith, Freedom, and the Future* (1912), pp. 290–294; *The Principle of Authority,* 2nd ed. (1952; orig. pub. 1913), pp. 371–383; *The Church and the Sacraments,* 2nd ed. (1947; orig. pub. 1917), pp. 297–303; and *Justification,* chap. 7.

[9] *This Life and the Next,* 2nd ed. (1946; orig. pub. 1918), chap. 3; our quotations are from pp. 27–28.

the course of this study, we will examine these divine attributes in the context of the "moral reconcilement" of the atonement.

Although the 'holy love' expression is most often expressed in exactly those words, the wider idea is just as prevalent, and conveyed in many different ways. Occasionally, he reverses the words, as for example: "The judgment is loving holiness. It is saving judgment."[10] Sometimes other adjectives are added (as in "ethical holy love"[11]), or substituted (e.g., "righteous love"[12] and "holy grace"[13]). One of the pair may be emphasized by the use of italics or an initial capital,[14] or both words may be capitalized to refer to God as 'Holy Love.'[15]

This simple word combination is often expanded to become a longer phrase, as for example when verbs are added to remind the reader that God's holy love is active and not merely ontic: "the holy, searching, sanctifying love which made the cross of Christ."[16] Sometimes the process of exchanging, expanding, and embroidering produces a moving paragraph: "But when we read behind the cross, and not only feel it, the heart of fatherhood is that *moral* tenderness which is so much more than pity. ... Today we are learning new depths of that *moral* tenderness which is the soul of grace, and that *holy* kindness which is the source of Atonement."[17] At other times, it must be admitted, the effect can be rather oppressive, of words piled on top of words: "For both Jesus and Paul," writes Forsyth, "the reconciling act was God's act of judgment-grace, holy mercy and righteous love."[18]

Perhaps enough has been said. Instead of adding example to example, we conclude from this sample of Forsyth's diverse use of 'holy love' that this distinctive way of speaking of God's attributes was prominent in his writings, extended over the whole of his major writings, and was so important to Forsyth that he developed an almost endless variety of ways to employ it.

---

[10] *Justification*, p. 148.
[11] *The Church, the Gospel and Society* (1962; orig. pub. as articles, 1905), p. 28.
[12] *Authority*, p. 151.
[13] *Cruciality*, p. 204.
[14] See *This Life and the Next*, p. 28, quoted above, and *Freedom*, p. 219.
[15] See for example *Freedom*, p. 291.
[16] *Cruciality*, p. 201.
[17] "The Holy Father" (1896), in *God the Holy Father* (1957), p. 26.
[18] "The Preaching of Jesus and the Gospel of Christ: [VII] The Meaning of a Sinless Christ," *Expositor* 8th series, vol. 25 (April 1923): 310

2. 'HOLY LOVE': AN EXPRESSION WITH A HISTORY

The phrase 'holy love' did not originate with P. T. Forsyth, although his usage is (as we have just seen) very common and interestingly complex. Which theological writers might have been influential for Forsyth with regard to this expression? In this section, we intend to explore this matter, beginning with the period of Forsyth's education and early ministry, and then looking back from there to others in the succession of writers who utilized this phrase. Although we cannot hope to offer an exhaustive treatment, the results will show an established tradition – in fact, at least two distinct traditions – concerning God's 'holy love.' The work begun here will not only supply a context for our discussion of Forsyth's use of 'holy love,' but also perhaps spur others on to further investigation of this subject more generally.

2.1 ISAAC DORNER AND MARTIN KÄHLER

In the 1870's, the predominant influence in theology was Albrecht Ritschl, whose impressive three-volume work, materially on reconciliation but especially in its last volume a virtual systematic theology, had been published in the previous decade, between 1870 and 1874.[19] In the early 1880's, however, two major systematic theologies appeared in Germany, both offering clear alternatives to the Ritschlian way. The first of these was *A System of Christian Doctrine* from the pen of I. A. Dorner,[20] while the second was Martin Kähler's *Die Wissenschaft der christlichen Lehre*.[21] Both were widely acclaimed as major works: Dorner's contribution was acknowledged by a prominent contemporary as "a work extremely rich in thought and matter,"[22] while Kähler's

---

[19] Albrecht Ritschl, *The Christian Doctrine of Justification and Reconciliation:* [vol. 3] *The Positive Development of the Doctrine,* trans. H. R. Mackintosh and A. B. MacAuley (Edinburgh: T. & T. Clark, 1900).

[20] I. A. Dorner's *Christliche Glaubenslehre* (1879–1881) was published under the English title, *A System of Christian Doctrine,* trans. Alfred Cave and J. S. Banks, Clark's Theological Library, 4 vols. (Edinburgh: T. & T. Clark, 1880–1882). On Dorner (1809–1884), see Claude Welch, *Protestant Theology in the Nineteenth Century,* vol. 2, 1870–1914 (New Haven: Yale University Press, 1985), pp. 273–282.

[21] Martin Kähler, *Die Wissenschaft der christlichen Lehre von dem evangelischen Grundartikel aus im Abrisse dargestellt* (Neukirchen: Neukirchener, 1966; 1st ed., 1883).

[22] Otto Pfleiderer, *The Development of Theology in Germany since Kant and its*

systematic theology has been characterized as "perhaps the greatest one volume work of dogmatics to appear between Schleiermacher and Barth."[23] Both works used the phrase 'holy love' repeatedly, and were well-positioned to be influential for P. T. Forsyth, who according to one religious writer, "thinks in German with one half of his brain and in English with the other."[24]

In fact, the anonymous writer just quoted, in the course of a survey of Principal Forsyth's library, noticed many volumes by German writers, including Isaac August Dorner (1809–1884), who was one of the most notable figures of the mediating school of theology. His four volume *System of Christian Doctrine* sees "holy Love as the supreme unity,"[25] but the capitalized noun is a revealing clue to Dorner's understanding of the relation between love and holiness. "Love is the centre, or the heart of God – God, in the Godhead, in such a way indeed that it holds the principles of all the divine perfections united in itself," declares Dorner, who then explains that God's holiness is included in his love: "Justice or self-preservation so largely pertains to love that it is itself a kind of love, namely, God's love for Himself."[26] Dorner further developed his views on God's nature in his posthumously published volume on Christian ethics, in which he speaks of God's holy love as self-assertion and self-impartation, as both absolute and communicative: "The two together and inseparably one constitute *holy love.*"[27] In Dorner's writings, Forsyth found much to ponder: a developed moral view of God, a prominent place for God's holiness, and (to choose one aspect that seems to have been particularly influential) a reasoned account of God's self-love. All this was

---

[23] *Progress in Great Britain since 1825,* trans. J. Frederick Smith, 2nd ed. (London: Swan Sonnenschein, 1893), p. 156.
Carl E. Braaten, "Revelation, History, and Faith in Martin Kähler," in Martin Kähler, *The So-Called Historical Jesus and the Historic, Biblical Christ* (Philadelphia: Fortress, 1964), p. 8.
[24] "Ministerial Libraries: V. Principal Forsyth's Library at Hackney College," *British Monthly* 4 (May 1904), p. 267.
[25] Dorner, *System of Christian Doctrine,* vol. 1, p. 456.
[26] Dorner, *System of Christian Doctrine,* vol. 1, pp. 455, 456. For other references to holy love in these volumes, see vol. 1, pp. 461–462 (within a discussion of divine immutability); and vol. 3, pp. 121, 122, 138.
[27] I. A. Dorner, *System of Christian Ethics,* ed. A. Dorner, trans. C. M. Mead and R. T. Cunningham (Edinburgh: T. & T. Clark, 1880–1887), p. 68; see also pp. 69, 75, 78–80, 91, 93, 197, etc. It was this volume that the interviewer for *British Monthly* noticed in Forsyth's library.

comprehensively presented, as both dogmatics and ethics, with God's holy love as a prime ingredient. Martin Kähler's use of the term was more frequent, and his influence on Forsyth more marked. In the preface to one of his greatest works, Forsyth wrote that he owed much to Kähler, to whom (he admitted) footnote references could have been made repeatedly. The English theologian regarded his German contemporary as a 'giant,' one of "the most powerful minds of the world in the region ... of theology."[28] Like Forsyth, Kähler had been a disciple of Ritschl who then rejected or modified many of his teacher's convictions. His writing on the atonement is decidedly Forsythian, as for example when he says: "A reconciliation with God is for sinners morally impossible and for the God of holy love impossible, if the barrier of guilt is not taken away, if the wrath of the Holy One has not been expressed and the immutability of His world-order maintained."[29] The 'holy love' formulation recurs, too, in Kähler's systematic theology, first published in 1883 and revised twice in the following decades. The Congregationalist Sydney Cave, after quoting Kähler's conviction that it is "precisely in this surrender of the Son that the Triune God perfects the final revelation of His holy love," adds a note that "the English reader will find much of Kähler's teaching expressed in the vivid, poignant writings of P. T. Forsyth."[30]

Here, then, are two noteworthy theological works which appeared around 1880, at a time when P. T. Forsyth was questioning the liberal Ritschlian assumptions of his early theological training. Both

---

[28] *Person*, pp. viii–ix.
[29] Martin Kähler, *Zur Lehre von der Versöhnung* (1898), p. 367, quoted in J. K. Mozley, *The Doctrine of the Atonement* (London: Gerald Duckworth, 1915), p. 171.
[30] Sydney Cave, *The Doctrine of the Work of Christ*, London Theological Library, ed. Eric S. Waterhouse (London: University of London Press, 1937), p. 209. The quotation from Kähler is from *Wissenschaft der christlichen Lehre* (1905 ed.), p. 365. In *The Doctrine of the Person of Christ* (London: Duckworth, 1925), pp. 223–224, Cave drew attention to the close similarity of a sentence in Forsyth's *Person*, p. 333, with a sentence from Kähler's *Wissenschaft der christlichen Lehre* (1905 ed.), p. 339. Later, Cave explained that "Forsyth probably did not have [Kähler's] book at his side when he wrote. But having assimilated [Kähler's] argument, he brought forth the best and most important of it in his own apologetic" (Robert McAfee Brown, "P. T. Forsyth and the Gospel of Grace," PhD dissertation, Columbia University, p. 68; Cave's words are quoted indirectly by Brown, who mistakenly substituted the name of Kaftan for Kähler's).

Dorner and Kähler point the way to a new understanding of the cross, and of God's nature, and use the holy love formulation to describe God's attributes. Forsyth's thought subsequently turned in the direction indicated by these two German theologians, without slavishly following either. It seems a reasonable conclusion that Dorner, and even more Kähler, were important influences in his use of the term.

2.2 EARLIER GERMAN THEOLOGY

The use of this distinctive combination, frequently employed by Forsyth, and used before him by Kähler and Dorner, did not originate with them. Its history can be traced (albeit partially and imperfectly) through the two previous generations of writers in the nineteenth century. It will be convenient to follow this trail in reverse historical order, looking first at the decade preceding Kähler and Dorner, and then pressing further back still.

Writing in the 1870's, Albrecht Ritschl did not employ the phrase 'holy love' in his constructive discussion of God's attributes as a preliminary to justification and reconciliation.[31] This is an understandable decision in the light of his conviction that "the conception of love is the only adequate conception of God,"[32] and his concomitant drastic undervaluation of the divine holiness. However, Ritschl knew of others who explained the attributes of God in terms of holy love, referring especially to Phillipi and Crell.[33]

In Ritschl's theology, as to a somewhat lesser extent in Schleiermacher at the beginning of the century, it is God's love which is consistently theologically dominant. A different position is taken by our next example of German-speaking theologians who used the 'holy love' formulation, Gottfried Thomasius (1802–1875). For him, love is not the essence of the divine personality, and holiness is not a mere satellite of love.[34]

---

[31] See especially paragraph 34, "Love as determination of the nature of God in relation to the Son and the Kingdom of God," in Ritschl, *Justification and Reconciliation,* vol. 3, pp. 270–284.
[32] Ritschl, *Justification and Reconciliation,* vol. 3, p. 274.
[33] Friedrich A. Phillipi, *Kirchliche Dogmatik,* vol. 2, pp. 20ff., quoted in Ritschl, *Justification and Reconciliation,* vol. 3, p. 272. Ritschl adds that "the Socinian Crell (*Jahrb. für deutsche Theol.* xiii. p. 256) proceeds exactly as does Philippi."
[34] Gottfried Thomasius, *Christi Person und Werk: Darstellung der evangelisch-lutherischen Dogmatik vom Mittelpunkte der Christologie aus* (2nd ed.,

Although there were undoubtedly others in mid-nineteenth century Germany who used the phrase holy love,[35] the earliest German-speaking theologian to give sustained attention to the holy love of God (so far as I have been able to ascertain) is Ernest Sartorius (1797–1859), better known for his early espousal of a kenotic christology. From him we choose the following characteristic sentence, written in 1840: "The holiness of God which condemns the sinner, and the mercy which atones for him, are contrasts which do not mutually negative or blunt one another, but which, when their difference is composed by means of Divine self-denial in the vicarious satisfaction of Christ, are united in most holy love, and perfectly reconciled in His atonement."[36] Sartorius's stress on the harmony of attributes is quite similar to Forsyth's emphasis three generations later. The many references to God's holy love in this work, combined with its timely English translation in 1884, prompt the writer to wonder if it was part of Forsyth's reading in the formative years before the holiness of God's love became for him such a strong personal reality.

Finally, the earliest German theologian to use the holy love formulation – albeit infrequently – was however a notable member of the mediating school that stemmed from, and to some extent reacted to, the earlier and monumental work of Schleiermacher. According to Hendrikus Berkhof, C. I. Nitzsch's *System of Christian Doctrine,* first published in 1829, was "the leading systematic theology of this school."[37] Here, Nitzsch (1787–1868) twice uses the phrase 'holy love' in his concluding discussion of the divine attributes.[38]

1856–1863): see Robert S. Franks, *The Work of Christ: A Historical Study of Christian Doctrine* (London: Thomas Nelson, 1962; first pub., 1918), pp. 594–607; for particular references to holy love, see pp. 600, 601.

[35] Robert Flint, in *Agnosticism* (Edinburgh: William Blackwood & Son, 1903), p. 594, cites Bruch, *Lehre von den Göttl. Eigenschaften* (1842), and Moll, *De Justo Attributorum Dei Discrimine* (1855).

[36] Ernest Sartorius, *The Doctrine of Divine Love; or, Outlines of the Moral Theology of the Evangelical Church,* trans. of *Die Lehre von der heiligen Liebe* (1840–1856) by Sophia Taylor; Clark's Foreign Theological Library, n.s. vol. 18 (Edinburgh: T. & T. Clark, 1884), pp. 174–175. See also pp. 154, 165, 167, 170, 246, etc.

[37] Hendrikus Berkhof, *Two Hundred Years of Theology: Report of a Personal Journey,* trans. John Vriend (Grand Rapids, Michigan: Wm. B. Eerdmans, 1989), p. 63.

[38] C. I. Nitzsch, *System of Christian Doctrine,* trans. R. Montgomery and J. Hennen from the German ed. of 1844 (Edinburgh: T. & T. Clark, 1849), pp. 168, 172.

2.3 EXAMPLES IN THE ENGLISH-SPEAKING WORLD

When we turn to theologians writing in English before Forsyth's time and once again survey the field in reverse chronological order, we make two significant discoveries. First, the phrase 'holy love' is not a common one in British and American theology, thus making Forsyth's frequent use of the term all the more noticeable, and therefore, we believe, more important. And second, towards the end of our search through the century, we find an extended deliberate use of the phrase in question in an undervalued Scottish theologian.

To substantiate the first point, we note that the two most prominent Congregational theologians in the latter part of the nineteenth century, both of whom were important influences on Forsyth's thinking, did not use the phrase. A. M. Fairbairn (1838–1912) contrasts the Fatherhood and sovereignty of God in his best-known book, *Christ in Modern Theology* (1893), and speaks of "love and righteousness, which we may term the paternal and regal attributes of God" as an inseparable unity, but he does not go on to combine these attributes in the same phrase.[39] Neither does R. W. Dale (1829–1895) use this formulation, partly (one suspects) because he did not read German, and arguably because he puts great emphasis on the righteousness of God and very little on the divine love.[40] In the Anglican tradition, it seems, neither John Henry Newman (1801–1890) nor F. D. Maurice (1805–1872), both widely read and often quoted by Forsyth, used the phrase. Maurice, who was very influential on Forsyth, especially during his student years, preferred to emphasize love among God's attributes, "absolute, unqualified love."[41]

In other writers, the phrase occurs in only an incidental way. In an 1886 article, the Unitarian James Martineau writes that "the source whence we come [is] not a fermenting chemistry, but a holy love."[42] A few years earlier, the Anglican Walter Senior included the phrase in a sermon on the jealousy and mercy of God (Exodus 20.5–

---

[39] A. M. Fairbairn, *The Place of Christ in Modern Theology* (London: Hodder & Stoughton, 1893), p. 441; see the entire paragraph.
[40] On this last judgment, see H. D. McDonald, *The Atonement of the Death of Christ: In Faith, Revelation, and History* (Grand Rapids, Michigan: Baker Book House, 1985), p. 248.
[41] F. D. Maurice, *The Kingdom of Christ*, p. 133, quoted in Charles R. Sanders, *Coleridge and the Broad Church Movement* (New York: Octagon Books, 1972; 1st ed., 1942), p. 184.
[42] James Martineau, *Essays, Reviews, and Addresses:* vol. 2, *Ecclesiastical: Historical* (London: Longmans, Green, 1891), p. 526.

6).[43] In *The Nature of the Atonement,* John McLeod Campbell speaks of the suffering of Jesus as "the sorrows of holy love."[44] And an old Shaker hymn speaks of God's love is this way:

>Those who're faithful in their duty,
>Are the objects of pure love.
>Yea such souls are clad in beauty;
>Love's their treasure, holy love.
>O they are the gems of heaven,
>Rightful heirs to worlds above.[45]

But all of these are isolated instances, occasional and undeveloped.

In the light of the recurring incidence of the holy love formulation in German theology, it is surprising that it is not until we have travelled six decades back from Forsyth's career that we find an English-speaking writer who frequently uses this distinctive phrase. In several books published around 1830, Scots lay theologian Thomas Erskine (1788–1870) wrote about "that holy love of God, which was manifested in the gift and work of Christ," and did so with a verve and tenderness that is often striking in its eloquence. Erskine praises both holiness and love in an even-handed way, without resorting to a theological middle ground, as for example when he defines the Father's love as "a shoreless, boundless, bottomless ocean-fountain of love, of holy, sin-hating, sin-destroying love, which longeth over us that we should be filled with itself – and be by it delivered from the power of evil."[46] In common with Forsyth, Erskine locates this love in the atonement; a recent commentator remarks that "the only love of which he knows in relation to God is that concrete love of the Cross which gives all for our sakes, and does so precisely because it is bound up inseparably with justice and the demands of God's holiness. It is . . . irreducibly holy love."[47]

---

[43] Walter Senior, *God's "Ten Words": A Course of Lectures on the Decalogue* (London: Richard D. Dickenson, 1880), p. 77.

[44] John McLeod Campbell, *The Nature of the Atonement and its Relation to Remission of Sins and Eternal Life,* 4th ed. (London: Macmillan, 1873), p. 115.

[45] Harold E. Cook, *Shaker Music: A Manifestation of American Folk Culture* (Lewisburg: Bucknell University Press, 1973), p. 243.

[46] Thomas Erskine, *The Brazen Serpent, or Life Coming through Death* (Edinburgh: 1831), pp. 34–35, 122–123, quoted in Trevor A. Hart, *The Teaching Father: An Introduction to the Theology of Thomas Erskine of Linlathen,* Devotional Library, eds. James B. Torrance and Michael Jinkins (Edinburgh: Saint Andrew Press, 1993), pp. 73, 58.

[47] Hart, *Teaching Father: Thomas Erskine,* p. 20. Noting that Erskine often used the expression 'holy love,' Hart adds that the phrase is "more commonly associated" with Forsyth. For further examples from Erskine's writing during

2.4 SOURCES BEFORE THE 1820S

We have traced the use of the phrase 'holy love' – in both German and English – to the late 1820s. Where might this terminology have been used before that date? The obvious possible source is the 'father of modern theology,' Friedrich Schleiermacher (1768–1834). His discussion of the divine attributes in *The Christian Faith* is divided into three widely-separated sections, the second of which relates to human consciousness of sin and includes holiness, and the third of which relates to redemption and includes love. In a short section entitled "God is Love,"[48] Schleiermacher maintains that "love alone and no other attribute can be equated" with "the Divine Essence," and that "we cannot say that God in Himself is justice or holiness." In himself God is love, but towards us God is holy. Love (and to a lesser extent wisdom) are "expressions of the very essence of God," while the other divine perfections, including holiness, are "mere attributes." Still, Schleiermacher adds, it is possible to see the work of God's holiness as preparatory to the work of redemption, so that holiness and the other 'non-essential' attributes "merge for us in the divine love ... and the divine love is holy and just love inasmuch as essentially it begins with these preparatory stages; in the same way it is almighty and eternal love." Here is the closest Schleiermacher gets to our chosen expression: "the divine love is holy and just love." Could this fragment of a sentence have been the source of the mediating school's interest in God's holy love?

Perhaps it would be helpful to explore the sources of Thomas Erskine's theology. From what source does his use of holy love stem? It is possible that reading Schleiermacher's treatment of the 'merging' of holiness into love might have triggered the formulation in his mind, although this seems like a long chance. Within English-speaking writers, Samuel Taylor Coleridge (1772–1834) would be a possibility, but a perusal of his distinctly religious works turns up no sign of the phrase,[49] and the author of a recent and

---

[48] the period 1828–1831, see pp. 27, 107, 117, 119, 120, and 147.
Friedrich Schleiermacher, *The Christian Faith*, eds. H. R. Mackintosh and J. S. Stewart (Edinburgh: T. & T. Clark, n.d. [1928]), pp. 730–732; this one-volume systematics was published in 1821, followed by a second edition in 1830, from which the English translation was made.
[49] Samuel Taylor Coleridge, *Confessions of an Inquiring Spirit, and Some Miscellaneous Pieces*, ed. Henry Nelson Coleridge (London: William Pickering, 1849); Coleridge, *Aids to Reflection*, vol. 1, ed. Henry Nelson

acclaimed biography of Coleridge comments that "Forsyth's phrase sounds a common nineteenth century usage," but confirms that it is "not specifically Coleridgean."[50] On the German side, Immanuel Kant (1724–1804) discusses the attributes of God in *Religion within the Limits of Reason Alone,* characterizing "the universal true religious belief" in God as a *"holy* Legislator," *"benevolent* Ruler," and *"righteous* Judge."[51] But he expressly disallows what Forsyth and others assert when they speak of God's holy love. Kant writes, "His justice cannot be represented as *beneficent* and *exorable* (for this involves a contradiction); even less can it be represented as dispensed by Him in his character of *holy* Lawgiver."[52] It is unlikely that Kant would be a source for the holy love expression.

Our search for a source of this distinctive phrase has reached an end, but not a firm conclusion. In a personal letter, Hendrikus Berkhof says that he was influenced in his own use of the term[53] by "the so-called mediating form of theology, *Vermittlungstheologie,* between modernism and orthodoxy or between Schleiermacher and his critics." Then, turning to the quest for origins, he writes:

> My conclusion is that this terminology was suddenly in the air (cf. Paul about *dunameis tou aeros!*). . . . We cannot say more than that these 'stylish' words were suddenly used and imitated by innumerable people. And after a certain period the terminology was 'out'. How happy I was when I 'discovered' the first use of 'existentialism' in the young Schleiermacher's lectures to his students! But was it really the first use? And if so – *'cui bono?*'[54]

It is indeed a good question: to know who first used the phrase would bring little lasting advantage. However, the search for the origin of 'holy love' has brought some benefit, and in conclusion the following constructive comments can be made: (1) Although a first use has not been ascertained, the idea of God's holy love which Forsyth later adopted was developed in the German mediating theology of the mid-nineteenth century. (2) With regard to the

---

[50] Coleridge (London: William Pickering, 1848).
Richard Holmes, personal letter, 5 January 1992; see his *Coleridge: Early Visions* (London: Hodder & Stoughton, 1989).
[51] Immanuel Kant, *Religion within the Limits of Reason Alone,* trans. Theodore M. Greene and Hoyt H. Hudson; Harper Torchbooks (New York: Harper & Brothers, 1960), p. 131.
[52] Kant, *Religion within the Limits of Reason Alone,* p. 132.
[53] See Hendrikus Berkhof, *Christian Faith: An Introduction to the Study of the Faith,* trans. Sierd Woudstra (Grand Rapids, Michigan: William B. Eerdmans, 1979), especially pp. 118–133.
[54] Hendrikus Berkhof, personal letter, 23 February 1992.

doctrine of the divine attributes, the main concern of this school was to affirm the importance of holiness as a constituent element of God's nature. Not content to envisage God's nature as a centre of love with various circling satellites, they insisted that holiness, too, was a moral attribute of the divine nature. (3) The term 'holy love' was not quickly appropriated by English-speaking theologians, and P. T. Forsyth was among the first to take over the phrase from the mediating school and use it in a deliberate and creative way in the English-speaking context.

3. THE INTRODUCTION OF HOLY LOVE IN FORSYTH'S THEOLOGY

In setting out to trace the development of Forsyth's thought concerning holy love, we choose as our starting-point the first time the phrase is mentioned, and then follow its progress from 1891 to 1896, until it was well-established as a distinctive feature of his writing.

3.1 *THE OLD FAITH AND THE NEW* (1891)

In April 1891, P. T. Forsyth gave the chairman's address of the regional Congregational Union of which his church, Clarendon Park in Leicester, was a part. An expanded version was published later that year as a pamphlet entitled *The Old Faith and the New*. It marks the public acknowledgment of a turning point in Forsyth's Christian experience, and the inauguration of a vigorous speaking and writing career that for thirty years would seek to infuse new life into the old theology. We must add immediately that Forsyth did not have in mind a repristination of Calvinistic orthodoxy, but rather its revision in the light of modern biblical criticism and current theological thinking. "It is clear to me," he told his colleagues, "that we ought to review the strength of the old Evangelicalism in order to repair the defects and avert the dangers of the new." More specifically – and here he introduced his theme – "the Cross and the Kingdom represent among us two tendencies, which have not yet found their reconciliation."[55] So, in the course of his paper, Forsyth strove to yoke a primary emphasis on the objective atonement with a prominent but nevertheless derivative emphasis on the kingdom of God. His task was to combine

---

[55] *The Old Faith and the New* (Leicester: Midland Educational Company, 1891), p. 7.

something of the modern thought of Albrecht Ritschl and Johannes Weiss with the 'old faith' of the historic Christian tradition.

The sustained argument of Forsyth's address need not detain us, but two considerations in connection with it are important at this stage. First, this essay reveals several new emphases in Forsyth's theology, and in particular a concentrated interest in the holiness of God. From the very first page, we hear the soon-to-be-familiar indictment of modern theology's sentimentality, and the concomitant lack of "the high severity and ethical *verve* which are bred of mortal moral strife." At the outset, too, we hear Forsyth's charge that "we cease to be Evangelical . . . when the love of God takes the place in religion which is due to His holiness, and when the divine justice is conceived to be more engaged in the war with wrongs than in the war with sin."[56] Within brief compass, we discern a plethora of distinctive Forsythian themes: of moral reality and a moral atonement, of Christ's satisfaction to a holy God rather than to an offended monarch, of Christ's obedience and human penitence, of God's self-reconciliation, and (along with many other examples that could be mentioned) of the absolute centrality of the cross of Jesus Christ.

Even more importantly in light of the present concerns of this chapter, we hear Forsyth discussing the subject of God's holiness and love in terms well-known to the reader of Forsyth's later writings. Isn't it possible, he asks, to view the cross "too much as a declaration of the love of God with too little relation to the holiness which made that love really divine?" He criticizes those who interpret God's nature in terms of human nature, instead of the other way around, and then adds: "The love of God is conceived too wholly in the form of humane and cultured sentiment, and too little in the terms of the Saviour's holiness." And he speaks memorably of "a God who was love to the white heat of holiness."[57]

Finally and most specifically, in *The Old Faith and the New* Forsyth uses the distinctive word-combination 'holy love' for the first time. Referring to the atonement made in Christ's death, he writes, "It was the recognition by perfect holiness [i.e., Christ] that the judgment was the judgment of holy love." Then, later in the same paragraph, he speaks of "the law which Christ satisfied" as "the law of holy love."[58] As it would be in Forsyth's later writings,

---

[56] *Old Faith and the New*, p. 3.
[57] *Old Faith and the New*, pp. 17, 18, 15.
[58] *Old Faith and the New*, pp. ii, iii (in the Appendix).

'holy love' here refers to God, and especially to the divine qualities that are prominent in the atonement.

We must be careful, however, not to exaggerate the importance of this first usage of the term 'holy love.' Although this 1891 address is a turning-point, and the introduction of 'holy love' seems to be no coincidence, nevertheless when we consider Forsyth's writing in the months following that address, we find Forsyth experimenting with another contrast. Instead of comparing God's love and holiness, we note a recurring emphasis on the contrast between faith and love. In October 1891, for example, he contrasts "the Catholic note of [human] love" with "the Protestant note of faith."[59] At the beginning of the following year, Forsyth wrote an article focusing on this contrast. In answer to the question, "What then is the common bond and principle of our church life in the New Testament?", he writes, "The readiest answer of the day is, Charity," but the biblical answer "is not Charity but Faith."[60] We are justified by faith, Forsyth asserts; "Let us look to this faith and God will look to our love."[61]

Later in 1892 this theme returns, with the same contrast between love and faith. But here the point is carried much further, and changes significantly in emphasis. A belief in love "is not faith," says Forsyth, making the familiar point, but then he adds – "even when the Love is unearthly and infinite."[62] With the elaboration of that last clause, our author has combined with the human response to God's activity a concern for the impetus behind that divine action. Forsyth's attention shifts from the contrast of human love and faith to the divine qualities that demand such responses. Before very long, those qualities or attributes of God would be repeatedly summarized by the expression, 'holy love.' But here Forsyth uses another word – grace – which (as we will see much later) is its virtual equivalent:

> Saving faith is faith in "a love which is more than love" in its contact with human wreck and sin. It is faith in the grace that forgives. It must be nearly time to restore the word grace to the place in our Christian speech from which it has been ousted by love – by love conceived in reference to human sorrow rather than to human sin.[63]

---

[59] "Teachers of the Century: Robert Browning," *Modern Church,* 15 October 1891, p. 451.
[60] "Faith and Charity," *Congregational Monthly* 5 (January 1892), p. 14.
[61] "Faith and Charity," p. 15.
[62] "Shelley," *Independent,* 5 August 1892, p. 523.
[63] "Shelley," p. 523.

The message of God's grace was to become a constant emphasis in P. T. Forsyth's writing, but before it did, the message was endorsed by English Congregationalism's leading preacher and elder statesman. R. W. Dale, returning to his pulpit after a lengthy summer holiday that had included a three-week visit by Forsyth, chose "The Meaning of Grace" as the subject of his first sermon. After announcing his text, Dale began:

> A few weeks ago I was talking with one of the most accomplished of living Congregational ministers – a man much younger than myself – about the present condition of religious thought in the Congregational Churches of England, and he said, Don't you think that it is about time to bring back the word Grace into Congregational preaching? The question was a most exact expression of my own judgment.[64]

3.2 "REVELATION AND THE PERSON OF CHRIST" (1893)

Thus publicly encouraged, Forsyth's next writing task was a substantial essay called "Revelation and the Person of Christ." A great deal of the work on that paper was done during that summer visit with Dale at Llanbedr in Wales, and the collected essays were published early in 1893 under the title *Faith and Criticism*. Only in the last half-dozen pages does Forsyth turn to the concerns of our thesis, but when he does speak of redemption, he compresses a great deal in a short compass.[65] Several points are notable. In line with his later writing about the principle of authority, he says here that it is based only on "the evangelical foundation of a redeemed conscience." Echoing his discussion with Dale, he claims that "the extinction of our guilt is a pure, unbought, inexplicable act of miraculous grace." And, in a series of compact paragraphs, he writes of God's holiness, and of his holy love. Here, without drawing the contrast as starkly, or arguing the case as earnestly as he would later, Forsyth speaks of the work of Christ as "the true practical

---

[64] R. W. Dale, "Dr. Dale at Home Again: Sermon on the Meaning of Grace," *Independent*, 23 Sept 1892, p. 633. In a letter to George Barber, written 14 August 1892, Dale confirms the source: "Forsyth said a good thing the other day – he thought that 'the time has come to get back the word *Grace* into our preaching'; word and thing have too much disappeared" (A. W. W. Dale, *The Life of R. W. Dale of Birmingham*, 2nd ed. [London: Hodder & Stoughton, 1899], p. 636).

[65] "Revelation and the Person of Christ," pp. 138–144, in *Faith and Criticism: Essays by Congregationalists* (London: Sampson Low Marston, 1893), pp. 95–144; our quotations are from pp. 140–142.

recognition of God's holiness," and of "God Himself meeting the law of His nature and satisfying in man His own holiness." Following the emphasis of his title, Forsyth looks at redemption in the light of God's self-revelation. He writes:

> It is too much ignored that the revelation in Christ[,] being a revelation of holy love, must be condemnation as earnestly as mercy. In Christ God did not simply show pity on men, but God was in man expiating sin to His own holiness. . . . Such is the work of Christ – to realize and transfer to us the experience of God's holy love in the conditions of sin.

A detailed explanation of Forsyth's doctrine of the atonement must wait until later in our argument, but at this point we note the central place that Forsyth gives to God's holiness when he speaks here of redemption. Associated with that discussion is his use of the term 'holy love.' This conjunction of interests in "Revelation and the Person of Christ" – of atonement, holiness, and the holy love of God – is precisely what we discovered in Forsyth's address two years earlier. There, in *The Old Faith and the New,* in a discussion of satisfaction, the same elements were discernible. In this similarity, Forsyth sets a pattern for his future theological writing.

The years following *Faith and Criticism* were difficult ones for Forsyth. The exhilaration of a call to the prestigious Emmanuel Church in Cambridge early in 1894 was severely dampened by his wife's chronic illness and his own weakness. In September, the same month as the pastorate in Cambridge began, his wife died, and soon after Forsyth suffered a nervous breakdown, the effects of which extended well into 1895.[66] Such illness, combined with the pressures of a new pastorate, were not much suited to writing. A short review written near the beginning of this period, however, reveals his growing concentration on the cross of Jesus Christ. What our world needs, argued Forsyth, is not so much new theories of the work of Christ, but a revitalized sense of the atonement: "no less the classic sacrifice and no less the exhibition of an infinite love, but much more the act of grace in the cancelling of guilt, and the founding of a new relation for one that had otherwise been utterly lost."[67] The same stress on a vital and personal connection between Christ and the believer was the distinctive characteristic of an article for the fledgling *Expository Times,* in which Forsyth claimed that "the

---

[66] [Jane T. Stoddart], "Dr. P. T. Forsyth, of Cambridge: A Special Biography," *British Weekly,* 7 March 1901, p. 531.
[67] "A Pocket of Gold," *Independent and Nonconformist,* 8 March 1894, p. 187.

world's last ethical certainty [lies in] the experience of guilt abolished by holy love."[68]

As we look back over the history of Forsyth's writing between 1890 and 1895, we sense in him a combination of increased confidence and diligent searching. The articles of this period, including *The Old Faith and the New* (1891), "Revelation and the Person of Christ" (1893), and "The Divine Self-Emptying (1895), are written with a mature self-assurance. They stress – and not in an undeveloped way – the theological themes that Forsyth would reiterate in the decades to follow: the centrality of Christ, the authority of experience, a modified kenotic christology, the value of biblical criticism, the importance of the cross, and many others. It would be wrong to call this 'the early Forsyth,' because the distinctives of Forsythian theology are already well established in these essays.[69]

At the same time, however, we sense something of a struggle in Forsyth's writing during this period. He seems to be searching for a way of expressing the spiritual realities that are bearing down on his own heart, and exploring the modern scholarly territory for a way of organizing in his own mind the variety of theological points he wishes to make. We note his experimentation with the idea of 'the cross and the kingdom' in 1891, which, though luminous, faded into the background in his future writings. He tried the contrast between faith and love, but found it wanting.

But there is an emerging theme in these writings, more clearly seen with the benefit of hindsight but discernible nevertheless. In *The Old Faith and the New,* Forsyth strove to be appreciative of new insights while at the same time asserting the priority of the Christian tradition; the result was an emphasis on the primacy of the cross. His repeated contrast between human faith and love was transformed into a concern for the divine love and grace. Without abandoning the accent on the experiential, Forsyth rejected the subjective focus of contemporary Ritschlian theology in favour of more attention on the perfections of God as they relate to Christ's cross. In addition, and of at least equal importance, there is an increased concern in the writings of the early 1890s for God's

---

[68] "Mystics and Saints," *Expository Times* 5 (June 1894), p. 403.
[69] John Rodgers notes the uniformity in Forsyth's authorship since 1893: "From this time on all of Forsyth's writings centre on Grace. While there is development and growing maturity in his writing we are not faced with a radical break" (John Rodgers, *The Theology of P. T. Forsyth: The Cross of Christ and the Revelation of God* [London: Independent Press, 1965], p. 7).

holiness, vitally experienced in the context of human sin and guilt. Accompanying these emphases – the cross, God's attributes, and especially the divine holiness – and closely related to them, we recognize the emergence in Forsyth's theology of the distinctive expression, the 'holy love' of God.

3.3 "The Holy Father" (1896)

Forsyth's search for an organizing principle and a distinctive voice found its answer in the 1896 sermon, "The Holy Father." The Congregational Union of England and Wales was meeting that autumn in Leicester, where twenty years earlier Forsyth had been a young radical in the cause of an undogmatic Christianity. Now, however, he was at the centre rather than around the fringes of Congregationalism, having been asked to preach at the opening service of the semi-annual meetings. London Road Church, which seated 1100 people, was packed to overflowing, and by the time Forsyth rose to speak, the sanctuary was becoming very warm. "Dr. Forsyth's appearance has the indefinable air of distinction," wrote one reporter. "Tall and somewhat slender, with his expressive face 'sicklied o'er with the pale cast of thought,' he impressed one as being a man of deep conviction as well as great ability." His 55 minute sermon was heard by "an appreciative and sympathetic audience," who were carried along by Forsyth's "clear-cut, literary style, now alliterative and antithetical, and now epigrammatic and aphoristic. ... He packs profound thought into carefully selected words."[70]

Widely acclaimed by the religious press, and frequently reprinted in the days and months that followed, Forsyth's sermon was an impassioned argument for the equal priority of holiness with love in any conception of God's fatherhood. God as Father is not a dispenser of cheap grace, or an easy-going vendor whose business is automatic forgiveness. Instead Forsyth insisted that "there is a height and a depth in the Father beyond His utmost pity and His kindest love. He is *Holy* Father and Redeemer, and it is His holiness of fatherhood that is the source of our redemption and sonship."[71] It was typical of Forsyth's preaching, and indeed of his writing generally, to draw vivid distinctions which need not imply that the

---

[70] *British Weekly,* 1 October 1896, p. 376.
[71] "The Holy Father" (1896), in *God the Holy Father* (London: Independent Press, 1957), p. 3.

opposite might not hold some truth as well. In other places, Forsyth would write of love as redemption's source, but nevertheless the point is well made for the reinstatement of holiness prominently within the divine nature. Even within this sermon, the counterbalance is applied in the repeated discussion of the relation between love and holiness, and in the increasingly frequent use of the phrase which yokes the two and emphasizes their inseparability: 'holy love.'

We will have sufficient opportunity to describe Forsyth's views on God's attributes in Christ's atonement, but we pause here to point out several prominent characteristics of his thought which are introduced and elaborated here, accents that are heard here for the first time in his writing, which then sound continuously in the articles and books that followed:

First, its fundamental *Christocentricity:* Forsyth based his sermon on a text that put God's attributes in the context of the relationship between the Father and the Son who knew and revealed him. "Christ's own prayer was 'Holy Father,'" announced Forsyth, referring to John 17.11. "That was Christ's central thought about God, and He knew God as He *is*. The new revelation in the cross was more than 'God is love'. It was this 'Holy Father'."[72] Repeatedly Forsyth points to Christ's self-consciousness as a crucial factor in our understanding of God's nature.

Secondly, its *mediating* character: There were theological errors on both sides of the debate which Forsyth surveyed, and in the cause of correcting these he chose the 'holy love' formulation. Without going into the details, he writes: "We have been over-engrossed with a mere distributive equity, which has made God the Lord Chief Justice of the world. Or we have recoiled from that to a love slack and over-sweet."[73] As we will see, these extremes (adopted respectively by orthodoxy and liberalism) were consistently critiqued as Forsyth strove to present a theology that treated holiness and love as equally essential in the divine nature.

Thirdly, its focus on *the cross:* Quoting Goethe, Forsyth reminds his hearers in this sermon (and often elsewhere) that the church must adjust her compass at the cross. "The Church takes her moral bearings there. She discovers God's moral world and authority there. She reconstructs man's conscience from there, from the word,

---

[72] "Holy Father," in *Father*, p. 3.
[73] "Holy Father," in *Father*, p. 4.

revelation and nature of the cross."[74] From this point on, Forsyth was determined to know nothing else except Christ and him crucified. In his authorship of the next twenty-five years, it was the cross (and not the kingdom, social improvement, philanthropy, the established church, or anything else) that was his burden to preach and teach. It was the subject from which he often started out, and to which, almost regardless of the starting point, he invariably returned. It will be clear that in speaking of Christ's cross Forsyth does not refer merely to the death of Jesus, but to the atoning accomplishment within that reality. As he says, "The divine Father is the holy. And the Holy Father's first care is holiness. The first charge on a Redeemer is satisfaction to that holiness. The Holy Father is one who does and must atone."[75]

Fourthly, its expression in terms of *holy love:* From this point on, Forsyth expressed the interplay between divine attributes and the atonement in Christ with the help of this distinctive expression, the 'holy love' of God. Several times in this essay the formulation is used, as for example when he claims that "we make too little of the Father when we do not rise beyond *love* to *grace* – which is holy love, suffering hate and redeeming it."[76] Moreover, even where the term is not used, the contrast and combination of God's love and holiness permeates this sermon, and quotations could be offered from almost every page, including phrases like "the holy severity of the love he spurned," or "the Father's love of His own holiness."[77]

With this sermon on "The Holy Father," Forsyth found his voice, his characteristic message. Henceforth, the cross would be his constant theme, and the contrast of God's love and holiness the explanatory framework. As John Rodgers confirms, this essay with its stress on "the God of Holy Love" was "the first clear statement of the central category of his theology. It lies at the heart of all that he ever wrote."[78] A final excerpt from the 1896 address summarizes that message, and more importantly expresses his future direction:

> The soul of divine fatherhood is forgiveness by holiness. It is evangelical. It is a matter of grace meeting sin by sacrifice to holiness, more even than of love meeting need by service to man. To *correct* and revive that truth, to restore it to its place in the proportion of faith,

---

[74] "Holy Father," in *Father,* p. 23.
[75] "Holy Father," in *Father,* p. 4.
[76] "Holy Father," in *Father,* p. 7; see also pp. 23, 26.
[77] "Holy Father," in *Father,* pp. 14, 27.
[78] Rodgers, *Theology of P. T. Forsyth,* p. 8.

would be to restore passion to our preaching, solemnity to our tenderness, real power to our energy, and moral virility to our piety.[79]

'To correct, revive, and restore that truth' – the truth of God's holy love effective on Christ's cross – from 1896 on, that was Forsyth's mission.

4. THE EXPERIENCE OF HOLY LOVE

When we compare the writings discussed in the previous section with the published writings of the preceding fifteen years, we notice a significant difference in theological emphasis. Indeed, Forsyth invites us to examine the difference: "I should confess," he confided in a 1906 article, "how different and how poor my views of the Cross were in my youthful theologizing days till God taught me what sin was and the theology of its cure."[80] The P. T. Forsyth who speaks in the 1890s is very different from the young minister printing sermons at his congregation's request a decade or so earlier.

4.1 THE YOUNG MINISTER: 'THE EARLY FORSYTH' (1876–1885)

One such sermon, preached about a year into his first pastorate at Shipley, was called "Mercy the True and Only Justice."[81] Although a text is noted (Psalm 62.12), the sermon is a topical treatment of "the relation between justice and mercy ... in the eternal divine nature."[82] As such, it promises to treat the very realities – God's holiness and love – that concern us in this paper. The subject is introduced in terms quite familiar to readers of Forsyth's mature writings: a Christocentric emphasis, a distinction between metaphysical and moral reality, and an insistence that every attribute of God is equally fundamental and necessary. All three principles are quickly abandoned, however. Christocentricity makes way for pluralism, moral realism is replaced with metaphysical confidence, and the equality of attributes is shelved in favour of one central attribute with various aspects. To the question, "Which quality is the more fundamental in God, justice or mercy?", Forsyth briefly surveys the major world religions, and then concludes that it

---

[79] "Holy Father," in *Father*, p. 5.
[80] "The Place of Spiritual Experience in the Making of Theology," *Christian World*, 15 March 1906, p. 12; reprinted in *Revelation Old and New: Sermons and Addresses* (1962), p. 78.
[81] *Mercy the True and Only Justice: A Sermon* (Bradford: T. Brear, n.d.).
[82] *Mercy the True*, p. 3.

is mercy: "There is no doubt this is the essence of Christianity. God is Love. ... All his qualities are but aspects of that. God is endless, universal, unweariable, awful Love. Every other predicate is a quality only, a side of Him. This is His being, His energy, His purpose, His result – Love."[83]

For this assertion, regarding which 'there is no doubt,' there is also no argumentation offered. Instead, Forsyth immediately offers for comparison "the popular conception ... that God is, above all things and primarily, just," then caricatures the corresponding view of the atonement in this way: "Mercy had a hard fight of it to get the upper hand, and only succeeded after justice had been appeased by an awful victim, on whom it spent its fires." The result is "the whole immoral theory of substitution."[84] The remainder of the sermon is a rebuttal of that position from a classic liberal stance. For example, Forsyth claims that "it is God's *nature* to forgive," just as water quenches thirst, and parents forgive their children;[85] later he would criticize this view as representing the easy forgiveness of a love devoid of holiness.[86] Throughout, sin is not taken with the seriousness Forsyth later accorded it, and after unworthy theories have been roundly criticized, the atonement is not mentioned again. Indeed, such an omission is understandable: if sin is so easily pardoned, a death for sinners is virtually unnecessary. "The ethic of the redemption did not rise to a real atonement," Forsyth wrote once about Ritschl's theology. "The effect on man eclipsed the effect on God."[87] The same could with much justification be said of the early Forsyth.

From the perspective of Forsyth's later work, this sermon about the divine perfections has serious deficiencies. The initial assumption, that God's essential attribute is love, is followed by a devaluation of divine justice to merely an aspect of something much more important. "Justice is but a form and application of love," says Forsyth. "Divine justice is simply love taking shape."[88] The later Forsyth consistently opposed such reductionism as denigratory to God's holiness. And indeed, when we evaluate this essay in the light of that criticism, we see that righteousness and holiness are words that do not appear. While God's love is known in a variety of ways,

---

[83] *Mercy the True*, p. 5.
[84] *Mercy the True*, pp. 5–6.
[85] *Mercy the True*, pp. 6–7.
[86] See our discussion of this point in Chapter Seven, section 5.1.
[87] *Church and the Sacraments*, p. 88.
[88] *Mercy the True*, p. 8.

including pity, kindness, mercy, and grace, the justice and wrath of God are not expressions of his holiness, but rather are "simply love taking shape" and mere fatherly discipline along the way. We are reminded of Albrecht Ritschl's contention that the goodness and Fatherhood of God could be summarized in one pre-eminent truth:

> He has revealed Himself to the Christian community as love. There is no other conception of equal worth beside this which need be taken into account. This is especially true of the conception of the Divine holiness, which, in its Old Testament sense, is for various reasons not valid in Christianity, while its use in the New Testament is obscure. ... The conception of love is the only adequate conception of God.[89]

Forsyth, of course, had studied with Ritschl just five years previously, and by his own confession had 'imbibed mightily' from him.[90] This early sermon bears the marks of that influence.

As we look through the writings that came from Forsyth's pen in the years that follow, we find similar sentiments expressed. In an 1878 sermon, he quotes approvingly the words of a modern poet: "'Sympathy is the last consecration of love. It is love itself, perhaps.'" These words, comments Forsyth, "contain the secret of Christianity."[91] In the same year, he spoke of "loving the Almighty Love and sympathising with the Almighty Sacrifice."[92] And in the following year he asserted that "a sympathy which is perfect, and a love that overcomes everything" is "the prime meaning of the revelation of Christ."[93] His mature contempt of religion founded on sympathy stands in stark contrast to these early views.

In these years of his first pastorate, which included the Leicester controversy about 'the terms of religious communion,' Forsyth writes little of human sin, and seems to restrict the death of Christ to an exemplary influence. In fact, the central figure of Christianity is rarely mentioned in the writings of this period. In his desire to "welcome even the opinions that traverse our own on the gravest points, if the spirit that prompts them is one with our own,"[94] Forsyth is unwilling to affirm even a fraction of what he later thought important, even crucial. In 1879, he wrote, "I would avoid

---

[89] Ritschl, *Justification and Reconciliation*, vol. 3, pp. 273–274.
[90] *Positive Preaching*, p. 285.
[91] "The Strength of Weakness," *Christian World Pulpit* 13 (6 February 1878), p. 87.
[92] *"Maid, Arise:" A Sermon to School Girls* (Bradford: T. Brear, n.d.), p. 17.
[93] *The Weariness in Modern Life* (no publication data), p. 15.
[94] "A Larger Comprehension the Remedy for the Decay of Theology," in *Public Conference on the Terms of Religious Communion* (London: Judd, n.d.), p. 21.

the offensive vanity of dogmatising. I would but testify."[95] Thirty years later, such a view was still common, but it was definitely not Forsyth's:

> We are in a time when a spirituality without positive content seems attractive to many minds. And the numbers may grow of those favouring an undogmatic Christianity which is without apostolic or evangelical substance, but cultivates a certain emulsion of sympathetic mysticism, intuitional belief, and benevolent habit. . . . [But, concludes Forsyth:] Upon undogmatic, undenominational religion no Church can live.[96]

The same emphases are discernible in the writings of the early 1880s. A sermon called *Corruption and Bribery,* preached in 1881, is, considering its subject matter, remarkably reticent about sin.[97] In an 1882 funeral address, Forsyth could fairly be described with his own words as 'a lover of love.'[98] As late as 1885, in his installation sermon at Cheetham Hill in Manchester, Forsyth regarded the cross as only one 'factor' of the incarnation, and merely one aspect of revelation.[99]

4.2 A TRANSITIONAL TIME (THE MID-1880S)

During this period, however, and especially towards the end of it, we notice a change in Forsyth's thinking on some subjects, and also the introduction of new accents in his theological writing. That his views were changing is signalled by his contribution to a discussion on "The Obligations of Doctrinal Subscription." Forsyth must have surprised his confrères from the Leicester controversy of five years previously, by advocating ministerial subscription to "an abbreviated form of the Apostles' Creed." "Some of the older men would welcome it as a bulwark against what they take to be the Universal Abolitionism of the juniors," Forsyth explained. "And the juniors would find it a covert from the tempest of suspicion and the violence of contempt which they sometimes experience from the senior quarters."[100] Here is language not so much of the young rebel

---

[95] *Weariness in Modern Life,* p. 13.
[96] Preface to *Work,* 2nd ed., p. xxxi.
[97] *Corruption and Bribery: A Sermon* (Bradford: T. Brear, n.d.).
[98] *In Memoriam: Andrew Baden, Esq., F.I.A.* (Died February 9th.) (Bradford: William Byles & Sons).
[99] *The Pulpit and the Age* (Manchester: Brook & Chrystal, 1885), pp. 8–9.
[100] "The Obligations of Doctrinal Subscription: A Discussion. – II," *Modern Review* 2 (April 1881): 280.

but of the emerging mediator, likely somewhat chastened by the tempest himself.

The fresh emphases in Forsyth's theology emerge toward the end of this period, that is to say, in the mid-1880s. In January 1884 Forsyth preached on "Pessimism," with Schopenhauer especially in view. "I do not find much in that strange, passionate, and loveless character to impress me with a sense of moral dignity, to say nothing of moral exaltation or insight," Forsyth observed, adding that Schopenhauer "was more sensible of the pains of the world than of the sins of it."[101] This moral critique – the moral principle as a key theological concept – is distinctive of Forsyth's later writing, and makes its first significant contribution in this article. Its importance to Forsyth is not limited to theological critique, or even spiritual diagnosis of sin, however, but also extends to the interpretation of God's remedy for humanity's moral crisis: "The solution of life is not to be found in grappling with pain, but in the conflict with sin," and therefore, "in the cross, the greatest [miracle] of them all."[102]

In later years, Forsyth would have pressed home this argument with an application of the atonement to human sinfulness, the inexorable holiness of God's love, the objective accomplishment of the cross, and the grace that has done all and won all. But, although the new themes are emerging, they are not yet fully developed in 1884. Instead, the power dissipates, and within a few sentences Forsyth speaks in a positive way about "the lovers of Divine loveliness," and of the virtue of love towards God (instead of emphasising God's love towards us, as he would later).[103] Here there is brief mention of "the pure and holy Jesus," and of the need for "a new solemnity in our sympathy with the sin-bearer,"[104] but this is not yet the holy love of God revealed in Christ. This sermon seems to reflect an uncertainty in the preacher about what should be central in Christian teaching, an intellectual conflict between divine action and human apprehension, between objective and subjective atonement, between the moral reality – Christ – that confronts and conquers sin, and the personal religious response to that reality.

It was, I believe, a struggle not yet decided. The moral concentration, the unflinching consideration of sin, 'the glory of

---

[101] "Pessimism," *Christian World Pulpit,* 16 January 1884, p. 43.
[102] "Pessimism," p. 43.
[103] "Pessimism," pp. 43–44.
[104] "Pessimism," pp. 43, 44.

the crucified' – these emphases were relatively new to Forsyth's sermons, and would later become important and even programmatic for his mature theology. But the key ingredient of divine holiness was still largely missing, much less its distinctive combination with God's love in the expression that is our focus of attention in this thesis. In the mid-1880s, Forsyth could still be fairly considered "a lover of love,"[105] an emphasis that went back in an unbroken line to *Mercy the True and Only Justice,* preached in 1876. During this period, the human focus was pronounced. But at the end of this first ten years of Forsyth's ministry, as we have just seen, there was a new concern emerging – a moral concern for the seriousness of sin, the importance of the cross, and the priority of God's grace. This newer voice is not yet sure of itself, and certainly not well-established, but it *is* emerging. William Bradley rightly observes that this sermon "contains the germ of his later thought," but the significance of "Pessimism" is much larger than that. This 1884 sermon reveals P. T. Forsyth in the uncomfortable place between two theological perspectives, the old liberalism still prominent but the new 'positive' theology making its presence felt more and more.

Such a claim is based on the examination we have carried out so far into the progress of Forsyth's thought in his early years, and on the comparison with his mature writings. But our judgment about the important place of the sermon under consideration at present does not rely entirely on the wider context. Within the published text of "Pessimism," there is further indication that this is a time of change for the author:

> Our first affections die, and our once bright and young ideas that stung us into intellectual life these tarnish and lose their charm and their power. But two things stay with us as we age, if we grow in grace and good – our one deep love and our one great sin.[106]

Then in the closing minutes of his sermon, Forsyth uses plural pronouns to speak for his congregation in St Thomas's Square in London, but more importantly, he speaks also for himself, and explains something at least about what has brought about this change of thinking:

> We are being forced into anxiety, not by abstract sin but by concrete sins, individual and especially social, here and now. We are being forced

---

[105] See for example "The Argument for Immortality Drawn from the Nature of Love: A Lecture on Lord Tennyson's 'Vastness,'" *Christian World Pulpit* 28 (2 December 1885), especially pp. 363–364.
[106] "Pessimism," pp. 43–44.

P. T. Forsyth and God's Holy Love

out of our ignorant optimism by the spread of social information, and by a truer idea of the real dangers science brings to soul. Our faith is becoming less a cherub's creed, and more a warrior's breath, less a thing of seraphic strain, and more a thing of battle and scars. The glory of life is becoming less the smile of the angel, and more and more the glory of the crucified.[107]

4.3 THE CHARACTER OF FORSYTH'S THEOLOGICAL CONVERSION

The autobiographical comments at the conclusion of the last section propel us toward an examination of Forsyth's theological conversion.[108] This is far from being an incidental or merely introductory concern, because it is our conviction that Forsyth's theological use of the 'holy love' combination arose from, and reflects, his own personal experience. He changed his mind, and prominent among the vital ingredients of this transformation are the divine attributes of love and holiness, the very aspects of God's character that concern us in this study. Where once Forsyth was preoccupied with the sympathetic side of that nature, he became more and more conscious of the divine holiness, and incorporated that new perspective with the old. A study of this 'conversion,' then, will shed useful light on our main concern.

Although the verdict varies on how to describe Forsyth's experience – was it a gradual reorientation or a more precipitous life-change? – and on when it occurred, we have it on the author's own authority that such a change did indeed take place.[109] Lecturing to young theological students in the United States, he asked rhetorically, "Might I venture here to speak of myself? Will you forgive me?" The immediate context of this uncharacteristic autobiographical revelation, which we quote at some length, was a discussion on the place of biblical criticism in preaching:

> There was a time when I was interested in the first degree with purely scientific criticism. Bred among academic scholarship of the classics and philosophy, I carried these habits to the Bible, and I found in the subject a new fascination, in proportion as the stakes were so much higher. But, fortunately for me, I was not condemned to the mere scholar's cloistered life. I could not treat the matter as an academic quest. I was kept close to practical conditions. I was in a relation of life, duty, and responsibility

---

[107] "Pessimism," p. 44.
[108] See especially Robert McAfee Brown, "The 'Conversion' of P. T. Forsyth," *Congregational Quarterly* 30 (July 1952): 236–244.
[109] *Positive Preaching*, pp. 281–285.

for others. I could not contemplate conclusions without asking how they would affect these people, and my word to them, in doubt, death, grief, or repentance.

As Forsyth pondered, he came to realize that here was a crisis for his ministry, a time to choose. To one side, there was his personal scholarly fascination with biblical criticism; to the other, the pastoral needs of a church. With an outward glance at "the state of mind and faith in the Church at large," he made his decision:

> I became convinced that they were in no spiritual condition to have forced on them those questions on which scholars so delighted and differed. They were not entrenched in that reality of experience and that certainty of salvation which is the position of safety and command in all critical matters.

Consequently, the focus of his ministry changed from the "questions on which scholars so delighted" to the vital experience of salvation through Christ.

An experience of such importance in the pastoral sphere is bound to leave a mark on the minister who faced it. Indeed, it would be closer to the truth to suggest that behind such an important professional conclusion lies a personal discovery of similar or perhaps even greater significance. Therefore it does not surprise us to hear Forsyth immediately add:

> It also pleased God by the revelation of His holiness and grace, which the great theologians taught me to find in the Bible, to bring home to me my sin in a way that submerged all the school questions in weight, urgency, and poignancy. I was turned from a Christian to a believer, from a lover of love to an object of grace. And so, whereas I first thought that what the Churches needed was enlightened instruction and liberal theology, I came to be sure that what they needed was evangelization, in something more than the conventional sense of that word.... There was something to be done, I felt, before they could freely handle the work of the scholars on the central positions.
>
> And that something was to revive the faith of the Churches in what made them Churches; ... to banish the amiable religiosity which had taken possession of them in the name of Christian love; and to restore some sense not only of love's severity, but of the unsparing moral mordancy in the Cross and its judgment, which means salvation to the uttermost.... What was needed before we discussed the evidence for the resurrection, was a revival of the sense of God's judgment-grace in the Cross, a renewal of the sense of holiness, and so of sin, as the Cross set forth the one, and exposed the other in its light.

And so, explains Forsyth, "my own course seemed prescribed." Turning from "the scholar's work" of biblical criticism, he took up "those theological interests ... which come nearer to life than science, sentiment, or ethic ever do." Although still a believer in criticism's methods and in many of its results, he was convinced that such was not the modern need. "What is needed," he concluded, "is no mere change of view, but a change and a deepening in the type of personal religion, amounting in cases to a new conversion." These last words about the need for conversion, which Forsyth applied to the people around him, were just as appropriate as self-description.

This testimony, spoken in 1907 and published the same year in *Positive Preaching and Modern Mind,* tells the important and indeed dramatic story of "a new conversion," a theological sea-change. After that experience, P. T. Forsyth's theology never failed to measure God's love by the greatness of his holiness, and his writing testified to that concern with the repeated occurrence of the words that concern us in this thesis: 'the holy love of God.'

4.4 EARLY EVIDENCE OF 'THE LATER FORSYTH' (1887–1891)

Having seen the reality of Forsyth's theological conversion, can we determine with any confidence the approximate timing of such a change? I believe we can. Let us return to Forsyth's 1891 address called *The Old Faith and the New,* with its distinctive stress on God's holiness and the introduction of that interesting phrase, the 'holy love' of God. As we pointed out in the previous section, the distinction of the title refers to what R. W. Dale had called the new evangelicalism,[110] which according to Forsyth was "in some danger of ceasing to be evangelical at all," in danger of sacrificing the gospel's moral rigour for sentimentalism and social relevance, and giving to God's love the place due to his holiness.[111] In the face of these tendencies, Forsyth said, we should take the best of the new back to "the old Evangelicalism," in order to build a better theology on those firm foundations:

> We should go back with our corrections to seek correction. When we have softened our father he will have but the more to teach us. We should evolve our new more frugally from the old, dropping no more than we must, and retaining much that in our first extravagance we have cast away. For it has long been our misfortune to have revolted from the old creed in our revolt from the old men, when we ought to have been

---

[110] R. W. Dale, *The Old Evangelicalism and the New* (London: Hodder & Stoughton, 1889).
[111] Forsyth, *Old Faith and the New,* p. 3.

taught to elicit the new from the old, and translate its form without the loss of its moral and intellectual power.[112]

Once again, the plural language here is nevertheless personal. The revolt from the old men, and the old creed, was a precise description of Forsyth's course of action. His mentors John Hunter and Baldwin Brown, his teachers Albrecht Ritschl at Göttingen and Samuel Newth at New College, and his heroes F. D. Maurice and G. W. F. Hegel – all represented to a greater or lesser extent the liberal departure from 'the old faith' once delivered to Forsyth's Congregational forebears. Now in 1891, the man who formerly cast away the old was championing the faith he once tried to destroy. Coincident with this change of emphasis, a friendship developed with the most renowned of 'the old men,' R. W. Dale – "a friendship, and intimacy indeed," elaborates Jessie Forsyth Andrews, "which was a deep joy to my father."[113] In the summer of 1892, in fact, Forsyth holidayed with Dale at the latter's cottage in Wales.

Further confirmation of this view is found later in *The Old Faith and the New,* where the author turns to the subjects of intellectual truth and personal religious experience, in the significant context of biblical criticism. Once again Forsyth combines with passionate exposition – in this case, of the relation between the cross and the kingdom – an intensely personal, indeed autobiographical, concern. Faith in Christ's cross, he says, "is essential to the kingdom. Attachment to Christ's ideas, truths, or principles, like sonship, without personal attachment to himself is ineffectual. It leaves us enlightened, even softened, but unredeemed."[114] The similarity to the passage quoted above from the Beecher lectures at Yale some sixteen years later is palpable: it was Forsyth's preoccupation with critical questions without a prior commitment to the crucial realities to which the Bible testified that left him as a 'believer' but not yet a Christian. It is little wonder that a reviewer commented, "There is manifestly an autobiographical element in the pamphlet."[115]

One more example from this 1891 address will suffice, although once again we quote at some length. The argument complete, Forsyth adds the following testimony:

---

[112] *Old Faith and the New,* p. 7.
[113] Andrews, "Memoir," in Forsyth, *Work,* 2nd ed., p. xv.
[114] *Old Faith and the New,* p. 26.
[115] Review of Forsyth, *The Old Faith and the New,* in *Congregational Monthly* 4 (December 1891), p. 321.

P. T. Forsyth and God's Holy Love 33

> Our youth begins in surprised impatient joy. We are all reformers and our sires were fools. We discover soon that even the spirit of the age can fail, and that many of our contemporaries are not wise. For they will not at our bidding part with the folly of the creeds. A little longer and we misdoubt our own complete wisdom. Still longer and we are troubled most with the *sin* of our fathers and brethren. And at last we give in. No sin has hampered us like our own. We were on too good terms with our own conscience. We can never trust our breezy selves again. We have all our world and all our hope to reconstruct at the foot of the Cross. Our new views must arise from our new selves.[116]

This paragraph reverberates with references to the writer's own experience. The opening words are reminiscent of the Preface to *Mercy the True and Only Justice* (1877), where Forsyth proclaimed with pseudo-humility and mock respect, "It is high time that we should have, on behalf of the young and less thoughtful, more plain-speaking on subjects which the wiser heads agree at least to leave open questions, and which the party of thought in religion as well as in science are tearing open in spite of us."[117] At the Leicester conference in 1877, Forsyth and others campaigned for an untheological Christianity and a minimalist approach to church membership, but the Congregational Union (led that year by R. W. Dale) rebuffed their attempts, unwilling to part with the evangelical kernel of the Christian 'creed.'[118] It is difficult to say just when Forsyth doubted his own 'complete wisdom,' but it is hard not to see an example of that cocksure quality in the letter announcing his early departure from his theology course at New College in 1874.[119] And of course, the reference to the awareness of sin is paralleled in Forsyth's later comment about God's holiness and grace bringing home to him his sin.[120] The result of this chain of events was a soul humbled, and then rebuilt, at the foot of the cross. From this 'new conversion,' Forsyth developed 'new views,' which although dynamic in their growth, were held consistently for the remainder of his life.

Our conclusion, then, is that the experience which Forsyth described in his Lyman Beecher lectures of 1907 is also reflected in

---

[116] *Old Faith and the New*, p. 27.
[117] *Mercy the True*, p. 2.
[118] See Mark D. Johnson, *The Dissolution of Dissent, 1850–1918*, Modern European History: A Garland Series of Outstanding Dissertations, gen. ed William H. McNeill (New York: Garland, 1987), chapter 2.
[119] Forsyth's letter is quoted in full in the minutes of the Council of New College, London, 1 October 1874; NCL ms 145/1 in Dr Williams's Library, London.
[120] *Positive Preaching*, p. 282.

The Old Faith and the New; therefore this conversion experience occurred before 1891. Can we be more specific yet? Does anything in Forsyth's own writing or in the reporting of his ministry suggest that his 'new conversion' occurred before 1891? Forsyth wrote only one major work before 1891, and it is situated in a convenient place for us to ask the pertinent questions. *Religion in Recent Art* is the result of a series of lectures given in 1887, concurrently with the Manchester Exhibition. Two chapters on Wagner were added later, and the substantial result – more than 350 pages – was published in early 1889. Forsyth shows a wide appreciation of four Pre-Raphaelite painters, and of the composer and pessimist Richard Wagner. In these lectures, he vividly conveys his aesthetic appreciation of both gallery and opera house. But it is not a book in which the author opens his personal life to our consideration. The spiritual power he feels is obvious;[121] the specific life-changing effects are not portrayed. And so, in terms of autobiographical evidence, our search for more information about Forsyth's 'conversion' in *Religion in Recent Art* draws a blank.

However, when we consider Forsyth's treatment of God's holiness and love in this work, here again we are a world apart from the early writing of *Mercy the True and Only Justice* (1877). Even though Forsyth's focus here is on interpreting the various works of art, most of which were painted or composed without Christian intent, still he speaks of his own perceptions in Christian terms. Some of his intermittent theological comments speak of the holy love of God without, however, using that precise formulation. For example, after referring to the cross of Jesus Christ, he adds, "It is in Him that we not only perceive love's unspeakable loveliness, but share love's eternal power. . . . It is a love that lavishes upon the sorrowful world a power of redemptive passion . . . and a solemn fear holier than beauty's most breathless awe."[122] In another place, he explains that "as there is awe in beauty and a tragedy in life, so there is fear in love and a high discipline in love's fear."[123] Furthermore, scattered throughout the work are phrases that remind us of Forsyth's later writings: "We hear enough of love as the charm and happiness of life. We do not hear enough of it as the moral principle of life."[124]

---

[121] See for example his description of "The Scapegoat" by Holman Hunt in *Religion in Recent Art* (1889), p. 200–211, and especially pp. 203–204.
[122] *Religion in Recent Art*, p. 50.
[123] *Religion in Recent Art*, p. 84.
[124] *Religion in Recent Art*, p. 149. In the light of this and similar evidence, we must disagree with W. H. Leembruggen, who places *Religion in Recent Art* before

"We have divided our Christ; and, while we have kept His humane compassion and His helping hand, we have ceased to fathom His awful soul, or sound the dread depths of sin and grace with keen-eyed sanctity."[125] And finally, although Forsyth does not in this volume speak of the 'holy love' of God, he does write about the "sanctity of love," "the forgiving love of God who is a consuming fire," and even of "[l]ove unholy and pitiless."[126] On the basis of this evidence, it would seem that *Religion in Recent Art* was written after the religious experience described in 1891, and shares the same theological perspective as Forsyth's later writings. Although the unusual nature of this book makes it rather difficult to draw comparisons with Forsyth's more theological writings, it would seem to be written from the newer point of view.

4.5 THE DAWNING OF HOLY LOVE

In section 3 of this chapter, we noted the emergence of an emphasis on divine holiness together with the first and then increasing use of the distinctive expression, the 'holy love' of God. In the present section, we have first traced Forsyth's theological pilgrimage from the drastically different content of *Mercy the True and Only Justice* in 1877 to the transitional time of 1884, illustrated by the ambivalence of the sermon called "Pessimism." Then we established the reality of Forsyth's conversion, with its strong associations with our concern for God's holiness and love, and followed Forsyth's autobiographical comments about that experience back to *The Old Faith and the New* (1891). Thus we have narrowed the likely date of his theological conversion to a period between 1884 and 1891. Moreover, we have described the writings in the earlier part of this period as ambivalent and sometimes contradictory. Indeed, it is not until *Religion in Recent Art* (lectures given in 1887 and published in January 1889) that Forsyth seems to be more sure of himself, more distinctively himself, theologically speaking. Such a conclusion must have a tentative quality, because the unusual subject matter of this last-mentioned book makes comparisons somewhat difficult.

Forsyth's realization of the importance of God's holiness; Leembruggen, "The Witness of P. T. Forsyth – A Theologian of the Cross," *Reformed Theological Review* (1945): 24.
[125] *Religion in Recent Art,* p. 201.
[126] *Religion in Recent Art,* pp. 270, 208, 329.

We conclude, therefore, that Forsyth's life-changing and theology-transforming experience occurred in the middle to late 1880s, emerging decisively into view in his aptly-named April 1891 address, *The Old Faith and the New,* in which he spoke of God's holy love for the first time. This new perspective was developed in his essay on "Revelation and the Person of Christ" (1893), and then found its public power and its distinctive accent of holy love in the sermon, "The Holy Father" (1896).

Before leaving this discussion of the timing of Forsyth's theological conversion, we pause to consider another question. Is our conclusion that this experience occurred within a period of several years in the latter half of the 1880s an admission of inadequate knowledge of what was undoubtedly a very personal experience? Or is it an indication that Forsyth's experience was not a sudden conversion but rather a more gradual change of mind? An essay by Forsyth (discovered in the course of research for this thesis) sheds light on this question. "A New Year Meditation," published early in 1895, is a sermon whose theme is well expressed by a sentence in its opening paragraph: "The soul has its own chronology."[127]

"There are stages ... in our spiritual progress," Forsyth avers at the beginning of a paragraph with autobiographical importance. Then he continues:

> We can remember when we get beyond this book or that, for instance. We recall a time when we were overpowered by a style of English that now makes us laugh, when we were even as the uncircumcised readers of the *Daily Telegraph.* We had, perhaps, our days of fluent sentiment, or turgid phrase, or affected sententiousness, or studied judiciousness, or artificial quietness of manner. We had a time, perhaps, when we thought literature a much more precious thing than Gospel.

It may be obvious, but nevertheless it is worth noting that Forsyth is describing his own experience in some detail. He tells us elsewhere that in early years he had affected the speaking style of Carlyle, and readers of Forsyth can appreciate his self-conscious comments about turgidity and sententiousness. As for literature, his early papers on Coleridge and Tennyson are proof enough of this devotion.[128] Later comments within this same paragraph speak of other stages: "of sombre and fashionable pessimism," of preoccupation with "culture"

---

[127] "A New Year Meditation," *Evangelical Magazine* 103 (1895): 29.
[128] *Coleridge's 'Ancient Mariner': An Exposition and Sermon from a Modern Text* (Bradford: William Byles and Son[s], n.d. [likely before 1883]); "The Argument for Immortality Drawn from the Nature of Love: A Lecture on Lord Tennyson's 'Vastness,'" *Christian World Pulpit* 28 (2 December 1885).

and "reforms." These too have their referents in Forsyth's past, indicated in writings which we have already noted.

Having established the autobiographical quality of this passage, then, we return to the text in order to answer the questions asked earlier:

> We may remember days when our belief was as much more easy as it was more shallow than now, when the millennium seemed very near and feasible, social reform the ruling passion, and forward movements the one thing needful. We may have changed our opinions. We may have changed in a deeper way, found ourselves out, turned ourselves out and taken in Christ. We may have gone through something worth calling conversion, and changed all our notions of what the soul and its sin count for among things. *We can almost remember the year* when words like 'spiritual,' 'righteousness,' 'redemption,' became incandescent for us.[129]

Amid several ideas which recur in Forsyth's subsequent descriptions of his theological conversion – the 'forward movement' of the higher criticism, a concern for sin, the new centrality of Christ – are highlighted, the new prominence of 'righteousness' and 'redemption,' later to become the holiness of the cross. Then Forsyth adds that he can almost remember the year such monumental words took on an urgent personal and professional importance. The timing of that sea-change was therefore not tied down to a particular day, or a discrete event. Rather, it was a transformation to be looked back on with the benefit of hindsight. For Forsyth in 1895, there was no doubt that such a change had occurred, but whether it happened (say) in 1884 or 1886 was difficult to determine, because the process had been in some ways a gradual one.[130]

More important than any decision about the date of Forsyth's experience, however, is our contention that the experience itself is intimately related to the attributes of God as they are revealed in Christ's atonement for sin. It was the cross of Jesus that confronted the theologian's sin and transformed his subsequent thinking. Our investigation so far in this chapter has revealed the tension between

---

[129] "New Year Meditation," pp. 33–34; emphasis added.
[130] Jessie Forsyth Andrews ("Memoir," in *Work,* p. xvi), in speaking of this "re-orientation," confirms that "it was not sudden," but seems to suggest that it occurred in the early 1890s, coinciding with the death of Forsyth's wife and his subsequent ill-health. Such a suggestion provides no explanation for Forsyth's sense of sinfulness, the reason for which may never be explained. In addition, as we have seen, his writings seem to indicate an earlier date.

God's love and holiness in Forsyth's thinking – not so much in the sense of the strife or harmony of God's attributes, as will be our concern in the later chapters of this study, but in the comparative emphasis which Forsyth gave first to love, and then to holiness within the context of God's holy love. While the early Forsyth later described himself pejoratively as "a lover of love," in his later writings, it was the divine holiness that assumed a new and commanding importance.

We conclude this section with a quotation from Sydney Cave, who was both a student of Forsyth's and a successor to his principalship, and "probably as close to Forsyth as any man ever was."[131] Cave dedicated his volume on soteriology "to the hallowed memory of Dr. P. T. Forsyth, through whose teaching the Cross became the centre not only of the writer's religion but of his thought."[132] Of most interest to us is the observation that Forsyth reflected the reality of God's holy love in his own experience:

> We knew that this naturally proud man had been humbled by the grace of God; we felt his awe of God's holiness, and, although there might be much that we [as students still in our teens] could not as yet understand, this, at least, we knew – the greatness of the Gospel, the awful majesty of God and the surprising wonder of His love. . . . [Principal Forsyth] did not fear men, but more than any I have known, he served God with awe and godly fear, and the love he trusted was the holy love he had seen in all its splendour in the Cross.[133]

---

[131] Robert McAfee Brown, *P. T. Forsyth: Prophet for Today* (Philadelphia: Westminster, 1952), p. 19.
[132] Cave, *Doctrine of the Work of Christ*, p. vi; on holy love, see e.g. pp. 264–265.
[133] Sydney Cave, "Dr. P. T. Forsyth: The Man and His Writings," *Congregational Quarterly* 26 (April 1948), pp. 112, 118.

Chapter Two

Literature Survey

The exercise involved in detecting the source of an author's ideas may be engrossing, but it is less profitable than the exercise involved in inquiring what his ideas actually were, how he held them together, and whether they were true.

Alec Vidler

In the previous chapter, we have seen the prevalence of the term 'holy love' in Forsyth's writings. Looking back through his authorship, we have noted the emergence of this expression in the 1890s, and examined the close connection between Forsyth's theological development with regard to the attributes of God, and the gradual but very significant changes that were occurring in his own life. We also explored a background of a different kind, namely the usage of this distinctive phrase in the earlier part of the nineteenth century.

Now, before launching into a study of the knowledge of God's attributes, and in particular God's holy love, we pause to evaluate the state of the discussion so far on this matter. In this chapter we no longer work backward from Forsyth's repeated usage to the developments in his own life and in the theological scene before that, but rather trace the subsequent scholarly reflection on Forsyth's doctrine of the atonement, his view of God's attributes, and his use of the term 'holy love.'

1. FORSYTH'S VIEW OF ATONEMENT AND ATTRIBUTES IN ACADEMIC CONTEXT

P. T. Forsyth was, according to the respected historical theologian Claude Welch, "a major thinker who gave new life to nonconformist theology."[1] At the centre of that theology is the cross of Jesus Christ, and not surprisingly the secondary monographs consider Forsyth's doctrine of the atonement in some detail, as do several theses and many articles. However, two somewhat contradictory qualifications must be added to this consensus. The first is well-expressed by Sydney Cave: "I have long felt that one of the greatest books on the Atonement would have been the book Forsyth might have written but did not write."[2] *The Work of Christ* was given as lectures, and is not as comprehensive as might be wished, while *The Cruciality of the Cross* is a small book of occasional papers. A second consideration must be set alongside the first, however. The cross was the centre of Forsyth's thinking, dominating virtually everything he ever wrote. In addition, much of that writing examines the cross, and applies it to important contexts. *The Soul of Prayer* is a soteriologically oriented spirituality and *This Life and the Next* is eschatology under the cross. *Positive Preaching and the Modern Mind* is a powerful plea for proclamation of this central reality of the Christian faith, and *The Christian Ethic of War* is less an apologetic for a just war than a sketch of theological ethics in the light of Christ's saving death. Foremost among his writings, though, is *The Justification of God*, which probes the problem of suffering at a time when world war was causing innumerable deaths and unparalleled grief, and comes to the conclusion that only the cross of Jesus Christ can take modern evil seriously enough. The atonement is everywhere in Forsyth's writing, and this fact is reflected in the secondary literature.

While those books written about Forsyth and his theology have been on the whole general introductions to his work with a special emphasis on his understanding of the cross,[3] several of the doctoral

---

[1] Claude Welch, *Protestant Thought in the Nineteenth Century*, vol. 2, 1870–1914 (New Haven: Yale University Press, 1985), p. 236. In the light of our discussion in the previous chapter, it is interesting to note that in the same sentence Welch adds that Forsyth was a "lively kindred spirit to [Martin] Kähler."

[2] Sydney Cave, "Dr. P. T. Forsyth: The Man and His Writings," *Congregational Quarterly* 26 (April 1948): 117.

[3] Only one of the published monographs – Clifford Pitt's *Church, Ministry and Sacraments: A Critical Evaluation of the Thought of Peter Taylor Forsyth*

theses and dissertations about P. T. Forsyth have focused on specific areas of his thought.[4] Dividing these theses into groups according to the broad traditional groupings of systematic theology reveals a strong preference for the second article of the creed: almost half of the authors have written about the person and work of Christ.[5] Although no one has yet concentrated on Forsyth's doctrine of the Holy Spirit (perhaps understandably, in light of his rather occasional treatment of the subject), there has been considerable interest in his treatment of other issues usually studied in relation to the Spirit: church and sacraments, preaching, spirituality, and church government.[6] By contrast, there are comparatively few theses on Forsythian theology that relate to the diverse subject matter which might be considered first article concerns; those which have been completed include work on revelation and authority and on theodicy.[7] As a result of this cataloguing of doctoral work about Forsyth,[8] it can be seen that the present study, concentrating as it does on God's attributes as seen in the atoning work of Christ, treads well-travelled territory with regard to soteriology (which indeed is hard to avoid in Forsyth's writing!), but attempts to break new ground in the matter of the characteristics of God's nature. For this reason, our treatment in what follows is from the perspective of the doctrine of God, looking first at the knowledge of God, then more specifically at the divine attributes, and finally (and most closely of all) at the divine love and holiness – what Forsyth calls the 'holy love' of God. Although the context (atonement) will be familiar, the theme of our study (the attributes of God) will be much less well

---

[4] (Washington, D. C.: University Press of America, 1983) – is a specialized work. See Section 6 of the bibliography for full details of theses mentioned in this paragraph.

[5] Among those who concentrate on Christology are Newman, Allen, Gardner, and Jones, while the following are concerned especially with soteriology: Rosenthal, Mikolaski, Gardner, Rodgers, and Rosser.

[6] On church and sacraments, see Bosse and Pitt; on preaching, Wismar and Parker; on spirituality, Hsü; and on church government, Norwood.

[7] Both Sturm and Wilson have written on revelation and authority, while Vicchio and Gardom contribute works on Forsyth's theodicy.

[8] In the interests of completeness, the remaining theses comprise general treatments of Forsyth's life and thought (Bradley and Brown, who chooses the grace of God as his unifying theme), examinations of his contribution to Biblical studies (Jackson and Stewart), and studies of the intellectual background to Forsyth's thought (Simpson and McKay). Several theses compare Forsyth and other theologians (Thompson, as well as others already mentioned in other contexts just above).

known to students familiar with the secondary literature on Forsyth's theology, as these specific areas have not yet been considered by writers of books, theses, and dissertations about Forsyth's theology.

2. EARLY RESPONSE TO FORSYTH'S THEOLOGY

We have noted in the previous section the paucity of references to God's attributes in the scholarly monographs and theses on Forsyth's theology. Nevertheless, there has been some attention given to the concerns of this thesis in the 115 years since "a curious reader" of Forsyth's first printed sermon first felt compelled to publish a reply.[9] In this section, we propose to survey the more notable contributions of the first respondents to Forsyth's writing, as it relates to our theme, proceeding for the most part chronologically from 1878 until the mid-1940s, that is, from the first reaction to Forsyth's writing until just before the explosion of interest in his theology after the Second World War.

The first such response, to which we have just referred, is a tract called *Justice and Mercy,* which is of some interest to our study because of its concern with the relationship between holiness and love. Admittedly, the value of its scattered arguments is eroded by its pedantic comments and caustic insults, but the anonymous author makes some observations which are worthy of note. He (or she) rightly observes that "if assertions could establish anything, this sermon would be a model for imitation."[10] More substantially, the contradiction implied in Forsyth's metaphysical agnosticism is pointed out. The author writes, "We are told almost at the beginning that, – 'We get no satisfaction about the metaphysics of the divine;' and then in the next paragraph we are treated to a very remarkable disquisition on the fundamental qualities of God."[11] This was a complaint that would have continuing validity concerning Forsyth's writing. Perhaps most significantly, Forsyth's reviewer turns to the assertion that it is God's nature to forgive: "Is it not equally, and in all respects, God's *nature* to be just?"[12] This would become Forsyth's position, stated so powerfully a generation later in "The Holy Father." On the whole, however, such questions are

---

[9] *Justice and Mercy: A Review of a Sermon Published by Rev. P. T. Forsyth, M.A.*, by "A Curious Reader" (Bradford: M. Field, n.d.).
[10] *Justice and Mercy: A Review,* p. 4.
[11] *Justice and Mercy: A Review,* p. 4.
[12] *Justice and Mercy: A Review,* pp. 5–6.

swamped by invective: Forsyth's views on God's wrath "are not held by any sane person," says the reviewer; other opinions are "mere chimeras, bogies conjured up by rash and hasty generalizations," whole sections of his sermon are "a blot on the character of the Christian pulpit" and "a disgrace to the intelligence."[13] Fortunately, future critics were themselves saner.

Foremost among them was J. K. Mozley. Although he was not the first to write about Forsyth,[14] this Anglican theologian was the first to study his theology in any detail. Indeed, Mozley's deeply sympathetic but not uncritical treatment led A. M. Hunter to call him "the finest of Forsyth's interpreters."[15] With regard to the general soteriological background of our study, Mozley's judgment is apropos: "No one in modern times has penetrated nearly so far as has Forsyth into the moral reality of the Cross."[16] More importantly, Mozley was the first to identify the specific subject of Forsyth's combination of divine attributes: "How often he recurs to the thought that the full truth is not that God is love, but that God is holy love."[17] Then, after an impressive tour of Forsyth's theology, Mozley adds that "any full treatment of that theology" would have to consider, among other concerns, "the relationship between holiness and love."[18] Both comments are suggestive, although the author does not follow them up.

While Mozley wrote about Forsyth in the early 1920s, the next significant contribution concerning Forsythian theology did not come until 1939. Around this time, Karl Barth was informed about what Forsyth had written, and he is reported to have answered, "If Forsyth had not said what he said when he said it, I would have said he was quoting me."[19] Another quotation, more reliable perhaps and arguably more useful, comes from another voice in the same theological quarter. "Forsyth is the theologian the practical man needs!" wrote the great theologian's son, Markus Barth, to a

---

[13] *Justice and Mercy: A Review*, p. 7.

[14] Besides the reviews of Forsyth's books, see the articles by K. C. Anderson, John Forster, E. Griffith-Jones, J. Warschauer, E. Hermann, Robert E. Ziegler, and Edwin H. Kellogg in Section 7 of the Bibliography.

[15] A. M. Hunter, "P. T. Forsyth Neutestamentler," *Expository Times* 73 (January 1962): 104.

[16] J. K. Mozley, *The Heart of the Gospel* (London: SPCK, 1925), p. 85. These conclusions were first published as "The Theology of Dr. Forsyth," *Expositor*, 8th series, 23 (February, March 1922): 81–98, 161–180.

[17] Mozley, *Heart of the Gospel*, p. 82.

[18] Mozley, *Heart of the Gospel*, pp. 108–109.

[19] A. M. Hunter, *P. T. Forsyth: Per Crucem ad Lucem* (London: SCM, 1974), p. 12.

practical British audience in 1939. He continued, "I cannot understand why his works are not much more widely read, why such a man of interdenominational importance is not installed as a teacher and herald in thousands of hearts."[20] Among the five aspects of Forsyth's theology which the younger Barth examines is God's holiness; he comments: "That God is *more* than our loving Father, that the Cross reveals Him as the Holy One, is seldom heard. ... This Forsyth brings out most clearly."[21] In the course of a discussion about the harmonious love and justice of God, Markus Barth uses Forsyth's 'holy love' expression, then concludes with the comment:

> The right relation of Law and Gospel, of our fear and faith over against God, has been the subject of endless theological struggles in Germany. By developing the thesis that there is no rivalry in God between His attributes, *e.g.*, between His justice and his goodness, Forsyth might, if known, have been a landmark in the controversy and a pioneer towards its solution.[22]

A more critical observation comes from Forsyth's younger colleague, Alfred Garvie. Where J. K. Mozley and Markus Barth understand Forsyth as stressing the unity of holiness and love, Garvie makes the charge that Forsyth, in his love for antitheses and his aversion to some modern theological trends, "often sets love and holiness in opposition to one another."[23] This misunderstands the older theologian's intention, which (as we will see) is in fact exactly the opposite. To ease his professed distress at Forsyth's antitheses, Garvie could have profitably reflected on his colleague's use of the 'holy love' combination, or, indeed, on his own use of the expression some twenty years previously.[24] The Canadian theologian John Mackintosh Shaw makes a similar point: love and holiness "are not two attributes of God to be set over against each other or simply contrasted with each other in the way that Forsyth has tended, following traditional thought, to do. They are rather two aspects of the one self-communicating and self-imparting attribute."[25]

---

[20] Markus Barth, "P. T. Forsyth: The Theologian for the Practical Man," *Congregational Quarterly* 17 (October 1939): 437.
[21] M. Barth, p. 439.
[22] M. Barth, pp. 439–440.
[23] A. E. Garvie, "Placarding the Cross: The Theology of P. T. Forsyth," *Congregational Quarterly* 21 (October 1943): 351.
[24] Alfred E. Garvie, *The Christian Doctrine of the Godhead or The Apostolic Benediction as the Christian Creed* (London: Hodder & Stoughton, [1925]), pp. 211–212.
[25] J. M. Shaw, "The Theology of P. T. Forsyth," *Theology Today* 3 (October 1946): 369.

However, what Shaw affirms against Forsyth is actually what Forsyth himself believes: that attributes aren't distinct entities, "something loose within God which he could manipulate," but instead "God Himself behaving, with all His unity."[26] These criticisms are in some ways surprising ones, because both Shaw[27] and Garvie follow Forsyth in using the 'holy love' formulation. The latter, for example, employs the expression as a name for God and as a designation of the divine attributes, but also argues for speaking of love alone, and of God's Fatherhood without "qualification by various epithets" – this last corrective issued apparently with Forsyth in view. It seems that when Garvie uses the expression 'holy love,' he means that God's love is holy, while when Forsyth uses it, "the antithesis of holiness and love is theological rhetoric."[28] The criticism is at least unproven, at worst hypocritical.

Other early students of Forsyth's thought conclude that his stress on holiness is not meant in any opposition to love, but in conjunction with it. "It should be realised," affirms R. L. Child in the *Baptist Times,* not only that holiness is fundamental in this Congregationalist theologian's thought, but also that "Forsyth is thinking all the time of a completeness and self-sufficiency in God which are nothing other than the perfection of Infinite Love. 'Holiness is love morally perfect; love is holiness brimming and overflowing.'"[29] This characteristic quotation from Forsyth well expresses his intention in speaking of God's 'holy love,' an expression which Child echoes throughout his series of articles on Forsyth's theology.

3. THE POST-WAR RENAISSANCE IN FORSYTH STUDY

To this point, we have noted the emergence of several themes in the early consideration of Forsyth's theology, in particular as they relate to our proposed examination of God's attributes of love and holiness. Our discussion has brought us past the devastating end of World War II to 1948, the centennial year of Forsyth's birth. This post-war era was a time of renewed and vigorous interest in the life

---

[26] *The Work of Christ* (1910), p. 117.
[27] John Mackintosh Shaw, *Christian Doctrine: A One-Volume Outline of Christian Belief* (Toronto: Ryerson Press, 1953), e.g., pp. 37–38, 47, 206–208; within the latter context, see quotations from Forsyth on pp. 214, 216.
[28] Garvie, *Christian Doctrine of the Godhead,* pp. 227, 229.
[29] R. L. Child, "P. T. Forsyth: Some Aspects of His Thought," *Baptist Times,* 20 May 1948, p. 9; the source of the quotation from Forsyth is not indicated.

and work of this British theologian, whose last books had been written during the First World War. Since his death in 1921, interest in Forsyth had waned. It is almost true to say that the essays by J. K. Mozley (1922) and Markus Barth (1939) discussed above are the only significant writing on Forsyth between the wars. The only exceptions to this were provoked by John McConnachie's description of Forsyth in 1933 as "that Barthian before Barth."[30] In 1934, for example, T. Hywel Hughes wrote an article which concluded, "The resemblances between the two are more superficial than real, whilst the differences are essential and profound,"[31] and in 1940, Robert Franklin Thompson completed a thesis (more thoughtful, but with less clear-cut conclusions) on the same subject.[32] While both Hughes and Thompson refer to Forsyth's stress on God's holy love, any comparison with Karl Barth's treatment of the divine attributes as interlocking pairs would have to wait until volume 2, part 1 of Barth's *Church Dogmatics* was published.[33]

In contrast to this modicum of interest in Forsyth's theology in the late 1930s, the post-World War II period saw a renewed interest in his theological contribution, and the emergence of a thriving publishing industry. The only reprinting of Forsyth's works in the 25 years since his death was a new impression of *The Person and Place of Jesus Christ* in 1930, and a 1938 second edition of *The Work of Christ*, to which Jessie Forsyth Andrews had added a Memoir. Then, within just four years (1946–1949), the Independent Press in London republished eight of Forsyth's most important titles, adding several more in the decade that followed. At the same time, new academic interest was marked: in the space of fifteen years, a total of fourteen doctoral theses or dissertations were written about Forsyth (compared to only one – Thompson's – previously), and four of these were published. There was a similar

---

[30] John McConnachie, foreword to F. W. Camfield, *Revelation and the Holy Spirit: An Essay in Barthian Theology* (London: Elliot Stock, 1933), p. vii.
[31] T. Hywel Hughes, "A Barthian Before Barth?" *Congregational Quarterly* 12 (July 1934): 308.
[32] Robert Franklin Thompson, "Peter Taylor Forsyth: A Pre-Barthian" (PhD diss., Drew University, Madison, New Jersey, 1940).
[33] Karl Barth, *Die Kirchliche Dogmatik,* vol. 2, pt. 1, *Die Lehre von Gott* (Zurich: Evangelischer Verlag) was published in 1940, too late for Thompson's attention; the English translation, *Church Dogmatics*, vol. 2, pt. 1, *The Doctrine of God* (Edinburgh: T. & T. Clark) did not appear until 1957. See especially the treatment of "The Grace and Holiness of God," pp. 351–368, and "The Mercy and Righteousness of God," pp. 368–406.

Literature Survey 47

proliferation of journal articles on Forsyth's life and work, with eight in 1948 alone.[34]

This scholarly attention devoted to Forsyth in the last fifty years has resulted in a variety of interpretations of his theological stance, although it must be admitted that because much of that study has been more devoted than scholarly, the variety is not overly wide. Nevertheless, the fact that several scholars were writing about Forsyth at roughly the same time, with very little history of scholarship to argue or agree with, resulted in some diversity of opinion. When we turn to examine this burgeoning crop of books, theses, and articles written since the mid-1940s, and look in particular at the treatment of Forsyth's views on God's love and holiness, we notice three distinct positions. These positions are distinguished not only by their differing perceptions of the relative importance of the two attributes in question, but also come to clearly different conclusions about Forsyth's characteristic choice of words to refer to the divine attributes: the holy love of God.

3.1 THE PREEMINENCE OF GOD'S HOLINESS

The first position discernible within the newer writing on Forsyth stresses an aspect of his thought that all commentators acknowledge as central to his theology – the holiness of God. Perhaps Samuel Mikolaski represents this position most clearly. After completing a DPhil at Oxford on the objective atonement in Dale, Denney, and Forsyth (1958), Mikolaski wrote articles on the latter's theology for the *Evangelical Quarterly* (1964), contributed a survey article on Forsyth to the widely-used textbook *Creative Minds in Contemporary Theology* (1966, 2nd ed., 1969), and introduced him in Forsyth's own words in the book, *The Creative Theology of P. T. Forsyth: Selections from His Works* (1969).

"No theme is more dominant in Forsyth's writings than the holiness of God and the reality of the moral order," wrote Mikolaski. Such holiness can be seen in two ways: "First, it is public and universal; second, it is God's nature and exhibited in the acts of God."[35] In considerable detail, Mikolaski outlined Forsyth's theology, returning again and again to God's holiness as the key concept in understanding many doctrinal areas, among them the

---

[34] For full details, see the relevant sections of the Bibliography.
[35] Samuel J. Mikolaski, "The Theology of P. T. Forsyth," *Evangelical Quarterly* 36 (January-March 1964): 32.

moral order ("The Biblical idea of the righteousness of God is what we mean by the moral order"), human sin ("Sin and guilt are measured not in abstraction but against the righteousness of the holy God"), and the atonement ("The Cross reveals the public righteousness of God").[36] Although his exposition is closely footnoted, the seasoned reader of Forsyth may detect something of an imbalance in the references to holiness and, as the above quotations show, to righteousness – an uncommon word from Forsyth's pen. There is also a corresponding lack of emphasis on the love of God. While Forsyth *did* stress God's holiness, and indeed campaigned for its return to theological discourse both in the pulpit and the academy, it is our contention (to be detailed in Chapter Six below) that this did not imply any diminishment in the doctrinal importance of the divine love. Mikolaski's references to that love, by contrast, are not only infrequent, but when God's love is mentioned it is almost always within a context where God's holiness is more important.[37] All of this suggests that he undervalues the role of the love of God in Forsyth's theology.

Such a view is confirmed, in our opinion, by Mikolaski's neglect of Forsyth's use of the 'holy love' combination. In the three substantial articles we have been examining, the holy love of God is only mentioned twice.[38] In one entire article set aside to a detailed study of Forsyth's doctrine of the atonement, these distinctive words which are so typical of Forsyth's soteriology are not referred to or used even once. Such an omission is extremely unusual, and when combined with Mikolaski's overwhelming concentration on God's holiness to the neglect of his love suggests that he sees Forsyth through the eyes of a tradition where holiness is God's pre-eminent attribute, and divine love the experience of only a fortunate few.

From a very different perspective, Clifford Anderson McKay comes to a similar conclusion. In a 1970 doctoral dissertation for Vanderbilt University, McKay asserts, "The most crucial single category for Forsyth is the category of holiness. . . . Holiness is the

---

[36] Mikolaski, "Theology of P. T. Forsyth," p. 32; Samuel J. Mikolaski, "P. T. Forsyth on the Atonement," *Evangelical Quarterly* 36 (April-June 1964): 79, 85.
[37] See, for example, Mikolaski, "P. T. Forsyth on the Atonement," p. 83; and S. J. Mikolaski, "P. T. Forsyth," in *Creative Minds in Contemporary Theology*, ed. P. E. Hughes (Grand Rapids: Wm. B. Eerdmans, 1966), p. 319.
[38] Mikolaski, "Theology of P. T. Forsyth," p. 33; and Mikolaski, "P. T. Forsyth," p. 313.

heart of Forsyth's theological work."³⁹ In a dispassionate style, McKay ably describes and critiques Forsyth's views of conscience, holiness, the cross, and faith. Surprisingly, he does not at any point discuss the crucial fact that for Forsyth, God's holiness is an integral part of a whole personality whose character is equally that of love. This neglect leads him to criticize Forsyth for a separation between moral and personal categories.⁴⁰ The force of such an argument is lessened, however, when Forsyth's insistence on yoking holiness and love in God's nature is given due emphasis. God's holiness is *loving* holiness, with the practical result that in Forsyth's view, the clash of sin and law is not in any way a mechanical conflict, but rather a matter of personal relationship, a confrontation between sinful, needy humanity and the holy, loving God. Therefore McKay's description of Forsyth's theology, for all its acuteness, lacks an important dimension. Failure to recognize the dynamic personalism of a God defined as holy love leads him to make the same error as Mikolaski: the balance between holiness and love is tipped in favour of holiness.

3.2 HOLINESS AS AN ASPECT OF GOD'S LOVE

Gwilym Griffith's 1948 volume about Forsyth's theology was the first monograph about Forsyth, and was published to coincide with the centenary of his birth.⁴¹ While valuable as a brief introduction to his thought, unfortunately the treatment is for the most part only cursory. A short chapter is given over to God's holiness, but an unprofitable comparison with Rudolf Otto steals most of the attention. The love of God is mentioned only briefly, and holy love not at all. Still, Griffith notes "Forsyth's insistence upon the category of the Divine Wrath (not indeed as limiting, or contradicting, the Divine Love, but as an aspect of it)."⁴² This view, mentioned but not explored, serves to introduce the second position we identify concerning love, holiness, and holy love: Griffith interprets Forsyth as seeing holiness as an aspect of love.

---

³⁹ Clifford Anderson McKay, Jr., "The Moral Structure of Reality in the Theology of Peter Taylor Forsyth" (PhD diss., Vanderbilt University, Nashville, Tennessee, 1970), p. 112.
⁴⁰ McKay, "Moral Structure of Reality," p. 279.
⁴¹ Gwilym O. Griffith, *The Theology of P. T. Forsyth* (London: Lutterworth Press, 1948).
⁴² Griffith, *Theology of P. T. Forsyth*, pp. 72–73.

The same position is advanced in a book of wider scope and greater importance. William Bradley's early work on Forsyth represents a substantial contribution to our understanding both biographically and theologically.[43] Prepared for a PhD at the University of Edinburgh and published in 1952 in the heyday of Forsyth studies, the work combines a sketch of the theologian's life, information about his early intellectual development, and detailed theological exposition. This latter part of the book travels widely over Forsyth's views, from the doctrines of God and humanity, through the work and person of Christ, to the church. Bradley refers to "Forsyth's emphasis upon holiness, wherein he differs from every theologian of his generation,"[44] and his exposition of Forsyth's thought accurately reflects that heavy emphasis. Bradley sounds the characteristic notes of his theology of God's attributes which we will expound in the following chapters, including the holiness of the Father, the dangers of both legalism and sentimentalism, and the moral accomplishment of the cross.[45] In addition (and here Bradley goes beyond Mikolaski), Forsyth's stress on God's love is noted, and the distinctive phrase 'holy love' quoted often to illustrate this dual emphasis.

There is much here that is worthy of note, but instead of pre-empting aspects of the discussion later in our pages, we observe that Bradley is uncomfortable with the tension that this contrast seems to create, moving quickly to reduce holy love to love. In explaining the usefulness of Forsyth's idea, Bradley comments, "With the idea of holy love he had discovered a means of giving moral content to love."[46] Here, Bradley characterizes God's holiness as an aspect of his love. Although that is certainly part of Forsyth's intention, as a grammatical view of the words 'holy love' alone would confirm, our reading of Forsyth leads us to suggest that this conclusion stops short of the whole truth Forsyth wanted to affirm, which was to restore the theological place of God's holiness, not to secondary status under love, but to a primary place inseparably yoked with the love of God. In another place, Bradley explains: "God's nature is holy love; therefore, both judgment and grace only represent this love in its response to man's particular state. Love

---

[43] W. L. Bradley, *P. T. Forsyth: The Man and His Work* (London: Independent Press, 1952).
[44] Bradley, p. 102.
[45] Bradley, pp. 119–121.
[46] Bradley, p. 82.

will be expressed as judgment where sin abounds; yet because God is love, His judgment is accompanied by grace."[47] This interpretation of Forsyth subtly reduces the reality of God's holiness by making judgment "only" a divine response to sin. To say that love is expressed as judgment bypasses the personal holiness of God, in preparation for considering it as merely an aspect of God's love. This view sees love as the *real* nature of God, and holiness as only an expression of that. In himself God is love, but we experience that as holiness.

3.3 THE IMPORTANCE – AND PRIORITY – OF HOLY LOVE

Two interlocking conclusions emerged to compete with the positions outlined above, and both concerned God's holy love. The first was a recognition of the importance of this expression in the context of Forsyth's theology, while the second was an elaboration on the first, asserting more clearly why 'holy love' was important.

It can be recognized from the preceding discussion that the attributes of God – and in particular, the divine love and holiness – are prominent features in Forsyth's writing. Moreover, our survey of the secondary literature up to this point has illustrated the initial realization of that importance, and the subsequent development of a variety of interpretations concerning the relation of these attributes. Forsyth's distinctive combination of words, the 'holy love' of God, has played an integral part in that academic debate. While there has not yet been any sustained discussion of this important topic in Forsyth's theology, there is nevertheless a small chorus of scholars who acknowledge the prominence of 'holy love' in his writing.

We have already noticed J. K. Mozley's early observation that Forsyth repeatedly uses the term, and Markus Barth's opinion of its theological usefulness. Subsequently, both William Bradley and John Rodgers spoke of this theme in Forsyth's writing. James Daane goes further, however, asserting that holy love is more that just an important theme:

> The basic motif of Forsyth's theology is the burning Holy Love of God revealed at the Cross, where it overcomes sin and Satan and reestablishes communion with man the sinner. This objective disclosure of Holy Love is experienced by man in his moral self, i.e., in his conscience; here he knows that Holy Love is, therefore, grace. Forsyth was not a

---
[47] Bradley, p. 195.

systematic theologian; but all the other rich and suggestive motifs of this restlessly questioning theologian are intended as an expanding exposition of this basic motif of God's Holy Love.[48]

While recognizing the importance of the formulation, Daane's assertion overstates the case, we believe. Although the contrast may be slight, we prefer Donald Bloesch's conclusion: "In Forsyth's view the heart of evangelical faith lies in the message of the cross. Soteriology was even more important for him than Christology" – and, we would add, the atonement even more important than the doctrine of God's attributes. Although our focus in this thesis will be on God's love and holiness, these are revealed in the course of God's saving involvement with the world through Christ and his cross, and that cross is the "basic motif" in P. T. Forsyth's theology. Bloesch concludes, "Forsyth saw the cross of Christ as the creative moral crisis of history, the point where divinity and humanity, time and eternity, judgment and grace met for a new creation."[49] God's holy love may be an important interpretive phrase in Forsyth's theology, but the atoning death of Jesus is the centre from which a whole variety of themes emanates, the personal event that spawns many "rich and suggestive motifs" – such as grace, kenosis, ethics, judgment, and many more.

If it be granted that this formulation about God's attributes, 'holy love,' is a prominent aspect of Forsyth's theological enterprise, what did the literature on that theology contribute to an understanding of the term beyond William Bradley's views examined earlier? The answer came in a book published in the same year – 1952 – that Bradley's book appeared, in which the author argued that the turn-of-the-century theologian had a vital message for contemporary people. Robert McAfee Brown's *P. T. Forsyth: Prophet for Today*[50] was a slimmed-down version of his massive doctoral dissertation for Columbia University, and a persuasive argument for the central place of God's grace in Forsyth's theology.

---

[48] James Daane, "Apostle of Grace," review of John H. Rodgers, *The Theology of P. T. Forsyth: The Cross of Christ and the Revelation of God*, in *Christianity Today*, 24 September 1965, p. 20.
[49] Donald G. Bloesch, "Peter Taylor Forsyth," in *Evangelical Dictionary of Theology*, ed. Walter A. Elwell (Grand Rapids, Michigan: Baker Book House, 1984), pp. 422–423.
[50] Robert McAfee Brown, *P. T. Forsyth: Prophet for Today* (Philadelphia: Westminster Press, 1952); see also Robert McAfee Brown, "P. T. Forsyth," in *A Handbook of Christian Theologians*, enlarged ed., eds. Dean G. Peerman and Martin Marty (Nashville: Abingdon, 1984; original ed., 1965).

And since Forsyth believes that grace is just another word for holy love (an assertion that Brown documents), the important place he accords to grace is a confirmation of our conviction that God's holy love is an important element in Forsythian theology.[51]

Before speaking of holy love, however, Brown adds his voice to the consensus that God's holiness is "one of the basic elements in his theology." For Forsyth, claims Brown, "holiness is something central to the very nature of the Godhead." But then he immediately adds: "On the other hand, holiness is something very different from love."[52] It would seem that Brown takes a different approach to God's attributes than either Mikolaski or Bradley, being less willing to conflate them, and decidedly unwilling to merge one into another.

The same tendencies are found in a book on Forsyth's theology by John Rodgers.[53] While the works by Griffith, Bradley and Brown were published in the early years of the Forsyth renaissance, Rodgers's book appeared at the end of that period, in 1965, the year of the last Independent Press reprinting of any of Forsyth's works. This University of Basle thesis affirms the prominence of divine holiness in no uncertain terms. Rodgers writes, "There is no one point at which Forsyth stood so alone as in his conscious, explicit relating of all doctrine to a fundamental understanding of God as holy."[54] Then, turning to a discussion of holy love, Rodgers asserts that this formulation ensures that God's love is unique and "and can only be understood as an expression of his holy self."[55] Far from making one attribute more important than another, he sees both as aspects and expressions of God's nature. Two points are especially important to Rodgers in regard to God's holy love. The first is expressed in his heading, "Holiness and Love as a Unity in God's Holy Love," in which he stresses that God's attributes are not to be read off human nature, but that both love and holiness should be theocentrically defined. The second point is this: "Holy love works, acts, redeems in the Cross of Jesus Christ. It is he 'in whom the

---

[51] Brown, *Forsyth: Prophet for Today,* p. 76, who quotes Forsyth, *The Holy Father and the Living Christ,* Little Books on Religion, ed. W. Robertson Nicoll (London: Hodder & Stoughton, 1897), p. 19, reprinted in *God the Holy Father* (1957), p. 7.
[52] Brown, *Forsyth: Prophet for Today,* p. 75.
[53] John Rodgers, *The Theology of P. T. Forsyth: The Cross of Christ and the Revelation of God* (London: Independent Press, 1965).
[54] Rodgers, p. 30.
[55] Rodgers, p. 36.

holiness goes out as love, suffers the judgement, and redeems as grace."⁵⁶

Both Brown and Rodgers interpret Forsyth's use of God's holy love as stressing the conceptual difference between these two attributes while at the same time maintaining that love and holiness are integrally related within God's nature. Both, however, devote comparatively little space to this claim. Brown is content to note that Forsyth equates holy love with grace, and then concentrates his attention on Forsyth's explicit use of the latter term. Rodgers, for his part, keeps the holy love of God in view throughout by constantly using the term, especially in capitalized form as a name for God, but beyond the discussion we have cited, does not often use it substantively. It is our view, to be substantiated in the remainder of this thesis, that Brown and Rodgers are substantially correct in this interpretation of God's holy love.

4. HOLINESS, LOVE, AND HOLY LOVE: THE DEBATE ILLUSTRATED

To conclude this chapter, we listen in on a conversation of sorts involving these three views of God's attributes. The American theologian Nels Ferré, who holds a more pronounced version of the *second* position we have outlined, interprets P. T. Forsyth as holding the *first* of the views we have presented. Before we elaborate on that, however, perhaps a word of introduction would be in order. "An almost constant debate," observes Ferré, "seems to go on between those who make love central and those who make holiness central to the nature of God."[57] With only a nod to the unity of the divine attributes, Ferré asserts, "God is entirely love and love is entirely holy, for holiness is the infinite purity of love or internal self-consistency of its nature;" in other words, holiness is functional while love is eternal.[58] He adds that Forsyth, "with a noble intention to combat the sentimentalism of liberalism, but with lack of perspective and systematic horizon," advocates the priority of holiness in God's character. Ferré dismisses this view because holiness "is not that completely inclusive outgoing concern which

---

[56] Rodgers, p. 42, quoting *Positive Preaching and [the] Modern Mind,* 1st ed. (1907), p. 254.
[57] Nels F. S. Ferré, *The Christian Understanding of God* (London: SCM, 1951), pp. 114–115.
[58] Ferré, *Christian Understanding of God,* p. 115.

must win the victory, and therefore it cannot solve the problem of evil."⁵⁹

Yet Ferré forgets that the holiness of which Forsyth speaks is characterized by love, a holiness accompanied constantly by all God's other attributes. The earlier theologian's concern is not to replace love with holiness, but to insist that God's love is holy love. For Forsyth, wrote Kenneth Hamilton in a reply to Ferré, "one love alone mattered – the holy love found in the Cross."⁶⁰ Hamilton's article in *Canadian Journal of Theology* is unique in its consideration of our topic. At issue, he explains, is how to eliminate the rivalry between God's love and holiness. As for Ferré, "his plan for reconciliation is for the Kingdom of Love to annex the Kingdom of Holiness," while Forsyth's (according to Hamilton) is the converse.⁶¹

Hamilton's vigorous refutation of Ferré's position has much to interest us, although it might be wished that he had gone further and considered Forsyth's position in more detail. Moreover, having clarified some points of difference between love and holiness, and what Ferré characterizes as the 'family' and the 'juridical' perspectives,⁶² Hamilton says only a little about Forsyth's distinctive position. What does Forsyth's use of the word-combination 'holy love' tell us about the relation between holiness and love? If we are to understand and perhaps answer that question, what is required is an investigation into the work of Christ that pays particular attention to the attributes of God. Building on the work done hitherto concerning Forsyth's doctrine of the atonement, and continuing the discussion presented above concerning God's attributes, we propose to do precisely that in the remainder of this thesis.

---

⁵⁹ Ferré, *Christian Understanding of God*, pp. 116, 117.
⁶⁰ Kenneth Hamilton, "Love or Holy Love? Nels Ferré versus P. T. Forsyth," *Canadian Journal of Theology* 8 (October 1962): 230.
⁶¹ Hamilton, "Love or Holy Love?" p. 229.
⁶² Nels F. S. Ferré, *Evil and the Christian Faith* (New York: Harper, 1947), pp. 46–47, quoted in Hamilton, "Love or Holy Love?" p. 233.

Chapter Three

The Knowledge of God

Your God has to be, let's be blunt about it, your own personal and temporary improvization.

Don Cupitt

In the previous chapters we have, in effect, presented a variety of contexts from within which to view the specific concern of this thesis, P. T. Forsyth's understanding of the holy love of God revealed in Christ's cross. In Chapter One, we explored something of the background to that expression in earlier theological writers of the nineteenth century; Forsyth was seen as a notable English-speaking theologian who adopted an expression used by several nineteenth-century theologians writing in German. Then we turned to see the emerging use of 'holy love' in Forsyth's own theology; it first appeared in 1891 and by 1896 its place was established and secure. We also discovered that Forsyth's own experience of being turned 'from a lover of love to an object of grace' mirrored his early theological pilgrimage; he moved from a Ritschlian emphasis on the sole priority of God's love to a distinctive position that championed the cause of God's holiness without neglecting the divine love. Then in Chapter Two, we surveyed the secondary literature relating to Forsyth's views about the attributes of God, thus describing the scholarly context within which the present work is conducted; we found that while there has been considerable discussion of Forsyth's doctrine of the atonement, there is considerable scope for further study of his view of God's nature and attributes, and hence a place for this exploration of his characteristic phrase, the 'holy love' of God.

The Knowledge of God

In this chapter we turn from context to content, although these two are not entirely separate or easily separable; as we have seen, Forsyth's theological contribution is closely related to his own spiritual experience. While it would be tempting to investigate immediately the specific question of how P. T. Forsyth forges his distinctive idea of God's holy love, such a task requires a more general introduction to his views concerning the knowability of God's attributes.

If we are to appreciate his conclusions when he speaks of God's holy love, a necessary preliminary (we repeat) is to consider the epistemological foundation on which Forsyth builds. How can we presume to investigate the specific matter of God's attributes without an assurance that God is knowable? From what source does such knowledge actually come, according to Forsyth? As we will see shortly, this "evangelical theologian hailed as a modern prophet by both his admirers and his critics,"[1] has created a division of opinion on this subject. In order to understand this debate, we must follow his argument quite closely.

"Everything does turn," Forsyth asserts, "on our footing, on our starting-point, our notion of reality." In theology generally, and in this study in particular, our point of departure is important. Specifically, Forsyth asks:

> Do we find it in the *Word* or in the *World,* in a given Revelation or in innate thought, in the super-rational or in the rational, in the experience of supernatural grace or of natural culture, in the sense of the holy or in that of the merely spiritual?[2]

We propose to explore Forsyth's answer to this multifaceted question by means of a wide-ranging discussion about general and special revelation, and more specifically about the possibility of a natural theology and the reality of God's self-disclosure in Christ and his cross. In the process of this discussion, we will be introduced to Forsyth's theological method, his doctrine of sin, and his view of the person of Christ. All these (and more that lie outside the purview of this study) are connected in Forsyth's mind. Therefore, the present chapter will investigate Forsyth's view of what he calls 'reality,' and particularly the possibility of knowing the moral reality of God. Following that, we will go on in Chapter Four to

---

[1] D. G. Bloesch, in *Evangelical Dictionary of Theology,* ed. Walter A. Elwell (Grand Rapids, Michigan: Baker Book House, 1984), p. 422.

[2] *The Principle of Authority,* 2nd ed. (1952; orig. pub. 1913), p. 178; see also *Positive Preaching and [the] Modern Mind,* 1st ed. (1907), pp. 247–249.

consider the attributes of God as part of that knowledge which is attained to.

1. THE POSSIBILITY OF A NATURAL THEOLOGY

Where does Forsyth stand in the perennial theological debate about a topic variously described as general revelation or natural theology? Is his point of departure, to use his terminology, in the *Word* or in the *World*? Is it possible to know God apart from, and perhaps prior to, God's Word? Is there a natural knowledge of God, more widely accessible and authoritative to a wider audience, which obviates or at least relativizes the necessity of the particular, historical, inscripturated, and experienced revelation concerning Jesus Christ? Could we perhaps find the nature of God (for example) in an inner sense of God's presence, in the course of history, or in some intellectual scheme? Finally and specifically, in our study of what Forsyth calls the holy love of God, what attitude should we take to the various sources that may claim to contribute to our understanding of that holiness, that love, and that God?

On the face of it, Forsyth's general answer to this complex web of questions is clear, and consistent with the Christocentric emphasis noted earlier in this chapter. He says:

> We cannot discover a God of holy love in the career of history so far as gone, nor in the principles of a rational idealism; we can but meet Him at the point where it pleased Him to appear as Saviour, and greet Him at the historic spot He chose, to set for ever His name and nature there.[3]

The knowledge of God is not found by careful examination of contemporary history or by close philosophical reasoning from the human side; rather, God has taken the initiative, chosen the ground, and revealed "His name and nature" in Jesus Christ. The words we may use to call on God and the content of that understanding are given incarnationally. In Christ, God is revealed and known, and it is to this revelation that those who would consider his attributes must look.

Throughout his writings, Forsyth reiterates the impossibility of a natural theology. In 1893 he contributed an essay to a volume called *Faith and Criticism,* which, in the light of the advance of Biblical criticism, attempted to do for Congregationalism and the Free Churches generally what *Lux Mundi* had done for the Church of England. Forsyth's paper, "Revelation and the Person of Christ,"

---

[3] *The Justification of God,* 2nd ed. (1948; orig. pub. 1916), p. 192.

was described by leading Free Church theologian R. W. Dale as "brilliant and vigorous."[4] Provocatively, Forsyth asserted that to look for God's revelation in the realm of nature is "the very genius of Paganism." He wrote, "If we will use words carefully, there is no Revelation in Nature. There can be none, because there is no forgiveness.... For the conscience, stricken or strong, she has no word. Therefore she has no Revelation."[5]

But if not in nature, perhaps in human nature? No, says Forsyth, it is impossible to find a saving revelation in our hearts because they contain only "a broken reflection" of God, and "the heart's voice is the voice of a sinful heart." Forsyth rejects natural theology, arguing that if revelation springs from nature, whether the cosmos or the heart, the natural world or the natural man, then "it is inevitable that Christ should come to be viewed as only a medium or preparation for this experience," which, once attained, can safely ignore him.[6] The force of these assertions is unmistakable; in a review, B. B. Warfield notes that Forsyth is teaching "the impossibility of a natural theology."[7]

But a voice has been raised against that conclusion. With the advantage of surveying Forsyth's work as a whole, Ralph C. Wood identifies "Forsyth's negative natural theology" in the place he allows for the conscience:

> Forsyth insists that Jesus Christ alone can transform the natural conscience into a 'new creation' ruled by God. Yet the universal cry of the stricken soul remains the basis for moral response to the God of the cross. Hence the double and sometimes contradictory emphases in Forsyth's theology: as Evangelical, he stresses the scandalous particularity and unsurpassability of God's self-disclosure in Jesus Christ; as Liberal, he locates the heart of Christian faith within the troubled human conscience.[8]

Wood's particular concern – to relate Forsyth's view of grace and nature to the arts – is beyond our remit, but as it relates to the question of natural theology his charge must be taken seriously. If

---

[4] R. W. Dale to E. A. Lawrence, 6 May 1893, quoted in A. W. W. Dale, *The Life of R. W. Dale of Birmingham*, 2nd ed. (London: Hodder & Stoughton, 1902), p. 659.

[5] "Revelation and the Person of Christ," in *Faith and Criticism: Essays by Congregationalists* (London: Sampson Low Marston, 1893), pp. 99, 100.

[6] "Revelation and the Person of Christ," pp. 100–101.

[7] B. B. Warfield, review of *Faith and Criticism*, in *Presbyterian and Reformed Review* 5 (1894): 356.

[8] Ralph C. Wood, "Christ on Parnassus: P. T. Forsyth among the Liberals," *Journal of Literature and Theology* 2 (1988): 84–85.

the conscience rather than Christ is really the "basis" or foundation for true knowledge of God, our concentration on the value of the revelation in Christ is an effort of only secondary value. If human moral awareness is really "the heart of Christian faith," if conscience is where the centre of the matter is, then our efforts in discerning the attributes of God should be directed away from the holy love of God revealed in Christ's cross, and turned inward to the place where God's word and activity are decisively revealed. So, how are we to make sense of the contradictory interpretations by Warfield and Wood? The solution lies in Forsyth's carefully nuanced view of the conscience.

2. CONSCIENCE AND CHRIST

P. T. Forsyth writes about the conscience with a verve that conveys his conviction of its importance. One commentator says: "For a searching analysis of conscience from both the psychological and religious side Forsyth's teaching equals that of Kierkegaard in whom he found a kindred spirit."[9] This is an area, perhaps, that benefits more than others from Forsyth's twenty-five years experience of pastoral work.

The first thing that becomes apparent as we look at the conscience from Forsyth's perspective is his rejection of any suggestion that human nature retains any natural innocence, or that some aspect of human nature escaped the crippling effects of sin. In his view, there is no way back to some past Eden, and no hope for the theologian of rediscovering an unfallen conscience created in the image of God. Forsyth rejects that avenue of inquiry. "We must take man in his actual historic situation [of sin and guilt]," he writes, "and if we do this the so-called natural conscience does not exist. It is an abstraction; and what exists is the historic product, the sinful conscience."[10] Forsyth decided there was little use in contrasting a theoretical, 'natural,' unfallen conscience with either its sinful or redeemed counterpart. Such a decision commends itself for its practical nature, and avoids a great deal of unfruitful speculation. More importantly, it reveals a Christocentric emphasis that turns theologian and preacher alike away from speculating on the past to

---

[9] A. F. Simpson, "P. T. Forsyth: The Prophet of Judgment," *Scottish Journal of Theology* 4 (1951): 152.
[10] "The Cross as the Final Seat of Authority" (1899), in *The Gospel and Authority: A P. T. Forsyth Reader*, ed. Marvin W. Anderson (Minneapolis, Minnesota: Augsburg, 1971), p. 173.

concentrating on the decisive events of God's history with humanity, and in particular to the redeeming death of Jesus Christ on the cross, the preaching of the gospel to human consciences, and the personal experience of God's holy love.

However, another contrast was important for Forsyth, and in a potentially confusing shift of terminology, he also adopts the adjective 'natural' to describe the *sinful* conscience *apart from the gospel*. Having concluded that there is no return to innocence, Forsyth speaks of "the natural conscience, doomed by its endless internecine strife, now accusing now excusing itself, and delivered over to individual death and social disintegration."[11] Such a sinful conscience, as yet unchallenged by the gospel, and unmet by Jesus Christ, is nevertheless a disturbing presence, eliciting variously "a vague sense of imperfection," "a dim disquiet," and "an inner schism and a real sense of retribution, however vague, when conscience does bite." There is no knowledge of God in such an experience, only a fear of awful self-realization or public humiliation: "It is the fear of judgment, indeed, but the judgment of exposure to man, not of inquisition by God."[12] Here Forsyth maintains that apart from the gospel, individuals lack any sense that inner judgment is God's judgment. When the conscience deliberates in a pagan context, Forsyth asserts, there is no sense of a divine judge, and no knowledge of God.

The natural, sinful conscience described in the previous paragraph, however, is something of a construction, Forsyth admits, not exactly hypothetical, but nevertheless an unusual variety of conscience, not often found in the Christianized western world: "in civilised communities to-day it does not exist."[13] Instead, in a Christian milieu informed but largely unmoved by the revelation of Jesus Christ, elements of this historic revelation are incorporated into the public perception. The human conscience envisions a deity that matches the sense of experienced judgment. The vague sense of guilty embarrassment felt by the so-called natural conscience is compounded and exacerbated by the preaching of the gospel, with

---

[11] "The Evangelical Basis of Free Churchism," *Contemporary Review* 81 (1902): 684–685. See also *Authority*, p. 119. Forsyth is here following John Calvin (See his *Institutes of the Christian Religion*, 2 vols., ed. John T. McNeill, trans. Ford Lewis Battles; Library of Christian Classics, gen. eds. John Baillie, John T. McNeill, and Henry P. Van Dusen [Philadelphia: Westminster, 1960], 2.1.11), who quotes Augustine and Paul (in Ephesians 2.3) in support of his position.
[12] *Positive Preaching*, p. 149.
[13] *Authority*, p. 403.

the result that, for practical purposes, the natural conscience does not exist, either in its abstract and unfallen state, or in its sinful pre-Christian version.

> What does exist [Forsyth writes] is a historic product, deeply, permanently, and universally moulded by the Christian ethic of sin and redemption.... The solemnity of the moral world within each of us is the accumulated and condensed sanctity of centuries of belief, ages of conscience, and millions of wills bowed before the holy order and urgency which wakes human faith, or, if we break with it, makes human tragedy.[14]

A crucial addition is made here to Forsyth's idea of the conscience. Humanity is not merely fallen, but the dilemma of its sinful nature is made acute by the revelation of Jesus Christ in his holiness. It is like a Pandora's box, which, after being opened, cannot be shut. Karl Barth expresses it well: "Once awakened by His revelation, our conscience can never again forget or deny that God knows."[15] But it is important to note that for Forsyth (as for Barth) any inner sense that wrongdoing is challenged by God is a product of the preached gospel. Before that and apart from that, God is not known to any significant extent.

Forsyth is deliberate about the distinction created here. In a development that parallels the apostle Paul's conviction that the law deepened the soul's gloom (Romans 7.13), Forsyth maintains that the gospel's pervasive influence in a society deepens the soul's agony, and increases its perception of guilt. "The Gospel creates far more sense of sin than it finds in the natural conscience and its accusals," he says, and the cumulative effect is a spiritual struggle in which the "conscience is always trying to put itself right, but deepening its despair in every effort, and so blinding its spiritual eye to the very Gospel it is scared into seeking."[16] In this situation, the power of sin reaches its peak, obscuring the truth, heightening the guilt, and increasing the desperation of the person confronted by the gospel.

The influence of the Christian tradition not only creates a sense of sin, but also conveys an indistinct and rudimentary knowledge of God. The sinner realizes that behind the judgment stands a judge. On the human side of the truth, the sense of sin becomes profound; on the divine side, the God of Christian faith is revealed as judge.

---

[14] *Authority*, p. 403.
[15] Karl Barth, *Church Dogmatics* 2/1, p. 546.
[16] *Authority*, p. 119.

According to Forsyth, then, the conscience is a function of the will and an internal moral sense of things, which in response to the gospel (even in its general and cultural presence in a society) is conscious of sin, and of standing guilty before a judge.

At times, the gospel of Jesus Christ breaks free from its cultural captivity. In those specific situations where the Christian message meets individuals, Forsyth believes, the conscience is aggravated by the glory of God in the cross of Christ. Contemplating that cross, he says, "You cannot cease to ask what charge conscience has against you. Then you magnify that to God's charge. If your heart condemn you, His condemnation is greater."[17] Conscience accuses, and in the Christian context it is God who accuses through the conscience.

Only in this context of a society informed by Christian norms and pervaded by Christian culture can we begin to understand Forsyth's further discussion of this matter in *The Cruciality of the Cross*.[18] Because of this identification, Forsyth can boldly conclude:

> Only let society confess the primacy of conscience [and not philosophy or science], and, provided thought be free, it is a mere matter of time till it declare the supremacy of God. ... Conscience involves God; and under His guidance it will evolve Him before all eyes.[19]

We will examine this passage in some detail in a later section, but our concern here is to underline Forsyth's *Sitz im Leben*. His context is not a hypothetical paganism but turn-of-the-century Christian Britain. The "society" he speaks of in the above quotation is a Christianized one which was not only willing but inclined to "confess the primacy of conscience." In addition, the knowledge of God that results is not conceived in opposition to God but brought to light "under His guidance." That is to say, the thinking that will "evolve Him before all eyes" is not the attempt of a natural sinful conscience – Forsyth has already called that the impossible effort of a pagan heart.[20] Rather, it is the pursuit of a mind and conscience already deeply influenced and challenged by the revelation in Christ. "Every conscience we interrogate has this long social history for its *prius*, and indeed, its progenitor," claims Forsyth, referring to the influence of two millennia of Christian teaching. "That is the true and typical human conscience as things are."[21]

---

[17] *The Work of Christ* (1910), p. 166.
[18] *The Cruciality of the Cross*, 1st ed. (1909), pp. 126–133.
[19] *Cruciality*, p. 126–127.
[20] "Revelation and the Person of Christ," p. 99.
[21] *Authority*, pp. 403, 404.

More important than even these considerations, however, is Forsyth's contention that this judge who accuses us is to be identified not with some anonymous divine power, but with Jesus Christ. "Conscience," asserts Forsyth, "is the Word of God within us."[22] In a Christian context, under favourable intellectual conditions, and with divine guidance, conscience will "evolve" a knowledge of God. But this is not a knowledge obtained apart from God the Son, as we discover towards the end of this passage:

> For there is no possibility of going to the bottom of the matter and leaving out Jesus Christ. This error of so many thinkers is a historic evasion. Christ was and is the conscience of mankind and of God. He called Himself man's final judge. Was he deluded? He stands in the whole race as conscience does in every man.[23]

Forsyth's is a carefully nuanced description of conscience, although we have reservations about some of the assumptions on which it is built. In particular, it seems that his view suffers from an overly optimistic view of his 'Christian' society. Even in such a society, conditions are often far from ideal, marred by human error and sin. Despite the cultural influence of Christianity, the pervasive hold of sin is greater.[24] In addition, Forsyth's view fails to take seriously enough other cultures where the name of Christ is much less well-known.

Having said this, however, Forsyth still insists that the voice of conscience should be identified with Jesus Christ. "As Judge of all the earth, as the Conscience of the conscience, Christ is absolute in His judgment."[25] According to Forsyth, all revelation is in Christ.

3. CONSCIENCE AND CORRELATION

If God meets humankind in the context of the conscience, perhaps that context can provide some clues to the nature of God. Further, perhaps these clues can together help the searching soul to attain the salvation it seeks. Indeed, the real moral needs that shape the human pursuit for contentment may be the crucial advance

---

[22] *Cruciality*, p. 132.
[23] *Cruciality*, p. 132.
[24] In other places, as we will see shortly (see section 5 below), Forsyth takes greater care in stressing sin's power to intervene between God's revelation and human apprehension.
[25] This quotation is from Forsyth's untitled article in *The Atonement in Modern Religious Thought: A Religious Symposium* (London: James Clarke, 1900), p. 81.

indications of the divine moral solution to those needs. Such a framework for theological thinking has been developed in Paul Tillich's three-volume systematic theology, which proceeds on a pattern of "existential questions and theological answers" that Tillich calls a method of correlation.[26] It has been suggested that Forsyth's thought illustrates a similar correlation.[27] By this interpretation, conscience would be the human faculty which provokes an existential disquiet, identifies the problem, and then leads us to understand the divine solution. Having first provided the self-knowledge of sin, conscience subsequently points to the saving knowledge of God in Jesus Christ, the Lord of the conscience. In order to gain a greater insight into Forsyth's views of natural theology and to understand better how Forsyth gains a knowledge of God's attributes, we propose to explore this claim. How does Forsyth's thought compare with Tillich's? Is there a method of correlation at work here?

There is some reason to think that Forsyth's thought proceeds on correlative lines, for he utilizes the conceptual framework of dilemma and solution, and elaborates the themes of sin and salvation at length. For example, in the concluding chapter of *The Justification of God,* Forsyth summarizes his argument in this way: "Life begins as a problem, but when it ends well, it ends as a faith: a great problem, therefore a great faith. Ordinary experience gives us the first half, it sets a problem; but the second half, the answer of faith to us, comes from God's revelation of grace."[28] The form of Forsyth's thinking resembles that employed in a scheme of correlation.

However, there are also differences between Forsyth and Tillich on this methodological matter. Whereas Tillich employs the correlation as a comprehensive theological framework, Forsyth's use of the question and answer pattern is restricted to the matter of conscience. Further, while conscience is a major concern for Forsyth, Tillich treats it only briefly, in connection with the ambiguities involved in the ethical life.[29] Neither of these contrasts, however, precludes the possibility that Forsyth's theological method resembles Tillich's pattern of correlation. In order to identify the

---

[26] Paul Tillich, *Systematic Theology,* 3 vols. (Digswell Place, Welwyn, Herts.: James Nisbet, 1953–1964), vol. 2, p. 14.
[27] David Widdicombe, thesis in preparation for Oxford University.
[28] *Justification,* p. 208.
[29] Tillich, *Systematic Theology,* vol. 3, pp. 43, 48.

similarities and determine the differences, we will briefly compare the views of the two theologians. Our specific concern will be to ascertain whether Forsyth uses the idea of conscience in the pursuit of a natural theology.

There is both a balance and an order in Paul Tillich's use of the method of correlation. The balance is indicated in his definition of correlation as the "interdependence of two independent factors," namely "existential questions and theological answers," which have their own autonomy but also mutually inform each other.[30] Despite this balance, however, Tillich maintains that there is an order: questions precede answers. "In using the method of correlation," he writes, "systematic theology proceeds in the following way: it makes an analysis of the human situation out of which the existential questions arise, and it demonstrates that the symbols used in the Christian message are the answers to those questions."[31] He explicitly gives a theoretical priority to the questions. In addition, some critics have noted that "in actual practice the content as well as the form [of the theological answers] became influenced, if not determined, by the philosophical questions."[32]

For Tillich, then, the questions of life open the door to the answers. Although he speaks of "the method of correlation, in which questions and answers determine each other,"[33] such even-handedness belies the possibility that at times the questions are programmatic, developing the answers (at least in part) independently of revelation, and yielding a natural knowledge of God. To adopt John Powell Clayton's felicitous terminology, the *question* has become a *quest:*

> In the *Systematic Theology,* Tillich would seem to have conflated two very different sorts of activities in the particular way he used the phrase 'the question of *x*.' He would seem to have held that 'the question of *x*' includes both forming a question about *x* and undertaking a quest for *x*. For Tillich, 'the question of God', for instance, means both undertaking a quest for God and forming a question about God or even the word 'God'. But these clearly are not identical activities.[34]

---

[30] Tillich, *Systematic Theology,* vol. 2, p. 14.
[31] Tillich, *Systematic Theology,* vol. 1, p. 62.
[32] Stanley J. Grenz and Roger E. Olson, *Twentieth Century Theology: God and the World in a Transitional Age* ([Carlisle]: Paternoster Press, 1992), p. 121. They refer to George F. Thomas and Kenneth Hamilton, among others.
[33] Tillich, *Systematic Theology,* vol. 2, p. 107.
[34] John Powell Clayton, *The Concept of Correlation: Paul Tillich and the Possibility of a Mediating Theology,* Theologische Bibliothek Töpelmann, Bd.

By contrast, P. T. Forsyth's correlation of human dilemma and divine solution refuses to move from one to the other, except insofar as God has revealed the Word to humanity through the preaching of the gospel. Although Forsyth is convinced that the answer fits the question, in no sense does he think that the question leads to the answer. This is clear as we follow his uncharacteristically well-outlined argument in *The Justification of God*. First, he asserts that the human problem is a genuine one, felt keenly by most people. But there is nothing merely theoretical about it: "The problem is disquieting, anxious, and even tragic," as "apostles of negation" such as Strauss and Nietzsche make very clear.[35] Like Tillich, Forsyth takes the existential situation of humanity seriously.

A solution exists to the problem, however, and humankind is not left in pessimism and despair. "The Christian message is that the answer is there, and is the gift of God. It is provided."[36] This is the key to our argument. The priority of grace in Forsyth's theology is exhibited at just this point where natural theology attempts to bridge the gap between sin and redemption. Salvation in Christ is not deduced from moral principles, nor is Christ introduced to the soul by conscience. Instead, "the practical solution of life by the soul is outside life. . . . The key is in the Beyond. . . . The solution of all is indicated as outside all."[37] The answers, then, have priority over the questions.[38]

But would it not be true to say that indications in our lives point the way to God's answer, even if that answer must be appropriated by grace? Yes, answers Forsyth, the lines of morality, thought, and history do converge. "But can we reach faith in that way?" he asks. "No, we cannot."[39] God purposefully makes his way through history,

---

37 (Berlin: Walter de Gruyter, 1980), p. 180. Clayton notes that this point is also made by Alistair M. Macleod, in *Tillich: An Essay on the Role of Ontology in his Philosophical Theology* (London, 1973), pp. 31ff.

35 *Justification*, p. 209.

36 *Justification*, p. 210.

37 *Justification*, pp. 212, 213.

38 In a brief but interesting discussion, Karl Barth counters Tillich's view with the query, "Should not the theological answers be considered as more fundamental than the philosophical questions and as essentially superior to them?" and then goes on to suggest a correlation in terms of covenant. Karl Barth, "An Introductory Report," in Alexander J. McKelway, *The Systematic Theology of Paul Tillich: A Review and Analysis* (Richmond, Virginia: John Knox, 1964), p. 13.

39 *Justification*, pp. 212, 216, 217.

leaving traces of his presence in a general revelation, but sin stands in the way of human discernment of the Holy One. Consequently, it is only by the condescending mercy of God that we may know the divine. God is not deduced or even introduced by conscience. On the contrary, "He emerge[s] on the soul's experience with the miracle of grace."[40] There is indeed a human problem, but it does not contain its own solution within it, knowable apart from God's definitive revelation in Jesus Christ. Eloquently, Forsyth maintains that the solution to life's moral problem is not the conclusions of a natural theology, but the person of the Saviour:

> We cannot solve life by moral thought or effort but by trust, which unites us with the invincible, eternal, moral act of God in Christ. Christianity is not the sacrifice we make, but the sacrifice we trust; not the victory we win, but the victory we inherit. That is the evangelical principle. We do not see the answer; we trust the Answerer, and measure by Him."[41]

We conclude that Forsyth does employ a contrast between human questions and divine answers that Paul Tillich might well recognize as the beginnings of a correlation. But there is a fundamental difference in their use of this pattern. While Tillich's view of the human existential situation plays a significant role in determining the nature of the theological response, Forsyth refuses to let the dilemma determine the solution. For Tillich, the question in some way has a priority over the answer, while Forsyth's conviction is that the answer shows us the true nature of the question. For the German-American theologian, the dilemma has the power to lead into the solution, while for his British counterpart, the answer meets the question on the Answerer's terms. Forsyth maintains, then, that there is a correlation between dilemma and solution. "The problem of problems is the moral problem. . . . , the practical problem of sin. The answer of all is a moral one. It is redemption."[42] But even though both problem and solution lie in the moral realm, in no way does any natural knowledge indicate the answer. Revelation, like redemption, is all of grace.

---

[40] *Justification*, pp. 219–220.
[41] *Justification*, pp. 220–221.
[42] *Justification*, p. 221.

4. CONSCIENCE AS A POINT OF CONTACT

How then are the existential question and the providentially provided answer related? Forsyth maintains that the revitalizing power of Christ's saving death coincides with the need of human lives. While denying that conscience has any power to define the salvation that God provides, Forsyth nevertheless freely admits, and indeed deliberately asserts the fact that the gospel meets individuals in the context of conscience. To deny a correlative role (in the Tillichian sense) to the place of conscience does not imply a denial of the reality of the conscience or of its place in the dynamics of the divine-human encounter. In humanity's moral nature Forsyth finds the contact point for the gospel.

However, to avoid misunderstanding, Forsyth prefaces a discussion of the conscience's role as point of contact with a lengthy cautionary assertion that

> in religious knowledge the object is God; it is not the world, it is not man. And that object differs from every other in being for us far more than an object of knowledge. He is the absolute subject of it. He is not something that we approach, with the initiative on our side. He takes the initiative and approaches us. Our knowledge is the result of His revelation. We find Him because he first finds us. That is to say, *the main thing, the unique thing, in religion is not a God Whom we know but a God Who knows us.*[43]

The inherent danger in mentioning the conscience in this regard, Forsyth realizes, is the temptation to construct a theology with a human foundation. And if humanity is the subject, God is reduced to the object of human scrutiny. Instead Forsyth urges that God is always the subject under whose initiative redemption is revealed.

Having stated this cautionary principle, Forsyth turns his attention to the human side of the relationship in which God's initiative is paramount. The first point he makes regarding the point of contact is that our knowledge of God is personal, reciprocal knowledge: "We have here the point of attachment in natural experience for the knowledge we have of God, insofar as the relation is knowledge. It belongs to that order of knowledge where person meets person."[44] In contrast to this, Forsyth claims, those who see revelation as propositional must "appeal to some previous truth to authenticate it, to some rational *a priori*, with which it must

---

[43] *Authority*, pp. 148–149; his emphasis.
[44] *Authority*, p. 154.

mortise." But Forsyth asserts that "revelation is not God's gift of truth, but of Himself."[45]

Furthermore, it follows that "this *a priori* is not in the region of the reason but of the will."[46] It is Forsyth's concern to avoid any suggestion of a natural theology in the sense defined by the Vatican Council of 1870, which decreed that "God can certainly be known from created things by the natural light of human reason."[47] We have already seen that Forsyth severely circumscribes the claims of human reason; here he draws the line once again: "It is not a rational test but a moral recognition."[48]

Related to the personal nature of human knowledge of God is another contention about the point of contact: "It is not a passivity but a receptivity, a loyalty, an obedience."[49] The reader is cautioned not to confuse receptive persons with passive containers. "It is the response of a will to a will, of the whole finite person to a whole person, absolute and holy. It is therefore ethical in its nature, and not merely impressive or sympathetic."[50] The emphasis here is on God the giver rather than human ability.

At every point Forsyth is keen to deny the possibility of a human claim to be even in part the originator of this knowledge, and therefore the author of salvation. Does God perhaps nurture to fruition the small human beginnings of salvation? No, there is no "germ whose innate resources Revelation develops," only "a recognising power, a receptivity."[51] Could response to God's revelation, then, be construed as an autonomous assertion of human discernment? No, says Forsyth; if the choices are to be put that starkly, we must recognize that we are not called to judge, but to be judged. "We do not sit in judgment on the reasonableness of God's truth," but instead the believer "recognises Another, greater and bigger, Who is revealed." Yet this recognition is also a choice, an act of faith, and so Forsyth goes on to speak of this receptivity more subtly. It is not a matter of the human will being "enabled to assert its own principle," but a far more drastic occurrence, "the

---

[45] *Authority*, p. 155.
[46] *Authority*, p. 168.
[47] Quoted in Walter A. Elwell, ed., *Evangelical Dictionary of Theology* (Grand Rapids, Michigan: Baker, 1984), s.v. "Natural Theology," by J. Van Engen.
[48] *Authority*, p. 171.
[49] *Authority*, p. 174.
[50] *Authority*, p. 157.
[51] *Authority*, p. 157.

redemption of [man's] impotent will.⁵² Human receptivity is not an inherent human possibility somehow immune from sin's debilitating effects, but rather a God-given capacity. Forsyth consistently maintains the priority of the divine subject, and the inability of humanity to know God apart from God's own revelation.

Reference to a landmark controversy concerning this subject may be beneficial. In their stormy debate about natural theology, both Emil Brunner and Karl Barth shared Forsyth's view on the primacy of grace. But the two great mid-twentieth century theologians differed on the matter we have just been discussing, the point of contact. After doctoral study in his native Switzerland, Brunner lived in England for two years (1913–1914), where he became acquainted with the work of P. T. Forsyth, then at the height of his career. Nearly half-a-century later in an interview on British television with Vernon Sproxton, Brunner put forward Forsyth's name when asked who he thought was the "greatest British theologian of recent times."⁵³ It is perhaps not coincidental, then, to hear a Forsythian echo in Brunner's views. In *Natural Theology,* the English translation of Brunner and Barth's 1934 debate, Brunner says: "This point of contact is the formal *imago Dei,* which not even the sinner has lost, the fact that man is man," with "capacity for words and responsibility." The first of these terms, 'capacity for words,' Brunner explains, means that among God's creatures "he and he alone is receptive of the Word of God." But the Swiss theologian cautions that this receptivity does not refer to "acceptance or rejection of the Word of God. It is the purely formal possibility of his being addressed." Brunner's second term, 'responsibility,' refers to the work of conscience: "This knowledge of sin is a necessary presupposition of the understanding of the divine message of grace."⁵⁴ The receptivity of conscience is precisely Forsyth's concern in discussing the point of contact.

Barth's essential objection to this view is that lurking behind the idea of receptivity is "a remainder of some original righteousness, an

---

⁵² *Authority,* p. 172.
⁵³ Emil Brunner, "Emil Brunner on his Faith and Work," interview by Vernon Sproxton (8 February 1961), *Listener,* 16 February 1961, pp. 307–308. For a discussion of Forsyth's possible influence on Brunner, see Samuel J. Mikolaski, "P. T. Forsyth," in *Creative Minds in Contemporary Theology,* ed. P. E. Hughes (Grand Rapids, Michigan: Eerdmans, 1966), pp. 333–337.
⁵⁴ Emil Brunner, "Nature and Grace," in Karl Barth and Emil Brunner, *Natural Theology,* trans. Peter Fraenkel (London: Geoffrey Bles, The Centenary Press, 1946), p. 31. For the specific reference to conscience, see p. 25.

openness and readiness for God" that is already well on the way to supplying "everything connected with the 'natural' knowledge of God."[55] For his part, Forsyth will have none of this possibility. Human receptivity to divine grace is not knowledge of God, and the ability to be addressed is not an assertion of human prerogative. Or, to use his own words: "The action on a sensitive surface is not the same thing as the appeal to a judge," "response is other than proof," and "God has points of affinity and attachment in us which are not criteria."[56] Forsyth insists that revelation, acting on the human will, elicits the choice of faith, "but it is a receptive choice on our part, it is not a creative."[57] He maintains the priority of God's grace, even and especially in the matter of faith's response.

At the same time, Forsyth stresses the reality of human response in the place he accords to moral awareness. "The conscience owns, in a sense of guilt, the approach of the absolute Conscience, His entrance, both on history and on the soul, with a sheer regenerating power, more miraculous in its action than continuous."[58] The conscience acknowledges the Conscience; humanity confesses Christ. So Forsyth's answer to the question, 'Does conscience commend the gospel and prepare the way for it?' is in the negative. Rather, the gospel transforms the human subject in such a dramatic way that the conscience can only assent.

Forsyth's provocative contrast between conscience and Conscience indicates the commanding priority that he gives to God's action, and consequently to revelation in preference to any reliance on natural theology. Although Forsyth is unwilling to deny the importance of conscience as the human moral context to which the gospel appeals, he repeatedly maintains that "the greatest conscience of all the world" is God's.[59] He insists that our point of view is that of God meeting the conscience in its need, rather than the conscience preparing the way for God. No human preparation paves the way for salvation, and no moral effort spurred on by

---

[55] Karl Barth, "No!", in *Natural Theology*, p. 89.
[56] *Authority*, pp. 145–146.
[57] *Authority*, p. 174. In a recent article about the disagreement between Brunner and Barth, Trevor Hart identifies the idea of capacity as "that upon which the whole debate hinges," and concludes that a distinction like Forsyth's – between receptivity and aptitude, passive and active capacity – is required; see Hart, "A Capacity for Ambiguity?: The Barth-Brunner Debate Revisited," *Tyndale Bulletin* 44 (Autumn 1993): 289–305.
[58] *Authority*, p. 196.
[59] *The Christian Ethic of War* (1916), p. 115; see also *Cruciality*, p. 132.

conscience can bring redemption closer. Nevertheless, Forsyth does insist that conscience is the point of contact to which the revelation of God in Christ pertains.

5. THE POWER OF SIN, AND THE LIMITED VALUE OF GENERAL REVELATION

After giving considerable attention to Forsyth's view of God's action in the human conscience, we turn to evaluate its usefulness. Can conscience provide knowledge of God's interest in humanity, either as judge or Saviour? Here we discover that Forsyth argues that human sinfulness drastically limits the good that might be gained from such revelation. He often combines two effects. Human sin, he contends, leads to a sense of guilt which is not merely troublesome but immobilizing. He speaks of "the helplessly guilty conscience of man," and of "the conscience in its impotent despair."[60] Not only is sin felt keenly, and individual culpability recognized, but the conscience senses the inability to solve its own dilemma. The existential situation of guilt is certainly a real problem, but the seriousness of sin prevents us from having even a dim intuition of the answer. People from varying theological approaches can agree on the reality of personal guilt, but Forsyth's conviction about human inability to know God's saving solution to the sinful human situation prompts him to draw an absolute line between question and answer, a line which cannot be crossed by the natural theology of a Tillichian correlation, which at this point reveals its naïvety about the effects of sin.

Forsyth says that the fall of man "is his moral tragedy, the fall not from happiness but from holiness – the tragedy not simply of gloom but of guilt. Behind all the tragedies of incident lies the tragedy of guilt."[61] But guilt is more than culpability. The voice of conscience conveys the voice of divine judgment, and individuals are therefore left without excuse. Sin is shown to be exceedingly sinful. Unfortunately for the individual in his or her anguish over sin, conscience can accuse but not absolve. "It repents, but the penitent conscience cannot forgive."[62] Guilt is within its purview, but atonement is not. As Forsyth says, "It is awake enough to cry for

---

[60] *Authority*, p. 58; "Revelation, Old and New" (1911), in *Revelation Old and New: Sermons and Addresses* (1962), p. 22.
[61] *Justification*, p. 50.
[62] *Authority*, p. 182.

redemption, but not enough to take the Christian redemption home, far less to bring it to pass around."[63] Similarly, for those who hear the gospel preached, this redeeming revelation creates a crisis. "It is an absolute and eternal alternative. It is the human soul's last dilemma. Christ does force the last stand and the last verdict of the conscience for Himself or for His enemies."[64] The weakened conscience requires the power to act in a way that could bring forgiveness, but exactly this is lacking in the sinful conscience. So we have "a moral, a practical problem, ... of the will and conscience."[65] In short, conscience reveals the human dilemma to be one of guilt standing before judgment, while pervasive human sinfulness prevents any apprehension of God's solution in Christ Jesus.

Here we find Forsyth standing in a distinguished tradition that includes John Calvin and the apostle Paul. While speaking forthrightly and without equivocation about the knowledge of God revealed in the cosmos, both seriously qualify the utility of that knowledge. Paul says that "what may be known about God is plain to [persons], because God has made it plain to them," and that his power and divinity have been revealed in the creation (Romans 1.19–20). Furthermore, with regard to the Gentiles, Paul says that "the requirements of the law are written on their hearts, their consciences also bearing witness, and their thoughts now accusing, now even defending them" (Romans 2.15). There is a general revelation, in creation and conscience. But surrounding all of this in Romans 1–3 is Paul's conviction that God's righteous anger is quite appropriately directed towards these very people "who suppress the truth by their wickedness" (Romans 1.18). On all without exception, sin has destroyed the potential good that God's general revelation might have accomplished. The end result is that although God has spoken, "there is no-one who understands" (Romans 3.11).

Similarly, Calvin speaks of a "twofold knowledge of God," distinguishing between "the sort of knowledge with which men, in themselves lost and accursed, apprehend God the Redeemer in Christ the Mediator," and "the primal and simple knowledge to which the very order of nature would have led us if Adam had remained

---

[63] *Positive Preaching*, p. 331.
[64] *The Preaching of Jesus and the Gospel of Christ* (1987; orig. pub. as articles in 1915), pp. 96–97.
[65] *Positive Preaching*, pp. 331–332.

The Knowledge of God

upright."[66] Forsyth follows Calvin closely on his discussion of the efficacy and value of that natural knowledge of God. We note the following comparisons:

First, Calvin and Forsyth agree that there is knowledge of God in both creation and conscience. According to Calvin, not only has God "revealed himself and daily discloses himself in the whole workmanship of the universe" (1.5.1), but God complements this outer witness with an inner one: "God has sown a seed of religion in all men" (1.4.1). Although Forsyth considers the conscience in greater depth, Calvin writes that God has placed in human minds "an awareness of divinity" (1.3.1), and as a result, "the distinction between good and evil is engraved on their consciences."[67]

Secondly, in comparing Forsyth's sketch of God's nature on the basis of general revelation, we discover that Calvin draws a similar picture. Starting from the fact that God is the Creator of the visible universe, Calvin says, "With what clear manifestations his might draws us to contemplate him!" Then he adds, "This very might leads us to ponder his eternity; for he from whom all things draw their origin must be eternal and have beginning from himself." This leads to the conclusion that the cause of creation must be "his goodness alone," which is closely related to God's love and mercy (1.5.6). Or again, starting from the evidence proffered by God's rule in society, "proofs of his powers just as clear are set forth." God is a governor who "declares his clemency to the godly and his severity to the wicked and criminal." In his capacity as judge, the Lord reveals "the unfailing rule of his righteousness." He hates sins, and will finally judge all sinners. Yet his severity is tempered by mercy and kindness (1.5.7). Therefore, Calvin moves from the fact that God is Creator to his power, eternity, and goodness, and deduces from God as moral governor the fact of his righteousness and kindness. If the opinion be advanced that this kind of creative theologizing is restricted to Christians, Calvin adds, "This way of seeking God is common both to strangers and to those of his household, if they trace the outlines that above and below sketch a living likeness of him" (1.5.6).

Thirdly, however, the force of Calvin's decisive qualifying phrase which we have noted earlier – "if Adam had remained upright" (1.2.1) – drastically reduces the value of this knowledge of God. The

---

[66] Calvin, *Institutes*, 1.2.1. Subsequent references to the *Institutes* are made parenthetically in the main text.
[67] John Calvin, Commentary on John 1.5, quoted by McNeill in Calvin, *Institutes*, p. 43, note 2. For related references to conscience, see also 1.3.2 and 1.5.15.

God of conscience has indeed planted "a seed of religion in all men," but so great is the force of human sin that there is "none in whom it ripens" (1.4.1). There is a divinely implanted kernel of truth yielding the conviction that "there is some sort of divinity; but this seed is so corrupted that by itself it produces only the worst fruits" (1.4.4). Similarly, although God reveals himself in the universe he made, "most people, immersed in their own errors, are struck blind in such a dazzling theatre" (1.5.8). Despite the clarity of the revelation, we "sit idly in contemplation" of the creation, but disregard the Creator" (1.5.11). Even worse, we build idols, and "attribute to anything else than the true source the praise of righteousness, wisdom, goodness, and power" (1.5.15). Although God has revealed his attributes in nature, sinful humankind has blinded itself to true holiness and real love.

This leads to a fourth point. We have already seen that for Calvin as for Forsyth, God has revealed himself in creation and conscience, and his word there is both true and substantial. But human sin has smothered that truth and corrupted it, so that the natural knowledge of God is never brought to fruition. Calvin's conclusion, therefore, is that "if men were taught only by nature, they would hold to nothing certain or solid or clear-cut, but would be so tied to confused principles as to worship an unknown god" (1.5.12). Left to examine the corrupted remains of God's revelation, whether in conscience or creation, humanity is helpless. "We have not the eyes to see," says Calvin, "unless they be illumined by the inner revelation of God through faith" (1.5.14). The twofold knowledge of God that Calvin describes is reflected in Forsyth's distinction between revelation and *real* revelation. In Calvin's words, "No religion is genuine unless it be joined with truth" (1.4.3). Or, in the words of the theological tradition, natural knowledge of God is ineffectual unless revealed knowledge is added.

So, in summary, conscience does not provide knowledge of anything resembling a Saviour, but under the pervasive influence of sin, promotes a disquieting sense of judgment. The limited knowledge of God provided by human moral awareness in a Christian context can only accuse and not forgive. The conscience is so weakened by sin that it can only appreciate God's supremacy as judge. It cannot contribute to, but only cry out for, salvation. Conscience is not a voice that reveals, but "the persecuting voice" that judges. "And every now and then," Forsyth asserts, conscience calls, "and we quail."[68]

Forsyth speaks about the limited epistemological value of conscience in various other ways. In one context, he asserts that the effect of conscience varies a great deal within the same individual. Sometimes it registers "no more than a vague sense of imperfection" while at other times we experience "an inner schism and a real sense of retribution."[69] In another place, Forsyth refers to conscience and creation: "They but suggest God rather than they assure Him to us," and "they suggest Him to individuals rather than make Him sure to the world."[70] If this is knowledge of God, it is certainly a dangerously variable, and therefore imperfect, revelation.

Because of these factors, all of which are rooted in the power of sin, the general revelation that God has made in conscience and creation fails to achieve its potential impact. Repeatedly, Forsyth circumscribes the role of conscience. Although it has a certain usefulness, it possesses no authority, and confers none. Although even sinful eyes can make out a vague outline of God's nature, thanks to the revelation in creation and conscience, the full reality of God's holy, loving desire to save is entirely unknown. Forsyth rejects the possibility that conscience could introduce the gospel, or that reason could deduce the salvation God would then go on to reveal. Rather, saving, authoritative truth cannot be found outside of God's redeeming revelation in Christ.

Further, Forsyth also denies that the insights of conscience are apologetically useful. In one discussion, he considers the possibility that a limited natural theology might be effective for merely defensive purposes, as it were. When Christians are challenged that their faith rests on illusion, perhaps a useful reply might be that the revelation of God in Christ is true "because it fits to what was in us before." In this line of thinking, God's revealed truth would be commended because it conforms with mystic experience, rational thinking, or "the response of the conscience." Forsyth's answer to this possibility is to turn the tables once again from human assertion to divine authority. It is not an argument from natural theology but God's revitalizing effect on redeemed humanity that convinces sceptics of the truth of the claims of Jesus Christ. Christianity is reasonable and not illusory "because it brings something so new and

---

[68] *Cruciality*, p. 129.
[69] *Positive Preaching*, p. 149.
[70] "Revelation, Old and New," in *Revelation Old and New*, p. 15.

powerful that it means a new creation."[71] The gospel needs no defenders, no authorities to stand on its side, because it is the final authority. According to Forsyth, we cannot

> refer the Gospel to have its claim tried before some native God-consciousness or ideal on man's side; as if there were some sure and supreme natural knowledge of God prior and permissive to the Selfrevelation of God. A lower revelation may prepare for the higher, and provide a psychology for it, but it cannot measure, and therefore cannot test it nor vouch for it. There is no final and innate revelation of God in human nature, nothing so much deeper and surer than the Gospel that it can lend it a license – there are only points of attachment or modes of action, an economy for a revelation when it comes.[72]

6. THE GOSPEL RECONSTRUCTS OUR VIEW OF CONSCIENCE

The priority of the grace of the gospel has been a recurring theme in our discussion of Forsyth's view of conscience. More than any other factor, it is that gospel that contradicts any claim of conscience to be more than a context for salvation. Forsyth asks provocatively, "How is the natural man to verify a gospel which takes the confidence out of human nature and its instincts, and destroys the egoism which is its first certainty?"[73] Not only is the gospel a 'higher' authority and therefore the measure of all others, but it is also the dynamic force that confronts those authorities – whether they be human reason, spiritual experience, or even the voice of conscience – with a pre-emptive strike that shakes any confidence we may have had in them. The gospel calls all other authorities to account, even those that may serve God's purposes.

The gospel does more than destroy our confidence in lesser authorities, however. Provoked by conscience, but prevented by sin, the human soul is in a dilemma that only the gospel of Jesus Christ can untangle. The power that conscience cannot supply is seen in the power that raised Jesus Christ from the dead. That powerful salvation is a gift of God that transforms the sinful conscience in its guilt into "the evangelical conscience, shaped by faith in the redeemer,"[74] or what Forsyth variously describes as "a saved and

---

[71] *Authority*, pp. 195–196.
[72] *Authority*, pp. 121–122. A recent work to make use of the idea of 'point of contact' in apologetics is Alister McGrath, *Bridge-Building: Effective Christian Apologetics* (Leicester: Inter-Varsity, 1992), especially pp. 17–91.
[73] *Authority*, p. 118.
[74] "The Cross as the Final Seat of Authority" (1899), in *The Gospel and*

enlightened conscience,"[75] and "a conscience washed in pure water."[76] That new conscience "was first created on the Cross by the offering of holiness to the Holy One."[77] Central to this whole discussion and absolutely essential is the atonement provided in Christ's sacrificial death, an act that recreates the conscience.

The cross meets individuals in various ways. For one, repentance comes through being challenged by Christ. Recognizing "the supremacy of the moral in God and His holiness created repentance," says Forsyth.[78] Also, God's act of atonement prompts our trustful response; "the Gospel must *create* the power to believe it."[79] Indeed, the unique thing in Christianity is regeneration that undoes the effects of sin: "It renews a lost moral power in the guilty soul, and removes the grand obstacle in the will to the realisation of our true nature."[80]

It is Christ the revealed Lord who informs every mention of conscience in Forsyth's theology. Through the historic figure of Christ, and especially Christ crucified, God confronts individual conscience. In considering the conscience, then, as in much else, Forsyth (in Goethe's phrase) adjusts his compass at the cross. It is there that God is known, and in the Christ of the cross that a right view of humanity is formed. Forsyth comments, "The Church takes her moral bearings there. She discovers God's moral world and authority there." And, turning specifically to our present concern, he adds, "She reconstructs man's conscience from there, from the word, revelation, and nature of the cross."[81] Such a reconstruction yields significant conclusions. Forsyth looks back to the voice of conscience and concludes that it is "the Word of God within us."[82] In other (non-Forsythian but traditional) words, he affirms the reality of a general revelation of God's will in conscience, which nevertheless is the voice of Christ as pre-existent Word.

We are now in a position to make sense of the contradictory claims of B. B. Warfield and Ralph C. Wood with which we

---

Authority: A P.T. Forsyth Reader, ed. Marvin W. Anderson (Minneapolis, Minnesota: Augsburg, 1971), p. 173.
[75] *Authority,* p. 77.
[76] *Preaching of Jesus,* p. 120.
[77] *Positive Preaching,* p. 327.
[78] *Authority,* p. 180.
[79] *Authority,* p. 119.
[80] *Authority,* pp. 159–160.
[81] "The Holy Father" (1896) in *God the Holy Father* (1957), p. 23.
[82] *Cruciality,* p. 132.

introduced this discussion. While Wood identified Forsyth's natural theology in the place he gives to conscience, Warfield read Forsyth as denying the possibility of a natural theology. Our careful examination of Forsyth's view of conscience has revealed that, far from being a "basis for moral response," as Wood claimed, conscience is merely the context in which the gospel meets humanity. And although God indeed meets humanity at the place of its moral need, it is incorrect to claim that Forsyth "locates the heart of Christian faith within the troubled human conscience."[83] Instead, that central reality is the redemption accomplished on the cross of Christ, where the divine Conscience met the need of human consciences. Wood identifies the beginnings of a natural theology in Forsyth's writings, but as we have seen, Forsyth holds that despite the fact that God has spoken in human conscience, sin seriously obscures that revelation.

Warfield, on the other hand, in his contention that Forsyth holds to "the impossibility of a natural theology,"[84] probes closer to the essence of Forsyth's position. In the matter of 'real' knowledge of God, knowledge that has the power to redeem, Forsyth insists that the natural person has no rights and no ability whatever. Further, the revelation of God in Christ is the judge of all other glimmers of truth, however revealed. The holy, loving God revealed in Jesus Christ radically critiques every other supposed authority.

7. IMPLICATIONS FOR THE PRESENT STUDY

We turn now to consider what value these conclusions hold for our central concern, the study of God's attributes. What are the practical results of Forsyth's view of general revelation on the subject of knowing God's nature?

We have seen that P. T. Forsyth affirms the reality of God's general revelation, but drastically limits the ability of humanity to apprehend it. We have also established that he accords radical epistemological priority to the revelation of God in the cross of Christ. On this basis alone, then, and not because of any natural theology, Forsyth suggests that conscience can perceive something of the outlines of the Christian God:

---

[83] Wood, "Christ on Parnassus," pp. 84–85.
[84] Warfield, review of *Faith and Criticism*, in *Presbyterian and Reformed Review* 5 (1894): 356.

> I would bear you back upon your own conscience, and bid you listen to its voice. Our moral coinage, whose is its image and superscription? ... Man is more than a consciousness, he is a conscience. He is not only aware of himself, he is critical of himself. There is in the soul a bar, a tribunal; our thoughts and actions are ranged before it; judgment is passed there.... We fear this judge, this critic, in our own heart; we go as far, at times, as to hate him.... We cannot get rid of this judge. He is not in our power. We cannot unmake him, though he be against ourselves. Then we did not make him....
>
> Who is this judge that follows us like our shadow? ... Conscience is something spiritual, a thinking being, a living moral mind.
>
> And what follows from the fact that this spiritual 'other' is our judge? Could any judge be a real judge who was not vested with power to enforce his threats and give his reward? ... This judge is one clothed with power; the judge of humankind must be invested with superhuman power to enforce the law he lays upon the human conscience.... The judge must have absolute power. There must be no crevice of the universe into which the culprit could creep and reckon on escape. And for such a moral being who has all power over man we have one name – God. Conscience is the Word of God within us; and moral responsibility means responsibility before God, the living God, and Christ, His living Grace.
>
> For there is no possibility of going to the bottom of the matter and leaving out Jesus Christ. This error of so many thinkers is a historic evasion. Christ was and is the conscience of mankind and of God. He called Himself man's final judge. Was he deluded? He stands in the whole race as conscience does in every man.[85]

From this passage, we conclude that the presence of Christ in the conscience yields a picture of God as a supreme judge, who knows the soul, has power to enforce the divine law, and possesses the ability to pursue the lawbreaker. This figure outlined in the conscience is not merely an impersonal fomenter of inner disquiet, but an omniscient, omnipotent, and omnipresent divine Judge. But for Forsyth this knowledge is not a 'natural' one, derived from human ability to follow the clues and derive a reasonable conclusion. Instead, it is precisely because the special revelation of Jesus Christ has been preached widely that conscience has any positive role. We recall Forsyth's distinction between the hypothetical natural conscience and the actual sinful conscience confronted with the gospel. Speaking first about the natural conscience, Forsyth insists:

---

[85] *Cruciality,* pp. 127–132.

In civilised communities to-day it does not exist. It is a mere abstraction of thought. What does exist is a historic product, deeply, permanently, and universally moulded by the Christian ethic of sin and redemption which for two thousand years has been shaping European morals.[86]

Christianity has become widespread and its doctrines and practices an accepted part of the culture, and it is within the context of this situation that the conscience operates. The pervasive influence of centuries of popular Christian teaching, the gospel of Christ's person and work, has had an indelible effect, Forsyth believes, on the human perception of God in the conscience.

In 1911, Forsyth made the same distinction and applied it to the specific matter of God's attributes in a masterful address called "Revelation, Old and New." To people who say that "all life is one vast revelation," he responded:

Truly revelation is the greatest of miracles, and the spiritual life is one vast miracle of revelation, because of the Holy Ghost. But it is not a miracle diffused over creation. The Omnipresence of God is not yet His nearness. Immanence is not yet communion. To know that God is there is one thing, to know that we are known of God is another.[87]

There is a radical gulf yawning between the vague information of general revelation and the saving Word spoken by God in the person of Jesus Christ. For someone to realize that there is nowhere to flee from the judging voice of conscience is a far cry from the intimacy of relationship with the living God. Similarly, any sense of divine rectitude inferred from God's judgment in the conscience is only a pale imitation of the holiness revealed in the purity and obedience of Christ. The information gleaned from general revelation may be useful in a very limited way, but it provides no foundation for spiritual life or theological construction.

There is, then, a contrast in Forsyth's writing between revelation and *real* revelation. It is a distinction at once inelegant and useful. The former, described more traditionally as general revelation, is not to be denied, whether in nature, reason, or heart. "It would be heartless and soulless to deny it."[88] But the value of such revelation is drastically limited, and its content devalued, by the pervasive sin that obscures it. When sin's facility to create a "moral wreck" is recognized, says Forsyth, "that is the time for real revelation. . . . You need the revelation indeed, the one certainty for which you

---

[86] *Authority*, p. 403.
[87] "Revelation, Old and New," in *Revelation Old and New*, p. 19.
[88] "Revelation, Old and New," p. 15.

would exchange all the mere impressions you ever felt."[89] We must, like Forsyth, adjust our compass at the cross and learn of God's attributes at the place and in the person of God's revealing. The cross of Jesus Christ is the epistemological point of departure, Forsyth insists, and *"no real revelation is possible except as Atonement and Redemption."*[90] God's holiness and love are known there, in Christ who reveals the Father's pure and passionate will to save.

8. A CHRISTOLOGICAL STARTING-POINT

Forsyth's reply to the question with which we began, about whether our point of departure is in Christ or culture, Word or world, revelation or reason, Holiness or spirit,[91] is clear: "Our human knowledge of the Father, as distinct from surmises, analogies, or deductions about a Father . . . is derived from Christ, and is entirely dependent on his will and nature."[92] Jesus Christ, the Word of the Father, is the starting-point for theology. Christians "regard Jesus and his full gospel as God's supreme revelation, as God's ultimate word." Consequently, our thinking on the nature of God and his holy love must be governed and guided by what God has given in Christ.[93]

There is an essential Christocentricity throughout Forsyth's thought. No matter what doctrinal concern is being considered, Forsyth sees its meaning in terms of Jesus Christ. For example, creation is "the arena or the base of God's salvation" through Christ; the church "confesses the sin of the world only because it confesses still more humbly and gladly the absolute holiness of the Saviour;"[94] and "it is only as we share the Redemption of Christ that we know what Redemption is."[95] Such examples could be multiplied, but Forsyth draws the important conclusion: "Christianity is Christ."[96] Obviously, the person of Jesus Christ stands at the centre of Forsyth's theology. But his view is not a reductionist one that would leave theology nothing else but the person of the Saviour. Rather, Christ is the centre and source of knowledge, as Forsyth

---

[89] "Revelation, Old and New," p. 15.
[90] *Cruciality,* p. 210; Forsyth's emphasis.
[91] *Authority,* p. 178, quoted in section 1 above.
[92] *The Person and Place of Jesus Christ* (1909), pp. 112–113.
[93] *Person,* p. 243.
[94] *Person,* p. 325.
[95] *Religion in Recent Art* (1889), p. 280.
[96] *Person,* p. 168.

memorably says: "In Christ we have the whole of God, but not everything about God, the whole heart of God but not the whole range of God."[97]

Despite this consistent Christocentricity, a word seen more often in Forsyth's writing is "theocentric," a word commonly put to polemical use against those who emphasize a humanity-centred religion: "There is a form of Christianity which makes everything (God included) minister to the worth of man, and renders nothing to the righteousness of God. It is humanist egoism. It is anthropocentric. And Christ was theocentric."[98] Even Forsyth's assertion that he is trading in theocentric religion is justified by a reference to the revelation of Jesus Christ. The *theos* of theology is to be measured by the *Logos* of God, and knowledge of God is possible because Jesus Christ has revealed the Father.

Although this assertion could be illustrated in many ways, perhaps one of the most striking instances of it in Forsyth's writing concerns the connection between assurance of salvation and the doctrine of election. Without delving into the details of his views, expressed in chapter 19 of *The Principle of Authority*, we note the emphatic conclusion: "Now for this tremendous certainty there is no other foundation than the historical revelation and salvation in Christ as the eternal and comprehensive object of God's loving will and choice, the Captain of the elect."[99] With this affirmation, Forsyth also implies a rejection of other ways. Specifically, he says, "We cannot start with a view of God reached on speculative or other similar grounds, and then use Christ as a mere means for confirming it or giving it practical effect. That would mean a certainty higher than Christ's, and superfluity of Christ when the end had been reached."[100] Although Forsyth does not elaborate on the matter here, this Christocentric principle is also applicable to the matter of God's attributes. They ought not to be deduced from speculation and then confirmed by scripture; that would be to give a higher authority to words and reason than to Christ the revealed Word.

---

[97] *Person*, p. 257.
[98] *Justification*, p. 176. For further on this, see *Authority*, chap. 20, "Theocentric Religion," and in particular p. 376.
[99] *Authority*, p. 353.
[100] *Authority*, p. 353.

9. A QUESTION OF ONTOLOGY

At the forefront of Christ's testimony about himself is his claim to be one with the Father. Our knowledge of God rests on this relationship of identity, which Forsyth calls "a native and unique unity with God, which all Christology is but an imperfect attempt to pierce."[101] Compelled by Christ's self-revelation, he ventures an explanation of that unity between God the Father and God the Son. Provocatively, he begins with a critique of the Chalcedonian definition: "The formula of the union of two natures in one person is essentially a metaphysical formula, and the formula of a Hellenic metaphysic, and it is more or less archaic for the modern mind."[102] Forsyth, influenced significantly by Immanuel Kant, argues instead for a metaphysic of ethic:

> Some metaphysic is here involved, certainly, but it is a metaphysic of the conscience. It starts from the conviction that for life and history the moral is the real, and that the movements of the Great Reality must be morally construed as they are morally revealed. The spiritual world is not the world of noetic process or cosmic force, but of holy, i.e. moral, order, act, and power.[103]

This could be seen as "the metaphysic not of substance but of energy, of spiritual energy especially, and most especially of redemption, through the faith which answers redemption. It is the metaphysic not of Being but of the Holy Spirit."[104] Forsyth's distinction may be fine – witness the contrast between "cosmic force" and "spiritual energy" – but his concern is to protest against an abstract view of God. More positively, he wishes to speak in terms of personality, but "even human personality is no mere receptacle; it is a power. And God can only be in it by some mutual involution, as power interpenetrates power, or, even more intimately than that, as person lives in person, as the Father dwells in the Son of his love."[105]

---

[101] *Person*, pp. 40–41.
[102] *Person*, p. 229. Compare his caustic comment: "The Chalcedonian or Athanasian form of the belief [in the person of Christ], which is embalmed in the current formula of two natures in one person in Christ, may be said to have been seriously shaken wherever modern conditions have been realised" (*Person*, p. 217).
[103] *Person*, pp. 222–223. See also "Faith, Metaphysic, and Incarnation," *Methodist Review* 97 (September 1915): 702.
[104] "Faith, Metaphysic, and Incarnation," p. 716.
[105] "Faith, Metaphysic, and Incarnation," p. 712.

It is not surprising, therefore, that Forsyth suggests a change to the traditional Chalcedonian language. Rather than speak of natures, with the implication of independent entities, Forsyth substitutes "modes of being." Therefore the incarnation can be described thus: "The Son, by an act of love's omnipotence, set aside the style of a God, and took the style of a servant, the mental manner of a man, and the mode of moral action that marks human nature."[106] Forsyth's desire is to transfer the Christological debate to the ethical sphere. In a very creative way, he suggests an improvement to the traditional view: "It might be better to describe the union of God and man in Christ as the mutual involution of two personal movements raised to the whole scale of the human soul and the divine."[107] These two movements, of kenosis and plerosis, are "the categories in which God and man meet. They meet in action rather than in being; and the unity of being is just such as is required for mutual action and communion."[108]

Perhaps in this last sentence we can discern an uncomfortable tension in Forsyth's attempt at a renewed, moralized christology. While asserting that these two movements of self-emptying and self-fulfilment "meet in action rather than in being," he immediately goes on to speak of "the unity of being" necessary for such action. We observe that in speaking of persons, ontology cannot be avoided. Being and acting are not separate; the one who *acts* is always the *one* who acts. Modes of being not only act, but are. Although the stress may be shifted to God's action in Christ, and not without benefit, the need to speak of being remains. In a later article, significantly entitled "Faith, Metaphysic and Incarnation," Forsyth concedes that "to think as thoroughly as we are saved is to become metaphysical in spite of ourselves." And he adds, "It is not to metaphysic that we need ever object, but to archaic metaphysic made final and compulsory."[109]

This ambivalent attitude to the metaphysics of christology met deserved criticism. H. R. Mackintosh, although broadly sympathetic with Forsyth's conclusions, promptly declared that "a metaphysic of the conscience is none the less metaphysical."[110] And Colin Gunton, in a book which has as one of its main aims to prove that

---

[106] *Person*, p. 307.
[107] *Person*, p. 333.
[108] *Person*, p. 336.
[109] "Faith, Metaphysic, and Incarnation," pp. 705, 701.
[110] H. R. Mackintosh, *The Doctrine of the Person of Jesus Christ* (Edinburgh: T. & T. Clark, 1978; orig. pub. 1912, 2nd ed., 1913), p. 303.

The Knowledge of God

"the unity between God and man in Jesus can be expressed in ontological terms," points out in a brief discussion of Forsyth's christology that "those who have no explicit ontology will almost certainly employ an implicit one unconsciously."[111] This is what we see in Forsyth's language about the mutual involution of movements: it is an attempt to describe being in terms of acting. Yet he is determined to hold the substance of the Athanasian position without the 'substance' language of the Athanasian Creed. He realizes the need for ontological language, even though he is unwilling to use the language of the tradition. His rhetorical questions bring out the point:

> The soul intrusts itself to God-in-Christ forever. But what ground or stay is there for such an unshakable faith unless we have an unshakable Christ? And how can we have an unshakable Christ for an eternal soul if we have not in him our soul's eternal God? And how can we really have God in him without some suggestion of ontological continuity, however defined? . . . We have God in Christ, not simply through him.[112]

For our purposes, this "ontological continuity" enables Forsyth to draw two important conclusions. The first is that to know the Son is to know the Father. "The son, then, knows the Father with the same knowledge as the Father has of himself. . . . The power that Christ gave was the power to know the Father in him; . . . to know the Godhead of the Father by the incarnate Godhead of the Son."[113]

The second corollary of the fact that we have God in Christ is that Christ's idea of God is determinative for our idea of God. True faith, says Forsyth, "can only be based on what is involved in the idea, the experience, of God that proceeds from Jesus himself." We must "bring all other religious truth to this test." This is especially important when considering God's attributes. We must make sure that "our notion of what God is," and particularly "those conceptions of Absoluteness, Omnipotence, and the rest which would be called common-sense notions," are put to this test: Are they taken from Jesus "as God's ultimate word"?[114] This is a fundamental point for Forsyth, not least because of his contention, to be considered in some detail later, that holiness "is the essence of Christ's idea of God."[115]

---

[111] Colin E. Gunton, *Yesterday and Today: A Study of Continuities in Christology* (London: Darton, Longman & Todd, 1983), p. 170.
[112] "Faith, Metaphysic, and Incarnation," p. 704.
[113] *Person*, p. 114; the inconsistent capitalization is Forsyth's.
[114] *Person*, p. 243.
[115] *Positive Preaching*, p. 368.

10. THE INCARNATION AND THE ATONEMENT

The preceding discussion of the Son's unity with the Father leads us to consider Forsyth's view of the relation between the person and the work of Christ. Because Forsyth accords such a high epistemological value to Jesus Christ, we must be clear about his views on just where that value lies.

At the outset, it cannot be said that Forsyth neglects the subject of the incarnation. His writings show considerable interest in the doctrine of Christ's person, both in its historical development,[116] and in its contemporary restatement. Most notably, Forsyth sets forth a nuanced version of the kenotic theory of the incarnation in *The Person and Place of Jesus Christ*.[117] In fact, he insists that a strong doctrine of Christ's person is a practical theological necessity:

> Where does the moral soul and self find the moral reality for which it craves? Where can it find it but in God, and God's supreme, eternal, moral action. A person can only rest in a person, a soul in a soul. Nature and soul are alike unreal till they are settled on that rock. And that rock is practically Christ, for experience it is Christ.[118]

Further, incarnation and atonement are clearly ordered and related in P. T. Forsyth's thought. On the one hand, Forsyth concedes that "for theological science, Incarnation is the logical *prius*. It is at the rational base of Atonement." However, he adds that it is an ethical rather than a metaphysical act, and that "it is the atoning Redemption that is at the practical base of belief in the Incarnation and prescribes its nature."[119]

According to Forsyth, salvation through the cross of Christ precedes our knowledge of his person. If we are to know what God is like, then, we must look to Christ, and if we are to understand Jesus Christ's personality, we must look to his actions, and above all to his greatest deed:

> The personality is revealed as it becomes effectuated in deeds. It is incarnated in action. Its object is not just to reveal itself and give play to

---

[116] For example, see *Person*, chap. 3 for a comparison of Athanasian, Socinian, and Arian views of Jesus, and Forsyth's unpublished lecture notes on the person of Christ, in the New College, London (NCL) manuscripts held by Dr Williams's Library, London.
[117] See *Person*, chaps. 11–12.
[118] *Christ on Parnassus: Lectures on Art, Ethic, and Theology* (1911), p. 273. The omission of a question mark at the end of the second sentence is telling.
[119] *Justification*, pp. 90–91.

its powers, but to do something, or get something done, in course of which it is revealed. . . . Personality is an energy.[120]

Theological reflection on Christ's person can only follow the experience of reconciliation through his death. "In a word," says Forsyth, "the work of Christ, realised in the Church's experience through faith, becomes the avenue and the key to the person of Christ. Soteriology is the way of access to Christology."[121] In support of this view, Forsyth here (and elsewhere) quotes the reformer Philip Melanchthon: "The knowledge of Christ is to know his benefits."[122] In this way, he puts a high priority on religious experience: "Only the saved have the real secret of the Saviour. This is the religion of the matter, which carries its theology."[123] It would seem that although the incarnation is the "logical *prius*" for theological science, the logic is determined at the cross.

The atonement, therefore, interprets the incarnation. In reiterating the point made in the previous paragraph, Forsyth begins to explain the significance of the incarnation: "The only real access to the Incarnation, and the key to the moral quality of its self-emptying, is by the way and the experience of a moral Atonement."[124] The incarnation is a moral reality, with humble condescension a key aspect.

The atonement for sin effected on the cross is the clue to the incarnation, and "prescribes its nature," that is, its nature as moral. "The metaphysic is one of ethic, of action, not of being; it is of will rather than thought."[125] Although we have encountered this distinction already in Forsyth's thought, and will have occasion to consider it later in more detail, we note here that Forsyth points to the cross in order to interpret the incarnation.

In all of this, it is apparent that Forsyth's intention is not to split off the incarnation from the cross, but to hold them together. This is asserted in a vivid way in *The Cruciality of the Cross*. After

---

[120] "Christ's Person and His Cross," *Methodist Review Quarterly* 66 (January 1917): 10.
[121] "Christ's Person and His Cross," p. 10.
[122] *Person*, p. 220; the Melanchthon reference is to the preface of his *Loci Communes Theologici* of 1521. A modern translation is found in Wilhelm Pauck, ed., *Melanchthon and Bucer,* Library of Christian Classics, vol. 19 (London, SCM Press, 1969), p. 21.
[123] *Person*, p. 219.
[124] "Does the Church Prolong the Incarnation?" *London Quarterly Review* 133 (January 1920): 7.
[125] *Justification,* pp. 90–91.

claiming that Jesus's death was not "an otiose appendix" but rather "His life finding its object at last," Forsyth adds: "If we take care what we mean, it is more true to speak of the atoning life of Christ than of His atoning death. He is the atoning person, whose crisis, effect, and key is in His death."[126] And, in probably the last article he wrote, Forsyth made this distinction: "Christ did not become incarnate *and* redeem; He became incarnate *to* redeem. His redemption is both the crown and the key of His Incarnation."[127]

When all this has been appreciated, we still must conclude that there is a deficiency in Forsyth's theology at this point. When he says, in distinctive epigrammatic style, that the focus should be on "the Son made sin rather than the Word made flesh," and then adds provocatively that "the incarnation has no religious value but as the background of the atonement,"[128] Forsyth opens himself up to criticism. J. K. Mozley, for example, while approving of Forsyth's stress on the atonement, asserts that his Congregational contemporary places too little emphasis on the incarnation as valuable in its own right. Even though Forsyth had good reason to react to a christology that "was prepared to go near to saying that incarnation itself was redemption," Mozley concludes that "at this point, Forsyth was over-much dominated by polemical necessities."[129] Seen on its own, Mozley says in another place, the doctrine of the incarnation "does not necessarily drop to a level of a misty doctrine of divine immanence, though I should admit that some of our Christian mysticism now so much in vogue has dangerous inclinations in this direction."[130]

The "polemical necessities" to which Mozley refers are not to be underestimated. At least three separate theological conflicts can be discerned which would have influenced Forsyth's decision to focus on the atonement:

First, in 1890 the publication of *Lux Mundi,* a collection of papers by Oxford Anglicans, created considerable interest for several reasons. The inerrancy of Holy Scripture was abandoned and Biblical criticism taken seriously; and a kenotic theory of the incarnation

---

[126] *Cruciality,* p. 139.
[127] "Does the Church Prolong the Incarnation?" *London Quarterly Review* 133 (April 1920): 212.
[128] *Positive Preaching,* p. 182.
[129] J. K. Mozley, "The Theology of Dr. Forsyth," in *The Heart of the Gospel* (London: SPCK, 1925), pp. 94–95.
[130] J. K. Mozley, *The Doctrine of the Atonement* (London: Gerald Duckworth, 1915), p. 212.

was advanced.[131] But more important for our present purposes is the book's subtitle, "A Series of Studies in the Religion of the Incarnation," which signalled the dominant position of that doctrine in the Anglo-Catholic theology of the time, which in turn had been strongly influenced (as Forsyth had been earlier) by the incarnational theology of F. D. Maurice. Of the authors in *Lux Mundi*, R. C. Moberly's view is representative when he writes that "the whole of our Christian creed . . . [is] really contained in the one crucial doctrine of the Incarnation."[132]

Secondly, an over-emphasis on God's immanence was the target of Forsyth's pen in the New Theology controversy of 1907. R. J. Campbell, preaching to large congregations at the City Temple in London, served up an attractive combination of romanticism, monism (some would say, pantheism), and idealism that concentrated on the immanence of God.[133] Forsyth correctly saw that the doctrine of the atonement was at stake. The New Theology, he said, "speculates about a Christ made flesh, but it never gauges the true seat of Incarnation – a Christ made sin."[134] Here we notice again Forsyth's tendency to telescope the significance of the incarnation into the atonement.

Thirdly, an unwillingness to defend the historicity of the virgin birth, then under considerable attack from the biblical critics, may also have contributed to Forsyth's limited stress on the inherent value of the incarnation. "The temper and tendency of our time is against the old emphasis on [the virgin birth], especially on critical grounds," Forsyth wrote in 1907. He noted in particular that "the higher criticism claims the right to dismiss" the witness of the birth narratives in the gospels of Matthew and Luke,[135] and the fact that the virgin birth is not mentioned in Paul's arguments about the uniqueness of Jesus Christ.[136] Like a metaphysical theory of

---

[131] See J. K. Mozley, *Some Tendencies in British Theology: From the Publication of "Lux Mundi" to the Present Day* (London, SPCK, 1951), pp. 17–20; and Alasdair I. C. Heron, *A Century of Protestant Theology* (Cambridge: Lutterworth Press, 1980), p. 65.

[132] R. C. Moberly, "The Incarnation as the Basis of Dogma," in *Lux Mundi,* ed. Charles Gore (London, John Murray, 1890), p. 247.

[133] For a well-told and judicious account of the controversy, see Keith W. Clements, *Lovers of Discord: Twentieth-Century Theological Controversies in England* (London: SPCK, 1988), chap. 2.

[134] "Immanence and Incarnation," in *The Old Faith and the New Theology,* ed. C. H. Vine (London: Sampson Low Marston, 1907), p .48.

[135] *Positive Preaching*, pp. 19–20.

[136] *Person*, p. 261.

incarnation, such a miraculous birth "must be taken on the authority of the Bible or the Church." It would be better, Forsyth averred, to see the incarnation as "a moral reality rising (as in the New Testament) from the experience of forgiveness in the Gospel and from the certainty that Christ has there done on us a work that none but God could do."[137] The critics thus bypassed, the problem of the virgin birth receded into the background of Forsyth's thought, no longer theologically necessary.[138] The dogmatic stress moves elsewhere: prospectively to the cross, and retrospectively to Christ's pre-existence and "the Lamb slain from the foundation of the world" (Revelation 13.8).[139]

Polemical considerations, then, led Forsyth to emphasize the atonement in a way that gave short measure to the incarnation as valuable in its own right. Nevertheless, his emphasis on the atonement is worthy of commendation, as further exploration and explanation within this thesis will show. In addition, Forsyth's position does at least attempt to consider Jesus Christ in his entirety, recognizing that "to preach only the atonement, the death apart from the life, or only the person of Christ, the life apart from the death, or only the teaching of Christ, His words apart from His life, may be all equally one-sided, and extreme to falsity."[140] Forsyth was consistent on this point, from the assertion in 1893 that "His person was absolutely one with His work,"[141] to the 1917 article which argued for "the complete unity of his death with his personal life."[142] Yet it is also a theological stance which sees a clear relationship between incarnation and atonement: Forsyth insists that "the Godhead that became incarnate in Jesus Christ did so not to convince, but to save. Godhead became incarnate so far and in such fashion as the purpose of redemption prescribed."[143]

---

[137] *Justification*, p. 89; Cf. *Positive Preaching*, p. 36, where Forsyth says that the virgin birth is not "experimentally verifiable and creative of experience."

[138] See the discussion in *Positive Preaching*, pp. 19–21. Forsyth's fellow Scot, James Orr, took a more aggressive apologetic approach in his *The Virgin Birth of Christ* (London: Hodder & Stoughton, 1907).

[139] See *Person*, p. 271. J. K. Mozley notes that "in *Positive Preaching* [pp. 19–21], he does not answer what he regards as the one theologically legitimate question with regard to it, 'Was such a mode of entry into the world indispensable for Christ's work of redemption?'" (*The Heart of the Gospel*, p. 95).

[140] *Cruciality*, p. 82.

[141] "Revelation and the Person of Christ," p. 120.

[142] "Christ's Person and His Cross," *Methodist Review Quarterly* 66 (January 1917): 18.

[143] *Person*, pp. 219–220.

11. THE CENTRALITY OF THE CROSS

We have noted at the beginning of this chapter that, in answer to his own question about the correct epistemological starting-point for theological inquiry, P. T. Forsyth's answer was: 'The Word rather than the world.' Knowledge of God comes from Jesus Christ, and not from any natural or solely human source. To know God, he asserted, we must begin with the ontological identity of Jesus Christ with God the Father, as revealed in the history of Jesus, recorded in New Testament scripture, and made contemporaneous in human experience.

Forsyth is not content to leave the matter there, however. As we have seen in our discussion of atonement and incarnation in the previous section, he insists that we ask a further question: Where is the centre of this revelation? His answer: Just as the Son is "the sole means for realising the Father," so "the gospel of the Cross [is] the sole channel of the Father's revelation (as distinct from mere intimation), the sole vehicle of the Father's self-giving."[144] Just as theology is Christocentric, the shape of christology is cruciform. The cross occupies the central place in Forsyth's theological system, a fact which will be shown repeatedly as our argument progresses. Rather than multiply examples to illustrate this, perhaps it will be sufficient to attest the conclusion. Writing in 1915, J. K. Mozley commented:

> Systematic is not a word that one would naturally apply to Dr. Forsyth; yet I know of no theologian of the day who has fewer loose ends to his thought. To adopt a phrase of his own he never attempts to set up in his theology a subsidiary centre, but at every point which he reaches in the gradual development of a position . . . , one knows that there is a straight line back, as from any point on the circle's circumference to its centre, to that which is the moral and therefore the only possible centre of the world – the Cross of Christ."[145]

As Forsyth often emphasized, revelation is found in redemption.[146] Just as the atonement of Christ's cross is the centre of Forsyth's theology, so the atonement will be the backdrop for the following discussion of God's attributes, and in particular, the holy love of God. To those divine perfections we now turn.

---

[144] *Missions in State and Church* (1908), p. 216.
[145] Mozley, *Doctrine of the Atonement*, p. 182.
[146] See "Revelation and the Person of Christ," pp. 116–124 passim.

Chapter Four

The Attributes of God

The endless wonder is the conjunction in Christ, and most in His Cross, of moral majesty and spiritual mercy, of infinite holiness and intimate love.

P. T. Forsyth

The task in the present chapter of this study will be to introduce Forsyth's treatment of the attributes of God, in both general and specific terms. Although a discussion of those attributes which are our particular focus – love and holiness – will be postponed until the following chapters, in the present chapter we will gather together a number of Forsyth's insights into God's nature. These range from broad theological principles to specific illustrations about particular attributes. With these findings in mind, we believe that on this subject, Forsyth's distinctive contribution justifies Gordon Rupp's conclusion: "It seems likely that he will take his place among preachers and theologians who will be read profitably for many generations to come, not on grounds of theological antiquarianism, but as speaking that language of the centuries which makes all Christians contemporary."[1]

1. PROCEDURAL DIFFICULTIES AND POSSIBILITIES

As we consider the prospect of analysing Forsyth's view of God's nature, we note some preliminary difficulties. First, God's greatness defies human description, and even the best human efforts to

---

[1] Gordon Rupp, Foreword to *The Gospel and Authority: A P. T. Forsyth Reader: Eight Essays Previously Published in Journals,* ed. Marvin W. Anderson (Minneapolis: Augsburg, 1971), p. 7.

describe God's nature will be inadequate ones. This calls the entire task into question. Who can presume to speak of God's nature? Is Job's adviser right to assert that "the Almighty is beyond our reach"? In the matter of the attributes of God, there seems to be a very real danger of pondering things we do not understand, and writing about matters that are too wonderful for mortals to know, as Job himself admitted (Job 37.23, 42.3). Yet, the immeasurable and almighty One became humanly accessible in Jesus Christ, who not only invites faithful investigation, but also urges his disciples to put into words the truth they have discovered (see John 20.27, Acts 1.8). That truth, according to Forsyth, is not merely "a *tour de force* of revelation" similar to what Job experienced, but an actual moral victory, because "the Vindicator has stood on the earth."[2] The one whose character we desire to know has acted to reveal it.

Secondly, the sheer immensity of the task is daunting, and serves as a warning to keep a specific goal in view. The scope of our task is large, ranging far beyond merely the doctrine of God into christology, atonement and incarnation, as well as the doctrines of the Trinity and the Holy Spirit. Therefore, our focus will continually return to God's attribute of holy love.

There is a third, more mundane obstacle to the present study. Despite J. K. Mozley's assurance that "no theologian of the day . . . has fewer loose ends to his thought,"[3] Peter Taylor Forsyth wrote no systematic theology and penned no comprehensive monograph on the doctrine of God. While the question of authority and the problem of evil received Forsyth's in-depth, book-length attention,[4] nowhere does he treat the attributes of God (or for that matter, related questions like God's existence or the Trinity) in an ordered way. Therefore, we must turn to Forsyth's authorship as a whole in order to glean the material appropriate for our study. In addition to his books, several of Forsyth's published sermons and articles, numbering more than 300 in total, are important sources. Still, the absence of any systematic treatment of God's nature in Forsyth's writings makes it inevitable that there will be aspects of the doctrine of God's attributes about which he has made no published comment. This problem would be especially keen if our task was to make a

---

[2] *The Justification of God,* 2nd ed. (1948; orig. pub. 1916), p. 121.
[3] J. K. Mozley, *The Doctrine of the Atonement* (London: Gerald Duckworth, 1915), p. 182.
[4] See *The Principle of Authority,* 2nd ed. (1952; orig. pub. 1913), and *Justification.*

comprehensive survey of the attributes of God; too many gaps exist for a complete study. Fortunately, our attention will focus more particularly on the holy love of God, about which Forsyth spoke often and fully.

A fourth concern is Forsyth's imprecision. There are times when we wish that words were more carefully defined, and distinctions more clearly made. For example, W. L. Bradley mentions that Forsyth is "rather careless" in using the words sin and guilt interchangeably.[5] Robert McAfee Brown makes a similar point about the meanings of 'grace,' 'Christ,' and 'the cross,' often used almost interchangeably to convey the same meaning.[6] Or again, even though Forsyth devotes half a volume to carefully distinguishing dogma, doctrine, and theology, one does not have to look very far afield to find Forsyth using the words imprecisely.[7] Yet there are indications that the problem is not as great as these comments might suggest. In most of the above cases, the words do not have mutually exclusive meanings, but are closely related. In any event, the contexts in each case make the meaning clearer. Further, Forsyth's writing generally exhibits signs of precision; from a "superabounding vocabulary"[8] he chose his words conscientiously, and he revised his manuscripts fastidiously.

Nevertheless, reading Forsyth with analytical interest is sometimes rather frustrating. The considerations mentioned above may help to explain but do not entirely excuse the fluidity of meaning in Forsyth's terms. At times there is an overlap or melding of meaning in the terms with which we will have most to do (love, holiness, grace, etc.) which not only reflects God's multifaceted complexity, but also the author's imprecision. Occasionally these factors combine to resist systematic theological formulations.

Fortunately, several factors mitigate these disadvantages. P. T. Forsyth's best-organized volume, *The Person and Place of Jesus Christ*, is invaluable for our purposes because of its attention to the

---

[5] W. L. Bradley, *P. T. Forsyth: The Man and His Work* (London: Independent Press, 1952), p. 124.

[6] Robert McAfee Brown, *P. T. Forsyth: Prophet for Today* (Philadelphia: Westminster, 1952), p. 67.

[7] Compare chap. 1 of *Theology in Church and State* (1915) with chap. 8 of *The Person and Place of Jesus Christ* (1909). Brown notes this instance: Robert McAfee Brown, "P. T. Forsyth and the Gospel of Grace" (PhD diss., Columbia University, 1951), p. 581.

[8] "Principal Forsyth among the Wesleyans: Sermon at City-road Chapel," *British Weekly*, 17 March 1904, p. 611.

Son's kenotic retraction of attributes. Although kenotic christology is not the focus of the present work, the doctrines of God and Christ intersect at the incarnation, and Forsyth insists that it is in Jesus Christ that God's nature is known. Such a Christocentric view of God's nature will become clearer as we examine Forsyth's christology further. In addition, and just as important, the specific concern of this thesis, God's holy love, is one to which Forsyth repeatedly returns. Whether discussing the atonement or art, preaching or prayer, he sooner or later returns to the high motivation of the holy love of God.

Therefore, being conscious of the immensity of the task, relying on the diverse but less-than-systematic treatment of the doctrine of God's attributes which Forsyth has left us, and acknowledging the possibility of encountering some imprecision in his formulations, we proceed in this chapter to consider Forsyth's doctrine of the attributes of God, and specifically of two classical attributes, while leaving to one side for the time being the more specific notion of God's holy love.

2. REVEALED RATHER THAN DISCOVERED

Without leaving methodological concerns behind, we turn now to more substantive issues in Forsyth's view of the nature and attributes of God. When called upon to describe the God we know, what attitude should our minds adopt? Are we explorers in a country where the hitherto undiscovered features must be named and classified? Do we adopt the assertive, inquiring tone of a detective determined to find the clues and crack the code of God's identity? Should we think of ourselves as construction workers building a logical edifice of necessary propositions? Alternatively, could it be that the appropriate attitude in our quest to delineate God's nature is a willingness to relate with the object of our study, and a holy receptivity to know God as he gives himself to us? It is our conviction, based on our examination of Forsyth's view of natural theology in the previous chapter, that this latter option is the correct way, that the attributes of God are revealed rather than discovered, and that we are more objects of God's attention than subjects who scrutinize the divine nature.

Therefore, as Forsyth recognizes, there is something inherently risky about the nomenclature 'attributes of God.' The very word 'attributes' is presumptuous, as if the human task of attributing qualities to God were the first order of business in creating a custom-made religion; such a venture seems dangerously close to carving an idol for the studyroom shelf. Provocatively, Forsyth asks: Is theology "something thrown out by man about God, or something conveyed from God to man? ... Is it the best reasoned account we can give of God? Or is it the substantial account God gives of Himself?" In answering his own question, he says that theology "is not an account of the Christian consciousness but of God's revelation that creates that consciousness; a revelation which, indeed, emerges in man's consciousness always, and in its terms, but is not identical with it, and does not arise from it."[9] In opposition to theology dominated by anthropology, Forsyth insists on the priority of revelation. As we noted in the previous chapter, God gives himself to be known in Jesus Christ and his cross. Faith worships there, and theology, looking over her shoulder, takes notes. God in his multifaceted perfection has given himself to be known and therefore to be spoken of, thus giving impetus to the descriptive task of systematic theology.

Moreover, this is a revelation of God's nature through Jesus Christ. When we have seen the Son, Forsyth affirms, we have seen the Father, and the historically-observed attributes are God's own perfections. "That greatness was God's greatness. That love was God's love. That grace was God's immediate grace, and no echo, report, or image of it; it was God's grace as surely as that judgment, or that forgiveness, was God's."[10] Jesus revealed the Father.

This conviction that divine revelation takes priority over human discovery is particularly important in the whole matter of God's perfections. The God described in scripture is not a static entity or intellectual construct, but rather the personal Father of Jesus Christ. Attributes are convenient names for God's personally revealed being-in-action. Forsyth writes, "An attribute of God is God Himself behaving, with all His unity, in a particular way in a particular situation." For example, "the love of God is not an attribute of God; it is God loving. The holiness of God is not an attribute of God; it is the whole of God Himself as holy." An attribute is not "something loose within God which He could manipulate" but "God Himself, unchangeable God, in certain relations."[11] Time after time, Forsyth turns us away from a materialistic approach to the divine

---

[9] *Theology in Church and State*, pp. 7–9.
[10] *Person*, p. 89.
[11] *The Work of Christ* (1910), pp. 117–118.

perfections, and toward a holistic and personal view of the God whose being is known in action.

Forsyth's views contrast noticeably with the traditional stance of Protestant orthodoxy on this matter. Methodologically, both starting-point and procedure are different. Charles Hodge, the premier nineteenth-century American exponent of orthodoxy, who crowned a long career with the publication of his *Systematic Theology* while Forsyth was still a theological student, comments: "When we say that we can define God, all that is meant is, that we can analyze the idea of God as it lies in our mind; or, that we can state the class of beings to which He belongs, and the attributes by which He is distinguished from all other beings."[12] Despite a high view of scripture, Hodge grounds his doctrine of God instead on the more philosophical basis of a logical construct, "the idea of God as it lies in our minds." Only incidentally does he remark, as for example in his discussion on the spirituality of God, that "the scriptures confirm these views."[13] Hodge begins with a rationalistic conception of a God that can be classified and compared, and only subsequently turns to scripture for confirmation of his results concerning the attributes of God. Human nature, rather than the revealed reality of God in Christ, is often the prime referent for his study. Hence, Hodge approvingly cites Leibnitz's use of the *via eminentiae:* "The perfections of God are those of our own souls, but He possesses them without limit,"[14] and in another place employs the scholastic *via negativa:* "It is by removing all the limitations of power, as it exists in us, that we rise to the idea of the omnipotence of God."[15] Rather than make reference to the one who is "the exact representation of [God's] being" (Hebrews 1.3), Hodge's comparisons are with humanity's virtues, or lack of them.

The twentieth-century heir of Hodge's work is Louis Berkhof's *Systematic Theology.* In the light of scholarly work done in the interim on God's attributes, Berkhof exhibits some important differences of opinion compared to his more scholastic forebear. For example, Berkhof rejects the ways of causality, negation, and eminence because they "take their starting-point in human

---

[12] Charles Hodge, *Systematic Theology* (London: Thomas Nelson & Sons, 1871), vol. 1, p. 366.
[13] Hodge, *Systematic Theology*, vol. 1, p. 380. These words, some capitalized, are a subsection heading.
[14] Cited as Leibnitz, 'Théodicée,' Preface, *Works,* p. 469, edit. Berlin, 1840, in Hodge, *Systematic Theology*, vol. 1, p. 374.
[15] Hodge, *Systematic Theology*, vol. 1, pp. 407.

experience rather than in the Word of God. They deliberately ignore the clear self-revelation of God and exalt the ideas of the human discovery of God."[16] And yet the old system largely remains. In asserting God's goodness, for example, Berkhof begins not with Jesus Christ, but with "the fundamental idea" that God "is in every way all that He as God should be, and therefore answers perfectly to the ideal expressed in the word 'God.'"[17] Rather than allowing God's actual gift of himself to define God's nature, Berkhof's picture of God must measure up to a preconstructed ideal, in some ways determined independently of the incarnation of God in humanity.

For Forsyth, however, the very fact that God has given himself in his Son is the first *datum* in the knowledge of God. Indeed, "self-revelation is His very nature."[18] In condescending to be known in relationship with humanity, God is the one who, with transparent openness, makes his reality and nature clear. From this source we draw the raw material of a doctrine of God's attributes, and as a result of this invitation we speak of God's nature.

3. TWO REPRESENTATIVE ATTRIBUTES

With this view of things, how does Forsyth deal with the classical attributes? Our intention is not to be comprehensive in outlining the divine characteristics that have been the traditional concern of dogmatics, but rather to illustrate Forsyth's approach in this matter. More detailed attention will be given later to those perfections which are our central concern, but here we look at certain specific attributes in order to delineate Forsyth's treatment more generally.

3.1 OMNISCIENCE

Despite the lack of a comprehensive discussion on the subject of omniscience in Forsyth's authorship, there are enough occasional references throughout his work for us to see the outlines of his convictions about God's "all-seeing Self."[19] Before God made the world, "He had absolute and simultaneous intelligence as a necessary feature of his being." But then, like a prism held to the light, the creation refracted God's reality into discernible attributes, "and the

---

[16] Louis Berkhof, *Systematic Theology* (London: Banner of Truth Trust, 1958), p. 53.
[17] Berkhof, *Systematic Theology*, p. 70.
[18] *Religion in Recent Art* (1889), p. 157.
[19] *Pulpit Parables for Young Hearers* (1886), p. 111; see also *Work*, p. 54.

absolute intelligence of God in relation to the world becomes in its form omniscience." Forsyth sees, therefore, that "omniscience is only a detailed aspect of God's absoluteness."[20] Such a judgment takes a step further the principle that God's perfections are aspects of God's own self: these attributes are real, and make sense to us, in relation to the created world, but only as they are revealed ("refracted") in Christ.

Such an understanding of necessity is not to be confused with that imposed by any logical system, or with some supposed consistency demanded by creatures God made. Rather, Forsyth insists that God is free to carry out his purposes: "He limits himself in the freedom of holiness for the purposes of His own end of infinite love."[21] Forsyth would agree with a later theologian who insisted, "With whatever necessity God acts in Himself, He is always free in relation to these [creatures]."[22]

Further to this, God's omniscience is not to be viewed as an abstract or impersonal concept, but as God's real knowledge of actual people, concrete situations, and especially human need, all seen within God's relationship of communion with redeemed humanity. Forsyth makes this point in his at once deep and practical volume, *The Soul of Prayer,* in the context of a discussion about petitionary prayer: "To common sense the fact that God knows all we need, and wills us all good, the fact of His infinite Fatherhood, is a reason for not praying." But we must see omniscience Christologically, and Jesus "made the all-knowing Fatherhood the ground of true prayer." God is not merely omniscient, say, as a heavenly scorekeeper of human sin, but knows us with a love that wants to act on our behalf. Therefore (for example) petitionary prayer "is filial reciprocity. Love loves to be told what it knows already. Every lover knows that. It wants to be asked for what it longs to give. And that is the principle of prayer to the all-knowing Love."[23]

Consistent with his conviction that the picture of God's character must be drawn with constant and primary reference to Jesus Christ, Forsyth identifies Christ's omniscience with the omniscience of the triune God. Such omniscience was revealed in the incarnate Christ,

---

[20] *Person,* p. 310.
[21] *Person,* p. 311. The inconsistent capitalization of pronouns referring to God is Forsyth's.
[22] Karl Barth, *Church Dogmatics* 2/1, p. 562.
[23] *The Soul of Prayer,* 2nd ed. (1949; orig. pub. 1916), p. 63.

but God's accommodation to human flesh meant that the all-inclusive divine knowledge was retracted to a potential, and concentrated at a point. Forsyth writes: "In the matter of knowledge Christ, as God, Christ in his eternal form, had an intuitive and simultaneous knowledge of all; but when he put aside that eternal form of Godhead and entered time, his knowledge became discursive, successive and progressive."[24]

Forsyth meets opponents of such a kenotic understanding of the incarnation with a counter-question (which indeed applies to a wider circle of theological opinion): Is change an option for God? Arguing from the dynamic reality of what God has done in Christ, Forsyth asserts that the omniscience of God is capable, rather than incapable, of limitation, "only it is self-limitation,"[25] a choice made in utter freedom by the sovereign God. Put another way, this retraction of divine knowledge takes place within the context of God's wisdom. "We may modify much in our views as to Christ's omniscience, and similar things affected by His emptying of Himself. He accepted some of the limitations of human ignorance. He consented not to know with a nescience divinely wise."[26] In these formulations, Forsyth is pushing at the boundaries of logic. Yet, in a careful and balanced way, he maintains that the Eternal Son had a knowledge limited but still in reserve, an evolving intellectual life, and a growing omniscience. Such growth is only possible because "the goal is in the start."[27] There is divine wisdom in the evolving human knowledge of Jesus.

This discussion of omniscience illustrates Forsyth's stress on the will and knowledge of God working together. The same conjunction was noted above in connection with prayer: God not only knows what we need, but also has a keen desire to act on our behalf. Forsyth links God's complete knowledge with his comprehensive will, in the context of the divine Fatherhood, thereby avoiding the dangers of portraying God as an impersonal omniscience.[28]

---

[24] *Person*, pp. 310–311.
[25] *Person*, p. 311.
[26] *Positive Preaching and [the] Modern Mind*, 1st ed. (1907), p. 278.
[27] *Person*, p. 308.
[28] Karl Barth, too, links omniscience and 'omnivolence' with the Fatherhood of God; see *Church Dogmatics* 2/1, pp. 552–555.

3.2 CHANGELESSNESS

P. T. Forsyth's provocative starting-point for a discussion of what classical theology has called God's immutability – and what he calls "the changelessness of the eternal nature"[29] – is the growth of Jesus Christ. God the Son had a history: he grew in "personal consciousness" and triumphed in a process of "moral redintegration." "So far is growth, then, from being incompatible with the infinite, eternal, and almighty that it is demanded by it." That argument about the growth of the Son prepared the way for a dynamic view of God to set against traditional views of immutability. Given Christ's progress, Forsyth pithily concludes: "The conditions of time must lie within the possibilities of Eternity, the growth of man within the infinite mobility of the changeless God."[30]

With this last comment, Forsyth moves the centre of the discussion from Christ's growth through some thirty years, to the startling development of the incarnation. Renovating the terms of an old debate, Forsyth says that while deism's doctrine of God excludes the possibility that Christ is capable of containing divine attributes, "the principle of Christian theism is *infinitum capax finiti.*"[31] If the fact of God-with-us teaches us anything, it is that God's changelessness can encompass and include the very human traits of growth, change, and mobility.

Therefore, in the incarnate Christ we have "the whole perfect action of Godhead concentrated through one factor or hypostasis within it [by what theologians used to call an *apotelesma* in the Son] and directed manward both to create and redeem."[32] The concentration of God in the man Jesus Christ was a shared operation of the triune God, in which the perfectly divine Son became genuinely human. In a distinctive way, Forsyth describes the resulting life of Christ as comprising "two movements in mutual interplay, mutual struggle, and reciprocal communion." Applying this to immutability, Forsyth says, "We have the self-complete God who cannot grow, in whom all things are already, Yea and Amen; and we have the inchoate man who must grow, and stumbles as he

---

[29] *Authority*, p. 355.
[30] *Person*, pp. 308–309.
[31] *Person*, p. 309.
[32] *Person*, p. 338. The words in square brackets are Forsyth's footnoted comment, with the capitalization and punctuation adapted for my purpose here.

grows; and we have movement in each."³³ Despite the fact that theology in times past has resisted the idea of change in God, Forsyth asserts, "In Christ's life and work we have that divine mobility in which the living Son eternally was – we have that coming historically, and psychologically, and ethically to be." Once again, one of Forsyth's infrequent footnotes adds substance to his argument: "I ask leave to use the word mobility to express that uncaused self-contained vitality, that changeless change, in God which is the ground of the manward movement of which I speak."³⁴ Then turning to stress the Godward movement, Forsyth says that in the creaturely Christ, "we have his divine mobility, therefore, translated into human growth. . . . And we have them in the unity of one historic person."³⁵

In an article on the much-discussed subject of evolution, Forsyth touches on our particular concern in this section, God's changelessness. He observes that the slow but constant action of evolution is played out against a backdrop of a "fixed moral world" and a "uniformity of nature," which indeed is "a constant source for the world of change." Science depends on "this permanent element" that "holds change in a hand that knows no change." Even more significantly, this world of dependable nature and moral law points to a changeless reality behind the world, "a spiritual fixity at once final and fluid, whose true name is the Eternal God."³⁶ The truth revealed in Jesus Christ – that God is, among much else, 'changeless change' – was also indicated (though not explained further) elsewhere.

We began by noting Forsyth's emphasis that growth is not only a divine possibility, but an observed actuality in the incarnate Son. Now we note the other side of that reality, that God is "the changeless, self-sustained, absolute, and Holy One," who is still the one who condescended to us in Jesus. "Would entire faith be possible," Forsyth asks, "without that eternal and holy goodness, changeless behind all the love we trust? A love that could change we might love, but we could not trust it, however intense."³⁷ Forsyth sees God as changeless and therefore trustworthy, solid and therefore

---

[33] *Person*, p. 336.
[34] *Person*, p. 338.
[35] *Person*, p. 339.
[36] "Some Christian Aspects of Evolution," *London Quarterly Review* 104 (October 1905): 227–228.
[37] *The Cruciality of the Cross*, 1st ed. (1909), p. 144. In the original, the word 'Holy' is italicized.

dependable, a God whose ways may vary but whose promises are sure.

So Forsyth sets out with vivid clarity a view of God that in effect contradicts the old scholastic notions of immutability, setting in their place a Christologically-derived view of a God at once changeless *and* mobile.

3.3 SOME RESULTING GENERALIZATIONS

At this point, it would be appropriate to review some of the findings arising from Forsyth's teaching on omniscience and immutability, and state them in a general way. Certain principles have been discovered in our investigation, principles which apply not merely to one attribute or another, but to God's perfections more generally. To this we propose to add further general considerations discovered in Forsyth's discussions of other attributes of God.

First, the Christological evidence is the decisive and governing factor for our knowledge and description of the divine perfections. Although Forsyth may speculate about the pre-existence of God's omniscience or the necessary characteristics of an absolute God, his starting-point (formally if not materially) in every case is the actual revelation of God's attributes in Jesus Christ. In formulating his views on the divine perfections, Forsyth treats Jesus Christ as the touchstone.

Secondly, a related matter and a recurring theme within Forsyth's consideration of the divine attributes is God's freedom to act. In a challenge to the traditions of theological orthodoxy, Forsyth insists that God is what he is revealed to be, and any imposed constraints must give way before that primary fact. His refusal to define God's changelessness in a way that would restrict divine freedom is paralleled in his treatment of other attributes:

> Omnipotence means not that God should be able to do anything and everything that fancy may suggest; but that, in working his will of love, God is, from his own free resource, equal to all it involves, and is really determined by nothing outside himself. Omnipresence, as absolute independence of space, means that God is not hampered by space, but can enter spatial relations without being tied to them, can exist in limits without being unfree, or ceasing to be God.[38]

---

[38] *Person*, p. 309.

As we noted in relation to omniscience, Forsyth's view is that God is self-limited, with no necessity imposed from outside himself.[39] For God to condescend in incarnational grace is neither a denial of his freedom nor of his divinity. Scholastic theologians sacrificed the former, classic kenoticists gave up the latter, but the position Forsyth outlined claimed to retain both.

Thirdly, the attributes are personal characteristics of God expressed within a relational setting. While some theologies yield an abstract and impersonal God, the deity Forsyth describes is intimately involved with humankind – in creation, in covenant-making, and pre-eminently in redemption. The context in which Forsyth most clearly makes this point, however, concerns the incarnation of God the Son. It is in the Word made flesh that God's perfections are seen. For Forsyth this involves a kenotic retraction of certain attributes, but the general point is persuasive within a Chalcedonian framework as well.

Fourthly, Forsyth does not isolate God's perfections, but rather affirms that all are interrelated in one personality. In our brief discussion of God's omniscience, Forsyth's quoted comments referred not only to God's Fatherhood as revealed by the Son, but also to God's will, wisdom, holiness, and love. On immutability, the interconnection of attributes is similarly apparent. It is impossible to discuss one attribute without reference to the others. God is a many-faceted reality.

Fifthly, even in the limited discussion above we have noticed Forsyth's determination to hold together seemingly contradictory elements. Regarding omniscience, Forsyth maintained that God's "intuitive and simultaneous knowledge of all" became "discursive, successive and progressive"; and regarding immutability, he spoke of "the infinite mobility of the changeless God."[40] Concerning immanence, a subject that captured Forsyth's attention during the 'new theology' controversy, he later reminded his readers of "the paradox that all immanence is the immanence of the absolutely transcendent, and the humble visitation of the Most High."[41] Essential to maintaining such tensions is Forsyth's contention that the incarnation is a definitive expression of God's nature. "So we have the principle", he concludes, "that *limitation* is a power of Godhead, not a curtailment of it. Among the infinite powers of the

---

[39] *Person,* p. 311.
[40] *Person,* pp. 310–311, 309.
[41] *Authority,* p. 154.

Omnipotent must be the power to limit Himself, and among His glories the grace to bend and die."[42] A paradoxical conception of God as "changeless change" is a hallmark of his treatment of the attributes more generally.

Lastly, the perfections of God are described in the closest relation to the atoning work of Christ. God did not become human merely to display the characteristics of his personality, but to conquer sin and accomplish reconciliation. So for example, Forsyth sees God's attribute of omnipresence in the light of soteriology: "Everywhere, according to God's ubiquity, immanence, or what you will, His holy love is invincibly at issue with death, sin, and sorrow. Everywhere is redemption."[43] Similarly, in considering the independence and self-sufficiency of God, Forsyth states, "His blessedness is not to be self-contained, and in Himself enough, but it is to seek and to save."[44] In short, "His knowledge, his power, his presence were all adjusted to his vocation. His vocation was not to apply or exhibit omnipotence, but to effect the will of infinite love."[45] The effect of such conclusions is to transfer the emphasis from a preoccupation with aspects of God's being to a concern for what the multifaceted God has done. In a tone both commendatory and instructional, Forsyth commented that modern thought "regards the attributes of God less, and the purpose of God more."[46] God's redemption of humanity is always in view in Forsyth's treatment of the attributes.

4. THE FATHERHOOD OF GOD

In the autumn of 1896, when the Congregational Union of England and Wales met at Leicester for its semi-annual meetings, the Rev P. T. Forsyth was the preacher at the opening evening session. It was a sermon that caught the attention of a generation, and was quickly published, first in the religious weekly newspapers, then in both British and American periodicals of printed sermons, and then as a small book.[47] The sermon text, John 17.11, with its

---

[42] "The Divine Self–Emptying" (1895), in *God the Holy Father* (1957), p. 33.
[43] *Justification*, p. 123.
[44] "The Taste of Death and the Life of Grace" (1900), in *Father*, p. 64.
[45] *Person*, p. 320.
[46] *Authority*, p. 38.
[47] *Independent and Nonconformist*, 1 October 1896, and *British Weekly*, 19 and 26 November 1896; *Christian World Pulpit*, 7 October 1896, and *Homiletic Review* (1897); *The Holy Father and the Living Christ* (1897); for full details

stress on God's holiness, could serve well as a text for Forsyth's subsequent theological writing.

More to our present purposes, this printed sermon called "The Holy Father" introduces a crucial aspect of God's nature – Fatherhood. When the Old Testament occasionally mentions the idea, says Forsyth, "it is one of those gleams of vision in which the soul of Israel outran the spirit of its age. It transcended its own genius. It rose from the covenant God to the father God." But that name, Forsyth continues, "is as yet imported into God rather than revealed from Him. He *is like* a father more than he *is* a father. And He is Israel's father only." Turning to the New Testament, Forsyth asserts that "God is not simply 'Our Father,' but 'the God and Father of our Lord and Saviour Jesus Christ.'" Then referring specifically to his text, Forsyth makes this point: "Christ's own prayer was 'Holy Father.' That was Christ's central thought about God, and He knew God as He *is*."[48]

Such a stress on the Fatherhood of God was not unusual, of course. In the theology of Forsyth's teacher Albrecht Ritschl, it was positioned prominently, but always subsidiary to his concern for "the *summum bonum* – the kingdom of God." 'Father' is for him merely "the Christian name for God," an equivalent idea to God's love.[49] "It seems clear," wrote James Orr of Ritschl's conception, "that Fatherhood is simply with him a synonym for God's will of love, as it rests first on Jesus, and then on His disciples united with Him."[50] For Ritschl, God's Fatherhood was not a "central thought about God" around which other content might be ordered, as it was for Forsyth, but rather a piece of theological shorthand for the love of God.

The liberal theology that stemmed from Ritschl made far more of the idea of God's Fatherhood. In an 1897 lecture, Orr fairly summarized this view by saying that the divine Fatherhood was "the highest expression for what Christ has taught us to believe

---

[48] see "The Holy Father" (1896) in the Bibliography, Section 3. Citations here are to *God the Holy Father* (1957), pp. 1–27.
[49] "Holy Father," in *Father,* pp. 3–4.
Albrecht Ritschl, *The Christian Doctrine of Justification and Reconciliation,* [vol. 3,] *The Positive Development of the Doctrine,* trans. H. R. Mackintosh and A. B. Macauley (Edinburgh: T. & T. Clark, 1900), pp. 35, 273. See also Albrecht Ritschl, "Instruction in the Christian Religion," in *Three Essays,* trans. and ed. Philip Hefner (Philadelphia: Fortress, 1972), p. 225.
[50] James Orr, *The Ritschlian Theology and the Evangelical Faith,* 3rd ed. (London: Hodder & Stoughton, 1905; orig. pub. 1897), pp. 112, 114.

concerning God in His relations to men and disposition towards them," and further "that God is now regarded as universal Father, whereas formerly this relation of Fatherhood was limited to believers."[51] Like Orr, Forsyth criticized this view of "the essential and generous Fatherhood of God," because it makes forgiveness "a thing of paternal course, a direct, smooth and easy outflow of his kindly love. And so the word grace loses its meaning."[52]

To this mixture of ideas, with its emphasis on God's loving Fatherhood, Forsyth added a vital ingredient – the holiness of God. Jesus addressed God as "Holy Father."[53] God's passionate commitment to humanity included a commitment to the integrity of his own holiness; his fatherly love was a holy love. But this counter to the Ritschlian theologians' preoccupation with God's love did not lead Forsyth to neglect the central place of God's Fatherhood in the theological scheme of things. In fact, just the opposite was true: Fatherhood is "God's first and last relation to the world."[54] For all his reservations about the current use of the idea, Forsyth was convinced of its theological value.

This conviction is derived from the revelation of God in Jesus Christ, whose action as a witness to God Forsyth takes very seriously. This relationship was all-important: "The Redeemer was not His own apostle. He spoke most of His Father, much of Himself as His Father's Son, little of His achievements, and of the pain and cost of them next to nothing at all."[55] That emphasis on the Son's relationship to the Father was taught by such texts as Matthew 11.27, where Jesus asserts that the Son both uniquely knows and decisively reveals the Father. That in turn, according to Forsyth, forms the basis of our religion: "We believe in the Father because of Christ."[56]

A common practice among expositors of the attributes of God is to consider the divine names in scripture, but Forsyth concentrates on this one name. "We cannot put too much into that word Father.

---

[51] James Orr, *The Progress of Dogma* (London: Hodder & Stoughton, 1901), pp. 324, 325.
[52] "Ritschl on Justification," review of *The Christian Doctrine of Justification and Reconciliation,* vol. 3, by Albrecht Ritschl, trans. H. R. Mackintosh and A. B. Macauley, in *Speaker,* n.s. 3 (London, 1901): 630.
[53] The holiness of God's Fatherhood is more fully treated later, particularly Chapter Six, section 4 and Chapter Seven, section 6.2.
[54] "Holy Father," in *Father,* p. 3.
[55] "Holy Father," in *Father,* p. 19.
[56] *Person,* p. 40.

It is the sum and marrow of all Christian divinity."[57] Fatherhood is "the whole of God and the fulness of Christ. It is the very nature and totality of Godhead, and the source of man's redemption. ... No name so fits our whole soul's whole God."[58] Indeed, for God to be Father is "the very nature ... of Godhead." Clearly this is an important category for Forsyth, and it would not be going too far to say that Fatherhood is an attribute of God, if we understand the attributes to be essential characteristics of God's personal reality which are not in any way secondary to God's being.

However, lest the discussion veer too close to metaphysical speculation, Forsyth is quick to point out that "the whole Bible use of the word Father refers it to an act of choice and a purpose of redemption. God is Father ... by gracious adoption. ... God is, directly, the Father of Christ alone. He is our Father only in Christ." God's Fatherhood is exercised in election, redemption, and adoption. With regard to this last aspect, and against the liberal theology which interpreted Fatherhood primarily in terms of the creating love of God, Forsyth added, "We are all destined to be sons of God; but the sonship is in our destiny rather than in our origin or state." God is Father, Forsyth avers, "by gracious adoption and not by natural generation."[59]

Forsyth makes another correction to mistaken views when he says, "The Fatherhood of God *sans phrase* [without more ado] is not Christianity."[60] The parable of the prodigal son is not a mine for quarrying a complete doctrine of God, and indeed is misleading if used in such a way. Forsyth maintains that the waiting father of the story "does not stand for the whole of God, nor even for the whole grace of God." Although it well expresses the freeness of grace, the parable makes no attempt to explain the cost of that grace to a Holy Father.[61] God the Father is not merely a family figure, but "the Father in Heaven, the Father from above us all, the royal, the holy,

---

[57] "Holy Father," in *Father*, p. 5.
[58] "Holy Father," in *Father*, p. 24.
[59] *Positive Preaching*, pp. 214–215. Here Forsyth is following Ritschl: "As Father, God is not in the first instance the Creator of the world, but the Father of Jesus Christ, and through His mediation the Father of believers as the children won to Him through Christ. ... All men assuredly are not the children of God, but only the members of the community, who already through Christ are reconciled to God." Ritschl, *Leben*, vol. 2, p. 199, quoted in Orr, *Ritschlian Theology*, p. 115.
[60] *Faith, Freedom, and the Future* (1912), p. 174.
[61] "Holy Father," in *Father*, p. 8.

the absolute Father, of an infinite majesty."[62] Forsyth's warning here is applicable to a more general concern: the *via eminentia* yields mistaken results because God is significantly different from humankind. For Forsyth, holiness makes a "generic difference," not only in correcting the mistaken notion that "heavenly fatherhood is but earthly magnified,"[63] but in other contexts as well.

In a paradoxical way, God's Fatherhood is both an overarching and inclusive category, and at the same time, only one element within the Triune God. To illustrate the former assertion, Forsyth can speak variously of "a *universal and eternal* Fatherhood," of "the restoration to Fatherhood of the idea of sovereignty," and of judgment as "an element essential to a holy fatherhood."[64] In an interesting and eloquent construction, Forsyth illustrates something of the breadth of God's Fatherhood: "He is father of pity to human weakness, still more father of grace to human sin, but chiefly father of holy joy to our Lord Jesus Christ."[65]

The latter point (concerning the Trinity), though not repeated often in Forsyth's writing, is nevertheless stressed: "Christian faith is faith in the Justifier, the Reconciler, the Sanctifier, and not merely in God the Father."[66] Forsyth warns against thinking of God in terms of "a simple Fatherhood, detached from a positive saving Word."[67] The living God is "no glorified individual, but the Triune God who is the peculiar revelation of Christ. For the Christian God is not the Father, but the Father of our Lord Jesus Christ in the Spirit."[68]

In summary, Forsyth's view of God as Father is stated within the broad context of classical trinitarianism, issues from scripture, and particularly from Christ's own idea about God. Although such a distinctive stress on the divine Fatherhood was held in common with the theological followers of Ritschl, Forsyth consciously defined his position over against the liberal theology of the late nineteenth century. While he shared the Christocentrism of the era, he was also determined to feature the holiness of the cross. God was "The Holy

---

[62] *Justification*, p. 176.
[63] *Authority*, p. 170.
[64] "Holy Father," in *Father*, p. 10; *Freedom*, pp. 291, 248.
[65] "Holy Father," in *Father*, p. 3.
[66] *Authority*, p. 46.
[67] *Freedom*, p. 108.
[68] *Authority*, p. 230. We return to consider the relation of the Trinity to God's holy love in Chapter Seven, section 6.

Father," as Forsyth insisted in 1896; it was a theme that resounded in his writing for another twenty-five years.

5. EXPRESSIONS OF THE DYNAMIC GOD

Earlier in this chapter, in the service of a methodological point, we quoted Forsyth's conviction that an attribute is not "something loose within God which He could manipulate," so that, for example, "the love of God is not an attribute of God; it is God loving."[69] These words serve equally well to illustrate Forsyth's point that God's self-revelation is not static but active. Because of that, redemption more than revelation is the proper focus: "The great object of things is not the self-expression of the Eternal in time but His self-effectuation as holy in a kingdom."[70] Time and time again, Forsyth reminds his readers that, in effect, theology is not a still-life photograph but a constantly moving picture, and God is not an object for metaphysical analysis but an active moral subject.

As we will have occasion to note several times in this study, Forsyth's language is often bluntly disjunctive, offering an argument in the form, 'not *a*, but *b*,' when in other circumstances he might more wisely say, 'not so much *a* as *b*.' In the preceding quotation, God's self-expression is unnecessarily denigrated in favour of his self-effectuation, revelation contrasted harshly with redemption. In other places, Forsyth is less sweeping and more judicious, more satisfying to one who wishes to analyse an argument closely. It must be also admitted, however, that a more careful argument loses impact, and given a choice, Forsyth usually opts for vivid expression and striking contrast. Consider the following quotation, which begins with an assertion that apparently rules out the possibility of a theological anthropology:

> In religious knowledge the object is God; it is not the world, it is not man. And that object differs from every other in being for us far more than an object of knowledge. He is the absolute subject of it. He is not something that we approach, with the initiative on our side. He takes the initiative and approaches us. Our knowledge is the result of his revelation.[71]

Such a perspective, and such a style of theological argument, is a powerful challenge to a human-centred approach that trivializes

---
[69] *Work*, pp. 117–118.
[70] *Positive Preaching*, pp. 307–308.
[71] *Authority*, pp. 148–149.

God's attributes by reducing them to a manageable size. Here Forsyth insists that God takes the initiative and defines his own attributes through his revealed action.

This perspective gives a certain objectivity to the doctrine of God's nature. In the same way that Forsyth described his own life-changing experience as a turning from religious subjectivism to the realization that he was "an object of grace,"[72] he reiterates that for theology, too, God's action has the priority, and his revelation has the initiating role. The interplay of subjective and objective in Christian experience is a recurring theme in Forsyth's writing, with the objective indicatives of grace in the foremost place. He often echoed the words of Jesus, who told his disciples, "You did not choose me, but I chose you" (John 15.16), and of Paul, who wrote to one church, "You know God – or rather are known by God" (Galatians 4.9). The following are typical: "In the faith that answers revelation we are more sure that we are known than that we know. ... We apprehend that we are apprehended. ... We know only because we are known with the infinite knowledge of a Creator and Redeemer, known in a way that not only evokes faith but creates it."[73] Such is the initiating grace of God that his actions are prior in creation, in the cross, and in the believer's experience.

It follows therefore that "the God of the Bible .... is not discovered. He is not forced into the light, even of love, by any power outside Himself, not even by our misery."[74] God retains the initiative of divine sovereignty. Further, as Christians mature in their understanding of God, they "find the very notion of Him more and more of a given thing, a descending, commanding, authoritative thing."[75] Any description of God, any treatise on God's attributes, must flow from a recognition that knowledge of God is the gift of One who assumes Lordship over the discussion by making the first move.

It would be possible to conclude that the priority of grace in revelation would preclude human search and human discovery, but Forsyth insists that divine initiative and overarching providence do not preclude human response, but actually invite it. The God who

---

[72] *Positive Preaching*, p. 283.
[73] *Authority*, pp. 155–156.
[74] *Authority*, p. 372.
[75] *Authority*, p. 110.

"gives himself to be known" is also the one "who wills to be enquired of."[76]

God is known by his actions, contends Forsyth. This turn-of-the-century theologian, by his own admission, is "engrossed with will and purpose" rather than "structure or substance," and interested in action more than thought. Philosophical theology that is faithful to its task "is thus concerned about the nature of God the Saviour even more than God the Creator. . . . It regards the attributes of God less, and the purpose of God more."[77]

Forsyth's concern here is a matter of balance. By so emphasizing the dynamic activity of God, he is not ruling out the possibility of knowing God's nature. Just the opposite is true, in fact, because the active God is revealing his attributes. The content of revelation "is God with a special nature shown by express action," and the two are one: as God acts within history, he acts in accordance with His own nature.[78] Actions are the window through which we see God's attributes because "His will is a perfect and eternal appropriation of His nature."[79] Put another way, in revelation we find first God's purpose, and then God's nature, and so rather than separating divine activity and attributes, "it would be more accurate to say the goal and the ground are one," but still distinguishable.[80] In these excerpts from his thought, Forsyth is affirming in a more balanced way the importance of what he earlier had appeared to deny. His apparent anti-ontological bias is not thoroughgoing; therefore, our enquiry about God's nature is not disbarred from the outset. Rather, the expression of God's nature in moral action reveals the divine attributes.

6. GOD IS PERSONAL – AND FREE

"God is an eternal person; I am a finite person; yet we are persons both," asserts Forsyth,[81] and in a variety of contexts he elaborates this important point. The present section considers those contexts, and the importance in his theology of a personal God.

First, in a philosophical context, Forsyth contrasts God as personal with the view of God as a process, advanced by Hegel:

---

[76] *Person*, pp. 113, 75–76.
[77] *Authority*, pp. 37–38.
[78] *Authority*, p. 54.
[79] *Authority*, p. 101.
[80] *Authority*, p. 37.
[81] *Work*, p. 75.

"Being a philosopher he was great upon the idea. The whole world, he said, was a movement or process of the grand, divine idea." While a process lacks will, responsibility, and the possibility of moral action, Christianity witnesses to the moral acts of God. A process lacks divine initiative; for Christian faith, "divine initiative is everything." A theology which views God as a process working by general laws has detrimental results. For example, it discounts God's providence, sees prayer as self-referential, and generally considers religious experience as "a subjectivity, a resignation, [or] a sense of dependence." Christianity insists on the fact that in Christ, God acts. God acts in creation, to bring about "the whole existence of a moral world."[82] He acts in providence, answering prayer. God is active in judgment: "Could a personal soul be judged by a mere historic process?" asks Forsyth; "Does it not call for a personal God?"[83] Most notably, the Lord acts in reconciliation "between *two persons* who have fallen out, and not between a failing person on the one hand and a perfect, imperturbable process on the other."[84]

Secondly, Forsyth stresses the importance of a personal God in relation to philosophy's "doctrine of the absolute," which agrees with theology on "the existence of this ultimate power," but disagrees on its nature. "For one it is immanent and pantheistic, for the other transcendental and personal. For the one tendency it means the presence and emergence in all things of the timeless and absolute *Being,* for the other the invasive action in all things of an influence akin less to thought than to will in *creating* and freedom in *becoming.*"[85] The latter, Forsyth concludes, "is the more personal view, which lays the stress on choice rather than thought, on crisis rather than order, on free will rather than fated force."[86] Yet Forsyth wishes to retain the idea of an absolute God, and so he renovates the conception. To the question, In what sense is God absolute?, Forsyth's answer is, Morally. "Religion is our relation to the absolute as holy. Without such an absolute there is no faith, no obedience, because no authority."[87]

The third context in which Forsyth stresses the personal God is more psychological, and "might perhaps be described as Christian

---

[82] *Work,* pp. 67–70.
[83] *Cruciality,* p. 171.
[84] *Work,* p. 76.
[85] *Justification,* pp. 69–70; corrected slightly by *Justification,* 1st ed. (1916), p. 68.
[86] *Justification,* p. 72.
[87] *Authority,* p. 67.

Personalism, the culture of personality by means of Christianity. . . . [Its adherents] have a firm yet large grasp of the personality of God; and they cling to it as the chief guarantee of man's personality and its culture. Their object of life is the creation and development of personality, under such an influence as religion in chief."[88] One advocate of this position, contemporary with Forsyth, describes personalism as "a system of selves related through a supreme personality," and "the latest form of theism."[89] Forsyth's estimate is negative, indeed caustic: Christian Personalism is "high . . . egocentricity";[90] the antidote for this intellectual infection is more concern for "the holy personality of God" than "the growing personality of man."[91] But "it is not enough to say that in religion we are in contact with a living personality." God is more than that. Indeed, the one we know as personal knows us "with such a creative intimacy as love alone provides."[92]

A warning is necessary at this point. In thinking about God's nature, Forsyth avers, we must be careful not to draw easy parallels between human and divine personalities. "In all of us the personality is incomplete; and it misleads us in the most grave way when we use it as an analogy for the ever complete and holy personality of God."[93] In terms of the attributes of God, then, the *via eminentia* is not good enough: God "is not simply our own superlative. God is not thought raised to infinity."[94] Once again, Forsyth's critique of the position is thoroughgoing. The *via eminentia* is not merely more difficult because of the distance between God and humankind; it is a wrong way. "It is not a matter simply of affinity and intellectual love but of difference and of intellectual fear, rising from the limitation of our thought and not its absoluteness."[95] The most important consequences of such a view can be very simply stated. God is personal and therefore known in the context of a

---

[88] *Freedom*, pp. 266–267.
[89] R. T. Flewelling, "Personalism," in *Encyclopedia of Religion and Ethics*, vol. 9, pp. 771, 772. This should not be confused with a later idea, associated with Martin Buber and others, which stressed the personal nature of true relationships.
[90] *Freedom*, p. 267.
[91] *Freedom*, p. 271.
[92] *Authority*, pp. 149–150.
[93] *Positive Preaching*, p. 262.
[94] *Authority*, p. 99.
[95] *Authority*, p. 99.

relationship. "Religion is communion with God, the relation of a living person with a living person."[96]

The self-limitation implied by the personal God's willingness to become human in Jesus Christ does not however mean that God is unfree, as if his hands were tied: "God is not imprisoned in His personality. That were a crude Deism, and only another form of weakness. His is a *free* personality." There is no sense in which there is "a god beyond God" who imposes another will, foreign to the one revealed in Jesus Christ. Moreover, this freedom paradoxically includes the possibility of limitation: omnipotence would be impotence, explains Forsyth, if it was not able to be at home within earthly limits. "It is not Omnipotence if it cannot empty itself of immunities and descend and be found in fashion as nature or man."[97]

7. MORAL UNITY AND FUNCTIONAL DISTINCTIONS

When we gather the findings of the preceding sections, it emerges that P. T. Forsyth's view of God is that of a personal Father, revealed in Jesus Christ. He is the active God, working redemption on the cross and creating a kingdom in which adopted sons and daughters are active subjects. In this dynamic and saving work, God's attributes are revealed. Far from being atomized entities, these divine perfections express aspects of his individual and unified reality.

Earlier in this chapter we examined omniscience and immutability in some detail; other attributes have briefly been our concern at other times; and subsequent chapters will focus very specifically on God's love and holiness. Is it possible to make distinctions between these various attributes? Are these perfections of God classifiable, with some alike, and others different? Forsyth's first answer to this question is to resist it, and to emphasize that attributes are aspects of God's character. As God is one and indivisible, so is the divine personality. An attribute is not a detachable entity, "for it is only the Being himself in a certain angle and relation."[98] Forsyth is determined not to let consideration of the parts obscure the unity of the whole. God is entirely loving, completely holy, and so on. Revealed in Christ and known in relationship, this God acts in ways that can be named by discrete words like omnipotence or wisdom,

---

[96] *Authority,* p. 99.
[97] "Divine Self-Emptying," in *Father,* p. 35.
[98] *Person,* p. 309.

but these must always be understood within the context of a full-orbed view of the indivisible God.[99]

The nature of this unity of attributes is not only founded on God's essential oneness, but also on God's ethical nature. All God's attributes are ethical ones, because God is a moral reality. Forsyth's contention is that "God is God not physically but morally."[100] In a significant section of *The Principle of Authority,* he speaks of having one's "footing on reality," and asserts that such an authoritative foundation is not in experience which tends to subjectivism, nor in rationality which verges toward a new scholasticism. Feeling and thought are merely components of a broader reality, "that activity which we call life." He continues:

> We came nearer life when Neo-Kantianism taught us that the real was the moral. The will took the primacy from the intellect. *Bonitas est substantia Dei,* as Augustine said. The proper metaphysic is a metaphysic of ethic. It is the conscience that plants us on the bedrock of being. Morality is the nature of things. ... If we raise this to the Christian temperature we have the reality of things in a kingdom of moral relations infused with love.[101]

All of what Forsyth says about attributes – and especially about the distinctions that separate them – should be understood within this ethical framework.

"Morality is the nature of things," wrote Forsyth in the previous quotation, and of course Joseph Butler was the source, unattributed here but acknowledged prominently in a previous work.[102] Butler is an important influence on Forsyth's thought, not least because of this emphasis on moral reality. As has been mentioned previously,[103] Forsyth made a prominent place for the conscience, an emphasis encouraged by Butler's published sermons. The importance of the moral was strengthened by Kant's work on the practical reason, and especially (as Forsyth notes) by the neo-Kantian school. Rodgers identifies this as "one of the most decisive of the philosophical

---

[99] Forsyth expands further on this subject in "Veracity, Reality, and Regeneration," *London Quarterly Review* 123 (April 1915): 214.
[100] *Person,* p. 313.
[101] *Authority,* pp. 178–180.
[102] See *Person,* p. 256, and the epigraph to the 1st ed. of *Person,* p. iii, inexplicably omitted from the subsequent reprint editions. Later, Butler's *Analogy* appears in the only bibliography included in any of Forsyth's books: see *Justification,* p. 224.
[103] See Chapter Three, sections 3–5 above.

influences upon Forsyth,"[104] and suggests that perhaps Windelband especially was influential through his focus on the primacy of the will and the place of the conscience.[105]

Forsyth, however, was not only interested in the moral quality of human nature, but primarily in "the supreme ethical category known to us – the holiness of God as Jesus Christ revealed Him."[106] As we will see when we turn specifically to the subject of that holiness, in Forsyth's view the one God was characterized by holiness, and all the divine attributes should be seen in the light of God's holy love. This attention to the moral qualities of God's nature is identified by John McIntyre as a particularly significant development in the doctrine of the atonement. Just as Christological dogma was forged as a response to various challenges, so "controversy and soteriological formulation have gone hand in hand."[107] One such period, stretching "from the nineteenth into the twentieth century," saw the doctrine of the atonement develop in terms of what McIntyre calls "the ethicising of the attributes of God." Aspects of this included a recognition that the metaphysical attributes should not be allowed to dominate the "more moral" attributes, and that God's attributes interpenetrate each other.[108] For his part, Forsyth affirmed that "the main part of the modernizing of theology is the moralizing of it."[109] With his concentration on the comprehensive moral reality of God, Forsyth played an important role in this development, both as it related to the attributes of God and to the atonement.[110]

In the history of systematic theology, however, a desire to emphasize God's unity has not been enough to prevent the proliferation of ways to classify God's attributes. The great systematizer Charles Hodge comments: "On few subjects have greater thought and labor been expended than on this." Then he admits: "Perhaps, however, the benefit has not been commensurate

---

[104] John Rodgers, *The Theology of P. T. Forsyth: The Cross of Christ and the Revelation of God* (London: Independent Press, 1965), p. 269.
[105] See Rodgers, *Theology of P. T. Forsyth*, p. 271, and *Authority*, p. 5.
[106] "Immanence and Incarnation," in *The Old Faith and the New Theology*, ed. C. H. Vine (London: Sampson Low Marston, 1907), p. 57.
[107] John McIntyre, *The Shape of Soteriology: Studies in the Doctrine of the Death of Christ* (Edinburgh: T. & T. Clark, 1992), p. 16.
[108] McIntyre, *Shape of Soteriology*, pp. 22–23.
[109] *Positive Preaching*, p. 293.
[110] See Forsyth's extended treatment of "the moralising of dogma" in *Person*, chaps. 8 and 9.

with the labor."¹¹¹ The most common way of organizing the attributes has been in two, variously named, groups. Karl Barth summarizes this "classical line of approach" as essentially a distinction between God's nature and his action. Two groups of attributes are contrasted, groups variously described as negative and positive, quiescent and operative, internal and external, absolute and relative, immanent and transcendent, primitive and derived, metaphysical and moral, or incommunicable and communicable. This "twofold division" could be summarized as "attributes of the divine being and attributes of the divine activity," and in Barth's view, "we have no real need to look around for a radically new solution."¹¹² Barth declares that "God not only appears but is almighty, eternal, just, wise, merciful – not merely for us but in Himself."¹¹³

Having advanced his view that all attributes are moral ones, Forsyth treats the divine perfections in two classes. In one group he includes God's love and God's holiness, "and holy love ... is the supreme category of the Almighty."¹¹⁴ Contrasted to holy love is a second group composed of "the less ethical attributes like omniscience, omnipotence, or ubiquity."¹¹⁵ It is apparent that in the division of attributes, Forsyth is following the traditional pattern of attributes as communicable and incommunicable, relative and absolute, etc. Traditionally, holiness and love have been seen as attributes of the divine activity, while omniscience, omnipotence, and omnipresence have been considered as attributes of God's being.

Although this division resembles Forsyth's frequently made distinction between the moral and the metaphysical, we must take seriously his contention (detailed above) that all God's attributes are ethical ones, and that metaphysical questions should be answered in moral categories. God's being is to be understood, then, in terms of God's action. Forsyth places a priority not merely on the given reality (God in Christ), but on his accomplished deeds (the world's reconciliation). These deeds are the key to understanding the one who initiated them, or in Forsythian terms, redemption is the key to revelation.

---

[111] Hodge, *Systematic Theology*, vol. 1, pp. 374–375.
[112] Barth, *Church Dogmatics* 2/1, pp. 340–341. For these distinctions in the history of theology, see also H. Bavinck, *The Doctrine of God* (Edinburgh: Banner of Truth Trust, 1977), pp. 132–137.
[113] Barth, *Church Dogmatics* 2/1, pp. 335–336.
[114] *Person*, p. 316.
[115] *Person*, p. 295.

What are we to make of Forsyth's statement that some attributes are "less ethical" than others? The explanation comes in the context of his discussion of kenotic christology: "Omniscience and the rest are not so much attributes as functions of attributes, or their modifications."[116] While both love and omnipotence, for example, are equally God's attributes, Forsyth asserts that there is an order, even a subordination, involved. Love and holiness inform the will, while omniscience, changelessness, and the like are instruments of it. This is an important and luminous distinction. Taking his cue from the Christ's incarnation, Forsyth sees "the less ethical attributes" in their limited but genuine presence, acting at the behest of holy love, which is "the region, the nature, and the norm" of omnipotence, omniscience, omnipresence and the rest.[117] Although the language is pictorial, we gather that in some sense, the relative attributes find their place within, and operate under the direction of God's holy love in Jesus Christ.

Forsyth here is actually renovating the traditional distinction between nature and attributes in a way that maintains its validity and usefulness, but moralizes it. For *nature and attributes* he substitutes *attributes and functions of attributes*. This changed terminology was a Forsythian attempt to break static categories of thought that emphasized what God is, and replace them with dynamic categories that described what God does. The moral nature of God, God as holy love, determines the way ahead; other attributes act within that plan. This dynamic view of God means that God's action is not prevented by what he must be, according to some imported notion of impassability, immutability, or whatever.

At the same time as we commend Forsyth for the light shed on God's attributes with his distinction between God's activity and being, between holy love and relative attributes, between attributes and functions of attributes, we must also add that to characterize this distinction as a contrast between "ethical" and "less ethical" attributes seems indistinct and unprofitable. What Forsyth terms "functions of attributes" are nevertheless fully divine characteristics, aspects of the one holy, loving – and indivisible – God. Omnipotence, for example, is no less an attribute of God for being at the service of God's holiness. Immutability is not less important when it is qualified to include mobility for love's sake.

---

[116] *Person,* p. 309.
[117] *Person,* p. 313.

In conclusion, this chapter has examined Forsyth's view of the attributes of God in a general way, sketching various ingredients in Forsyth's doctrine of God's perfections: God is self-revealed and personal, the Father of Jesus Christ, active in history. But at every one of these points, Forsyth points beyond them to something that is for him more important: the holiness and love of God. Certainly God is self-revealed, but he is "a God self-revealed as absolute and holy Love."[118] God is not an impersonal Absolute, but rather "a moral Absolute" which is "the active revelation of the Holy One."[119] Yes, God is a loving Father, but "the new revelation in the cross was more than 'God is love.' It was this 'Holy Father.'"[120] Indeed, these two vital ingredients must be combined, and so P. T. Forsyth went on to say, "The nature of Godhead is Holy Love."[121] In the next chapter, we begin to examine the constituent parts of that distinctive theological contribution.

---

[118] *Authority*, p. 66.
[119] *Justification*, p. 74.
[120] "Holy Father," in *Father*, p. 3.
[121] *Person*, p. 313.

Chapter Five

The Prominence of Love

Truly we cannot exaggerate the love of God, if we will take pains to first understand it. But we have been taught to believe only in a beneficent and not in a sovereign God, in a tender God in no sense judge, in an attractive God more kindly than holy, more lovely than good. . . . Such a habit of mind, now that the lid is off hell, is suddenly struck from its only perch.

P. T. Forsyth

In the previous chapter, we considered the attributes of God in a general way; in this chapter we turn to one divine perfection in particular. There we noted Forsyth's emphasis that attributes are aspects of the whole personality, and therefore that any one attribute, whether it be omnipotence, love, holiness, or any other, will be an inadequate description of God. Here, however, we concentrate on love, acknowledging the value of focusing on one divine characteristic in the wider context of God's whole nature. Such an approach will not only confirm what has already been said, but will advance our understanding concerning this particular attribute of God.

Concurrent with a detailed examination of Forsyth's view of God's love, we wish to make three broad assertions: first, that Forsyth gives a prominent place to the love of God and considers it an important theological emphasis; second, that the cumulative result of his unsystematic references to God's love yields a reasonably comprehensive picture of that love; and third, that Forsyth considers love, by itself and without qualification, to be an inadequate description of God. We will see that although Forsyth vigorously describes the loving aspect of God's nature, he also insists that much more must be said if we are to understand God, and indeed his love.

To put it another way, two strands of thinking will be separated and examined in this chapter. The first is a theological message about the great and tender love of God, while the second is a description of Forsyth's critique of a distortion of that message in his particular era. A prominent church historian has written recently that P. T. Forsyth "was probably the greatest British theologian of the Edwardian age, indeed almost the only one . . . whose theological work can really be profitably read for its own sake seventy years later."[1] In this section we hear Forsyth the Edwardian critic applying that theology to the thinking of his own day; we also hear the enduring theologian sounding the timeless note of God's love.

1. THE PROMINENT PLACE OF GOD'S LOVE IN FORSYTH'S WRITINGS

We begin by looking at Forsyth's positive assertions about the love of God, within various contexts, in order to show that he gives this aspect of God's nature an important place in his theological writing.

1.1 GOD'S CHARACTERISTIC LOVE IS KNOWN IN CHRIST

If we would start our discussion of God's love where Forsyth begins, that point of departure is "Love's own account of itself in Christ." We should begin with "God's revelation of His love as dying for the ungodly. This is love original and absolute. Hereby know we love at its source."[2] The work of Christ, Forsyth declares, is according to the New Testament "the supreme and distinguishing act of God's love."[3] This is a basic point in Forsyth's theology, simply and often made. The love seen in the cross is the motivating love of God, earnest and passionate in its intention to rescue sinful humanity from all opponents. To look back in faith at that successful rescue mission, Forsyth asserts, is to see God's love decisively expressed and enacted: "The supreme form of God's love

---

[1] Adrian Hastings, *A History of English Christianity 1920–1985* (London: Collins, 1986), p. 118.
[2] "The Taste of Death and the Life of Grace" (1900), in *God the Holy Father* (1957), p. 59.
[3] *Faith, Freedom, and the Future* (1912), p. 14.

was a real act, central in history and critical for eternity."[4] When we later have occasion to note the tremendous importance that Forsyth gives to the holiness of God, it will be essential to recall these repeated assertions of 'love absolute and supreme' in the cross of Christ.

As we have noticed previously,[5] however, Forsyth holds the person of the Saviour in close connection with the redemption accomplished on the cross. To speak of the cross is to speak of Jesus Christ. Divine love, therefore, is not only acted out on the cross, but is enfleshed in Jesus Christ. "God's way of carrying home His love to the world was through a person,"[6] Jesus Christ, who as the Son of the Father revealed the divine love:

> For that sonship there was an inner condition in his nature, a native and unique unity with God, which all Christology is but an imperfect attempt to pierce. He knew the Father's love, and he was himself pure love, without the alienation, the self-will, the sin, that not only removes us far from God but severs us. For the peculiar revelation of his Father's love there was in Christ a peculiar being.[7]

Wherever in the career of God the Son we sample Forsyth's view, we discover that God's love was prominent:

First, the *pre-existence* of Christ was affirmed as true by the New Testament writers in order "to give full and infinite effect to the condescending love of God."[8]

Secondly, in the *incarnation*, "God in his vast act of creative love laid a limit upon himself."[9] Although Forsyth would not be willing to say (with Charles Wesley) that the Son "emptied himself of all but love," the kenotic aspect of Forsyth's christology serves to emphasize that love.

Thirdly, in Christ's *ministry*, "He was preoccupied with God's giving love,"[10] while in his *parables*, Jesus illustrated "the intensity and persistency of God's love," even if (as we will investigate later in this chapter) "they do not do justice to its nature."[11]

---

[4] *Positive Preaching and [the] Modern Mind*, 1st ed. (1907), p. 204.
[5] See Chapter 3, section 10.
[6] *Positive Preaching*, p. 346.
[7] *The Person and Place of Jesus Christ* (1909), p. 41.
[8] *Person*, p. 277.
[9] *Person*, p. 315.
[10] *The Preaching of Jesus and the Gospel of Christ* (1987; orig. pub. as articles in 1915), p. 73.
[11] "The Preaching of Jesus and the Gospel of Christ: [VII] The Meaning of a Sinless Christ," *Expositor*, 8th series, vol. 25 (April 1923): 298.

Fourthly, the love of God is further evidenced in the *faith and obedience* of Christ as he faced death. "To obey and trust a God with His face hidden and His hand stayed, to accept in loving faith such a will of God, was, for the Son of God, the height of all obedience, trust, and love."[12]

Fifthly, however, in Forsyth's view, it is in *the cross* of Jesus Christ more than anywhere else that the love of God is most prominently displayed. He accepts and asserts that this love of God is lived out and exemplified by Jesus in the cross. Echoing Paul's words in Romans 5.7–8, Forsyth says: "Love, to appear exceedingly lovely, dared to die."[13] Referring to the cross, he continues, "The infinite, ultimate love of God is there. ... It is the love of God for the godless, loveless, hating world that is there."[14] Such love was not only received by subjective impression, but was an objective act of God. Forsyth makes the same point in a frequently quoted epigram: "Do not say, 'God is love. Why atone?' The New Testament says, 'God has atoned. What love!'"[15]

1.2 THE LOVE OF GOD IN THE EXPERIENCE OF THE BELIEVER

We have seen in the previous paragraphs that God's love is seen in the person and work of Jesus, in his incarnation, ministry, teaching, obedience, and especially in his death. But this is only one way to express the centrality of God's love in Forsyth's theology. There are other ways to see the same truth, by holding up Forsythian theology at a different angle, so to speak. God's love not only shines from Jesus Christ, it also impacts the life of the believer. We can discern that love in its effects in humanity.

First, the divine love conveys to us God's knowledge of us. In his love, we know that we are known by him. God "knows us, in a special sense, with such a creative intimacy as love alone provides."[16] God's love provides the conduit of knowing. On the same subject, but even more importantly, it is God who initiates the communication of love. For Forsyth, God's love "is the *prius* and the creator of all our love to God." Then and only then can we consider the answering love from humanity's side, namely that "our

---

[12] *Preaching of Jesus*, p. 72.
[13] "Taste of Death," in *Father*, p. 68.
[14] "Taste of Death," in *Father*, p. 72.
[15] "The Holy Father" (1896), in *Father*, p. 4. Forsyth is apparently quoting another author, without attribution.
[16] *The Principle of Authority*, 2nd ed. (1952; orig. pub. 1913), p. 150.

love to Him is the creature of a love from Him to us which . . . flows from the springs of eternal reality."[17]

Secondly, it is divine love that converts, so that Forsyth can speak of "the evangelical experience of God's gracious love of us" and "the whole heart's capture by Christ's love."[18] Brought face to face with "the loving work of the Redeemer,"[19] faith "trusts all the love in the world in the fatherly love and salvation of God."[20] God's love can be trusted.

Thirdly, we experience the love of God in personal communion: "We feel, the more we are united with Him in true prayer, the deep, close difference, the intimate otherness in true love."[21]

And finally, when Christians face 'the taste of death,' they discover not only that God's love is stronger,[22] but that "all things work together in a final teleology of redemptive love."[23]

In each of these examples, Forsyth's obvious intention is to make apparent the wonderful intimacy of close relationship with a God who, in kindness and concern for his human creation, breaks barriers, wins redemption, and maintains communion in Christ, all for love.

1.3 THE LOVE OF GOD IN THE SYSTEMATIC THEOLOGY OF THE CHURCH

The love of God that is revealed in Jesus Christ and subsequently experienced and discerned by Christians in community is described and elucidated by systematic theology. Although P. T. Forsyth never traces the thread of love in a systematic way, he does see the various aspects of the theological agenda in terms of love. The present section intends to outline that agenda, to briefly show that Forsyth includes the love of God in a wide variety of dogmatic contexts. Much more could be said, but the following sketch will serve our present purpose, namely, to illustrate the importance and pervasiveness of God's love in Forsyth's writings.

If we were to start with God's eternal intention, with what Forsyth summarily calls "His purpose of love,"[24] we note that when

---

[17] *Authority*, p. 188.
[18] *Person*, p. 246; *Socialism, the Church and the Poor* (1908), p. 71.
[19] *Preaching of Jesus*, p. 91.
[20] *Rome, Reform and Reaction* (1899), p. 132.
[21] *The Soul of Prayer*, 2nd ed. (1949; orig. pub. 1916), p. 30.
[22] See "Taste of Death," in *Father*, especially the moving last section.
[23] *Authority*, p. 153.

he speaks of *election,* Forsyth bears witness to Jesus Christ as "the eternal and comprehensive object of God's loving will and choice, the Captain of the elect." Alluding to Ephesians 1.4, 11 and quoting Isaiah 42.1, Forsyth states: "The eternal election is in Christ, 'Mine elect in whom my soul delighteth.'"[25] In thus beginning with Christ, Forsyth is attempting to take seriously the loving character of God as revealed in the condescension of the incarnation and the salvation accomplished at the cross. While other systems make the fatal mistake of using election as "an attempt to explain the world and account for its two classes, the good and the bad," Forsyth insists that the doctrine is actually a description of what was accomplished by Jesus Christ.[26] That revelation can be briefly encapsulated in this way: "The certainty of revelation and faith is that in the universal Christ the world is chosen for salvation, and is saved in principle, and shall be saved in fact. The lost are lost by refusing that gospel in their mysterious and incalculable freedom."[27] Election, therefore, is "Love's mode of action, God's election of the world to salvation, and its effective and solidary salvation accordingly."[28] The electing God is Love personified.

Concerning *creation,* Forsyth notes that the divine attribute of love was prominent both in God's "eternal action of love which incessantly creates a moral universe,"[29] and specifically in making humanity: "In love we were created and endowed with freedom."[30] Moreover, "the [human] race which began in love is continued by love."[31] In the wisdom of God's *providence,* therefore, we discover that real power and true help "can only come from the love of the Eternal Heart."[32]

The gift of God in *Jesus Christ* is an "act of love,"[33] and it was on the cross, as we have seen, that "in His love and pity He redeemed us."[34] Further, since Forsyth keeps the cross and the *kingdom of God* in close relation, it comes as no surprise that the latter is called "a

---

[24] *Authority,* p. 52.
[25] *Authority,* p. 353.
[26] *Authority,* p. 356.
[27] *Authority,* p. 357.
[28] *Authority,* p. 359.
[29] *The Justification of God,* 2nd ed. (1948; orig. pub. 1916), p. 108.
[30] *Person,* p. 314.
[31] "The Empire for Christ," *Christian World Pulpit* 57 (16 May 1900): 305.
[32] *Religion in Recent Art* (1889), p. 45.
[33] *Socialism, the Church and the Poor,* p. 48.
[34] *Authority,* p. 13.

kingdom of love."³⁵ And, referring to *eschatology*, he speaks of God's love "and its secure triumph in the race."³⁶

When we turn to Christian practice, we discover Forsyth's view that *preaching* is "faith energised with love, and love announcing its word to a world."³⁷ *Prayer* is communion with the loving God: "We feel, the more we are united with Him in true prayer, the deep, close difference, the intimate otherness in true love."³⁸ For its part, Christian *ethics* came from "the greatest Love that ever entered history."³⁹

As the above survey indicates, the love of God is a prominent topic in Forsyth's theology, constantly and consistently appearing in his books and articles. In his view, the love of God pervades the ministry of Jesus, is communicated to every aspect of individual Christian experience, and is comprehensively formulated in the church's doctrine. Altogether, even though Forsyth's exposition of God's love may be occasional and unsystematic, it is nevertheless a substantial description.

Perhaps the most appropriate criticism of Forsyth's treatment of God's love is one of balance, especially in terms of relating love and holiness. Although we will return to consider this matter again later in this chapter, a reading of Forsyth's work leaves us wishing that he had devoted the same eloquence and intensity to interpreting God's love as to his holiness. J. K. Mozley's judgment is correct: "In saving love from the trivial associations which too often have gathered round it, Dr. Forsyth never quite does it full justice as a controlling idea and power. . . . Dr. Forsyth's insight into love is not quite equal to his insight in other respects."⁴⁰ Although discussion of God's love is consistently introduced in Forsyth's writings, the topic could be more prominent.

However, this judicious conclusion is open to two significant qualifications. The first is that Forsyth makes room in his theology

---

³⁵ *Justification*, p. 29.
³⁶ *Freedom*, p. 271.
³⁷ *Missions in State and Church* (1908), p. 241.
³⁸ *Soul of Prayer*, p. 30.
³⁹ *Marriage: Its Ethic and Religion* (1912), p. 149.
⁴⁰ J. K. Mozley, *The Doctrine of the Atonement* (London: Gerald Duckworth, 1915), p. 89. Responding to this point, W. H. Leembruggen points to "many noble passages in exaltation and understanding of love" in Forsyth's *Religion in Recent Art*, but then acknowledges that this was written just before Forsyth's realization "that the current talk on love lacked a certain quality; and that quality was holiness." Leembruggen, "The Witness of P. T. Forsyth – A Theologian of the Cross," *Reformed Theological Review* (1945): 24.

for a stronger emphasis on the love of God. He returns time and time again to the importance of God's love, stressing in the strongest terms its place in the mission of Jesus, the experience of believers, and the theology of the church. He clearly says that revealed religion should not countenance "a reduction of its note of love, a blanching of its tender mercy, and a flattening of its mystic strain."[41] And even more forcefully he declares, "We cannot love God too much, nor believe too much in His love, nor reckon it too holy. A due faith in Him is immoderate, absolute trust, and it has a creed to correspond."[42] The confession of God's perfect love cannot be overdone, and Forsyth would have no objection if those who followed him would magnify that love – that *holy* love – in its true dimensions.

A second factor that may cause us to reconsider our conclusion about the possible undervaluing of God's love in Forsyth's theology is a fuller understanding of God's love as holy. That investigation, in Chapter Seven below, will lead us to a fuller appreciation of Forsyth's treatment of the love of God.

2. THE CHARACTERISTICS OF GOD'S LOVE

When we gather together the material outlined above, it readily yields a dogmatic description of the love of God, which although not as full as one might wish, nevertheless presents a well-rounded picture of the love of God.

2.1 MULTIFACETED LOVE

Among the many facets of the divine love revealed in the person and work of Christ, the first that shines out from Forsyth's writings is its greatness, "the incredibility of anything so vast as God's love."[43] In the face of human sin in tragic proportions, we marvel at "God's love of His bitter enemies, and His grace to them in repaying their wrong by Himself atoning for them on the cross." The motivation for that cross-work of Christ was "His love's tremendous resource,"[44] which Forsyth cannot praise too highly: "Truly we cannot exaggerate the love of God, if we will take pains

---

[41] *Authority*, p. 417.
[42] *Justification*, p. 126.
[43] *The Cruciality of the Cross*, 1st ed. (1909), p. 90.
[44] *Cruciality*, p. 167.

to first understand it."⁴⁵ In those words of qualification, we detect the theologian's concern not only to praise but to comprehend the love of God, and to explain it in such a way that God's greatness is appreciated. As we shall see in subsequent chapters, Forsyth sees the specific region of divine love's excellency in "the moral greatness and wonder of it; meaning thereby especially its qualitative greatness – not merely its amount or intensity, but its holiness."⁴⁶

A related aspect of God's character of love is its perfection: "God's love in Christ was that absolute and eternal love for all mankind which involved the whole and holy God forever, from which love no power can separate us."⁴⁷ Such love is absolute: "The Love of God in Christ Jesus our Lord" is a love "which blesses all at the expense of none, and is perfect as God's Fatherhood is perfect."⁴⁸

Further characteristics of this love emerge as we turn the pages of Forsyth's authorship. The love of God is identified with "His heavenly kindness" and "the overflowing goodness of God's will towards us."⁴⁹ In including such attributes as goodness and kindness within the divine love, Forsyth simplifies the often long lists of attributes in some systematic theologies.

This love of God is startling in its breadth. It is not occasional or transitory but eternal, and it is not restricted to a few but poured out on all. In contrast to orthodoxy's tendency to limit God's love to certain moments in the history of salvation and to certain individuals, Forsyth would agree instead with Augustine's comment: "It was not from the time when we were reconciled to Him by the blood of His Son that he began to love us; He loved us from the foundation of the world."⁵⁰ Moreover, that love had an impressive comprehensiveness. Quoting the first few words of John 3.16, Forsyth emphasizes that "the world was the prime object of God's love. ... God loved not this or that individual, or group of individuals, only." A prophet could not save, being incapable of "a pity great enough, or a love." But Christ's love was large enough to

---

[45] *Justification*, p. 36.
[46] "The Preaching of Jesus and the Gospel of Christ," p. 292.
[47] "Faith, Metaphysic, and Incarnation," *Methodist Review* 97 (September 1915): 709.
[48] *Religion in Recent Art*, p. 150.
[49] *Justification*, p. 165.
[50] Augustine, *Joannis Evangelium Tractatus*, cx.6, quoted in James Moffatt, *Love in the New Testament* (London: Hodder & Stoughton, 1929), p. vii.

encompass all time and all people in a "universal, eternal salvation."[51]

Similarly, the love of God is faithful. Forsyth maintained that "God never ceased to love us even when He was most angry and severe with us."[52] Reconciliation, far from involving "a change in God from wrath to love," was instead a deliberate divine act that "flows from the changeless will of a loving God."[53] Just as the Father was always pleased with the Son, God's love for humankind issues in a passion to save that is eternal, wide, and constant.

Paradoxically, divine love is both transcendent and immanent. United with God, we sense "the deep, close difference, the intimate otherness in true love."[54] It is also omnipotent: "God's love in Christ was that absolute and eternal love for all mankind which involved the whole and holy God forever, from which love no power can separate us."[55] Further, love is also patient: "We preach the wondrous, endless, patient love of God as the message of Christ."[56] In fact, consistent with our more general conclusion in chapter 3 that the attributes describe aspects of a personal God, we see in this particular case that God's love can be defined in terms of the other attributes.

2.2 TRINITARIAN LOVE

A further, final point deserves separate treatment, particularly because the doctrine of the Trinity is an aspect of Forsyth's thought not much appreciated by his commentators.[57] For P. T. Forsyth, with his consistent Christocentricity, the love of Jesus Christ reveals God's nature, which is trinitarian love. The foundation of this view is the love between Father and Son, and within that relationship Forsyth's particular though not exclusive concern is the Father's love for the Son. Forsyth affirmed, on the basis of the gospel

---

[51] *The Work of Christ* (1910), pp. 115–116.
[52] *Work*, p. 105.
[53] *Work*, p. 180.
[54] *Soul of Prayer*, p. 30.
[55] "Faith, Metaphysic, and Incarnation," p. 709.
[56] "The Preaching of Jesus and the Gospel of Christ," p. 291.
[57] Rodgers rightly acknowledges "the trinitarian foundation of Forsyth's thought," and organizes his discussion of Forsyth's soteriology accordingly; see John H. Rodgers, *The Theology of P. T. Forsyth: The Cross of Christ and the Revelation of God* (London: Independent Press, 1965), pp. 280, 25, and 256. Such an arrangement is both luminous and decidedly un-Forsythian.

accounts, that "the Father dwells in the Son of his love."[58] That sense of communion, unity of purpose, and continual divine pleasure was revealed in the life of Christ. Indeed, it was from such evidence that the divine identity of Father and Son was realized. Here "passion gravitates to metaphysic," contends Forsyth, in a rare but strategically-placed acknowledgment of the value of things ontological. Such is the central importance of the divinity of Jesus Christ that Forsyth asks rhetorically, "Is unity of being not the postulate of a love so engrossing and complete as the genius of the Church's faith realised that of the Father and Son to be?"[59] Such reciprocal love was evidenced in their relationship on earth; and on that basis it was reasonable to conclude that "upon this personality [Jesus] the personal love of the Father forever rested, well pleased, in the depth and mystery of Godhead's eternal life."[60]

The love shared between the Father and the Son leads Forsyth to affirm that the Trinity is a communion of love. The God revealed in Jesus Christ is "a triune God who is an eternal home and society in Himself."[61] Forsyth uses this formulation more to stress the fact of communion than the distinctness of the Father, Son, and Spirit. Within this context, he has a striking way of describing the love shared by Father, Son, and Spirit that stresses both the unity of the Godhead and the intra-trinitarian relations: "The love beyond all love," he says, is "God's love of His own holy Self."[62] In another place, in the context of a discussion about God's concern for his own law, Forsyth says: "He loves it as He must love Himself, or His other self, His very Son, His Holy One, dearer to Him than all men and all prodigals."[63] God's love is at once essential and expressed, at the same time personal and interpersonal within the triune God. The divine self-love is a vivid description of the relationships of love within the holy Trinity.

The points already made – namely, the mutual love of Father and Son, and its context within the Trinity – lead to another. Forsyth accents the truth that the salvation accomplished through Christ occurs within a trinitarian context, namely "the incredible fact that we are included by God's strange grace in the same love wherewith

---

[58] "Faith, Metaphysic, and Incarnation," p. 712.
[59] *Person*, p. 242.
[60] "Faith, Metaphysic, and Incarnation," p. 714.
[61] "Holy Father," in *Father*, p. 25.
[62] *Preaching of Jesus*, p. 59.
[63] *Preaching of Jesus*, p. 109.

he loves his only begotten Son."[64] The work of Christ reveals God's intimate concern for humanity's best and ultimate interests, his intra-trinitarian love reaching out in compassion to the world, so that "we are incorporated into the inner life of God. We are loved not as His children but as members of his Son."[65] Reading the words of Jesus (in John 15.9) in a trinitarian framework, Forsyth reiterates that "God by His Grace and His Spirit includes us in His love for His eternal and holy Son."[66]

Finally, we note that Forsyth's theological discussion of God's love is conducted throughout in a dual context: of the Trinity, and of needy humanity. As truly God and truly man, Jesus encompasses the two: "He rejoices alike in the love of His Father and the love of His Redeemed, and in the communion of both."[67]

On the basis of what has been said to this point, we conclude that Forsyth's treatment of trinitarian love as Christocentric and personal is fresh and suggestive of insights. To contrast this society of love with the idea of God's self-love is a provocative and helpful reminder of the triune paradox: that God is both one and three. And to stress all this within the context of God's love for humanity in Christ's work puts the doctrine of the Trinity, often criticized as ethereal and academic, in the most practical context.[68]

3. AN ASSESSMENT OF GOD'S LOVE IN FORSYTH'S THEOLOGY

At this point in our consideration of Forsyth's theology of the love of God, we stop to critique several significant aspects of his thought. Forsythian theology takes as its noetic starting-point the cross-event, which reveals a love expressed in exemplary sacrifice and effected in saving, reconciling, forgiving action. This is not narrowly conceived, however, but is seen within the context of a Christologically-centred theology that concentrates on "Love's own account of itself in Christ."[69] On the whole, Forsyth's treatment of the divine love is traditional, but at particular points along the way – the atoning cross, love's choice in election, and the self-love of the triune God, for example – his accomplishment is distinctive.

---

[64] *Person*, p. 343.
[65] *Freedom*, pp. 34–35.
[66] *Person*, p. 115.
[67] "The Living Christ" (1897), in *Father*, p. 89.
[68] We return in Chapter Seven, section 6, to consider the subject of the Trinity in more detail, particularly as it relates to the atonement.
[69] "Taste of Death," in *Father*, p. 59.

His formulations are not immune to criticism, of course. Some of these are of an incidental nature, paralleling as it were the incidental nature of their presentation. Under this category, we would include several concerns of Forsyth's colleague, A. E. Garvie. First, he says with regard to the doctrine of the atonement, "Forsyth seems to me here unduly to narrow the purpose of God's love in the gift of the Son." Although short on further explanation, Garvie seems to mean that Forsyth's attention to the forgiveness of guilty consciences is less than the whole truth concerning Christ's work, and therefore an undervaluing of the love of God. In fact, Garvie acknowledges earlier on the same page that, far from narrowly defining Christ's work as *propitiation,* Forsyth also "recognizes *redemption* from sin and *reconciliation* with God as affected by the Cross of Christ."[70] Forsyth would go even further than that, recognizing the usefulness of the historical development of the doctrine of the atonement, and finding elements of truth in the various theories of Christ's work.[71]

Secondly, Garvie notes and apparently laments the fact that Forsyth does not expound "the New Testament conception of love in the distinctive words *agape* and *philia.*"[72] While such an approach may well have seemed obvious from Garvie's 1943 vantage-point, after the publication of Anders Nygren's landmark study *Agape and Eros* in the previous decade, it was by no means an obligatory (or even obvious) approach in Forsyth's day. Interestingly, Garvie does not specify how such a study might correct Forsyth's apparently inadequate view.

A third concern of Garvie's is more substantial. Considering Forsyth's assertion that "Jesus was more engrossed with the will of God than the needs of men in his last hours,"[73] Garvie comments: "We may agree that the relation of Christ to God must be primary, and to man secondary, yet His love for God need not be contrasted with His love for man."[74] Although in a technical way we may disagree with Garvie's last comment, because it does seem instructive

---

[70] A. E. Garvie, "Placarding the Cross: The Theology of P. T. Forsyth," *Congregational Quarterly* 21 (October 1943): 347.
[71] *Positive Preaching,* pp. 293–294; and especially *Work,* chap. 7, where "The Threefold Cord" of the atonement is disentangled, and the triumphant, satisfactionary, and regenerative strands are examined.
[72] Garvie, "Placarding the Cross," p. 351.
[73] Annotations to Robert Mackintosh, "The Authority of the Cross," *Congregational Quarterly* 21 (1943): 216, quoted in Garvie, "Placarding the Cross," p. 352.
[74] Garvie, "Placarding the Cross," p. 352.

to consider and contrast Christ's relationships to God and humanity, it is nevertheless true, in our view, that the result of that contrast is that Forsyth undervalues Christ's specific love for humanity. For example, he asserts, "As Christ's love to God was greater that His love to man, so His love for God's law was more intense than His sympathy with man's weakness."[75] It seems more correct to say that Christ's passion to save sinners and his devotion to his Father's will stemmed equally, and with equal force, from a loving nature. Nevertheless, we consider that Forsyth is right to point to the precedence of obedience to God, or as Garvie puts it, that the relation to God is primary. Although we may wish he had made more of God's love for humanity, Forsyth gets the order right: "He served men chiefly out of obedience to God; and His love to them was because of His love to God."[76] Taking these reservations into account, we believe that Garvie's concern remains undecided. However, when the important qualification of the following section is taken into account, the weight of evidence shifts to favour our contention that Forsyth makes a prominent place for God's love. That important qualification involves the theological context of his writing.

4. THE INADEQUACY OF LOVE ALONE AS A DESCRIPTION OF GOD

When P. T. Forsyth became Chairman of the Congregational Union of England and Wales in 1905, he was already acknowledged as a stirring preacher – witness the impact not only of "The Holy Father" in 1896,[77] but also of "The Cross as the Final Seat of Authority," a paper preached (for so it was) to the second International Congregational Council at Boston in 1899. A prominent historian of British Congregationalism reports that the latter was "the high-water mark of the Council," and that "the discussion that should have followed was abandoned and the meeting closed with the singing of 'In the Cross of Christ I glory.'"[78] Despite

---

[75] *Positive Preaching*, p. 156.
[76] *Positive Preaching*, p. 156. Ironically, I owe this reference to a longer, unpublished version of Garvie's paper: A. E. Garvie, "Placarding Jesus Christ the Crucified: The Theology of the Late Peter Taylor Forsyth," n.d. [likely 1943], p. 23. New College Library ms 537/1, Dr Williams's Library, London.
[77] See Chapter One, section 3.3 above.
[78] R. Tudur Jones, *Congregationalism in England 1662–1962* (London: Independent Press, 1962), p. 329.

the accompanying public esteem, however, Forsyth's published work to this point was comprised almost entirely of short works – sermons and lectures which had received an encouraging response both from the pew and the papers. For the most part, these small books, pamphlets, and periodical articles by the new Principal of Hackney College evaded the reviewer's attention and caused little stir. It was not until 1907 when Forsyth's first major book, *Positive Preaching and Modern Mind,* appeared that his ideas became the common subject of public debate.

In 1905, however, one of Forsyth's chairman's addresses, entitled "The Grace of the Gospel as the Moral Authority in the Church," provided the spark for a notable exception to that calm indifference.[79] In a combative article, Dr K. C. Anderson responded in detail to Forsyth's claims. Although the detailed substance of his argument need not concern us, an instructive paragraph from its last page may serve to set the context for our discussion in the present section. Anderson wrote:

> What are the reports that are coming in from all parts of the universe to-day? They all tend to one announcement, they all unite their voices to preach one mighty Gospel, the essential goodness of the world and of life; that the universe is cradled in love; that it is not only a unity, but a beneficent unity; that the life of man, the child of the universe, lies embosomed in one great Life; that the essence of things is good, and the purpose and the outcome good. But what is this but a confirmation of the essential Gospel of Jesus Christ? What He discerned in the depths of His own pure and serene heart, in His own sense of sonship, men are finding to-day in the great universe – the Father, the Eternal Goodness, the Universal Love. This is the eternal gospel of which all partial gospels are but phases.[80]

This estimate of divine love, derived most recently from Ritschl and Harnack, was a conspicuous aspect of the theological landscape in the early 1900s. Our chapter title, therefore, has an intended double meaning: not only is God's love more prominent in Forsyth's theology than has sometimes been acknowledged, but that love of God was indeed a prominent feature in current theology, to which Forsyth proposed a corrective.

Within such a picture of 'the universe cradled in universal love,' there was little room for any discussion of human sin, divine

---

[79] "The Grace of the Gospel as the Moral Authority in the Church" (1905), in *The Church, the Gospel and Society* (1962; orig. pub. as articles, 1905), pp. 65–127.
[80] K. C. Anderson, "Dr. Forsyth and Reaction," *Message Extra,* no. 1 ([Bristol, c. 1905]): 14.

authority (Forsyth's concern in the address that triggered Anderson's paper), or the holiness of God. Forsyth's view of love clashed head-on with this version of God's nature. The root of this deficient picture, in his view, was the isolation of one attribute – namely, love – from the wider view of God's nature:

> The Love of God ... has been removed from its New Testament setting. It has been treated as the mere superlative of romantic love. It has been detached from the idea of propitiation with which the Apostles identify it (1 John 4.10), and regarded as an infinite dilation of human affection (where the real revelation is held to be). Judgment is viewed but as a device of the Father instead of as a constituent of His Fatherhood as holy. Little wonder then that love has gone thin in the expansion, and lost power.[81]

Then, once love has been isolated, it tends to be magnified and distorted, as Forsyth points out. It did that in at least three areas:

4.1 Love Humanized and Romanticized

When loosed from its biblical moorings, the love of God is seen more as a somewhat expanded and refined version of human affection, rather than a description of the divine character revealed in Christ. "We do seem too much accustomed to-day to translate the love of Christ into the terms of human affection," comments Forsyth, with the result that the cross is surrender rather than redemption, and sacrifice instead of salvation. Then, having humanized God's love, we take a further step: "We idealize reciprocal love, and call it divine, instead of reading God's revelation of His love as dying for the ungodly." Here is theology growing from experience rather than scripture, natural theology challenging revealed religion. Forsyth supplies the corrective: "We should interpret our human affection by the love of God who first loved us," rather than vice versa.[82]

As Forsyth notes, it is possible to misconceive God's love as "the mere superlative of romantic love."[83] From a longer perspective, D. M. Baillie describes what happened:

> The rediscovery of the historical Jesus was such an illumination to many perplexed souls that they sometimes tried to make a religion out of that alone – out of the practice of gazing back into ancient Galilee and picturing Jesus as their Master in a very human and even sentimental

---

[81] *Justification*, p. 85.
[82] "Taste of Death," in *Father*, pp. 59–60.
[83] *Justification*, p. 85.

way. Thus religion became an eager and loyal, if sometimes sentimental, following of the Man of Nazareth, as a substitute for Christianity.[84]

Forsyth described his era in this way: "It is a liberal age, ... an aesthetic age, ... and love is everywhere, love is enough."[85] It was "an age of sentiment and sympathy,"[86] in which a romantic view of 'lovely Jesus' prevailed, and current theological discussion pictured Jesus as "more kindly than holy, more lovely than good."[87] The holy love of God revealed in Christ was relieved of holiness, then boiled down to "a love slack and over-sweet."[88] Not surprisingly for one who described his own personal experience as being turned "from a lover of love to an object of grace,"[89] Forsyth reserved some of his most scornful language for this audacious reduction of the divine love to manageable human proportions. The modern "seers and geniuses" have a startling lack of insight, he said. "They see into 'Love in the valley' – and how lovely – what they do not see into is love *in excelsis.*"[90] Their picture of God is dominated by his immanence, to the detriment of a proper apprehension of the divine transcendence.

4.2 AN EXEMPLARY DOCTRINE OF THE ATONEMENT

Another distortion that results from an over-emphasis on the love of God is a soteriology that restricts the cross to a subjective influence on humans. In the opening section of this chapter, we noted that God's love is an element in Forsyth's explanation of the various phases of Christ's life, including his death on the cross. However, the precise relationship of God's love and Christ's death is the occasion for some discussion in Forsyth's writings, as it had been throughout the history of doctrine. Instead of beginning with the dispute, we first note two points of agreement between Forsyth and those who hold a merely exemplary theory of the atonement.

First, both underline the priority of God's initiative. In fact, this view reflected a growing theological consensus that Forsyth had helped to shape. "In recent years," wrote H. R. Mackintosh in a

---

[84] D. M. Baillie, *God Was in Christ: An Essay on Incarnation and Atonement* (London: Faber & Faber, 1948), p. 41.
[85] *Rome, Reform and Reaction,* p. 235.
[86] *Missions,* p. 98.
[87] *Justification,* p. 36.
[88] "Holy Father," in *Father,* p. 4.
[89] *Positive Preaching,* pp. 282–283.
[90] *Person,* p. 229.

1915 article, "men who share this conviction as to where the crucial emphasis in redemption should be laid – on God, not man – have happily grown more conscious of agreement than of difference. They are united in holding that in Atonement the doer is God, even if they differ as to what was done."[91] The opposite emphasis was still made, and Forsyth was therefore critical of the anthropocentric religion that focuses on human effort, and believes "in love as a work instead of love as a faith, in the love we practise instead of the love we trust."[92] God's initiating love is the proper focus.

Secondly, Forsyth agreed with the exemplarists not only that it was *God* who loved in Christ's cross, but that Christ's death issued from and directly expressed God's *love*. There could be no question of minimizing or limiting the Lord's passionate commitment of love shown on the cross.

> The infinite, ultimate love of God is there. The gift and grace of God for the whole world is there. It is not simply nor chiefly the love of Christ for His brethren that is in the Cross. That was indeed uppermost in Christ's life; but in His death that is not direct but indirect; and the primary thing is Christ's obedience to God, and His action, therefore, as the channel of God's redeeming love. It is the love of God for the godless, loveless, hating world that is there. And it is there, not simply expressed but effected, not exhibited but enforced and infused, not in manifestation merely, but in judgment and decision.[93]

This quotation, however, takes us beyond initial agreement to the fundamental difference between the Abelardian view and Forsyth's position. Some said that the life of Jesus showed God's love capped by tragedy, but Forsyth insisted, "In Christ God did not send a message of his love which cost the messenger his life, but himself loved us to the death, and to our eternal redemption."[94] Nor did Forsyth sanction the more common view that Christ's death illustrated the ultimate in non-judgmental, sacrificial giving; that sort of religion "is in love with His love, and with His Cross as the summit of that love in self-sacrifice."[95]

What precisely is wrong with such a view? How does Forsyth critique it? His response has several elements. For one thing, an exemplary atonement reduces the cross to a lesson to be learned,

---

[91] H. R. Mackintosh, "Recent Thought on the Atonement," *Review and Expositor* 12 (1915): 351.
[92] *The Christian Ethic of War* (1916), p. 95.
[93] "Taste of Death," in *Father*, p. 72.
[94] "Faith, Metaphysic, and Incarnation," p. 708.
[95] *Justification*, p. 175.

and then left behind. "If the Cross is a kind of practical parable which God set forth of His love and His willingness to save, then when the parable has done its work it can be forgotten."[96] To say the cross is only an expression of God's love makes the revelation a word rather than a deed, designed to educate or impress.

In a later article on the same subject, Forsyth went even further. "Love which dies with no other object than to show love or create an effect is morally unreal," he wrote. "It is stagey love, . . . a device, . . . more or less of a pose, . . . and even tends to hypocrisy." An observer of Christ's ministry and death gets the impression, rather, that he was not intent on making an impression, but on accomplishing a work. The cross is certainly exemplary, but it is even more executory. "Christ in His death preached to men only because He was wholly offered to God."[97]

In Forsyth's argument against the Abelardian view, however, the most important factor was its characterization of a God "of sacrificing love without atoning righteousness, . . . of loving-kindness more than of loving power, of everlasting pity and no moral majesty, no holiness."[98] An exemplary martyr, even one sent from God, falls far short of the God revealed in Jesus Christ. One aspect of God's character has been taken to be the whole truth. Plucked from it's biblical context, the love of God no longer conveys its intended fullness of meaning. Specifically, "it has been detached from the idea of propitiation with which the Apostles identify it (1 John 4.10), and regarded as an infinite dilation of human affection (where the real revelation is held to be)."[99]

All of these responses to a merely exemplary theory of the atonement have a common factor: the Forsythian insistence on divine moral action. Never content to describe merely who God is, Forsyth always includes a stress on what God does. When noting "God's passion to save," for example, he immediately adds: "and his ceaseless action in saving."[100] Further, God would hardly be God if his compassion was only exhibited: "He is our God, not because He loved and pitied, but because in His love and pity He redeemed us."[101]

---

[96] *Work*, p. 102.
[97] *Preaching of Jesus*, pp. 111–113.
[98] *Justification*, p. 25.
[99] *Justification*, p. 85.
[100] *Person*, p. 343.
[101] *Authority*, p. 13.

Here is yet another example of what Stephen Sykes calls "the priority of the actual" in Forsyth's theology.[102]

4.3 MYSTIC LOVE

While the liberal approach tended to reduce divine love to human affection and the atonement to merely an example of that love to humankind, there was another stream of theological thought that focused on the concept of mystic love.[103] Mysticism is not to be identified with the liberal stream *per se,* but occupies a position of its own, somewhat independent of the wider theological stances of the day. Yet this mystic strain was sufficiently prominent within Christian teaching that it came under repeated scrutiny from Forsyth. Much of his criticism pivoted on mysticism's inadequate view of God's love. Before turning to that specific concern, however, a brief orientation to the topic would be in order.

According to Forsyth, mysticism can be variously defined. By one definition, "faith is essentially mystic" because it insists on "personal intercourse with the personal, historic, and living Saviour." But more commonly, mysticism refers to religion that makes "contemplation or intuition the goal and essence of the perfect life," while insisting on unmediated "direct contact between God and the soul."[104] Bernard of Clairvaux was included in the former category: Forsyth once confided to a friend that "Bernard is my favourite saint and his 'Canticles' an old delight."[105] Within the latter group Forsyth numbered the 14th century mystic Johannes Tauler (for whom Christ "may be but an annexe"), the Anabaptist Thomas Münzer, and Count Leo Tolstoi.[106] In addition to these, Forsyth almost certainly has in mind Dean W. R. Inge, whose *Christian Mysticism* was published in 1899. With these influences

---

[102] Stephen Sykes, "Theology through History," in *The Modern Theologians,* ed. David F. Ford (Oxford: Basil Blackwell, 1989), p. 9.
[103] See R. J. Campbell, "The Form of the Christian Doctrine of God," *Christian Commonwealth,* 29 August 1907, pp. 845–846.
[104] "Mystics and Saints," *Expository Times* 5 (June 1894): 401, 402.
[105] Letter from Forsyth to William Robertson Nicoll, 1 November 1905, quoted in T. H. Darlow, *William Robertson Nicoll: Life and Letters* (London: Hodder & Stoughton, 1925), p. 401.
[106] Forsyth, "Dr. Forsyth and Mysticism," letter in *Examiner,* 9 November 1905, p. 434; *Freedom,* pp. 84–85; and *Authority,* p. 243.

and others, Forsyth concluded that his was "an age when mystic has taken the control from ethic in religion."[107]

Turning back to the present concern of this paper, namely the conception of God's love, we note that Forsyth laid out the options with distinctive simplicity: it was a conflict, he said, between "the mediaeval idea of mystic love" and "the evangelical idea of faith."[108] Elsewhere, he explains:

> Faith was, as Melanchthon said, simply trust in God's mercy to the sinner in Christ. It was not fusion with God's nature even as love, it was not being sunk in the abyss of the divine, or filled to rapture with the inflowing of the Holy Spirit. It was not the translation of the soul into a divine substance, man becoming God through God becoming man. It was not seeing God, or feeling Him, but trusting Him, committing one's self, one's sins, one's soul, one's eternity to God in Christ, on the strength of God's act and promise in Christ's redemption. It was not elation, rapture, ecstasy – it was confidence. It was answering a person, a gospel, not a system, or a divine infusion. Its peace was not the calm of absorption, of losing ourselves in the ocean of God's love, but the peace of believing, of forgiveness assured and foregone in Christ, and trusted even amid repeated and cleaving sin.[109]

In this quotation, among many and varied declarations that 'Faith is not mysticism,' is the positive counterpart, also repeated several times, that 'Faith is trust *in Christ.*' According to Forsyth, the essential error in mysticism is "the rejection of all mediation," the bypassing of Jesus Christ in favour of union with God.[110]

To counter this error, Forsyth asserts the importance of the historical reality of Jesus Christ. "The true spirituality . . . is not the lone soul with the Alone" but rather "is in a historic Mediator;" "the moral soul finds such mediation the way to reality."[111] Nevertheless, Forsyth is unwilling to give up the word, preferring to redefine it:

---

[107] *The Church and the Sacraments,* 2nd ed. (1947; orig. pub. 1917), p. 283.
[108] *Authority,* p. 71.
[109] *Rome, Reform and Reaction,* pp. 146–147.
[110] "Mystics and Saints," p. 402; Wilhelm Herrmann, the noted German contemporary of Forsyth, vividly describes the result: "According to mysticism, Christ leads the man who becomes His disciple up to the threshold of blessedness. But then the mystic steps across that threshold, and at the highest point of his inner life, he has no longer to do with Christ but with God, for when a man really finds God, he finds himself alone with Him. ... But then, the revelation of God in history loses all its worth." Herrmann, *The Communion of the Christian with God: Described on the Basis of Luther's Statements,* 2nd English ed., trans. J. Sandys Stanyon, rev. R. W. Stewart (London: Williams & Norgate, 1906), pp. 30–32.
[111] *This Life and the Next,* 2nd ed. (1946; orig. pub. 1918), p. 49.

"Mysticism we must have if we are to have Christianity; but it must be the mysticism of history and not simply of the soul, the mystery of God manifest in the flesh and not of the soul on God's breast."[112]

Concomitant with the loss of the historic is a diminishing of the importance of the gospel. If Jesus can be bypassed on the way to something greater, the value of his sacrifice for sin fades in the theological distance. "The note of mystic love submerges the word of moral grace; and the wonders love can work in neglected hearts obscure the miracle of mercy to the evil soul."[113] Having challenged mysticism's tendency to discard Christ along the spiritual pathway to union with God, Forsyth then allows mysticism to return with its priorities rearranged, with Jesus Christ at the fore.[114] Indeed, it is Christ who is "the Creator of the possibility of that mysticism which keeps at its heart the moral crisis of the race, the mystery of sin, the miracle of its conquest;" in short, "the mysticism of the Cross."[115] That is where the true communion with God is centred — in the forgiveness and renewal of the cross of Christ. Such a union with Christ relies not only on the human nature God shared with us in Christ, but primarily on the fact that Christ was for us in his salvific death and resurrection: "This is the only source of a mysticism energetic and not merely quietist, a mysticism which is the fellowship of the divine Act rather than of the divine Being."[116]

The love of God is stressed overmuch by mysticism; it comes as no surprise, then, to hear Forsyth declare that we need to confront mysticism with the holiness of God. Indeed, that has already happened in Christ: "By His atonement to the holy He converted all worship, all mysticism, and all sacraments from the aesthetical to the ethical; and he set the longings or enjoyments of religious feeling on the eternal foundations of a moral redemption."[117] In effect, Forsyth affirms the place of spiritual experience — of abiding in Christ, of visions and revelations, of being hidden with Christ in God (John 15.4, 2 Corinthians 12.1, Colossians 3.3) — but will not

---

[112] *Freedom*, p. 15.
[113] *Authority*, p. 410.
[114] Mozley comments that, in making room for the mystic note, Forsyth "was far removed from the anti-mystical bias of such a theologian as Herrmann, with whom, in his emphasis upon the ethical, he had so much in common." J. K. Mozley, *The Heart of the Gospel* (London: Society for Promoting Christian Knowledge, 1925), p. 101.
[115] *Authority*, pp. 415, 410.
[116] *Preaching of Jesus*, p. 83.
[117] *Church and the Sacraments*, p. 296.

allow that experience to be reduced to the ecstasy of believers awash in the love of God. "Is Christianity mystic love?" he asks, and then answers his own question: "We all love love; our great need and quest is what will create it."[118]

These three trends in theology were all reductionist: romanticism reduced Jesus to one merely human, exemplarism reduced the cross to an example, and mysticism reduced Christian experience to the contemplation of a loving ideal. Forsyth confronted this reductionism with at least two arguments. The first was an insistence to take the love of God more seriously. These three contemporary theological views were doing less than justice to the very element they professed to exalt – God's love. Look at the cross, he insisted, and understand from that reality what love is like. Look into the depths of that love, and not merely on the surface. The second argument was of a different kind, and to it we turn in the concluding section of this chapter.

5. THE NECESSITY OF A WIDER CONCEPTION OF GOD'S NATURE

With some justification, then, Forsyth perceived his era as a romantic age in which the gospel realities were sentimentalized, the meaning of Christ's death reduced to a shining example, and God-given moral truth changed to the end product of a mystical quest. Mimicking its style of language, he described "the Naturalism of the age, with its brief, sweet beauty, and its quavering creed that 'Love is enough.'"[119] In that context, he addressed the age with an unpopular word: Love is not enough! His conviction is that to isolate love is to reduce it to only a pale imitation of its fully divine self. Once isolated, God's love is sapped of rich theological meaning. The Word of God, and particularly the New Testament, is contravened when love is plucked out and treated in isolation. Vital ingredients are lost in the transition. We have noted three such distortions, concerning romanticism, exemplary atonement, and mysticism, and Forsyth notes others as well. In theology, for example, the Fatherhood and sovereignty of God are reduced, making God's love "just paternity transfigured, maternity taken up to heaven."[120] "And the person of Christ becomes but then ill understood. For it has been well said that God's love becomes for us

---

[118] *Authority*, p. 243.
[119] *Religion in Recent Art*, p. 141.
[120] *Freedom*, p. 273.

a reality only in the Godhead of Jesus Christ."[121] In the field of Christian action, weakened love brings with it a weakened ethical stance: "The Church's victory can only be by way of its moral authority, which is grace, not love; mercy, and not pity. The morality of pity has no imperative."[122] And in preaching, God's theologcally-detached love "becomes a powerless thing, moving eloquence more than action, touching us when it should humble us, and wooing where it should make us wince;" in fact, to combat such a tendency, Forsyth reminded graduating ministers: "Your Gospel is not 'God is love,' but 'God so loved that He gave.'"[123] In short, when love is cut loose from its wider matrix of meaning, it is less than divine.

God's nature is not susceptible to a one-word definition, or at least not for long. God is indeed love, as 1 John 4.16 declares, but clustering around that Johannine assertion are several crucial elaborations of the definition. As Forsyth in several places reminds us, love is indissoluably connected with the incarnation and sacrificial death of Jesus and the resultant reconciliation and life given through him (1 John 4.9–10). In the face of this given complexity, what is required is a wider vision, a theological breadth with several vital ingredients.

The first of these is grace. God's love is not love that meets us on even terms. Rather, "it is the love of grace, which loves beneath it, and comes down to the lost."[124] That incarnate grace was also forgiving: "Love tasted death that it might overpass love and be worshipped as grace."[125] Forsyth counters Newman's poetic opinion that there might be "a higher gift than grace" with the assertion, "There is more in God than love. There is all that we mean by His holy grace."[126]

Secondly, love alone does not take human sin seriously enough. Here is a clear difference between a liberal theology and a 'positive' gospel: "The one views God's love chiefly in relation to human love, the other chiefly in relation to human sin."[127] The power of sin to interpose itself between God and humanity is consistently underestimated, Forsyth believes. But we dare not minimize "the sin

---

[121] *Freedom*, p. 271.
[122] *Church, the Gospel and Society*, p. 107.
[123] *Freedom*, p. 271; "The Courage of Faith," *Examiner*, 11 July 1901, p. 270.
[124] *Authority*, p. 371.
[125] "Taste of Death," in *Father*, p. 68.
[126] *Work*, p. 26.
[127] *Positive Preaching*, p. 212.

that brought death to God in the Son of God." Similarly, we must not lessen the importance given to God's judgment. "[Some say,] 'There is nothing to be afraid of. God is love.' But there is everything in the love of God to be afraid of. Love is not holy without judgment."[128] And a theology of God's attributes is not serious unless it deals with sin.

Thirdly, and most importantly for Forsyth, a full-orbed theology of God's nature must look into "the holy heart of the loving God."[129] Holiness is the aspect of God's perfections that most needs emphasizing in light of liberalism's concentration on love. "There is a height and a depth in the Father beyond His utmost pity and His kindest love. He is Holy Father and Redeemer, and it is His holiness of fatherhood that is the source of our redemption and sonship."[130] Our intention is not to downgrade the importance of that love, but to see it in its proper context. God is indeed a loving Father, but he is "revealed by a Cross whose first concern was holiness and the dues of holiness. See what manner of love the Father hath bestowed on us."[131]

Love, then, is an important and necessary part of P. T. Forsyth's description of God, as we have seen by examining his writing on the subject. Whether the perspective is the ministry of Jesus Christ, the Christian's experience, or systematic theology proper, he does not neglect God's love or denigrate it in any way. Further, the result of gathering together his views on this subject yields a sketch of God's love that is coherent and (considering that he has given the subject no full-length treatment) remarkably comprehensive. Further, as we have seen in the second half of this chapter, when love is isolated it becomes susceptible to distortion in a variety of ways. The life of Jesus can be reduced to a romanticized human affection, the cross can be reduced to a merely exemplary atonement, and the Christian life can be distorted as mystic communion, to mention only three examples. Forsyth was convinced that in conscious contrast to those approaches, we need to see God's love in a larger perspective, as wide as God's grace and as deep as the harm caused by sin. Something more is needed if theology is to describe God's nature competently. As he wrote in 1909, an emphasis on God's love alone is not enough:

---

[128] *Work*, p. 85.
[129] *Justification*, p. 182.
[130] "Holy Father," in *Father*, p. 3.
[131] *Positive Preaching*, p. 327.

We have been living for the last two or three generations, our most progressive side has been living, upon the love of God, God's love to us. And it was very necessary that it should be appreciated. Justice had not been done to it. But we have now to take a step further, and we have to saturate our people in the years that are to come as thoroughly with the idea of God's *holiness* as they have been saturated with the idea of God's love.[132]

---

[132] *Work*, p. 78.

Chapter Six

The Importance of Holiness

It is of the Holy Spirit that we make our theories of Atonement. They are part of the worship of the Act and Fact.

P. T. Forsyth

After establishing in the previous chapter that P. T. Forsyth made a prominent place in his theology for God's love, we move to a new task, an examination of the other divine attribute which he so often paired with love, namely holiness. As we will see, he considers God's holiness to be equally deserving of dogmatic attention. More than that, he believes that to bring the message home to his own generation, an extra emphasis is required. Because his hearers were so well-acquainted with God's love, it was the note of God's holiness which would have to be accented:

> I have sometimes thought when preaching that I saw a perceptible change come over my audience when I turned from speaking about the love of God to speak about the holiness of God. There was a certain indescribable relaxing of interest, as though their faces should say, "What, have we not had enough of these incorrigible and obtrusive theologians who will not let us rest with the love of God but must go on talking about things which are so remote and professional as His holiness!" All that has to be changed.[1]

We intend to show that Forsyth takes God's holiness with the utmost seriousness. While we postpone to the following chapter discussion of the relationship between holiness and love in the divine nature, it will be unavoidable to make some comparisons along the way. In Forsyth's theological writing, the two attributes are very

---

[1] *The Work of Christ* (1910), p. 79.

closely connected, and it would be artificial (as well as impossible) to separate the two strands entirely.

1. AN ACCENT ON HOLINESS

In stressing the importance of holiness in Forsyth's theology, we have three purposes. The first is descriptive: What is the divine holiness, in his view? Where is it revealed and known? How shall we understand it? In order to appreciate him fully when he speaks of "the holy love of God," we must have a clear understanding not only of love, but of holiness as well. A second purpose is to show that Forsyth has a full-blooded doctrine of God's holiness, in which that aspect of God's nature is not reduced to a secondary place. And third, our presentation of Forsyth's view of the divine holiness will be conducted within the context of his doctrine of the atonement, thereby preparing the way for our consideration in the next chapter of the strife or harmony of God's attributes, and particularly of God's love and holiness. Only if we have a firm hold of his meaning of these two divine attributes can we assess the question of their harmony (or lack of it) in his doctrine of the atonement.

1.1 A NEGLECTED EMPHASIS

When Forsyth considered the theological context in which his writing and teaching were carried out, two facts related to the attributes of God were paramount. The first has been noted in the previous chapter, namely, that God's love occupied a prominent place in contemporary discussion of the divine character. Indeed, in Forsyth's view, some theologians of his day overemphasized this aspect of God's nature. The second feature of theological debate regarding the attributes of God at the turn of the century is our concern in the present pages: God's holiness had virtually disappeared from the face of contemporary theology. Although there were exceptions to this judgment, particularly in the writing of those within the tradition of Protestant orthodoxy, Forsyth's considered opinion was that "the bane of modern and current religion is in the practical loss of the idea so closely identified with Love's might, majesty, judgment, and glory – the idea of the holy."[2]

---

[2] *The Justification of God*, 2nd ed. (1948; orig. pub. 1916), p. 107. The last quoted words are not an echo, but rather an anticipation, of Rudolf Otto's title.

Such was his conviction throughout his writing career, from the powerful early sermon in which he insisted that it was not enough to say "that God is love, but also that the Father is holy;"[3] to the urgent argument, expressed a generation later in *The Justification of God*, that amidst the horror and grief of widespread war, "nothing is more conspicuous in the popular Christianity now being shocked to its senses than the loss of the sense of the holy God amid the fair humanities of new religion."[4]

Evidence for this assertion sprang readily to Forsyth's mind. "A due sense of the holiness of God" has largely disappeared, he maintained, from so many aspects of contemporary religious experience: "from our public worship, with its frequent irreverence; from our sentimental piety, to which an ethical piety with its implicates is simply obscure; from our rational religion, which banishes the idea of God's wrath; from our public morals, to which the invasion of property is more dreadful than the damnation of men."[5]

In order to rectify such a loss, Forsyth stressed the centrality of holiness for the believer's experience and instruction alike. "This holiness of God is the real foundation of religion – it is certainly the ruling interest of the Christian religion,"[6] he maintained. In fact, "everything begins and ends in our Christian theology with the holiness of God."[7] From such comments, it is apparent that Forsyth was not merely lamenting the decline in interest in a mere constituent aspect of God's character, but decrying the eclipse of a central facet of the divine nature. To remedy such a situation would require more than simply giving new attention to a neglected item on the list of divine attributes; what was needed was nothing less that the restoration of holiness as the "ruling interest" of Christianity, and the reorientation of the church's theological thinking around that centre. For twenty-five years, that was Forsyth's ruling interest and constant task.

Forsyth wrote in 1916; Otto's *Das Heilige* was first published in 1917, and the English translation (and title) dates from 1923.

[3] "The Holy Father" (1896), in *God the Holy Father* (1957), p. 26.
[4] *Justification*, p. 109.
[5] *The Cruciality of the Cross*, 1st ed. (1909), p. 38, corrected slightly by the 2nd ed., pp. 22–23.
[6] *Cruciality*, pp. 38–39.
[7] *Work*, p. 78.

1.2 A CORRECTIVE TO ORTHODOXY

Before we turn specifically to examine Forsyth's view of God's holiness, we observe that within the theological scene of his day there was another influence that affected his formulations. Besides the *neglect* of God's holiness noted in the previous section, there was also (Forsyth believed) an *overemphasis* on that same holiness by some who represented the systematic reformulation of reformation doctrine. Protestant orthodoxy, in particular its Calvinistic variety, had constructed its doctrine of the atonement with undue emphasis on God's holiness to the detriment of his love, with the result that too much attention was devoted to God's law and divine judgment. In the same sermon that championed a new stress on God as the *holy* Father, Forsyth declared, "We have been over-engrossed with a mere distributive equity, which has made God the Lord Chief Justice of the world."[8] In a later book on the work of Christ, he elaborated on this point, and identified it as an important ingredient in the theological dynamic concerning attributes and atonement:

> There is no doubt we are in reaction from a time when that side of things was overdone. The juristic aspect taken alone, and taken in relation to legal demand rather than personal holiness – such *satisfaction,* when isolated, does not do justice to . . . *redemption* [or] . . . *sanctification.* And it tended to promote the fatal notion that holiness could be satisfied with suffering and death, or with anything short of an answering holiness effected and guaranteed. The satisfaction in it was offered to a distributive justice rather than to a personal holiness, to a claim rather than a person, to a regulative law rather than to a constitutive life.[9]

In Forsyth's critique of orthodoxy, illustrated in the previous quotation, several convictions recur. First, the errors of orthodoxy were largely ones of degree and matters of emphasis. A theological point of view that had much to commend it had been, so to speak, distended. At the same time as Forsyth asserted that this theology had to be surpassed, he also admitted that it had maintained the central truth of the gospel: "The old orthodoxies can never again be what they were; but one thing in them draws me and sustains me amidst much that is hopelessly out of date. And it is this, that they

---

[8] "Holy Father," in *Father,* p. 4.
[9] *Work,* pp. 229–230. Forsyth's playfulness with words, even in his most earnest paragraphs, is revealed twice in this passage, first in the assertion that "the juristic aspect . . . does not do justice" to other aspects, and then in his statement about "the fatal notion" that concerned "suffering and death."

had a true eye for what really mattered in Christianity." "The old Puritans," he reminds us, "stood at the centre of things with their religion of a moral Atonement, of a free but most costly Gospel."[10]

Secondly, a rationalistic concern for systematization had obscured the personal quality of the relation between God and humanity. This was clear to Forsyth in the resulting incongruity between legal satisfaction on the one hand, and the more personal resonances of redemption and sanctification. The way to resolve apparent theological conflicts was not rationalistic but personalistic, with reference to a personal God. The reconciliation of paradox, Forsyth believed, lies "in a supreme and absolute personality, in whom the antinomies *work*. . . . It is the category of personality that adjusts the contradictions of reason; which, after all, is not abstract thought but a person thinking."[11] No wonder that Forsyth could quite sharply speak of "the mere rationalism . . . of a crustacean orthodoxy which loses the perspective of theological values, rates all Christian truth alike, makes scriptural form final, and includes all its hard science as essential in its faith."[12]

Finally, and most importantly for our purposes, orthodoxy's over-concentration on the legal element in soteriology led paradoxically to a diminishment in the importance of God's holiness. In the older theology, Forsyth believed, holiness was sometimes construed as an outward constraint on God, and not the source of justification. He resisted any tendency to separate the Father and the Son, to characterize the atonement as a matter of God sending and demanding, while Christ satisfies and atones. Such a contrast – indeed, a separation – between the Father's exacting legal demands and the Son's loving intervention was anathema to him. What was required instead, Forsyth insisted, was "due acknowledgment of God's holiness, and the honouring of that and not of His honour."[13] The theology of the atonement, and the true conception of the divine holiness, must derive not from theories of feudal honour or the demands of impersonal systems, but from the person in whom God has revealed that holiness.

---

[10] *The Church, the Gospel and Society* (1962; orig. pub. as articles, 1905), pp. 121, 122.
[11] *The Person and Place of Jesus Christ* (1909), p. 71.
[12] "Faith and Mind, *Methodist Review Quarterly* 61 (October 1912): 629.
[13] *Work,* pp. 164–165.

EXCURSUS: FORSYTH'S THEOLOGY AS A THIRD WAY

As we have seen, P. T. Forsyth criticizes traditional theological positions with regard to their views on love and holiness. Specifically, liberalism comes under fire for a sentimental view of God's love that leaves no room for the holy judgment of God (see Chapter Five, section 4), while Protestant orthodoxy is charged with the neglect of that love and an overemphasis on God's holiness (as we noted in the previous section of this chapter). Forsyth defines his own position over against these others, and takes his stand in a place distinct from the traditional theological options.[14]

However, this 'third way' is not adopted with a view to inclusiveness, as if it was possible to bridge the gap between orthodoxy and liberalism, while embracing both. We therefore disagree with William Bradley's conclusion:

> In his conception of a holy God Forsyth demonstrates better than in any of his other theories the importance of his contribution to Christian thought; for it is here that he combines that which is true in the older orthodoxy with that which is necessary and good in liberalism. . . . Not until he developed his theme of holy love, however, did he succeed in bringing the two schools together in a satisfactory manner.[15]

While Bradley correctly sees the key role of Forsyth's view of holiness and the importance of God's holy love, and rightly refuses to identify Forsyth's position with either liberalism or orthodoxy, it seems to me that Forsyth's intention was not to 'bring the two together,' but to adopt a third stance which is *not* orthodoxy and *not* liberalism. Instead, he builds a new edifice of theology on biblical and Reformation foundations. We agree with R. S. Paul's conclusion: "Forsyth's position was unique at that time. It caused him to

---

[14] Many observers have pronounced on the subject of Forsyth's place on the spectrum of theological thought, but perhaps the most bizarre comment was made in the context of an announcement of his move from a Cambridge pastorate to a London teaching position: "The position of the new Principal of Hackney is not so easily definable. Sometimes he appears to be a mystic and a Cyprian, sometimes he speaks like a Genevan Calvinist; and then the tendencies of Maurice and the incisive critical faculty of the best present-day scholarship appear in all his words. Perhaps Dr. Forsyth has partly himself to blame, for he is apt to speak in enigmas after the fashion of the Delphic oracle. Or it may be the wise gowns of Cambridge can comprehend these involutions better than the workaday folk of commercial cities" (*Congregational Monthly* [Manchester], April 1901).

[15] W. L. Bradley, *P. T. Forsyth: The Man and His Work* (London: Independent Press, 1952), p. 119.

The Importance of Holiness 155

criticize not only the sterile orthodoxies in the Church, but also to be even more stringent against the Liberal reconstruction that was to govern most of our century."[16]

The confusion among some of Forsyth's interpreters about how to define his position may reflect a desire to place him in one of the two 'camps,' rather than accept his own definition of his theological place. Some of those interpreters have seen him, if not as a theological liberal, at least betraying his true colours by adopting elements of the liberal agenda. For example, Nels Ferré observes that Forsyth's *Principle of Authority* "shows the persistent power of the liberal synthesis" of "Christian content" and "general knowledge,"[17] while more recently Ralph Wood goes so far as to say that Forsyth "adhered to many of [Liberalism's] basic presuppositions."[18] More generally, Gwilym Griffith says that "what Forsyth was in revolt against was not liberalism but that Hegelian vogue which was working out into pantheistic humanism touched with evangelical sentiment."[19] Others perceive Forsyth in an entirely different way. One writer says that "many, if not most, of his contemporaries regarded him as one of the last representatives of a vanishing Calvinistic orthodoxy."[20] A. E. Garvie wrote of Forsyth, "Fundamentally a Calvinist, he yet considerably modified Calvin's doctrine."[21]

With that last comment we come somewhat nearer the truth. Forsyth worked out a theological position in dialogue with both Calvinistic orthodoxy and current liberalism. Although this process may be observed frequently in his writings, a major treatment of the subject is found in *Positive Preaching and the Modern Mind*,

---

[16] Robert S. Paul, "P. T. Forsyth: Prophet for the 20th Century," in Donald G. Miller, Browne Barr, and Robert S. Paul, *P. T. Forsyth: The Man, The Preachers' Theologian, Prophet for the 2oth Century: A Contemporary Assessment* (Pittsburgh: Pickwick Press, 1981), p. 64.

[17] Nels F. S. Ferré, *Searchlights on Contemporary Theology* (New York: Harper & Brothers, 1961), p. 87.

[18] Ralph C. Wood, "Christ on Parnassus: P. T. Forsyth among the Liberals," *Journal of Literature and Theology* 2 (March 1988): 83. See our discussion of Wood's conclusion in Chapter Three above.

[19] Gwilym O. Griffith, *The Theology of P. T. Forsyth* (London: Lutterworth, 1948), p. 26.

[20] John Webster Grant, *Free Churchmanship in England 1870–1940: With Special Reference to Congregationalism* (London: Independent Press, n.d.), pp. 227–228.

[21] A. E. Garvie, "A Cross-Centred Theology," *Congregational Quarterly* 22 (1944): 325.

chapters 6–9. In chapters 6 and 7 he engages first with liberalism, contrasting it with a 'positive' theology, then identifies aspects of current thought which ought to be part of a modernized theology. In chapters 8 and 9, Forsyth interacts with orthodoxy, identifying holiness and holy love as important concepts, and maintaining the place of judgment as a central soteriological category. Throughout, he defines his own position in relation to these two theological stances. Elsewhere, Forsyth succinctly sums up "the distinction between an orthodox, a positive, and a liberal Christianity":

> Orthodoxy urges the necessity of a certain theological system for salvation; liberalism grounds faith on general ideas or sympathies native to man but roused by Christ, who gave them unique expression winged by his great personality; while positive Christianity rests Christian faith on certain historic and saving facts, centring in the death and resurrection of Christ, as the new creation of the race. The spiritual destiny of the race is the work of Christ's atoning and creative death.[22]

Much more could be said about the distinctives of Forsythian theology – as evangelical, Reformed, and modern – but in the present context it is sufficient to note that Forsyth's theological project is an exposition of what he calls positive Christianity – a theology that exalts neither love nor holiness, but centres its insight on the cross of God's holy love.

1.3 A CHRISTOLOGICAL DEFINITION OF HOLINESS

What then is God's holiness? Forsyth offers a succinct definition: Jesus Christ is "the very incarnation of the holiness of God," and his cross "its supreme and complete assertion."[23] The theologian's conception of the holiness of God is derived from the person and work of Jesus Christ. "The holiness of God," says Forsyth in another place, is "the whole concrete righteousness of existence, self-sustained at white heat. For our God is a consuming fire." And he adds, "practically that is the holiness of God in Christ."[24] Holiness is not defined abstractly, but by direct reference to God incarnate in Christ Jesus, who is himself "God's holiness in human form."[25]

With such an emphasis on divine moral action, Forsyth is equally clear that "holiness is not the calm balance and self-possession of an

---

[22] *The Preaching of Jesus and the Gospel of Christ* (1987; orig. pub. as articles in 1915), p. 79.
[23] *Cruciality*, p. 160.
[24] *Cruciality*, p. 159.
[25] *Person*, p. 347.

infinite of Eternal Being." Instead, God's holiness is "more akin to the self-conquest, self-bestowal, and self-effectuation which belong to an eternal moral personality." Here, Forsyth decisively rejects the impersonal scheme deriving from Aristotle and Plotinus, which was refined by Thomas Aquinas and still perceptible in Protestant scholasticism, which thought of God as "the Supreme Being, inviolable, self-sufficing, and splendid."[26]

Having laid that foundation, or rather having accepted that "no one can lay any foundation other than the one already laid, which is Jesus Christ" (1 Corinthians 3.11), Forsyth builds on it when he speaks more conventionally about the divine holiness: "It is the perfection of God's moral nature. It is ethic upon the whole eternal scale. It is the eternal unity of God's free will with His perfect nature. It is the supreme expression of His absolute perfection. But His *moral* perfection, observe."[27] Closely and keenly balanced here are the perfection of God's nature and the practical expression in Christ of that nature in moral will. The holiness of God revealed in Jesus Christ is *moral* perfection, not merely ontological sinlessness but also purposeful obedience.

A similar conclusion is reached as the result of considering the Old Testament. The orientation of holiness is Godward:

> In the Bible, things, or places, or people are holy which are set apart for God; God is holy as He is set apart for Himself. Things are holy as they are for God; He is holy as He is for Himself. We are holy as belonging to Him; He is holy as belonging to Himself, as absolute possessor of Himself, by gift of none. ... For the creature to be holy is *to be for God;* for God Himself to be holy is *to be God.* His holiness is the complete accord of His will and His nature. It is not an attribute of God; it is His name and being and infinite value.[28]

A recurring theme here is the freedom of God to be God, or as we quoted in the previous paragraph, "the eternal unity of God's free will with His perfect nature." The counterpart of God's holy freedom is his saving love. In the wider context of these quotations and many others that focus on holiness, Forsyth speaks of the divine love. And so, typically, "The holiness of God is His self-sufficient perfection, whose passion is to establish itself in the unholy by gracious love."[29] Just as God's love is a holy love, God's

---

[26] *Church, the Gospel and Society,* p. 19.
[27] "A Holy Church the Moral Guide to Society" (1905), in *Church, the Gospel and Society,* p. 19.
[28] *This Life and the Next,* 2nd ed. (1946; orig. pub. 1918), pp. 28–29.
[29] *Positive Preaching and [the] Modern Mind,* 1st ed. (1907), p. 145.

holiness is holiness in the service of divine love. This, of course, is the subject which we reserve for fuller consideration in the following chapter.

1.4 A DISTINCTIVE TERMINOLOGY

Although the definition of God's holiness emerges in Forsyth's writing as he describes the death of Christ for our justification, it might be useful at this point to note the terminology he employs. The first thing we notice is the preponderance of the words *holy* and *holiness,* even in places where we might expect *righteous* and *righteousness.* These, it turns out, are virtual equivalents in Forsyth's usage, as for example when he says, "The righteousness which reconciles and secures everything is the holiness which destroys guilt in its very exposure. It is God's holy and atoning love making a new world in Christ's Cross."[30] The identification is explicit when Forsyth speaks of the church's failure "to see in the judgment of the cross God's righteousness, God's holiness, coming finally to its own,"[31] or when he freely substitutes one for the other in a paraphrase of scripture, as in "the kingdom of God and His holiness."[32]

While noting that Forsyth employs the two words as virtual synonyms, A. E. Garvie adds that in using the Old Testament word *holiness* to express the New Testament idea of *righteousness,* Forsyth "seems to me to alter its meaning."[33] In Garvie's haste to proceed to other matters, he doesn't very clearly explain this point, and comparison with the most comprehensive of Garvie's works turns up no further elaboration of this matter.[34] However, his contention seems to be that in its New Testament usage *holiness* is related to sanctification, and to use it in contexts where *righteousness* is the conventional word robs the latter of its "distinctive meaning," presumably justification. This criticism misses the mark, for several reasons. Exegetically, the contention that "holiness is more an Old Testament than a New Testament

---

[30] *Justification,* p. 22.
[31] *Cruciality,* p. 72.
[32] *Cruciality,* p. 40.
[33] Alfred E. Garvie, "Placarding the Cross: The Theology of P. T. Forsyth," *Congregational Quarterly* 21 (1943): 351. Within this context, further citations to Garvie are from this page.
[34] Alfred E. Garvie, *The Christian Doctrine of the Godhead, or The Apostolic Benediction as the Christian Creed* (London: Hodder & Stoughton, [1925]).

idea" may recognize its important place in the Old Testament, but ignores (as Albrecht Ritschl before him) the fact that words in the *hagios* group occur about 250 times in the New Testament, a total roughly equal to that of the *dikaios* family. For his part, Forsyth replies that "we cannot read even the gospels without finding on Christ's lips quite as much about Judgment as about Fatherhood," a fact which 'the lovers of love' fail to do justice to.[35]

Further, in the New Testament all three persons of the Trinity are called Holy – the Father only occasionally, the Son more often, and the Spirit frequently – and these references are by no means limited to a concern for sanctification. Finally, there does not appear to be a firm delineation of meaning in scripture between the two word-groups, thereby justifying Forsyth's almost interchangeable usage, as for example when he defines righteousness as "the absolute holiness of God."[36] When he does make a distinction, it is usually between the holy love of God and the righteousness that is ours by the grace of God: "What we on earth call righteousness among men, the saints in heaven call holiness in Him."[37] But even this distinction is not held consistently, because Forsyth also speaks of the consequent holiness of believers, and of the righteousness of God, again reflecting the biblical pattern. The real problem, one suspects, is not so much the terminological choice between *holiness* and *righteousness,* but rather a theological disagreement about whether divine holiness should have the prominence which Forsyth accords it, or whether the love of God should be given priority, as Garvie (following Ritschl) prefers.

Returning to our main concern, Forsyth does not discuss his thinking in preferring *holiness* to *righteousness,* but there appear to be several influences at work. First, there is a general preference to use fresh language to describe the old truths, as for example when *egoism* replaces *pride, personality* is used instead of *soul,* and *reality* bears the weight of *truth.* More often than not, *experimental religion* stands in for *faith,* and Forsyth speaks more frequently of the *absoluteness* or *finality* of Christ than his *finished work.* In one remarkable passage, a six-page discussion of salvation by works, the noun *work(s)* is only used once in its conventional sense.[38] While protesting against the modern tendency which "takes the Christian

---

[35] *Faith, Freedom, and the Future* (1912), pp. 247–248.
[36] *Preaching of Jesus,* p. 96.
[37] *Cruciality,* p. 39.
[38] *Rome, Reform and Reaction* (1899), pp. 237–242.

truths and terms and trims them down, under plea of filling them out,"[39] Forsyth is even more insistent "that we learn constantly to realize the great historic words, and to re-interpret them, and modernize their teeming truth. ... If we cannot restore, we can re-translate, re-interpret, and transform."[40] *Holiness,* then, comes across with a startling freshness that *righteousness* has lost from overuse.

A second influence, and a more important one because it concerns content more than impression, is a desire to avoid any confusion with phrases that were then becoming increasingly popular, *social righteousness* and *public righteousness.* In one passage of *The Cruciality of the Cross,* Forsyth makes this distinction clear. After reiterating his conviction that "righteousness eternal and absolute" is equivalent to "divine holiness,"[41] he goes on to speak of a proper view of Christian social concern:

> The new passion for righteousness, then, must end upward in a new sense of judgment. ... Social righteousness, unaccompanied by moral delicacy, inner penetration, and self judgment, could easily become another phase of Pharisaism. ... But to give God's judgment its due place in public righteousness is to raise ethic to religion, [and] righteousness to holiness.[42]

Forsyth's concern, therefore, is to rescue from its cultural captivity the reality of the holy God's action in making many righteous (justification). "The word justification has long gone out of our religious vocabulary," he said in 1905, "and I do not wish to force it back. It will return when the thing returns and demands a name."[43] Since the word *righteousness* had been co-opted (and sometimes sentimentalized) by those who stressed social transformation and social justice, Forsyth set out to refurbish the doctrine of justification by speaking of it in the language of holiness.

Within the context described above, Forsyth's emphasis on holiness served to accent certain theological points, and to this extent Garvie's observation is correct. To speak of holiness as Forsyth did is to emphasize God's sovereignty in justification, which is precisely what he wishes to stress. The absolute priority of grace is

---

[39] *Rome, Reform and Reaction,* p. 105.
[40] "Christ our Sanctification," *Wesleyan Methodist Magazine* 134 (1911): 732, 733.
[41] *Cruciality,* p. 171.
[42] *Cruciality,* pp. 173–174.
[43] "The Grace of the Gospel as the Moral Authority of the Church" (1905), in *Church, the Gospel and Society,* p. 113.

among Forsyth's highest concerns: the holy love of God is acting for our salvation, entirely apart from our deserving or our prior approval. Furthermore, if the use of *holiness* terminology prompts his hearers to see sanctification and justification as close theological relations, Forsyth will again be pleased, for this is a point he makes with considerable force elsewhere.[44]

In this opening section, we have noticed three prominent concerns in Forsyth's thinking about holiness. First, he wishes to highlight the deficiency he detected in contemporary theology on this topic. With the exception of a declining orthodoxy, current doctrinal thinking had so emphasized the love of God that the divine holiness was of little interest, except in support of a program of social amelioration. Secondly, regarding definition, Forsyth claimed that the holiness of God defines itself by its self-revelation, by giving itself to us. Just as God had deeply impressed upon Forsyth "the revelation of His holiness and grace, which the great theologians taught [him] to find in the Bible,"[45] so the Spirit had convinced him that "Jesus was the Holy One and the Just – nay, the very Righteousness of God."[46] Indeed, it was Forsyth's contention that all the words that cluster around holiness, including justice and righteousness, are understood through Christ. And thirdly, he used the word *holiness* in a particularly creative way, in order to recapture aspects of soteriological thinking, including a stress on divine sovereignty and grace.

1.5 THE HOLINESS OF THE CROSS

Central to these emphases is Forsyth's Christocentric focus on the holiness of the cross. It is particularly the atoning and reconciling death of Jesus that informs our knowledge of God's holiness. Therefore Forsyth insists that "holiness is not anything that can just be shown; it must be done. Here revelation is action."[47] Echoing this point, Colin Gunton notes Forsyth's "concern to allow the metaphor of justice to take shape, to be filled with its proper meaning, at the place where God takes upon himself the evil for

---

[44] See the discussion on "The cross as sanctification" in section 2.2 below.
[45] *Positive Preaching*, p. 282.
[46] *Missions in State and Church* (1908), p. 59.
[47] *Justification*, p. 167.

which he is held responsible."[48] If we are to appreciate God's holiness in its self-revelation, we must look to Christ's cross. That task is the major concern of this chapter. However, we do not regard the death of Jesus as merely an event, but a meaningful action which requires interpretation. The cross is not merely the symbol of a capital punishment, but shorthand for a matrix of meaning. We cannot simply read off love or holiness – much less *God's* love or holiness – from such an ambiguous event, but must see the cross as an interpreted event. Therefore, we now turn to an examination of Forsyth's doctrine of the atonement.

In considering P. T. Forsyth's soteriology, we begin by choosing a characteristic summary phrase to serve as an outline for our discussion. He memorably describes the death of Jesus Christ as "the offering of a holy self to a holy God from sin's side."[49] As we examine the various parts of this definition, our purpose throughout will be to highlight the importance he accords to God's holiness, and to describe and evaluate his treatment of this attribute of God. While we will not endeavour to present every aspect of the doctrine of the atonement, we aim to explore it in sufficient depth to accomplish the purposes outlined at the outset of this chapter: to describe Forsyth's view of the holiness of God, to understand the importance he ascribes to it, and to prepare the way for a fuller discussion in the following chapter of the strife or harmony of God's holiness and love in the cross.

2. "THE OFFERING": AN ATONING SACRIFICE

A central aspect of the atonement is its sacrificial nature. Stephen Sykes identifies this as the predominant theme in Forsyth's view of the atonement, although he also notes that the earlier theologian did not confine himself to this, or any, particular theory of the atonement.[50] Therefore, in this section, we first examine the wider context, and then focus more particularly on Christ's death as sacrificial. For Forsyth, the atonement as sacrifice finds its place within a broad theological framework. By this we mean not that the

---

[48] Colin E. Gunton, *The Actuality of the Atonement: A Study of Metaphor, Rationality and the Christian Tradition* (Edinburgh: T. & T. Clark, 1988), p. 106.
[49] *Cruciality*, p. 182.
[50] S. W. Sykes, "Theology through History," in *The Modern Theologians: An Introduction to Christian Theology in the Twentieth Century,* ed. David F. Ford (Oxford: Basil Blackwell, 1989), vol. 2, pp. 9–11.

atonement is one of a number of concerns of systematic theology, but that sacrifice is one motif among several in the doctrine of atonement.

In a chapter of *The Work of Christ* entitled "The Threefold Cord," Forsyth writes about the doctrine of the cross in three perspectives: satisfactionary, regenerative, and triumphant, explaining that through the Christian centuries the emphasis in atonement theory has changed. In the early church, victory over the devil was stressed; in the medieval and Reformation church the focus was on "the finality of [the Lord's] satisfaction, expiation, or atonement presented to the holy power of God"; while in the modern church, the sanctifying influence on man was notable.[51] But these are not exclusive of each other, as their combination in 1 Corinthians 1.30 shows: Christ is made unto us justification, sanctification, and redemption. "The whole history of the doctrine [of the atonement] in the Church," Forsyth claims, "may be viewed as the exegesis by time of this great text of the Spirit."[52]

2.1 THE CROSS AS VICTORY

The *Christus victor* aspect of the atonement is one that engaged Forsyth's pen throughout his career. In one of the small books of published sermons from the days of his pastoral ministry, Forsyth wrote about Christ "coping with the great Satan, a world-power, wickedness in high places." In a style reminiscent first of Luther and then of Milton, he vividly described not only the bold dramatic conflict ("But him He vanquished, and saw him fall like lightning from heaven"), but also the subtler battle in "the region of moral and spiritual nausea," where "the king of terrors is the old serpent, the spirit of the slime."[53] The note of triumph in the cross recurs in Forsyth's later sermons, as for example in "The Fatherhood of Death," where he claims, "The holiness of Christ was the one thing damnatory to the Satanic power. And it was His death which consummated that holiness. It was His death, therefore, that was Satan's final doom."[54]

---

[51] *Work*, p. 199.
[52] *Work*, p. 200.
[53] "The Taste of Death and the Life of Grace" (1900), in *Father*, pp. 53–55.
[54] *Missions in State and Church*, pp. 13–14; see also the following sermon, "Final Judgment Full Salvation," where the text is John 16.11: "The prince of this world hath been judged."

The focus on this triumphant aspect of the cross continued in Forsyth's lectures on the atonement in 1908–1909, from which we have quoted in the previous section. But it was during the war of 1914–1918 that Forsyth wrote most persuasively on the atonement in terms of victory. As tens of thousands died and grief touched the hearts of many, he tried to meet the intellectual and pastoral need for a theodicy. In his *Justification of God,* Forsyth put the emphasis on "the completeness of the Cross and its eternal victory."[55] Younger theologians, he claimed, had reduced the cross to sacrificial love, ignoring the aspect of judgment: "Their belief in Christ is impaired for want of a belief in the Satan that Christ felt it His supreme conflict to counterwork and destroy."[56] The result was portrayed in an article probably prepared during the same period. Forsyth wrote about

> the awful conflict and work for us sinners, caught amid spiritual powers that bemaze us, wherein God in Christ makes our bad cause His own . . . , Himself for us faces our fierce accuser, meets and conquers the evil power that holds us, and saves us from a world riot of spiritual wickedness which He alone can measure and manage, not we.[57]

This was not an isolated theory of the atonement, applicable only to the moment of death, but a doctrine that was integrated with the person of Jesus Christ. Forsyth maintained that Jesus was continually engaged in a battle – in every conflict, every decision, every act of forgiveness. "He was thus dying and conquering all His life, in word and deed," until "the finished victory on the Cross" crowned "the constant victory in His soul."[58]

In light of our wider purposes of considering the harmony of love and holiness in God's nature, it is interesting to note that Forsyth describes the victory in terms of both these attributes. God's love was powerfully at work in Christ's action. "At its height in the cross it was the silent deed . . . of destruction to Satan."[59] Love, out of passionate concern for humanity, dealt death to sin and sin's

---

[55] *Justification,* p. 223.
[56] *Justification,* p. 175.
[57] "The Preaching of Jesus and the Gospel of Christ: [VII] The Meaning of a Sinless Christ," *Expositor,* 8th series, vol. 25 (April 1923): 304. Several references in the first three pages of this article to the world war, and the lack of any sense of distance from the previous six articles published in the *Expositor* throughout 1915, lead to the conclusion that the seventh was written at about the same time and, for unexplained reasons, only published posthumously eight years later.
[58] *Justification,* p. 218.
[59] *Preaching of Jesus,* p. 106.

The Importance of Holiness 165

sponsor. Similarly, Forsyth describes the cross as a life-and-death struggle between sin and holiness:

> Sin is the death of God. Die sin must or God. Its nature is to go on from indifference to absolute hostility and malignity to the holy; and one must go down. There is no compromise between the holy and the sinful when the issue is seen from the height of heaven to the depth of hell, and followed into the uttermost parts of the soul. And that is the nature of the issue as it is set in the Cross of Christ. It is the eternal holiness in conflict for its life.[60]

Whether speaking specifically of the conflict between Christ and Satan, or more generally (as in the preceding quotation) in terms of a battle between "the holy and the sinful," Forsyth speaks vividly of the cross as a victory for God, and consequently for God's people. And it is a therefore a victory for the holiness of God exerted in Christ over the unholy alliance of sin, the devil, death, and hell.

2.2 THE CROSS AS SANCTIFICATION

A second aspect of Forsyth's doctrine of the atonement is that of regeneration or sanctification, which he sees as complementary to the victorious redemption which we considered in the previous paragraphs. A *Christus victor* atonement is incomplete without its obverse, the sanctifying aspect:

> To deliver us from evil is not simply to take us out of hell, it is to take us into heaven. Christ does not simply pluck us out of the hands of Satan, He does so by giving us to God. He does not simply release us out of slavery, He commits us in the act to a positive liberty. He does not simply cancel the charge against us in court and bid us walk out of jail, he meets us at the prison-door and puts us in a new way of life. His forgiveness is not simply retrospective, it is, in the same act, the gift of eternal life. Our evil is overcome by good. We are won from sin by an act which at the same time makes us not simply innocent but holy.[61]

In the latter part of this quotation, the key phrases are "in the same act" and "at the same time." The cross of Jesus Christ is the one source of both justification and sanctification, and the atonement therefore has a twofold reference. It is an event with objective significance to the relationship between God and humanity, conferring God's righteousness; it is also the beginning of a lifelong process of regeneration, inculcating holiness in committed human lives. Though distinguishable, these two are inseparable aspects of

---

[60] *Justification,* p. 147.
[61] *Work,* p. 202.

the same reality. With a more recent theologian, "one might even say that regeneration is the subjective pole of justification."[62]

It was Forsyth's conviction that Protestant orthodoxy had separated the inseparable, and had treated the atonement as an exclusively objective work, describing how Christ's cross had acted on God. It was no solution, however, to make the equal and opposite error of interpreting the cross as merely a subjective moral influence, as liberal theology had done. Both approaches were one-sided, he insisted: the one made the cross "something done wholly over our heads"; the other was "a weak religious subjectivism which has the ethical interest but not the moral note."[63] In both cases, the result was a disjunction between justification and sanctification, and between faith and works.

The solution, Forsyth averred, was "not change of accent but balance of aspects."[64] Rather than constantly measuring the theological disproportion in this matter, and first emphasizing one and then the other, the two aspects must be thought together. Instead of weighing in on one side of the argument between imputed and imparted righteousness, Forsyth spoke of justification and sanctification as held together *in Christ,* and specifically in Christ's holiness. In holy sinlessness and loving obedience, Christ presented to God "a Humanity presanctified," so that "the very nature of justification was sanctification," rather than sanctification a mere sequel.[65] Or, to express the same conviction in terms of its effect on humanity, through faith in Christ we participate in both these realities: "We are justified only as we are incorporate (not clothed) in the perfect righteousness of Christ." The vicarious work of Christ, and our participation in him, is the unitive factor. "It is this being in Christ for our justification," Forsyth claims, "that makes justification necessarily work out to sanctification, and forgiveness be one with eternal life."[66] Calvin before him had insisted, "By partaking of him," that is, Christ, "we principally receive a double grace: namely, that being reconciled to God through Christ's blamelessness, we may have in heaven instead of a Judge a gracious Father; and secondly, that sanctified by Christ's spirit we may

---

[62] Donald G. Bloesch, *Essentials of Evangelical Theology,* vol. 1: *God, Authority, and Salvation* (San Francisco: Harper & Row, 1978), p. 231.
[63] *Work,* p. 220.
[64] *Work,* p. 221.
[65] *Work,* pp. 224–225.
[66] *Work,* p. 215.

cultivate blamelessness and purity of life."[67] For us, Forsyth insists, Christ is not only justification but sanctification – at the same time.

2.3 THE CROSS AS SATISFACTION

The third strand of atonement doctrine that Forsyth identifies brings us specifically to the matter of sacrifice. In describing the cross as "*the offering* of a holy self to a holy God from sin's side,"[68] he draws particular attention to its sacrificial aspect. In the next three sections of this chapter (3–5) we will offer an exposition of the other elements in that quotation (the sinlessness of Christ, the divine holiness, and the human context), and in so doing will elucidate Forsyth's view of Christ's sacrifice. At this point it falls to us to note the place of sacrifice as one strand of 'the threefold cord.' Our concern throughout the chapter is to highlight the place of God's holiness in Forsyth's theology.

The "satisfactionary aspect," Forsyth says, gathers round it words like expiation, atonement, and justification.[69] His 1909 lectures on *The Work of Christ* are an examination of Christ's death with this theme particularly in mind. Although his treatment pays good attention to the related themes of victory, sanctification, confession, and reconciliation, the sacrificial aspect is to the fore. In the first lecture, for example, Forsyth recounts the story of a Belgian signalman whose sacrificial act of heroism prevented the crash of two passenger trains, thereby saving the lives of countless passengers. In an extended discussion, Forsyth draws out the essence of sacrifice, and the difference between God's sacrifice and ours.[70] A picture emerges of Jesus, "a life gathered into one consummate sacrifice," motivated not by duty but by love, willingly and deliberately going to the cross to save a world who hated him.[71]

According to Forsyth, what are the most important features of this sacrifice? First, he notes its continuity with the Old Testament sacrifices. To understand the use of phrases like "the blood of Christ," Forsyth contends that we must return to "the profound, moral, and spiritual religion of the Old Testament."[72] The imagery of sacrifice had been much misunderstood in the subsequent

---

[67] John Calvin, *Institutes* 3.11.1.
[68] *Cruciality*, p. 182 (emphasis added).
[69] *Work*, pp. 199–200.
[70] *Work*, pp. 11–28.
[71] *Work*, pp. 26–27.
[72] *Cruciality*, p. 184.

centuries, however, and so in the light of Christ's cross, the New Testament writers set out to restore the corrupted original meaning of the Levitical sacrifices. There were two truths in need of particular renovation, as Forsyth saw it: first, "the sacrifice is the result of God's grace and not its cause," and second, "the pleasing thing to God, and the effective element in the matter, is not death but life."[73] The material effect of these judgments will emerge in the course of our discussion of the atonement; we note at this point Forsyth's affirmation of the Old Testament as the context and counterpoint for understanding Christ's sacrifice.

The second point concerning this sacrifice is its integral connection with who Jesus is. The incarnation of Christ, his movement from pre-existence to earthly life, was a sacrificial act:

> His sacrifice began before He came into the world, and his cross was that of a lamb slain before the world's foundation. There was a Calvary above which was the mother of it all. . . . He renounced the glory of heavenly being for all he here became. . . . Unlike us, he *chose* the oblivion of birth and the humiliation of life. He consented not only to die but to be born.[74]

As Stephen Sykes notes, Forsyth's doctrine of the atonement, with its prominent place for sacrifice, finds a natural complement in a kenotic interpretation of the incarnation.[75] Quite consistently, Forsyth saw both incarnation and atonement as "the self-donation of God in sacrifice."[76]

Thirdly, we observe the wholehearted and complete nature of this sacrifice. There was nothing held back, no sense of reserve. Christ's death is "a real act or deed of gift once for all, the absorption and oblation of the whole self in a crucial and objective achievement."[77] There could be no sense of unreality or illusion in the cross, no sleight-of-hand with sins. After all, "Who was skilful enough to hoodwink the Almighty?"[78] Instead, God himself provided the atonement for sins, once for all.

A fourth factor is the importance of the will. In the Old Testament sacrificial system, the stress on the blood indicates a concern for life rather than property, and consequently for personal

---

[73] *Cruciality*, pp. 185, 186; see the entire chapter, "What is Meant by the Blood of Christ?" in *Cruciality*, pp. 175–218.
[74] *Person*, p. 271.
[75] Sykes, "Theology through History," in *Modern Theologians*, vol. 2, pp. 9–11.
[76] *Person*, p. 235.
[77] *Cruciality*, p. 182.
[78] *Work*, p. 54.

relationship rather than impersonal bargain. "Blood means essential, central, personal moral life," Forsyth argued, and at the heart of that life, and hence at the heart of sacrifice, is "the central will."[79] Therefore, the sacrificial death of Christ is an active self-giving, a deliberate offering of life to God. "The essence of all sacrifice, which is self-surrender to God, ... was made a moral reality in Christ's holy obedience."[80] We consider this matter further in section 3 of this chapter.

Fifthly, Christ's sacrifice was offered to the Father. "It was the total and active surrender of His will to the Father, and only so a perfect sacrifice for the sin of the world."[81] And yet, "The Holy Father was Himself the Saviour in His Son, making far more sacrifice than He received."[82] Sacrifice was not external to some impersonal deity; it was God's own work. This concern will be more fully explored in section 4 below.

Sixthly, the sacrifice that Christ made was a sacrifice for sin. This facet of Forsyth's doctrine of atonement is explored in greater depth in section 5 below.

2.4 A MULTIFACETED DOCTRINE WITH HOLINESS AS A COMMON THEME

Christ's sacrifice on the cross may be interpreted in various ways, and P. T. Forsyth has identified three of them as victory, sanctification, and satisfaction. Others could be added, and indeed he also employs such concepts as reconciliation, confession, and example to describe the atonement.[83] With such a wide variety of metaphors employed to describe the same reality, is there one common idea that runs through all or most of them? For his part, Forsyth suggests holiness as the key concept, or more specifically, the Son's perfect obedience to the Father, "the holy obedience to the Holy. ... It is the only idea which unites justification and sanctification and both with redemption. For the holiness which

---

[79] *Cruciality*, p. 191.
[80] *Work*, p. 164.
[81] *Different Conceptions of Priesthood and Sacrifice*, ed. William Sanday (London: Longmans, Green, 1900), p. 24.
[82] *Preaching of Jesus*, p. 56.
[83] Among many possible references, see respectively: *Work*, chap. 2, "The Great Sacrificial Work is to Reconcile," pp. 33–62; *Work*, chap. 5, "The Cross the Great Confessional," pp. 141–172; and, on the 'moral' or exemplary theory, *Preaching of Jesus*, pp. 111–113.

satisfied God and sanctifies us also destroyed the evil power in the world and its hold on us."[84] The divine holiness enacted at the cross of Christ is the "principle [which] co-ordinates the various aspects" of the atonement. "This one action of the holy Saviour's total person was, on its various sides, the destruction of evil, the satisfaction of God, and the sanctification of men."[85]

The influence of the holiness of God, Forsyth contends, can be traced in the development of atonement theories in Christian history. Through the centuries, the church has been occupied with the long process of moralizing theology, not least in its doctrine of the atonement. After noting the moral effect of Christ on Judaism, and of Paul on Pharisaism, he continues:

> And a great step in this movement was taken in the Middle Ages, when the work of Christ ceased to be regarded as a traffic with Satan for His captives, and became for Anselm a satisfaction made by Christ to the wounded honour of God. It was another step when the principles of a great social discipline like jurisprudence were applied to explain the situation. It was a real advance when the Reformation introduced the idea of public justice, instead of wounded honour, as the object of satisfaction. The much decried forensic idea was ethically far ahead of the previous idea which recognized in Satan rights of property in souls, ahead also of the feudal idea of the honour of God. And still we move up the moral scale as we substitute for retributive justice with its individualism, universal righteousness and eternal holiness with the social note. So also when we discard the idea of equivalent penalty in favour of Christ's obedient sanctity as the satisfying thing before God.[86]

And, Forsyth believes, the development of atonement doctrine continues apace with developments in his own day: "The more we modernize it the more we moralize it," and, most importantly, "the more ethical we become the more exigent is holiness."[87] The pressing theological claim of God's active holiness stands at the very centre of Forsyth's view of the atonement, both the "eternal holiness" of the Father and the "obedient sanctity" of the Son.

In making this claim, Forsyth is not treating holiness as an umbrella concept that includes all the others, or championing holiness to the exclusion of other aspects. Rather, he is suggesting that the central thing, the atoning element, is holiness, "that the active and effective principle in the work of Christ was the perfect

---

[84] *Work*, p. 222.
[85] *Work*, pp. 201–202.
[86] *Positive Preaching*, pp. 293–294.
[87] *Positive Preaching*, p. 294.

obedience of holy love which He offered amidst the conditions of sin, death, and judgment. The potent thing was not the suffering but the sanctity, and not the sympathetic confession of our sin so much as the practical confession of God's holiness."[88]

Such a position could be criticized as unduly narrowing the doctrine of the atonement. After all, the church has so far preferred a multifaceted doctrine, showing little interest in any tight circumscription of the meaning of the cross. Forsyth's stress on divine holiness, it might be argued, threatens to limit the scripturally-inspired diversity of views on the atonement. However, just the opposite is the case: his strong emphasis on the centrality of holiness is accompanied by an appreciation of the diversity of perspectives. The preferences of individuals will vary, he says, just as the church through the ages has first appreciated one perspective and then another. "Some souls, according to their experience, will gravitate to the great Deliverance, some to the great Atonement, and some to the great Regeneration. . . . And the Church is enriched by the complementary action of such diversities."[89] Forsyth acknowledges and appreciates this diversity, but claims that the central factor, the atoning element of the cross is holy, loving obedience.

Another possible objection to Forsyth's position is that the stress on holiness is an abstract or theoretical one, a step removed from the personal Saviour depicted in the gospels. This is precisely what Forsyth wishes to counter in his doctrine of the atonement. Repeatedly he protests against any impersonal theory of the cross, as for example when he insists that "what we are concerned with is not the satisfaction of a demand but of a Person."[90] At every point, whether in a discussion of the atonement, the believer's spiritual experience, authority, or theodicy, Forsyth stresses the dynamic and personal nature of the realities involved.

To summarize the conclusions of this section, we have seen that Forsyth's doctrine of the cross is one that speaks of the death of Christ in terms of a sacrifice. We have noted some of its leading characteristics, and will elaborate on some of these in the remainder of the present chapter. Forsythian soteriology is not limited to the sacrificial perspective, however, but incorporates other aspects as well, notably victory over evil, divine satisfaction, and

---

[88] *Work*, p. 201.
[89] *Work*, p. 233.
[90] *Work*, p. 204.

sanctification: "He subdued Satan, rejoiced the Father, and set up in Humanity the kingdom – all in one supreme and consummate act of His one person."[91] All these are held together in the personal holiness of the Lord Jesus Christ, in whom the holy love of God is revealed.

3. "A HOLY SELF": THE SINLESSNESS AND OBEDIENCE OF JESUS

In continuity with the Christian tradition, Forsyth spoke of Christ's perfection. Jesus, he said, was "the sinless Son of God, who lived from eternity in God's holiness," who became human and "lived that holiness out in the face of sin."[92] In short, "He was the incarnation of [God's] holiness."[93] Holiness, then, is not only the central idea in Forsyth's doctrine of the atonement, but also a prominent theological context for describing the character of the atoning Saviour.

Within that overarching concept, he identifies two aspects, the sinlessness and the obedience of Christ. This first aspect, Christ's "sinless perfection"[94] is not in itself the subject of much elaboration in Forsyth's writings. When he does mention it explicitly, he regards it as "a negative idea," an admirable ideal which "declares much but conveys little."[95] Just as an exemplary view of the atonement is inadequate on its own, so an ideal sinlessness, though perhaps impressive enough to evoke a feeling of personal unworthiness, cannot provoke a true sense of sin, nor deal with it effectively: "No mere worship of a most holy life can search, humble, confound and re-create us, as Christ has done to His classic own from His cross. It does not carry us beyond saint-worship."[96]

In light of the fact that descriptions of Jesus in terms of sinlessness are overly negative, Forsyth considers the more positive term, 'purity.' But that too is judged inadequate: "How much more than pure Christ was!"[97] What is seen in Jesus Christ is something much more active and deliberate, and so he concentrates his attention on the second aspect of Christ's holiness, namely obedience. In so doing, he redefines the terms of the debate,

---

[91] *Work*, p. 224.
[92] *Work*, p. 209.
[93] *Cruciality*, p. 194.
[94] *Work*, p. 212.
[95] "The Preaching of Jesus and the Gospel of Christ," p. 293.
[96] "The Preaching of Jesus and the Gospel of Christ," pp. 293–294.
[97] *Work*, pp. 159–160.

preferring to speak of "the perfect holiness of Christ's redeeming obedience, what is unhappily called His sinlessness."[98] Specifically, our attention is drawn by this turn-of-the-century theologian to see "in Christ's life one actively holy even unto death," an obedience aptly summarized as "the holiness of the Cross."[99]

The holiness of Christ's obedience is a key concept, enabling us to understand better certain aspects of his life. For example, the growth of Jesus which Forsyth so boldly affirms appears at first to be incompatible with perfect sinlessness. But when Christ's holiness is enlarged to include ongoing obedience, a theoretical place opens up for what the Bible asserts to be true. Forsyth speaks of "the progressive deepening of the man Jesus in this sinless life and holy work; his enlarging sense of the work to be done, his rising sense of the power to do it, and his expanding sanctity in the doing of it."[100] In short, while Jesus was always the sinless One, "He learned a redemptive obedience" in "the deepening mastery of a moral vocation."[101]

To choose another example, that obedience provides the explanation and deeper meaning of Christ's suffering: "It was suffering accepted and transfigured by holy obedience," Forsyth explains. Then, to counter the theory that Christ's sufferings were the sum total of what humanity deserved to suffer, he quickly adds that "the atoning thing was not its amount or acuteness, but its obedience, its sanctity."[102] It is the holiness of the Saviour's response to his Father's will that atones, and not the suffering that accompanied it. "The atoning thing is not obedient suffering but suffering obedience."[103] As Hebrews 5.8 says, although Jesus was the Son of the Father, nevertheless "he learned obedience from what he suffered."

In the atoning death and finished work, Forsyth maintains, God is not only shown to be holy, but acts in such a way as to establish that holiness. Holiness is not merely exemplified, but enacted. In a passage dedicated to bringing out this point, he describes this with a whole variety of verbs: "The active holiness of Christ . . . consisted

---

[98] *Positive Preaching*, p. 21.
[99] "The Preaching of Jesus and the Gospel of Christ," p. 293.
[100] *Person*, p. 349.
[101] *Person*, p. 126.
[102] *Work*, p. 157.
[103] *Work*, p. 205

in revealing the holiness of God," "putting it into final and universal effect among men," "conveying and establishing it."[104]

In the preceding discussion of these two aspects of Christ's holiness, it comes as no surprise that obedience rather than sinlessness is stressed; here again is the Forsythian preference for the active to the ontological. Such a view is justified, he believes, not only by the actual experience of Christ, but by the wider context of Old Testament sacrifice that forms the background to Christ's self-offering in holiness. In the Levitical sacrifices, the obedient will of the offerer is more important than the sinless purity of the victim. "The material sacrifice was, and was meant to be, but an outward symbol of the real inner sacrifice, which was the offerer's self-oblation. ... It was the living symbol of a life, *i.e.* of an obedient will."[105] Similarly, the cross was the dynamic outward expression of the Son's obedience to the Father.

The two facets of holiness are, of course, inseparable, and the obedience impossible without the sinless purity, as the New Testament in particular shows. What was a symbolic identification of offerer and oblation in the Old Testament becomes in the New a personal and actual identification, where Christ is both priest and victim. Once again, the stress is on the obedient will. The death of Jesus on the cross involved "no martyr passivity," asserted Forsyth; instead, "it was the work of a Messiah king with power over Himself. Christ never merely accepted His fate; He willed it." Then, referring to the last servant song of Isaiah, he adds, "The same great picture which presents the sheep before the shearers dumb deepens before its close to one who poured out His soul unto death."[106] The decision to accept death was a conscious acceptance of the Father's will; therefore, "Christ's sacrifice is essentially one of will in obedience."[107]

That will is not a new development, however, but of a piece throughout Christ's history, and so it is not merely the death of Jesus but "the work of Christ's person"[108] that atones and reconciles. Just as the cross has no meaning apart from the Saviour's holy obedience, so "the mere act of dying" has no salvific value, "but the

---

[104] "The Preaching of Jesus and the Gospel of Christ," p. 296.
[105] *Cruciality,* pp. 187–188.
[106] *Cruciality,* pp. 70–71; see Isaiah 53.7, 12.
[107] *Different Conceptions of Priesthood and Sacrifice,* p. 12.
[108] "The Preaching of Jesus and the Gospel of Christ," p. 296.

person in it."[109] Despite Forsyth's emphasis on the Son's holy obedience, particularly in the face of death, he can also quite eloquently describe "the beauty of holiness offered to [God's] sight in the perfect character of Christ."[110] Person and work belong together. In sinless obedience, Christ both exemplified and enacted the holiness of God.

Indeed, in the cross of this One, in this One whose life apparently ended on a cross, God shows humanity what genuine holiness is. Jesus Christ is "the normal holy man, the man holy with all the holiness of God."[111] Here in the obedience of a sinless Christ, Forsyth finds the revelation of God's holiness. In several important ways, Forsyth stresses the unity of the Father and the Son in holiness. In this section we have explored that holiness in terms of Christ's sinlessness and obedience. Now we turn to examine the Father's holiness.

4. "TO A HOLY GOD": THE ACKNOWLEDGMENT OF THE FATHER'S HOLINESS

In the preceding section, we have recorded Forsyth's conviction that Jesus Christ personally communicated the holiness of God. The sinlessness and obedience of Jesus revealed the divine holiness in human form. But Christ did more than proclaim that holiness and make it known in his own person. According to Forsyth, the Holy One of God also acknowledged God's holiness in the sense of confessing its righteousness in judgment.

In a chapter of *The Work of Christ* called "The Cross the Great Confessional," Forsyth spoke in the following way about the crucified Son of God: "He confessed in free action, He praised and justified by act, before the world, and on the scale of all the world, the holiness of God."[112] To be more specific, "He confessed God's holiness in reacting mortally against human sin, in cursing human sin, in judging it to its very death."[113] Sin and judgment are closely related, and the work of Christ proclaimed the rightness of the second following on from the first. This matter of God's judgment is a large question, prompting others: How can God forgive the guilty?

---

[109] Untitled article, *The Atonement in Modern Religious Thought: A Theological Symposium* (London: James Clarke, 1900), pp. 67, 68.
[110] *Work*, p. 208.
[111] *Work*, p. 215.
[112] *Work*, p. 147.
[113] *Work*, p. 150.

and, With what degree of seriousness does God take human sin? These are debated issues within the doctrine of the atonement. Forsyth maintains that the answers to these questions, and the solution to the problem of human sinfulness more generally, resides in Christ who confessed God's holiness.

4.1 THE CONFESSION OF SIN

We enter this debate by considering the question, What words does this confession speak? Regarding the specific content of Christ's confession of holiness, Forsyth first replies to previous work in this area. In his book, *The Nature of the Atonement* (1856), John McLeod Campbell had advanced the thesis that in Christ, God as man had made "a perfect confession of our sins. This confession, as to its own nature, must have been *a perfect Amen in humanity to the judgment of God on the sin of man.*"[114] While praising Campbell's "great, fine, holy book,"[115] Forsyth nevertheless wants to change the emphasis, because "what a holy God requires is the due confession of His holiness before even the confession of sin."[116] Being sinless, and therefore guiltless, Jesus could not confess sin. Indeed, repentance is only possible in the light of God's holiness perfectly confessed, recognized in union with Christ. Summarizing the distinction, Forsyth writes, "There is a racial confession that can be made only by the holy; and there is a personal confession that can be made only by the guilty."[117]

In 1899, Forsyth engaged views similar to Campbell's at a conference in Oxford which examined "Different Conceptions of Priesthood and Sacrifice". The fifteen participants had each responded in writing to a series of questions put by the organizer William Sanday; the collated answers were then circulated to the participants in advance of the discussions. In his written contribution, R. C. Moberly had advanced the view that Christ's sacrifice was "perfectly consummated in penitence,"[118] a position that he was to develop and defend in his book, *Atonement and*

---

[114] John McLeod Campbell, *The Nature of the Atonement and its Relation to Remission of Sins and Eternal Life,* 4th ed. (London: Macmillan, 1873), pp. 117–118 (emphasis in original).
[115] *Work,* p. 148.
[116] *Cruciality,* pp. 206–207.
[117] *Work,* p. 151.
[118] *Different Conceptions of Priesthood and Sacrifice,* p. 25.

Personality (1901).[119] In the conference discussions, Forsyth noted that "Dr. Moberly refers to Christ's sacrifice as 'consummating human penitence,'" and then advanced three objections. First, "historically we cannot find any trace of repentance – of a vicarious repentance – in His mind." Second, "vicarious repentance is a moral impossibility." And third, "There is nothing really atoning in penitence. Penitence cannot undo, and Christ did."[120]

Forsyth's first point is well taken; McLeod Campbell for his part only quotes Ps 119.136 in support of his specific thesis that Christ confessed human sin,[121] while H. R. Mackintosh comments that "there is nothing in the New Testament in the least resembling the view that Christ repented of our sins vicariously."[122] In Campbell's defense, George Tuttle notes that "account must be taken also of the long experience of the church in arriving at doctrinal statements as implied by the scriptures, even though not expressly stated therein," and mentions the Trinity and satisfaction as examples.[123] While agreeing that none of these three doctrines (like many others) are expressly stated in scripture, surely the two Tuttle introduces are more than 'implied,' while arguably Campbell's particular proposal is supported by "not even a faint allusion" in the New Testament.[124]

The second point – that repentance is only morally possible to the sinner – is the central one, and one which Forsyth later elaborated at some length:

> How could Christ in any real sense confess a sin, with whose guilt He had nothing in common? . . . Personal guilt Christ could never confess. There is that in guilt which can only be confessed by the guilty. "I did it." That kind of confession Christ could never make. That is the part of the confession that we make, and we cannot make it effectually until we

---

[119] See the discussion and comparison in R. S. Franks, *The Work of Christ: A Historical Study of Christian Doctrine* (London: Thomas Nelson and Sons, 1962), pp. 694–701.
[120] *Different Conceptions of Priesthood and Sacrifice*, pp. 123–124.
[121] Campbell, *Nature of the Atonement*, p. 115.
[122] H. R. Mackintosh, *Some Aspects of Christian Belief* (London: Hodder & Stoughton, [1923]), p. 88.
[123] George M. Tuttle, *So Rich a Soil: John McLeod Campbell on Christian Atonement* (Edinburgh: Handsel Press, 1986), p. 130. The entire chapter, "Christ's Confession and Repentance: Insights with Staying Power," pp. 126–135, is an insightful discussion of this question.
[124] Mackintosh, *Some Aspects of Christian Belief*, p. 88.

are in union with Christ and His great lone work of perfectly and practically confessing the holiness of God.[125]

The issue here is a fundamental one, involving distinctions between justification and sanctification, and between grace and human effort. Forsyth reacts against McLeod Campbell's effort to characterize the atonement in terms of the human response to Christ's work, to transpose confession of sin from response to grace to work of grace. It is a distinction between Christ's work accomplished at the cross, and Christ's work achieved in the Spirit. It is a confusion between what was done for us, and what is done in us. Therefore, where Forsyth would say (as in the quotation above) that repentance is created when Christ confronts an individual in his or her sin, Campbell might well protest that salvation is all by grace, and that Christ has already repented of human sin.

The third point, regarding the nature of the atoning element in Christ's death, indicates Forsyth's disagreement with the formal starting-point of Campbell's argument, namely the assertion by Jonathan Edwards that if satisfaction for sin is to be made, there must be "either an equivalent punishment or an equivalent sorrow and repentance."[126] Edwards adopted the first option without seriously considering the second. Conversely, Campbell rejected the first and spoke in favour of the second, "which is surely the higher and more excellent, being a moral and spiritual satisfaction."[127] While not referring to the exclusive options proposed by Edwards, Forsyth rejects both: the first, an equivalent punishment, must be seriously qualified if its truth is to be appreciated, while the second, equivalent repentance, has no real ability to change the divine-human relationship.[128]

Forsyth, together with Jonathan Edwards and McLeod Campbell, acknowledged the reality of God's wrath and the necessity of

---

[125] *Work*, pp. 148, 151.
[126] Campbell, *Nature of the Atonement*, p. 119, gives the reference to Edwards as *Satisfaction for Sin*, chap. 2.1–3.
[127] Campbell, *Nature of the Atonement*, p. 119.
[128] It is interesting to note that R. C. Moberly's son, a noted theologian in his own right, later took Forsyth's side in this debate. W. H. Moberly said that "we must distinguish within the conception of sacrifice between its primary aspect of sin-offering or propitiation and its secondary aspect as moral self-dedication." The latter aspect he identifies with the vicarious penitence theory advocated by his father, and quotes Forsyth's comment, "Penitence cannot undo, and Christ did," in support of his own argument. See W. H. Moberly, "The Atonement," in *Foundations: A Statement of Christian Belief in Terms of Modern Thought* (London: Macmillan, 1912), p. 303.

satisfaction, but then went on to make some subtle alterations to the classical theory. He rejected the need for equivalency, as we will see in the following chapter, and then went on to elucidate a carefully nuanced penal view of the atonement. In doing that, Forsyth employed some of Campbell's language about Christ's confession to good effect – but a confession not of sin, but of holiness. "He does not express the natural representative of the old humanity but creates the penitent faith of the new – 'the new man created unto holiness.'"[129]

4.2 THE CONFESSION OF HOLINESS

Turning from Forsyth's convictions about what the confession was not, he asserts more positively that the content of Christ's confession was "the holy God's repulsion of sin."[130] Only in Jesus Christ, Forsyth insists, can one know the scope and seriousness of sin. When God's holiness clashes with human sin, the awesome reality of God's perfect holiness and the full reality of sin's awfulness are revealed. And it is in that order: first the holiness, then the awareness of sin. In common with other Christians, Forsyth knew that from personal experience. To one audience he testified, "It also pleased God by the revelation of His holiness and grace . . . to bring home to me my sin."[131] The key in these quotations is the fact that it is the holiness of God that reveals the full seriousness of sin: "Only the absolutely holy can measure sin or judge it."[132]

Forsyth perceived that divine holiness shines a searching light on humanity, revealing a sinful nature, and therefore the critical need for salvation. Put succinctly, "It is holiness that makes sin sin."[133] Forsyth expands on this in his exposition of John 16.9 ("The Spirit will convince the world of sin, in that they believe not in Me."):

> Sin, you note, is not measured by a law, or a nation, or a society of any kind, but by a Person. The righteousness of God was not in a requirement, system, book, or Church, but in a Person, and sin is defined by relation to Him. He came to reveal not only God but sin. The essence of sin is exposed by the touchstone of His presence, by our attitude to Him. He makes explicit what the sinfulness of sin is; He even aggravates it. He rouses the worst as well as the best of human nature.

---

[129] *Work*, p. 210; the last words are from Ephesians 4.24.
[130] *Work*, p. 150.
[131] *Positive Preaching*, p. 282.
[132] *Justification*, p. 31.
[133] "Holy Father," in *Father*, p. 8.

> There is nothing that human nature hates like holy God. All the world's sin receives its sharpest expression when in contact with Christ; when, in face of His moral beauty, goodness, power, and claim, He is first ignored, then discarded, denounced, called the agent of Beelzebub, and hustled out of the world in the name of God.[134]

The rejection of Jesus Christ, then, is the epitome of sin, and in reference to his reality, God's holiness is known, and our sin measured. The holiness of God's love confronts "the egoism of human nature"[135] – and Christ is crucified again.

In the spiritual landscape Forsyth surveyed, such a strong sense of sin was the exception rather than the norm. "It is freely lamented in religious circles," he wrote toward the end of his life, "that no feature in the moral physiognomy of the day is more marked than the decay or absence of sin." The liturgical chorus is of "a general confession with the strong phrases pruned."[136] Forsyth, therefore, stressed his central conviction that Christ's confession of God's holiness reveals the effrontery sin offers to the Lord. As a result, the popular idea of sins as an accumulation of misdeeds must be superseded. Our concern is not merely sins, but sin.[137] Forsyth speaks of "the loving, unsparing moral realism of the New Testament" and "its sense of the sinfulness of sin rather than of the number of sins."[138] In one page, Forsyth uses words like "alienation" and "hostility" to describe the human situation; we are God's "antagonists"; most vividly, perhaps, he says, "As a race we are not even stray sheep, or wandering prodigals merely; we are rebels taken with weapons in our hands."[139]

The whole matter of sin can be described in terms of God's holiness. So, when the serious nature of sin comes home to individuals, it is a shocking realization not only of "the misery of moral impotence" and "the chagrin of perpetual failure," but of "our wound to the Holy. . . . The sting in sin is its wound to God, its stain to holiness."[140] In all of this, Forsyth's concern is to bring home to

---

[134] *Missions in State and Church*, pp. 56–57.
[135] *Socialism, the Church and the Poor* (1908), p. 28.
[136] "The Preaching of Jesus and the Gospel of Christ," p. 288.
[137] For a discussion of the implications of such a view for the Roman Catholic practice of the confessional, see *Rome, Reform and Reaction*, pp. 160–161.
[138] *The Principle of Authority*, 2nd ed. (1952; orig. pub. 1913), p. 45.
[139] *Positive Preaching*, p. 56.
[140] *Preaching of Jesus*, p. 3.

his hearers and readers the simple yet profound fact: "Sin is not a thing, it is a personal relation."[141]

In this attitude toward sin, once again Forsyth and Campbell share a common emphasis. Whether we say with Campbell that Christ confessed human sin and thereby exposed it to the holy judgment of God, or with Forsyth that Christ made the good confession of God's holiness in the face of sin's seriousness, the underlying conviction is the same: God in Christ reveals the true depth of human wrongdoing. The two theologians differ, however, in that one regards Christ's accomplishment as primarily a confession *of* sin, while the other sees it rather as a confession *about* sin, and God's holy response to human need.

There is nevertheless a striking similarity between McLeod Campbell's position, or at least a part of it, and Forsyth's view. When the earlier theologian says that "the feelings of the divine mind as to sin, being present in humanity [in Christ] and uttering themselves to God as a living voice from humanity, were the true atonement for the sin of humanity,"[142] we think of Forsyth's contention that Christ confessed God's holiness. The divine mind's view of sin is that of holy love acting to judge and save; on this both theologians would agree.

Moreover, Forsyth is willing to concede that the work of Christ confessed sin in some way. Although criticizing Campbell on this point, we note that Forsyth declines the opportunity to break the connection between Christ and confession of sins. His warnings are in relative terms. *The Nature of the Atonement*, he says, "speaks too much, perhaps, about Christ confessing human sin,"[143] and both McLeod Campbell and Moberly "come short" of the whole truth because "they do not get their eye sufficiently away from the confession of sin."[144] The explanation lies in the distinction already mentioned between what Christ does for us, and in us; Forsyth's meaning, then, would be that Christ confessed God's holiness for our justification, and then in the Spirit, confessed through the repentance of believers. "The confession, the revelation, the establishment of holiness in Christ's Cross is the only means for the due revelation and destruction of sin," which in turn "begets a conviction of sin and a repentance and confession of it, according to

---

[141] "The Preaching of Jesus and the Gospel of Christ," p. 300.
[142] Campbell, *Nature of the Atonement*, p. 124.
[143] *Work*, pp. 148, 149.
[144] *Cruciality*, p. 206.

our living faith. . . . And this is the only sense in which Christ could confess our sin."[145] To put it more succinctly, "our repentance was latent in that holiness of His which alone could and must create it."[146]

P. T. Forsyth and John McLeod Campbell share several theological distinctives: the close relationship of holiness and love, the attempt to balance these attributes in theological construction, a significant place for conscience, the stress on the finished work of Christ, the practical piety of the writing, etc.[147] But as we have seen significant differences remain concerning the nature of Christ's confession, and more broadly concerning the relation of justification and sanctification.

For Forsyth, then, the confession of God's holiness is the work of the holy Son. Being sinless, Jesus could not confess sin; nevertheless, he revealed the seriousness of sin in all its stark reality, signalled the need for an honourable and satisfactory remedy, and initiated and indeed accomplished the sacrificial work of atonement. Such a description, however, may leave the impression that it is enough for the Holy One to impress upon humanity the seriousness of sin, for the Son to acknowledge the Father's disagreement in principle with human pride and idolatry. But such a pronouncement, however solemn, well-meaning, and authoritative, makes no change in the situation. Humanity would still remain in sin, without hope of reconciliation. It is not merely a question of God's righteous attitude to sin, but of God's holiness in actually judging that sin. According to Forsyth, the content of Christ's confession of God's holiness was not merely a revelation, but a redemption. That matter of judgment will be a main concern of the following chapter; before that, however, we turn to note one further aspect of Christ's sacrifice, namely its context within the human situation.

5. "FROM SIN'S SIDE": THE HUMAN CONTEXT

There is a danger in examining the holiness of the Son and the holiness of the Father separately, as we have done in the previous two sections, because the reader may get the impression that these realities are somehow independent entities, detached from their

---

[145] "The Preaching of Jesus and the Gospel of Christ," p. 300.
[146] *Work*, p. 192.
[147] For further enumeration with references to *The Nature of the Atonement*, see W. L. Bradley, *P. T. Forsyth: The Man and His Work* (London: Independent Press, 1952), p. 102.

contexts. But the truth is exactly the opposite. It is precisely Jesus Christ, the sinless obedient Holy One, who confesses the holiness of God. Through Christ we know that holiness, and in him the holiness of God comes to saving effect. Similarly (and here we move to our present concern), Christ's holiness does not operate in a vacuum but operates *within the human context* in order to atone for sins. In this section, we will examine something of the way in which the divine holiness in Christ acts from within and for humanity. The death of Jesus Christ was "the offering of a holy self to a holy God *from sin's side.*"[148] As Hans Urs von Balthasar says, "The outstanding Congregationalist theologian P. T. Forsyth in his own way placed the heavenly sacrifice of the lamb at the nodal point where God and the world are joined in mutual relation."[149]

This is a profound truth in a twofold sense. First, Christ confessed God's holy judgment on sin "from amidst the deepest experience of it," that is, within the human sphere of activity and not from a distance. And second, that incarnational identification was "the experience not of a spectator but a victim."[150] It is certainly extraordinary that God should become part of our experience, but that was merely the beginning of the miracle, Forsyth believed; Christ went further, and underwent the judgment entailed by human sin. Not only was "the Word made flesh," but "the Son made sin."[151] The present section will explore in turn these two related aspects – identification with us and judgment of our sin – in Forsyth's treatment of Christ's humanity.

5.1 THE WORD MADE FLESH

Fundamentally, the incarnation meant God's self-identification with humanity in Jesus Christ: "He stood in the midst of human sin full of love to man, such love as enabled Him to identify Himself in the most profound, sympathetic way with the evil race."[152] Although Forsyth has in other places strong things to say about the inadequacy of mere sympathy, and the sentimentality of love alone, still there remains an important place for "a love which was as great as it was holy, ... which was as closely and sympathetically

---

[148] *Cruciality,* p. 182; italics added.
[149] Hans Urs von Balthasar, *Mysterium Paschale: The Mystery of Easter,* trans. Aidan Nichols (Edinburgh: T. & T. Clark, 1990), p. 35.
[150] *Work,* p. 206.
[151] *Positive Preaching,* p. 182.
[152] *Work,* p. 150.

identified with man as it was identified with the power of the holy God."[153] In standing beside us with the unique sympathy of the holy loving God, Jesus Christ made our context his own and identified with our need.

To go a step further, Forsyth makes it clear that solidarity was based on ontological identification with humanity, on Jesus in "His organic unity with us."[154] Jesus was "as truly of man as man is of nature. He was all men's creator in a true man's life."[155] Given Forsyth's acceptance of this reality, however, why are phrases such as these relatively rare in his writing? Arguments for the divinity of Christ are encountered more often than for his humanity. Moreover, when both are mentioned in the same context, Forsyth's purpose is usually to stress that Jesus was and is God, as in the characteristic assertion, "Christ is more precious to us by what distinguishes Him from us than by what identifies Him with us."[156] One critic goes so far as to say that Forsyth "makes Christ so unlike a human being that He has little in common with those He came to save."[157] And it must be admitted that in the present era when the divinity of Christ is over-emphasized, and docetic christology threatens a proper understanding of Christ's humanity, Forsyth's position seems inadequate.

Nevertheless, when Forsyth's views are considered in their own context, this criticism cannot stand. Forsyth's theological contribution was made during a time when evolutionary thinking had reduced Jesus to merely another figure in the developmental scheme of things, so that for many thinkers his humanity was the only certainty. Advances in biblical criticism emphasized the humanness of the documents, and of the authors of scripture. The movement to reconstruct the Jesus of history, from Reimarus in the eighteenth century to Strauss and Renan in the nineteenth, had championed the idea of a prophetic Jesus, to whom his impressed followers had mistakenly attributed divinity. In the light of such influences, Forsyth concluded, "We have no call to-day to prove the real manhood of Jesus. For that is universally owned; and [he adds poignantly] it is all that many can own."[158] We conclude that it is not surprising, then, that Forsyth does not stage a full-scale defence

---

[153] *Work*, p. 153.
[154] *Work*, p. 213.
[155] *Person*, p. 352.
[156] *Person*, p. 193.
[157] Bradley, *Forsyth: The Man and His Work*, p. 271.
[158] *Person*, pp. 327–328.

of Christ's human nature. Moreover, his distinctive and vigorously-argued kenotic christology highlights the very human limitations and weaknesses that Christ shared with humanity, taking them with utmost seriousness.

There is, we conclude, no serious defect in Forsyth's doctrine of Christ's humanity. As J. K. Mozley said, "P. T. Forsyth is one of the few great theologians who have refused to think about Christ in terms of the Two Natures' formula and yet have preserved the full value of the orthodox Christology."[159] Three factors must be held together "when we set out to consider the nature of God's union with man in Christ," says Forsyth: first, "the absoluteness, the freedom, of God," second, "the reality of [Christ's] human life, the conditions of its finitude, the necessity of growth," and third, the union of these two "in one historic personality – absolute God and relative man."[160] Although he considers that certain times demand emphasis on one aspect more than another, Forsyth does hold these aspects together.

It is important to remember at each point in the discussion the tendency of Forsyth's thought to emphasize the dynamic nature of God. Only rarely does he define Christ's human nature in ontological terms. More commonly, he allows the acted reality to define the concepts under discussion in this section, and the result is an active identity. Therefore, the place where we find Forsyth declaring and defending the real humanity of Christ is within a discussion of his work on our behalf, where he argues that not only is the atonement made by God through the Son of God, but it is also accomplished through Christ's humanity: "If Christ was the Son of man the reparation was made by man in Him. Christ was the new Humanity doing the one needful and right thing before God."[161]

There is a danger that combativeness regarding the emphasis of a particular aspect of the truth may occasionally lead to denial of a complementary aspect. We notice that tendency in Forsyth's presentation on this point. So strongly does he wish to emphasize the moral reality of the atonement that at times he risks giving up the very identification that makes the atonement efficacious. In one place he maintains that "the solidarity involved in His

---

[159] J. K. Mozley, "Christology and Soteriology," in *Mysterium Christi: Christological Studies by British and German Theologians*, ed. G. K. A. Bell and D. Adolf Deissmann (London: Longmans, Green, 1930), p. 183.
[160] *Person*, pp. 344–345.
[161] *Justification*, p. 169.

representation is due to His own act of self-identification and not to natural identity with us," and therefore "we need not get lost in discussing the metaphysic of it."[162] It would be wrong, however, to allow the wish to avoid unfruitful debate obscure Christ's real oneness with humanity, a principle Forsyth would also want to protect. The comment just quoted is, in fact, an uncharacteristic one, because Forsyth acknowledges a 'mystic' as well as a moral dimension to this subject: "When Christ died, all died. Dying with Christ is not a mere ethical idea, complete only as we succeed in doing it. It is a religious or mystic idea, which is ethical as taking effect in a holy act."[163] There is a metaphysical substratum to Forsyth thought, albeit not often acknowledged. As we pointed out much earlier,[164] the dynamic presumes the ontic, and no amount of minimizing it can eliminate it.

5.2 THE SON MADE SIN

Given Forsyth's conviction about Christ's 'organic unity' with humankind, we move now to advance the argument by attempting to be more precise about the meaning of God's self-identification with us in Christ. The Christian tradition has a variety of ways of making this point, and it will be useful to disentangle some of the key words. A key quotation from Forsyth follows:

> Whatever we mean, therefore, by substitution, it is something more than merely vicarious. It is certainly not something done over our heads. It is representative. Yet not by the will of man choosing Christ, but by the will of Christ choosing man, and freely identifying Himself with man. It is a matter not so much of substitutionary expiation (which, as these words are commonly understood, leaves us too little committed), but of solidary confession and praise from amid the judgment fires, where the Son of God walks with the creative sympathy of the holy among the sinful sons of men.[165]

From declarations such as these, we recognize that Forsyth is wary of a transactional view of vicarious sacrifice, not so much for what it asserts, but for what it neglects to say. Apparently, the view he rejects would see the atonement as an accomplishment that was disconnected from human involvement, yet an event essentially unfinished, awaiting human approval to make it complete. In such a

---
[162] *Work*, pp. 215–216.
[163] *Cruciality*, p. 53.
[164] See the discussion in Chapter 3, section 9.
[165] *Work*, pp. 225–226.

scheme, the real work of salvation would still have to be done. The vital ingredient in a truly substitutionary atonement, Forsyth believes, is the election in Jesus Christ of sinful humanity. Anything less puts the onus on individuals to decide for God quite apart from divinely-initiated action. God's autonomous act of grace in willingly identifying himself with sinful humanity pre-empts any proud assertion of human initiative in salvation. Forsyth is cautious, then, about the concept of substitution, because in the popular understanding, it includes both concepts he wishes to discard and others he wishes to maintain.

With such distinctions in mind, and this text from *The Work of Christ* in view, J. K. Mozley commented that "it is certainly not easy to penetrate to the heart of these ideas."[166] But it is important to press on deeper into Forsyth's substitutionary doctrine of the atonement, in order to understand more fully his view of God's holiness. While he wishes to avoid any suggestion that the atonement was an external transaction, Forsyth fills the word 'substitution' with considerable positive value, indicated by words like 'solidary' (an adjectival form of 'solidarity'), 'sympathy,' 'representative,' and 'identification.' Yet, these words lack something vital. 'Representative' can be misconstrued if it is too closely related to political democracies, whereas Christ is a king not dependent on those he represents for his power.[167] The idea of 'sympathy' can quickly turn to sentimentality. Words like 'surety' and 'guarantee' are inadequate, because they suggest mere assurance, and turn Christ into a broker.[168] What terms then can make sense of what Christ did and accomplished?

In a summary statement, P. T. Forsyth writes, "Reconciliation is effected by the representative sacrifice of Christ crucified; by Christ crucified as the representative of God on the one hand and of Humanity, or the Church, on the other hand." To be more specific, and for our purposes to go a step further in the exposition of Forsyth's view of substitution, "it was by Christ crucified in connection with the divine judgment."[169] The Saviour's work is not accomplished merely "from sin's side", but "from amid the judgment fires, where the Son of God walks with the creative

---

[166] J. K. Mozley, "The Theology of Dr. Forsyth," in *The Heart of the Gospel* (London: Society for Promoting Christian Knowledge, 1925), p. 84.
[167] *Work*, p. 210.
[168] *Work*, pp. 210–212.
[169] *Work*, pp. 145–146.

sympathy of the holy among the sinful sons of men.[170] Indeed, without this element of judgment, Christ's work would have been incomplete. In Christ's sacrificial death, divine holiness accentuates human sin, identifies with it personally and actively, and accepts, praises, and confesses the rightness of God's holy judgment on it.

In our examination of Forsyth's doctrine of the atonement in each of the previous sections of this chapter, we have met this aspect of judgment. In section 1, for example, we noticed the vital connection between the cross viewed as a victory and the divine judgment on evil and the evil one. In section 2, our dual focus was on the revelation of divine holiness in the sinless person of Jesus Christ, and the perfect enactment of that holiness in the obedient work of Christ. In our third section, we noted that the holiness of God encompassed not only his righteous attitude to sin but his effective judgment of it. Finally, in section 4, a similar point was made, namely, that to speak of a sacrifice made "from sin's side" is not only to affirm Christ's humanity but also his substitutionary act in relation to the judgment of God. On each occasion, we have considered the matter within its context, and developed the discussion of Forsyth's doctrine of the atonement to a certain point, but then delayed the larger enquiry. The time has now come to extend the lines of our argument specifically to the question of God's judgment. However, to do that in such a way as to honour the vital connections within his thought, we must no longer restrict our thinking to the divine holiness, but speak very specifically about a distinctive contribution from P. T. Forsyth's pen, the holy love of God.

---

[170] *Cruciality*, p. 182; *Work*, pp. 225–226.

Chapter Seven

The Centrality of Holy Love

Oh safe and happy shelter!
Oh refuge tried and sweet
Oh trysting-place, where heaven's love
And heaven's justice meet!
                    Elizabeth Cecilia Clephane

. . . with the grace uppermost.
                    P. T. Forsyth

In Chapter Five, we noticed that "the great, but much neglected, Scots theologian Peter Taylor Forsyth"[1] gave considerable prominence to the creating, covenanting, providing, and redeeming love of God. This love was revealed above all in Jesus Christ, the Son of the Father whose passionate intention was to save a world which had turned away from God. Forsyth accents that love as both the motivation for Christ's atoning death and the goal of his victorious sacrifice.

Then in Chapter Six, our concern shifted to the holiness of God, again revealed in Christ. As in the previous chapter, the discussion considered the divine holiness in relation to the human situation which Christ confronted and decisively changed in the work of his cross. Besides this emphasis on context, our attention was directed to both the sinless and obedient holiness of the Son, and the Son's confession of the Father's holiness.

---

[1] Kenneth Surin, *Theology and the Problem of Evil*, Signposts in Theology (Oxford: Basil Blackwell, 1986), p. 132.

Our study as a whole, and these two chapters in particular, have focused on two main concerns. From one perspective, the discussion has been concerned with the attributes of God, first in a general way and then more specifically as we looked at two of those divine qualities, love and holiness. At the same time, another agenda has been followed: we have been describing the doctrine of the atonement which P. T. Forsyth presents in extensive, although not systematic, detail. In the early chapters, we noticed that he sees the cross of Jesus Christ as the epistemological key; as he never tires of saying, revelation is redemption. Then in the two immediately preceding chapters, we have shown that God's love is the source and motivation of redemption, and God's holiness an integral element in the atonement.

This twofold agenda, with its contrasts between holiness and love and between divine attributes and the atonement, raises the question of whether these can exist harmoniously. Are there signs of strain in Forsyth's doctrine of the atonement, precisely in relation to these two attributes of love and holiness? To speak of the atonement in terms of God's love may give readers an understanding of the divine motivation for humanity's rescue, and may even lead them to praise the God who went to such lengths to accomplish salvation. Similarly, to speak of Christ's work in terms of God's holiness may leave hearers with an appreciation of the sinless purity of the Redeemer and perhaps even a sense of the seriousness of their sin. But to eschew one-dimensional perspectives and examine the work of Christ more comprehensively, in terms of both God's holiness and love, is to introduce the possibility of points of tension. To identify judgment as a key concept in the atonement, as we concluded in the last chapter, raises the dismaying prospect of a strife of attributes in the divine nature, and a conflict between the Father and the Son.

The purpose of the present chapter is to demonstrate Forsyth's conviction that there is no strife of divine attributes in the cross of Jesus Christ – that the judgment of the cross does not represent an inner clash in God's nature – and to show that central to the presentation of that conviction is his distinctive use of the expression 'the holy love of God.' Forsyth's repeated references to the divine love and holiness exhibit a calculated balance, which is worked out in his doctrine of the atonement. By interpreting the atonement in terms of God's holy love, he corrects and sometimes counters those theories that posit a conflict or tension in God's own nature as the object of Christ's atonement.

1. A STRIFE OF ATTRIBUTES?

That such a tension is a real possibility can be illustrated by noting some of the questions that arise as a result of our study so far. Against a background of God's overarching love, our consideration of holiness in the previous pages leads us to ponder some difficult queries. In section 3 of Chapter Six, for example, we saw that the holiness of the sinless Son was evidenced in his obedient work. But if there is an interpersonal dynamic involved between Jesus and his Father, a dynamic of divine command and answering obedience, does not Jesus' sense of doing God's will introduce a dangerous antinomy? What are we to make of the Son's obedience to the Father's command, if the result is suffering and judgment? Is it right that a *loving* God demands such far-reaching holiness, encompassing suffering and even death?

In Chapter Six, section 4, we noted Forsyth's conviction that Christ's work confessed the holiness of the Father. God is revealed as one who takes sin with utmost seriousness. When individuals are confronted with Christ's holy, loving work on their behalf, the holiness of the Son communicates to them the Father's judgment of their sin. But what sense are we to make of the fact that it is precisely in the death of Christ that this dynamic is initially shown? Is this an appropriate expression of the Father's holiness, or does it lie uncomfortably beside the love which the Father has for the Son?

And then in section 5 of the same chapter, we considered the human context of the atonement, and noted that the dynamic interaction of the incarnate holiness of Jesus and his Holy Father took place within as well as for humanity. The Word of God not only became flesh, in sympathetic solidarity with humankind, but (Forsyth contends) the Son who thus identified with us became sin. Christ died as a representative of sinners. But how can God's professed love for humanity be reconciled with the holy action of his judgment on sinners in the Son of his love?

If these questions arising from a consideration of Forsyth's doctrine of the atonement encourage us to look more closely at the question of whether there is a strife of attributes in the cross of Christ, a brief look at some historical examples makes the subject an urgent one. A popular conception of Christ's death had it that as a result of the loving death of Jesus on the cross, an angry God was changed into an accepting God. To characterize the atonement as a matter of judgment (as Forsyth does, although he also describes it as the work of God's love) is to risk turning God against God, the

Father against the Son, and holiness against love. Is this not an entirely unacceptable and immoral view that pits an angry divine holiness against a suffering divine love? And if we hold to the identity of Father and Son, is not the result a schizophrenic deity whose holiness lashes out at every sign of sin, but whose love desperately seeks to rescue humanity from that same sin? It seems inevitable that the contradiction must be eliminated by favouring one side or the other, leaving us with a God who is an intolerable tyrant, holy but not loving, or an indulgent and morally lackadaisical parent, loving but not holy. The result is a divided Trinity and a splintered divine nature.

John Stott, in the context of an argument that we will look at in more detail later, points out that such "crude interpretations of the cross" come in two varieties: "In the one case Christ is pictured as intervening in order to pacify an angry God and wrest from him a grudging salvation. In the other, the intervention is ascribed to God, who proceeds to punish the innocent Jesus in place of us the guilty sinners who had deserved the punishment."[2] Arguments of both sorts were in Forsyth's sights as he developed his doctrine of the atonement. They were all-too-easy to list as commonly heard during his time. F. W. Farrar, a fellow-contributor with Forsyth to the volume called *The Atonement in Modern Religious Thought,* cited several examples, and then drew the obvious conclusion:

When we read such lines as those of Sir Henry Wotton: –
> One rosy drop from Jesu's heart,
> Was worlds of seas to *quench God's ire,*

or as those of Dr. Watts: –
> Rich were the drops of Jesu's blood
> That *calmed God's frowning face,*
> That sprinkled o'er the burning throne,
> *And turned the wrath to grace:* –

or when we read such ghastly and revolting anthropomorphism as the phrase of Dr. Cumming, that Jesus "wiped away the red anger-spot from the brow of God"; – or of Professor Parkes, that "God drew His sword upon Calvary, and slew His only Son"; . . . when, I say, we read such phrases, they seem to be absolutely deplorable if they be placed side by side with the revelation that "God is Love," or with such passages as "I trust in the MERCY of God for ever and ever."[3]

---

[2] John R. W. Stott, *The Cross of Christ* (Leicester: Inter-Varsity, 1986), p. 150.

[3] F. W. Farrar, in *The Atonement in Modern Religious Thought: A Theological Symposium* (London: James Clarke, 1900), pp. 37–38. Farrar provides the emphasis in the quotations, but gives no further information about their original

Is Forsyth's doctrine of the atonement susceptible to this kind of interpretation? As we have seen in the previous chapter of this study, the lines of his soteriology converged at the point of judgment, and judgment is the crucial point of contention in theories that contain a clash of divine characteristics. Within a broad soteriological framework of victory, reconciliation, and sanctification, his central contention is that Christ's death is not only sacrificial, but expiatory, a self-offering judged satisfying by God. Within the human context, the interplay between Christ's obedient holiness and the Father's holy assessment of sin was marked by judgment. Is this 'interplay marked by judgment' really a euphemism for a conflict between God's love and holiness?

2. THE NOTE OF JUDGMENT

In contrast to those who took God's holiness less seriously and diminished the aspect of judgment in Christ's cross, Forsyth claimed that religion is impoverished "by reducing the idea of sin and dismissing the note of guilt."[4] Such a move is exactly the opposite of what is required, he believed. Modern humanity needs to face the reality of its alienation from God, and glimpse the decisive and finished work of Jesus Christ on its behalf. The gospel indicates that the holy God has dealt with the hard realities of an unholy humanity, and therefore, to excise holiness from the theological scheme of things is counter-productive: "It banishes from our Christian faith the one note which more than any other we have to-day come to need restored – the note of judgment."[5]

In a 1902 sermon with the title "Final Judgment Full Salvation," Forsyth expounded his convictions about sin, righteousness, and judgment. That sermon is for about half its pages a carefully organized exegetical treatment of John 16.9–11. Then a seamless transition leads to the second half of the paper, in which Forsyth expounds with characteristic passion and from a variety of perspectives the importance of judgment. The orderliness of the first part provides this beginning of a definition: "Judgment is not primarily punishment, nor is it a mere declaration of the state of the law, but it is the actual final establishment of righteousness upon the

---

source(s).
[4] *The Work of Christ* (1910), p. 229.
[5] *Work*, p. 229.

wreck of sin."[6] Even more important, perhaps, is the delineation of the text's three keywords in a Christocentric way. Forsyth portrays Christ declaring: "'I with My kingdom am the righteousness of God. To resist and renounce Me is sin. My victory is true judgment, and judgment begins at the house of God.'"[7] (This last phrase, it would seem, has been renovated by Forsyth, and in this context refers not only to the church but to Christ himself. As he repeats elsewhere, God took his own punishment.) From the beginning, Forsyth's treatment of judgment is centred on the positive accomplishment of Jesus Christ: the judgment in the cross leads to victory over sin and the establishment of righteousness.

Forsyth, then, does not minimize the reality of judgment in the cross, as some had done. It was his conviction that current theology had largely emptied of meaning the idea of judgment. Orthodoxy had postponed it to a fearsome last day (and then argued about the date), liberals rather vaguely located God's judgment in the flow of contemporary events, but our author points to the present tense of the verb in John 16.11 and takes another tack, which is his main concern, both here and elsewhere: "The Cross, I keep saying, is God's final judgment on the world."[8] Christ's death meant both victory and pardon – the defeat of Satan and the condemnation of evil, as well as the forgiveness of sins. These two, of course, are not discrete realities or separate outcomes, but aspects of the same sacrifice, with the victory over God's enemies a result of the judgment of sin in Christ. When Forsyth asserts that "the sin from which we are saved is a thing most damnable," and then adds that "by the judgment of God's holy love on our Redeemer, it is not only subdued, but (I speak with awe) it *is* damned – for ever,"[9] he asserts that the divine judgment extends across a wide range, from evil generally through specific sins to the devil himself.

For our purposes, it is important to note that this judgment on evil, sin, and the devil was accomplished through an historical incident, the death of Jesus Christ. It is impossible to separate the atoning meaning from the atoning event. So Forsyth says that on the cross "the judgment of our sins fell once for all on the Holy One

---

[6] *Missions in State and Church* (1908), p. 52.
[7] *Missions*, p. 53.
[8] *Missions*, pp. 72–73. The same point is discussed, for example, in *The Justification of God*, 2nd ed. (1948; orig. pub. 1916), p. 179.
[9] *Missions*, p. 76.

and the Just."[10] It is this stark reality, "the judgment of God's holy love on our Redeemer,"[11] that we have to come to grips with if we are to appreciate the problem of reconciling God's holiness and God's love. Without denying either present or future judgment,[12] Forsyth will not allow the offence of "the judgment death of Christ"[13] to be shifted away from the historical cross, either by diffusing the judgment throughout the historical process or postponing it to the eschatological future. Henceforth, by virtue of the cross, Jesus is now the criteria of judgment. "The wickedness of all the world was so judged on Christ that it is judged by Christ. It was so judged by His bearing of it that He mastered it, wielded it, and became by His Cross the Judge of all the earth."[14] Forsyth, therefore, makes judgment the central category for understanding the cross. However, when that much is said, we have not yet plumbed the depths of the seriousness of sin and judgment. This judgment involved profound spiritual and physical realities, which we now go on to explore.

3. GODFORSAKENNESS: THE TASTE OF SPIRITUAL DEATH

In considering Jesus of Nazareth, it is one thing to say that "he suffered death," while it is quite another to hold the conviction that "he [tasted] death for everyone" (Hebrews 2.9). Forsyth believed that the fact of Christ's death was a *significant* fact, with ramifications beyond the politically expedient sentence and the impromptu obituary notice. In a sermon on this text from the letter to the Hebrews, he attempted to explain the significance of Christ's sacrifice. "The whole efficacy of His death," Forsyth said, lay in the fact that "He experienced the worst of it, touched the bottom of it, nay, went under that. He felt the horror, the sordid horror of it, the Godforsakenness of it, the earthiness, the deadness of it. . . . He tasted the death in death, ... the death of the universal soul –

---

[10] *Missions*, p. 73.

[11] *Missions*, p. 76.

[12] The 'last judgment,' says Forsyth (in *Missions,* pp. 74–75), "is less coming than come. . . . All that is yet to come, with all its fearful expectation, is but the working out of that final and eternal solemnity which transpired when in the Cross of Christ the prince of this world was judged, and cast into the outer darkness."

[13] *Missions*, p. 101.

[14] *The Christian Ethic of War* (1916), p. 147; the point is elaborated on p. 158.

death eternal."[15] In the dramatic language of his sermon, Forsyth was bringing home the concrete reality of judgment. Nothing makes that point more strongly than the gospel narratives about the cross, and specifically Jesus Christ's cry of dereliction, "My God, my God, why have you forsaken me?" (Mark 15.34 and Matthew 27.46, quoting Psalm 22.1).

In considering Forsyth's interpretation of that godforsakenness, the first thing we notice is his determination to emphasize the horror of the Father's absence. Forsyth asks, "Did God not lay on Him the iniquity of us all, and inflict that veiling of His face which darkened to dereliction even the Redeemer's soul?" He tersely answers his own question: "The forsakenness is the worst judgment."[16] The awfulness of the cross was not to be minimized, and although our author's words are carefully chosen, they do not shrink from declaring the appalling theological truth of the Son forsaken by the Father.

Alongside this, however, Forsyth observes that Christ's response was continued trust and faithful obedience. "Yea, at the last the Father Himself grew silent to Him, and communion ceased, though faith and prayer did not."[17] Even though the sense of abandonment was palpable, the Lord Jesus could still cry out, "My God, *my* God. . . ." This faith in the absent God was no empty boast, no hollow shell of words, but resulted in "an obedience that did not fail even in the shadow of God's judgement, when, in a last crisis, the Son was denied the Father's power, communion, [and] aid. To obey and trust a God with His face hidden and His hand stayed, to accept in loving faith such a will of God, was, for the Son of God, the height of all obedience, trust, and love."[18]

Beside the fact of God's absence, it is important to place Forsyth's contention that nevertheless and at the same time, the Father was always present. This paradoxical conclusion is memorably illustrated when Forsyth describes the Son's dereliction in terms of "losing the Father's face (but not the Father)."[19] In the darkness of God's judgment on sin, Jesus lost conscious contact with

---

[15] "The Taste of Death and the Life of Grace" (1900), in *God the Holy Father* (1957), pp. 51–52.

[16] *Work,* p. 243.

[17] "The Holy Father" (1896), in *Father,* p. 21.

[18] *The Preaching of Jesus and the Gospel of Christ* (1987; orig. pub. as articles in 1915), p. 72.

[19] *Preaching of Jesus,* p. 20.

his Father, but on another level, the connection was unsevered. Elsewhere Forsyth explains, "God never left Him, but He did refuse Him His face." Then, apparently forgetting that previously he had spoken of the dereliction as the time when communion failed, he adds: "The communion was not broken, but its light was withdrawn."[20] Despite the terminological inconsistency, Forsyth's intent is clear: to affirm both the reality of the abandonment and the continuity of the Father-Son relation. In a more synthetic way, Forsyth maintained that "the dereliction was Christ's sense of the certainty but the elusiveness of the Holy Love."[21] The cry of dereliction revealed Christ's conviction that the holy, loving God was both real and hidden. The certainty was reflected in Christ addressing the Father, the elusiveness in his very real sense of God's absence.

The reality of godforsakenness prompts the question of its meaning, its inner content. What is God's reaction to the Sinbearer? "The truth is," maintained the Puritan Thomas Goodwin, whom Forsyth particularly admired, "it was an evidence of God's anger."[22] No, said Forsyth, the Father's silence "was not the Father's anger but His holy love, unspeakable by word or look, to be uttered only by deed, by Resurrection."[23] The holy love of God bound Father to Son, and Son to Father, even in the extremity of the cross. God's love was a continuing reality; it never ceased. At the same time, God's holiness judged sin. The holy love of God issued in saving wrath.

To explain this, Forsyth employed two distinctions. The first is the contention that "God could be wroth with the world and yet gracious and loving to individuals."[24] Although he buttresses his argument for this distinction with a plausible comparison to a political party and its members, the party incurring one's anger while its members still command respect, and with a measured

---

[20] *Work*, p. 243; cf. *The Cruciality of the Cross*, 1st ed. (1909), p. 73.

[21] "The Preaching of Jesus and the Gospel of Christ," *Expositor*, 8th series, vol. 25 (April 1923): 308.

[22] Thomas Goodwin, *Works*, 5: 194, quoted in Ronald S. Wallace, *The Atoning Death of Christ*, Foundations for Faith, ed. Peter Toon (Westchester, Illinois: Crossway Books, 1981), p. 101. On Forsyth's regard for Goodwin, see "Ministerial Libraries: V. Principal Forsyth's Library at Hackney College," *British Monthly* (May 1904), p. 270, and *Faith, Freedom, and the Future* (1912), pp. 117–119, 148–149.

[23] "Holy Father," in *Father*, p. 23.

[24] *Work*, p. 119.

rejection of religious individualism, Forsyth's comment is unconvincing. It fails to address the real problem, which is the apparent inner conflict in God if the Father's anger is directed toward his own Son. Given the representative function of Christ, to be angry at the world is to be wrathful to Jesus himself.

The second distinction which Forsyth mentions from time to time, though he never elaborates it in a systematic way, is quite similar to the first, namely that God is angry at human sin, but loving toward individual sinners. Although this distinction preserves the truth that created humanity retains the image of God, sinners and their sins are not easily separated. While usefully distinguishable in theory, sinners are persons who sin, and the wrongdoing cannot be pried away from the wrongdoer. In the same way, Jesus so identified himself with the sin of humanity on the cross (as we saw previously in our discussion of Christ made sin) that it would seem to be impossible to claim that God was angry at the sin, while the Sinbearer remained unaffected by the divine wrath. Being and act are inseparable, influencing each other in an integral unity.

While these two distinctions preserve important truths, they are not entirely satisfactory. We see Forsyth wrestling with this problem, and pointing to a more satisfactory solution, in the Addendum to *The Work of Christ*.[25] His starting-point there is yet another distinction, made earlier in the book, that "the wrath of God is not to be taken as a pathos or affection, but as the working out of His judgment in a moral order."[26] On further reflection, Forsyth avers that he wishes to avoid both extremes: the divine anger was not the expression of a passionate temper, nor was it an impersonal and mechanistic process. Instead, "there was in Christ's suffering the element of personal displeasure and infliction."[27] A comparison with human experience of God's anger reveals that such suffering is not exclusively from human causes, but an expression of the divine judgment. "Well, if it be so, that God's direct displeasure and infliction is the worst thing in sin's penalty, did the displeasure totally vanish from the infliction when Christ stood under it?"[28] J. K. Mozley points out that Forsyth's intention in this "important"

---

[25] Quotations from the six-page Addendum are difficult because fully two-thirds of the sentences are phrased in the interrogative. This indicates that Forsyth wants to assert his point with some delicacy. Though not uncertain of his intention, he wishes to tread carefully through the paradoxes and possibilities.
[26] *Work*, p. 239; see p. 118.
[27] *Work*, p. 240.
[28] *Work*, p. 243.

passage is to answer that question in the negative, and to press home "to its furthest conclusion" the assertion that "the judgment of God was on Christ, and not only through Christ on us."[29]

How can this be? Isn't this a contradiction of Forsyth's contention that there is no strife of attributes in God's nature? Forsyth replies, first, that such a conclusion fails to define God's anger carefully enough. "To begin with," he writes, "the anger of God means a great deal more than His passion, His temper, His mode of feeling, more than anger as an affection."[30] Instead, it is connected with "the sure changelessness of God's moral nature."[31] The wrath of God is not capricious, and carries no vindictiveness or hostility. Because "the judgment of God is perfectly compatible with His continued love,"[32] Christ could experience God's holiness in a genuinely personal way. To put it plainly, "The anger of God as the anger of love is without hate."[33] Love and hate are indeed incompatible and conflicting opposites; love and holiness can exist harmoniously in one nature.

The second element in Forsyth's defence is that a conflict of God's attributes in the atonement depends to a large extent on the way in which the Son perceives and receives the Father's anger at human sin. The cross was not an imposition on the Son, but a sacrifice willingly undertaken. So Forsyth asks rhetorically, "Did the complete obedience and reparation not include the complete acceptance of God's displeasure as an essential factor in the curse?"[34] Yes, and that acceptance was uncoerced, given graciously by God who willingly offered his own self for love's sake. Further, the gift of the Father is also the gift of the Son: "He accepted the divine situation – the situation of the race before God. By God's will He did so. By His own free consent He did so."[35]

Forsyth's third response to the suggestion that if Christ felt the Father's displeasure at human sin a dichotomy develops between God's holiness and love, is to stress the context of the Father-Son

---

[29] J. K. Mozley, *The Doctrine of the Atonement* (London: Gerald Duckworth, 1915), p. 186, note 1, quoting *Positive Preaching and [the] Modern Mind*, 1st ed. (1907), p. 314.
[30] *Work*, p. 118.
[31] *Work*, p. 239.
[32] *Work*, pp. 118–119.
[33] *Christian Ethic of War*, p. 185.
[34] *Work*, p. 243.
[35] *Work*, p. 150.

relationship. Just as the atonement was directed towards changing the relationship between God and humanity, Christ's experience of the wrath of God was not abstract but within a relational context. "What Christ bore was not simply a sense of the connection between the sinner and the impersonal consequences of sin, but a sense of the sinner's relation to the personal *vis-à-vis* of an angry God."[36] In other words, Christ's experience of the broken divine-human relationship, signified most poignantly in the cry of dereliction, led to the healing and reconciling of that relationship. God's involvement in the human situation occurred within the relationship between the Father and the Son. Here we return to the important idea of Christ's obedience: his will was one with the Father's will, and the result was at-one-ment.

In the cry of dereliction, we face the utter awfulness of the reality of judgment, and see the problem of the strife of attributes in its starkest terms. In striving to understand it, however, and examining Forsyth's arguments in relation to it, we begin to hear his contention that there is no strife of attributes in the cross. Although these comments in *The Work of Christ* (and particularly in the Addendum) are sometimes spoken tentatively, they are nevertheless profound. Forsyth accents the reality of judgment in the cross, and illustrates that in his discussion of the cry of dereliction. At the same time, in his considerable stress on the holiness of God, he refuses to reduce God's character to holiness, nor does he allow that holiness a more fundamental place than God's love. Similarly, he does not place love in a higher position and relativize divine holiness. Instead, he maintains the close relation between these two attributes, while insisting that they work together as God's holy love. That term is a key concept in Forsyth's contention that in the atoning cross all God's attributes work together in harmony.

4. THE GRAMMAR OF HOLY LOVE

We have already considered in detail the prominent place Forsyth gives to God's love among the divine characteristics (Chapter Five), and his equally strong conviction that the atonement makes no sense without sustained attention to God's holiness (Chapter Six). That concentration on divine holiness is so impressive that some have seen an imbalance in Forsyth's thought at this point.[37] And it

---

[36] *Work*, p. 243.
[37] This problem was given some consideration in Chapter Five, section 3.

must be granted that Forsyth is effusive in his praise of the holiness of God: "It is the first thing in God, His very being. His love is divine only because it is holy."[38] That quotation continues at length and in similar vein, as does Forsyth from beginning to end of his mature theological writing. Two further striking quotations will suffice to illustrate this, the first from the powerful sermon that first brought him widespread public regard:

> You can go behind love to holiness, but behind holiness you cannot go. It is the true consuming fire. Any real belief in the Incarnation is a belief in the ultimacy, centrality, and supremacy of holiness for God and man. We may come to holiness by way of love, but we only come to love by reason of holiness.[39]

Similarly, in a book written twenty years later, he says bluntly that theocentric religion "means the absolute supremacy of the holy."[40]

In addition to our comments previously about Forsyth's alleged undervaluation of God's love, a charge we believe to be not only unproven but also for the most part wrong,[41] there are several factors that account for Forsyth's impressive stress on God's holiness. His choice of the work of Christ as the centre of attention for several of his books, and the fact that the atonement is hardly ever far from view in the rest of his authorship, is part of the reason. While love is the context and the goal of the atonement, when one looks into the heart of the gospel, Forsyth insisted that "the holiness of God is a deeper revelation in the cross than His love."[42] Another significant reason for this stress on holiness arises from the theological context of his time. As we have seen, polemical considerations prompted Forsyth to stress the importance of God's holiness, both to liberals who tended to neglect it and to the representatives of Calvinistic orthodoxy who were more likely to absolutize it. Whatever his motivation, however, it is our contention in this section that alongside a high view of God's holiness, Forsyth places an equally high regard for God's love. He indicates this precisely through his constant inclusion of God's love with the divine holiness.

This claim may come as a surprise because there is no doubt that it was the divine holiness that occupied a greater proportion of

---

[38] *Justification*, pp. 128–129.
[39] "Holy Father," in *Father*, p. 5.
[40] *Justification*, p. 107.
[41] See Chapter Five, section 3.
[42] *Cruciality*, p. 205.

Forsyth's attention. He never shied away from any opportunity to rehabilitate the place of holiness in the church's theology and especially in its soteriology, because it was his conviction that "the greatest human need is not only holy *love,* but *holy* love."[43] Nevertheless, as the careful "not only" in the previous sentence can testify, his intention is to accord theological equality to the love of God.

In the quotations above which illustrated the supremacy of holiness, and in many others which make the same point, Forsyth's concern is not to champion one attribute among many, but to ensure that *both* love and holiness are given serious theological consideration. Despite his predominant focus on God's holiness, it is a notable fact that many of his references to this divine attribute speak of it in the context of God's love. For example he asks, how can we be sure that God's love "may not one far day succumb to some dark but mightier fate behind all?" The answer we need has been given in Christ's cross: "The revelation we need is not simply, God is love: it is the invincibility of that love by any other power that might rise against it; it is its ultimacy as the last reality."[44] What is at stake here is any diminishment of God's full reality. Repeatedly, Forsyth considered God's love in terms of God's holiness – holiness is the "intrinsic greatness of love;"[45] sanctity is the texture of love,[46] and so on. He never tired of describing love in terms of holiness. Sometimes the limited supply of divine attributes, dressed variously in adjectives and nouns, tumble around each other, but more often Forsyth's precise writing makes them dance in the cause of greater clarity and understanding: "The deeper the revelation *of* the love, the deeper is the holiness revealed *in* that love; and we are delivered from the wrath of God, *i.e.* His Holy judging demand, only by the gracious act of His holy atoning love."[47]

The simple observation that arises from these examples of Forsyth's marriage of holiness and love is the same one a student of grammar might make when considering Forsyth's phrase, 'the holy love of God.' Forsyth accords love the emphasis of a noun, while holiness is commonly given the place of an adjective. Both in his

---

[43] *Cruciality,* p. 168.
[44] "The Reality of God: A War-time Question," *Hibbert Journal* 16 (July 1918): 609.
[45] *The Person and Place of Jesus Christ* (1909), p. 68.
[46] *The Church and the Sacraments,* 2nd ed. (1947; orig. pub. 1917), p. 94.
[47] *The Principle of Authority,* 2nd ed. (1952; orig. pub. 1913), p. 119.

repeated inclusion of holiness's characteristics in love's nature, and in his use of the holy love formulation, Forsyth puts holiness as a modifier to love. This observation is not to imply that Forsyth reduces holiness to a secondary place, but rather to point out that he refuses to downgrade the first class status of love as an attribute of God. Indeed, the combined effect of (1) stressing love by giving it grammatical pride of place and (2) stressing holiness by concentrated discussion, is to emphasize the equal importance of these two attributes of God.

This brief exploration into grammatical analysis, although it accurately describes Forsyth's use of words and of larger phrases, is consistent with his general view of God's attributes. Among the divine characteristics, no one attribute is more important than another; each describes one aspect of God's nature. These words like holiness and love describe facets of God's character revealed in Jesus Christ, a person who cannot be divided but must be considered in his personal integrity. "Christ reveals to us God's holy love,"[48] claims Forsyth, and so it is with Christ that any discussion of divine attributes properly begins. It is futile to determine an order, a hierarchy between love and holiness; instead, each attribute can contribute to a greater understanding of God.

It will be apparent from what has been said already that Forsyth's position is best construed as a distinctive mediating view. Earlier, we considered three positions on this matter among Forsyth's interpreters.[49] We conclude that Forsyth does not champion the preeminence of God's holiness (as Samuel Mikolaski affirmed), nor does he support the view that would see holiness as an aspect of God's love (as Gwilym Griffith asserts). Instead, he takes a third way (as Robert McAfee Brown and John Rodgers confirm) and emphasizes the importance of both attributes by means of his distinctive formulation, the 'holy love' of God. Or, to put the matter in another way, in terms of the debate between Nels Ferré and Kenneth Hamilton,[50] Ferré is wrong to try and 'annex the kingdom of holiness to the kingdom of love,' while Hamilton in rebuttal is perhaps not careful enough to avoid the suggestion that the opposite would be a better arrangement. For his part, Forsyth takes a vigorous mediating position. In the atonement, it was not

---

[48] "Faith, Metaphysic, and Incarnation," *Methodist Review* 97 (September 1915): 713.
[49] See Chapter Two, section 3.
[50] See Chapter Two, section 4.

God's holiness demanding a sacrifice, or God's love providing it, but God's holy love sending and sacrificing for the sake of humanity.

5. THE HARMONY OF GOD'S ATTRIBUTES

Forsyth uses this distinctive combination of words, 'the holy love of God,' to express the unity of God's gracious love and his judging holiness, his positive regard for and redeeming judgment of the world. 'Holy love' encapsulates an important theological point he wishes to make. The Father was always well-pleased with the Son; this was true even when the Father's holiness was expressed in terms of judgment in Christ's cross. At one and the same time, God expressed his love for humanity represented in Christ and his holy concern to take sin with divine seriousness. In the cross, God's holy love is revealed in action, integrated in a decisive event.

Forsyth realized that to combine an emphasis on judgment with a prominent place for divine love raised a serious theological problem. In *The Justification of God,* after speaking of the reality of judgment, he adds: "Yet how does it comport with grace? Is the gracious God judge at all in His grace? How can Christ be at once the living embodiment of the moral law (and so both standard and judge) and also the living grace of God and the agent of reconcilement?"[51] Forsyth responds to these questions with the conviction that God's reconciliation of humanity in Christ was accomplished by a God at one with himself. In Christ, those attributes were in harmony; in his reconciling cross, the holy love of God was revealed and humanity redeemed. To illustrate this crucial collection of concepts, and to bring out further his distinctive contribution, we propose to compare Forsyth's view of God's holy love with a contemporary writer who knows his thought well.

5.1 THE PROBLEM OF FORGIVENESS

In their common passion to preach the atoning cross, P. T. Forsyth and the modern British expositor John R. W. Stott have a great deal in common, a fact that Stott acknowledges in his book *The Cross of Christ* by quoting approvingly from Forsyth about as often as he quotes Calvin, and more often than all others except Anselm and Luther. The similarities between the two will not be our primary concern, however. Instead, by comparing them closely on a

---

[51] *Justification,* p. 179.

specific point of contention – what Stott calls 'the problem of forgiveness' – our hope is to show more clearly how Forsyth maintains the harmony of God's attributes.

We begin the comparison of Forsyth's and Stott's treatments of the attributes of God in the atonement with a common quotation, which introduces a common conviction. The last words of the German poet and essayist Heinrich Heine were: "Le bon Dieu me pardonnera; c'est son métier" – "The good God will forgive me; it's his business."[52] Both theologians use the quotation as a springboard from which to launch into a discussion of the problem of forgiveness. Their common conviction is that God cannot ignore human sinfulness, as Heine presumed, but must consider his holiness as seriously as his love. My contention is that Forsyth and Stott, despite the convictions they share, and despite their common language about God's holy love, nevertheless perceive the problem differently and therefore diverge in their understanding of the solution. Between problem and solution stands a fundamentally different conception of the attributes of God, and of the atonement.

In a chapter devoted to "the problem of forgiveness," Stott argues that it is "constituted by the inevitable collision between divine perfection and human rebellion, between God as he is and us as we are." But the problem does not stop there, he says. "The obstacle to forgiveness is neither our sin alone, nor our guilt alone, but also the divine reaction in love and wrath toward guilty sinners."[53] This is precisely the problem which Forsyth sees, namely "the tragic conflict of man's egoism with God's purpose of holy love," and, he continues, "the crisis of that issue is the decisive Cross of Christ, decisive for all mankind and for all eternity."[54] The death of Jesus was the collision between God's passionate saving love and our rebellious insistence to go it alone, between the exacting divine holiness and our prideful disobedience. For both Forsyth and Stott, the problem of forgiveness was the clash between holy love and sin.

This is a problem to be seen in relational terms, and the solution must take both God and humanity into account. It is not merely 'the problem of sin,' but the problem of a broken relationship between the God who created humanity for communion with himself, and a race of individuals whose sin shattered that communion. In this too, Stott speaks for Forsyth:

---

[52] See Stott, *Cross of Christ*, p. 87.
[53] Stott, *Cross of Christ*, p. 88.
[54] *Authority*, p. 202.

We have located the problem of forgiveness in the gravity of sin and the majesty of God, that is, the realities of who we are and who he is. How can the holy love of God come to terms with the unholy lovelessness of man? What would happen if they were to come into collision with each other? The problem is not outside God; it is within his own being. Because God never contradicts himself, he must be himself and "satisfy" himself, acting in absolute consistency with his own character.[55]

Following Forsyth, Stott uses the holy love formulation (crediting Forsyth as the one "who coined – or at least popularized – the expression 'the holy love of God'"[56]), and utilizes the language of satisfaction in the sense of personal consistency. Both theologians are concerned that the church's theological explanation of this problem have integrity.

However, an additional theme runs through John Stott's description of the problem, and here the ways diverge. Stott believes that the problem of forgiveness consists in three aspects: first, God must overcome the obstacle of sin; secondly, he must do it in a way that is consistent with his own nature; and thirdly, he must also overcome the practical opposition between the conflicting claims of his own holiness and love. The solution to this threefold problem is Christ's substitutionary death for sinners. Stott writes:

At the cross in holy love God through Christ paid the full penalty of our disobedience himself. He bore the judgment we deserve in order to bring us the forgiveness we do not deserve. On the cross divine mercy and justice were equally expressed and eternally reconciled. God's holy love was 'satisfied.'[57]

In the penultimate quotation, Stott stated, "The problem is not outside God; it is within his own being." In this quote, the key phrase is that God's "mercy and justice were . . . eternally reconciled." John Stott sees both the soteriological problem and solution as comprised in part by an inner divine conflict. Such a position finds no parallel in Forsyth's writings. For Stott, God's nature must be adjusted if humankind is to be forgiven. The earlier theologian, by contrast, was convinced that God's disposition toward us didn't need to be changed; God's love for humanity was constant. In the relation of attributes and atonement, these two theologians see matters differently. The crucial difference is that for Stott, the problem of forgiveness involves a clash within God's own nature.

---

[55] Stott, p. 133.
[56] Stott, p. 131.
[57] Stott, p. 89.

5.2 THE BIBLICAL UNDERPINNING OF THE DEBATE

Forsyth disagreed. Although many instances of his argumentation could be quoted, an interesting and concise version of it appears in his published sermons. Sometime in early 1911, we may reasonably conjecture, this preacher-theologian discovered a text that wasn't really a text. But these words so appealed to him that those who read the sermons that resulted, and come across the more incidental treatment of this text elsewhere in his writings, can still sense the impact they made on Forsyth. The text in question was the deuterocanonical Ecclesiasticus 2.18, which speaks of the Lord in these terms: "as his majesty is, so is his mercy." After quoting the passage in the *London Quarterly Review,* Forsyth exclaims, "What a phrase! What an inspiration! To be in the Apocrypha too, outside the pale of reputable inspiration! There is no such mighty miracle anywhere as the union of God's most holy majesty and His most intimate mercy."[58] In much the same way as Calvin's attention had been arrested by Psalm 145 when he discussed the divine attributes in the *Institutes,*[59] this simple line from Ecclesiasticus captivated Forsyth's attention. On 30 April 1911, he preached on this text (albeit with Psalm 57.10 standing usefully nearby), and began by explaining that he had come across these "magnificent words" as a wonderful discovery.[60] Then, holding the text to the light, and slowly turning it like a fine diamond, Forsyth examined the majesty and mercy of God from various angles. As the sermon progressed, he wove those two attributes together with others: love expressed in mercy, and the majesty of holiness. Far from there being any strife of attributes in the divine nature, he concluded, all these are united and harmonized in Christ and his cross. "Therefore, as is His holy majesty, so is His endless mercy in the grace of Jesus Christ."[61]

---

[58] "The Soul of Christ and the Cross of Christ," *London Quarterly Review* 116 (October 1911): 209.

[59] John Calvin, *Institutes* 1.10.2.

[60] "Majesty and Mercy," *Christian World Pulpit* 79 (17 May 1911): 305.

[61] "Majesty and Mercy," p. 307. In addition, Forsyth preached on this text at a weekday evening service at Hackney College; see "Remember the Majesty of Mercy," among the "Manuscript Addresses to Students" preserved in Harry Escott, *P. T. Forsyth and the Cure of Souls: An Appraisement and Anthology of his Practical Writings* (London: George Allen & Unwin, 1970), pp. 121–122. For other references to this text, see *Revelation Old and New: Sermons and Addresses* (1962), p. 21, *Authority,* p. 182, and *Justification,* p. 121. A reference in *Positive Preaching,* p. 354, indicates he knew the phrase earlier; his

The convictions about the attributes of God that were crystallized in Ecclesiasticus 2.18 are repeated in many other places within Forsyth's authorship, and buttressed with the exegetical support of several other texts. He marshalls evidence from both Old and New Testaments to show that God's nature is a unity of various attributes. In 1 John 1.9 for example, God's multifaceted nature is seen as the source of reconciliation: "He is faithful and just to forgive us our sins." To the same effect, Forsyth quotes Isaiah 45.21, where the Lord is described as "a just God and a Saviour."[62] In addition to these scripture references, Forsyth's repeated use of the phrase 'the holy love of God' indicates the unity of two attributes held closely together.

All of this discussion of God's majesty and mercy and of his holy love receives its theoretical undergirding from Forsyth's view that an attribute is not "something loose within God which He could manipulate," but "God Himself, unchangeable God, in certain relations."[63] The resulting notion is of a personal God with various characteristics, hence the conclusion: "There can therefore be no strife of attributes."[64]

John Stott challenges these conclusions: "Was P. T. Forsyth correct in writing that 'there is nothing in the Bible about the strife of attributes'? I do not think he was."[65] In a chapter called "Satisfaction for Sin," Stott examines that concept from various angles, and concludes that "'satisfaction' is an appropriate word, providing we realize that it is [God] himself in his inner being who needs to be satisfied, and not something external to himself."[66] God's way of reconciling humanity, therefore, must satisfy his character; the enacted atonement must be consistent with the divine attributes. So far Forsyth would agree. But Stott goes on to argue that within this context it is nevertheless consistent to see "a divine 'problem' or 'dilemma' on account of this conflict" of attributes.[67]

---

comments in "Majesty and Mercy," p. 305, allow the possibility that his "discovery" of the text was indeed a rediscovery.

[62] *Revelation Old and New*, pp. 26–27; we will return later to another implication of this text.

[63] *Work*, p. 117. This contention is considered in some detail in Chapter Four above.

[64] *Work*, p. 118.

[65] Stott, p. 129.

[66] Stott, p. 123.

[67] Stott, p. 129.

Having noted Forsyth's exegetical support for a unitive view of God's attributes in the preceding paragraphs, we turn now to examine Stott's evidence for a strife of attributes in God's nature. The question that must be answered is put this way: "When we thus distinguish between the attributes of God, and set one over against another, and even refer to a divine 'problem' or 'dilemma' on account of this conflict, are we not in danger of going beyond Scripture?"[68] In reply, Stott gives prominent first place to an exposition to Hosea, chapter 11; he concludes from his examination of the passage: "Here surely is a conflict of emotions, a strife of attributes, within God," "a struggle between what Yahweh *ought* to do because of his righteousness and what he *cannot* do because of his love," "an inner tension."[69] Then Stott elaborates "this 'duality' within God" by means of a scriptural catena which contrasts God's grace and punishment, his wrath and love. In each contrast, "two complementary truths about God are brought together, as if to remind us that we must beware of speaking of one aspect of God's character without remembering its counterpart."[70]

Because these passages of scripture provide the justification for much of the argument that follows, it is important to be precise about Stott's intentions. Two quite different conclusions are drawn from this material. The first is that God's nature can be fairly described as a 'duality' of holiness and love; the second is that this duality creates a problem, dilemma, or conflict. For Stott, the Hosea passage illustrates "a conflict of emotions, a strife of attributes, within God," while the subsequently quoted catena is intended to bolster that argument. In fact, the nine excerpts – stretching comprehensively from Exodus through the Psalms and prophets to the gospels, Paul, and John – do not speak of any inner conflict in the divine nature, but instead bear impressive witness to Stott's other concern, the multifaceted nature of God. There is no suggestion in these texts that God may be inconsistent, either in himself or toward us, nor is there any indication from the texts themselves that these apparent opposites are problematic. For example, John speaks of the incarnate Lord who is "full of grace and truth" as one who embodies both of those attributes, precisely within the context of the Word made flesh (John 1.14); Paul says that "the kindness and sternness of God" is experienced variously, depending

---

[68] Stott, p. 129.
[69] Stott, p. 130.
[70] Stott, p. 130.

on one's circumstances (Romans 11.22); and Ephesians 2.3–4 asserts, with no trace of tension, both the reality of divine wrath and the love of "God, who is rich in mercy." Indeed, several of these texts stress that the duality in God's nature is a harmonious one. Exodus 34.6–7 pictures God's love issuing in forgiveness at the same time as the guilty are not left unpunished, while Psalm 85 says that love, faithfulness, righteousness, and peace are divine realities given to God's people, realities so closely related that they can be said to "meet together" and "kiss each other." Indeed, some of the very same passages, including Isaiah's description of Yahweh as "a just God and a Saviour" (45.21), are quoted by Forsyth to support his own view that there is no strife of attributes in God.[71]

If this view of the proffered scriptural catena of proof is correct – that it provides biblical warrant for the duality of God's nature but not for a strife of divine attributes – then we are turned back to look more closely at the text with which Stott's discussion begins, Hosea 11. Here, as in many places in scripture, the variegated personality of God is shown, and the contrast between God's tender love and fierce anger is especially sharp. In vss. 1–7, the Lord's soliloquy alternates between examples of his love shown in practical ways, and of Israel's disobedience which deserves divine punishment. The parental love that rescued the young Israel from Egyptian slavery was answered with idolatrous apostasy (vss. 1–2). God's providential care for the fledgling nation was met with an uncomprehending gaze (vss. 3–4). Therefore, because Israel turned away from God and would not repent, God's punishment was prepared (vss. 5–7). But the love which acted in the past to save and sustain is not exhausted, and even in the face of his son's sin, the Lord takes another approach:

> My heart is changed within me;
> all my compassion is aroused.
> I will not carry out my fierce anger,
> nor will I turn and devastate Ephraim.
> For I am God and not man. . . . (vss. 8–9).

In Forsyth's terms, even this is not a conflict of attributes, but rather proves the point even more dramatically that anger and compassion, holiness and love, can coexist in the same personality.

---

[71] For Isaiah 45.21, see *Work*, p. 118; for Romans 11.22, see *Positive Preaching*, p. 314, and *Cruciality*, p. 89.

What Hosea describes is not an ultimate contradiction, but a realistic appreciation of God's multifaceted nature.[72]

At the same time, it is helpful to recognize that the language of changed heart and kindled compassion is anthropomorphic and metaphorical. In his commentary on Hosea, James Luther Mays points out that such anthropomorphism is more like analogy than definition, enabling Hosea to represent Yahweh's thoughts and feelings as human, and therefore comprehensible. "But [the Lord] transcends the metaphor, is different from that to which he is compared, and free of all its limitations," continues Mays. "He is wrathful and loving *like* man, but *as* God."[73] God's personality is living and dynamic, and characterized by a wide range of emotional response, and the Father is not so quickly stymied as a human parent might be. Stott compares this passage to the dilemmas of parenthood: "All parents know . . . what it means to be 'torn apart' by conflicting emotions, especially when there is a need to punish the children."[74] But the Lord is "slow to anger, abounding in love" (Psalm 103.8), and his resources to deal with his disobedient children are both endless and infinitely creative. The conflict of emotions portrayed by the Hosea text is inconsequential in the light of God's wisdom, power, and holy love. Precisely in his response to his wayward children, he is God and not man.

Further consideration of this text leads to the conclusion that Stott speaks in too simplistic a way about how God *must* act in the light of his holiness. His compassion and anger are complementary aspects of a multifaceted nature. The outcome of these qualities ought not to be reduced to simple outcomes. To use the example at hand, Hosea 11 sees the love of God issuing variously in rescue, healing, and guidance (vss. 1, 4, and 5). The human situation is complex, and the divine resources many and diverse. In the same

---

[72] In an interesting postscript to this passage, Stott and David Edwards debate this subject, with Stott reiterating that "there are some scriptures which express, and some theologians who concede, the legitimacy of talking (though anthropomorphically) of 'a conflict of emotions, a strife of attributes' within God." In support of this, he refers again to Hosea 11.8–9, and quotes Brunner to the effect that God's holiness and love "'are equally infinite'" and combined in the atonement. See David L. Edwards with John Stott, *Essentials: A Liberal-Evangelical Dialogue* (London: Hodder & Stoughton, 1988), pp. 163–164. Here again the assertion of inner strife is supported by quotations which actually prove the inner compatibility of God's diverse attributes.

[73] James Luther Mays, *Hosea: A Commentary*, Old Testament Library (London: SCM, 1969), p. 157.

[74] Stott, p. 129.

way, in the face of sin God's holiness is not limited to a preconceived idea of wrath. Holiness stands for an aspect of the divine nature that in its fulness responds to each situation in a way that is congruent with the divine nature and appropriate to the particular situation. So in verse 9b, Yahweh declares to Israel that it is precisely as "the Holy One among you" that he resolves not to visit his wrath on them. God's holy love is not a contradictory formulation, like 'white blackness,' but a description of God whose nature encompasses love, holiness, and much more besides.

In the same way, God's love is not limited in the range of its responses. Because that love is a holy love, we should not restrict the love of God to an indiscriminate goodness or an easy forgiveness, which would be to reduce it to a pallid imitation of the real thing. Forsyth insists that kindness and severity are simultaneously operative in the divine character: "God never ceased to love us even when He was most angry and severe with us. It will not do to abolish the reality of God's anger towards us. True love is quite capable of being angry, and must be angry and even sharp with its beloved children."[75] To draw too strong a distinction between these two is to create a disjunction where there is in fact a personal unity.

For his part, as we have already seen, Stott affirms the duality of divine love and holiness, mercy and justice. But he immediately adds that "we must never think of this duality within God's being as irreconcilable. For God is not at odds with himself, however much it may appear to us that he is. He is 'the God of peace', of inner tranquillity not turmoil."[76] With the principle that the holy, loving God is a God of peace, Forsyth would of course agree (although with some qualification, as we will see shortly), but the earlier theologian refused to posit a fundamental cleavage between reality and appearance, between God's inherent "inner tranquillity" and his outer "turmoil," between God in himself and God toward us.

5.3 THE PASSION OF CHRIST

If Stott takes a step toward Forsyth in asserting the reconciliation of God's attributes, we could characterize our next point as Forsyth qualifying his position in such a way as to resemble more closely the stance Stott takes. Choosing his words carefully, Forsyth writes,

---

[75] *Work*, p. 105.
[76] Stott, p. 131.

It is surely impossible to say that the Jesus of the Passion felt no strain between God's pitiful and His righteous holy love. If the theoretical adjustment is hard for the theologian, how much harder the practical in the personal experience and act of the Redeemer. Reconciliation in a personality is always harder than adjustment in a system.[77]

The precise words and careful distinctions here alert us to a finely tuned idea. According to Forsyth, there is a strain in God's attributes exhibited in Christ, but no strife. To speak of "God's pitiful and His righteous holy love" is to admit the validity of the distinction. Christ felt the exigency of God's holiness directed toward the sins of humanity as well as the passion of the divine, saving love. These were experienced as strain, not strife, and although the difference is fine, Forsyth's intention to maintain both complexity and unity is clear. Moreover, the very carefulness of the language is proof of the fact that Forsyth wanted to hold together what some were separating; it was as if he had said, 'the holy, loving holy love.' He wanted to make clear that the love and holiness of God were one in the personality of Jesus Christ.

Given Forsyth's keen conviction that God's reality is revealed in Jesus Christ, what incident in Christ's life might have prompted this fine distinction between strain and strife? Where in the passion of Christ, mentioned by Forsyth in the previous quotation, might that tension be revealed? An answer appears in a sermon called "The Supreme Evidence of God's Love," preached at the historic King's Weigh House Chapel in London. We do not possess the text of this address, but Forsyth is reported (by means of lengthy indirect quotations) to have said that

Christ conceived His death not so much as an act of love towards man as an act of obedience towards God; and regarded its chief value as an agent and channel of God's purpose rather than as an act of love towards man. And in carrying on his thought through his sermon [the reporter continued], Dr. Forsyth emphasised the fact that both purposes were in Christ's mind, but that that of obedience was uppermost. Did not the agony in Gethsemane consist in the conflict between His obedience and His love? He clung to life because of His own love for His disciples. He had so much yet to do for them. They were not yet ready to be left. But there was a bond to God mightier still; and He laid down His life because of obedience to God. His wish was in conflict with His will.[78]

---

[77] "The Preaching of Jesus and the Gospel of Christ," p. 309.
[78] "Dr. Forsyth on 'The Supreme Evidence of God's Love,'" *Examiner*, 20 December 1900, p. 167.

It seems clear from this report of a conflict between Christ's obedience and his love, and the preceding quotation which tentatively introduced the idea of a "strain between God's pitiful and His righteous holy love," that the picture of Christ agonizing in the garden has introduced a qualification to Forsyth's repeated contention that there is no strife of attributes in the cross. The unity and harmony of the divine perfections, and Forsyth's consistency as well, seem threatened by this interpretation of the suffering in Gethsemane.

However, Forsyth's positive exegetical conclusion, we believe, is sound: the primary consideration for Jesus during this struggle in prayer is obedience. The repeated emphasis of the gospel accounts concerns the will – specifically, whether Jesus would carry out the Father's will. As Forsyth says according to the newspaper report of his sermon, the decision to be taken was "an act of obedience towards God," and even though love for the disciples was a factor in Christ's thinking, "that of obedience was uppermost."

The consequence of this priority given to holiness is, according to Forsyth, a lessened importance in Christ's passion and death as "an act of love towards man." With an emphasis on the very real friendship of the Lord for his followers, Forsyth says that Jesus "clung to life because of His own love for His disciples." This would seem to be a perspective that does not include a vital part of the truth. According to the witness of the gospels, Christ's love for humanity was not only – not even primarily – related to his hold on life. Christ was not only intent on doing God's will, but had a firm conviction that obedience to that will was in the disciples' best interests, in other words, an act of holy love. For example, in the synoptic gospels, Jesus claims that he will give his life as a ransom, thus bringing benefit to many (Mark 10.45, par. Matthew 20.28). In the gospel of John, he is reported as telling his friends that it is for their good that he is going away (John 16.7). Not only obedience to the Father but love for the ones the Father had given him motivated Jesus as he resolved in Gethsemane to go to the cross. Or to put it another way, Christ not only was intent to do as much as possible for the disciples during his earthly ministry; he was equally determined in his death to exert God's love in a way that would have results reaching far beyond that small group of followers. "Having loved his own who were in the world, he loved them to the end," comments the gospel writer (John 13.1 RSV). An even more consistent view of Christ's holy love would stress the suffering love of Christ in equal measure with the obedient holiness. As we have noted previously in Chapter Five, Forsyth occasionally fails to maintain the balance in this regard; our examination of his interpretation of the Gethsemane incident seems to bear this out.

If Christ is the revelation of the invisible God, if as Forsyth says, "the key to the prehistoric Godhead is the historic Jesus, and His historic obedience, even to the historic cross,"[79] then the Gethsemane drama is indicative of divine reality. If not as a 'strain' in God's nature, how should we interpret it? In the garden scene, we see a picture of God as a unity of holy love, complex but not logically contradictory, choosing to act in a way that is entirely congruent with his nature. Christ's inner dilemma at Gethsemane is a reflection of the complexity of personal decision-making, and bears some similarity to the situation in Hosea 11, examined earlier. While in that case God's anger gave way to compassion without compromising either, in the garden Christ became convinced that holy obedience was the way of filial love. A sacrificial death for sinners was a far greater good than the desire not to leave his closest friends. And just as in the Old Testament example, God's compassion for Israel did not lose its quality of holiness (see, e.g., Hosea 11.11), in Gethsemane Christ's obedience to the Father incorporated a filial love.

Such a view brings holiness and love in the closest relationship, which is precisely Forsyth's often-stated intention. Both obedience to God and love for humanity were indeed in Christ's mind in this agonizing decision, as he asserts in "The Supreme Evidence of God's Love." Christ determined in his time of prayer in Gethsemane that obedience to God's holiness, even to the point of death, was the way of accomplishing God's loving purpose. It is here at the heart of the atonement that we see the perfect combination of God's attributes, resulting in the harmonious expression of both judgment and grace. Neither is sacrificed; both are crucial.

In his lectures on preaching, Forsyth carefully asserts: "As the grace of God was on Christ, and not only through Christ on us, so also the judgment of God was on Christ and not only through Christ on us." Concerning that judgment, he continues:

> It alone meets the moral demand of holiness and completes it. Christ not only exercises the judgment of God on us; He absorbs it, so that we are judged not only by Him but in Him. And so in Him we are judged unto salvation. "The chastisement of our peace was on Him."

---

[79] "The Divine Self-Emptying" (1895), in *Father,* p. 43.

> In the Cross, then, we have the ethical consummation, perfect and prolific, of the old paradox of grace and judgment. During His life Christ was at one time pitiful, at another severe. He was merciful to one class, and stern to another. But in the Cross this separation of grace and judgment disappears, as the distinction of all classes disappears in the one issue of the universal conscience. And the goodness and the severity of God are perfectly one, as God is one in His passion of movement toward the sinner and reaction from his sin, of grace to the one and wrath to the other.[80]

Here, Forsyth accents the diversity of attributes which together make up God's nature, attributes that are expressed in a variety of ways in Christ's life. In different situations, one or another of them is to the fore, particularly revealed in the context of personal action. Despite the predominance of any attribute, the person of Christ is still a unified personality with many perfections. In the cross, Forsyth asserts, all these characteristics "are perfectly one." The love and holiness of God meet there, and issue in judgment and grace.

5.4 Drama and Dénouement

What then is the significance of the 'strain' in garden and cross, if it was not a strife between God's attributes of love and holiness? There is no denying that an observer can legitimately understand the passion of Christ in a way that raises questions about the unity of God's attributes. Despite the perfect harmony of attributes revealed in Christ's cross, a harmony which Forsyth champions, it is understandably difficult to be entirely consistent in this matter. One who expresses this well is the Scottish theologian John McIntyre, who says that a vital component in the drama of the cross is – not the conflict, but – "the juxtaposition of love and justice" in the action of salvation. He continues:

> No one can possibly read through day by day the events of Holy Week without feeling in his bones the heightening of the drama as Good Friday draws near, and its almost unbearable intensity on the following Saturday. Will God's justice demand the death of mankind, who not only disobeyed Him in the First Adam, but who are now about to slay the second Adam, who for love of man was made man? Or will the love of God, this great mystery present in the Creation, guiding Israel through some 1500 years her history and now sojourning among men, break the bonds of hell and go free again in the farthermost parts of the

---

[80] *Positive Preaching*, p. 314.

earth and in the deepest places of men's black hearts? Will the love or the justice have the final say? The dénouement, which we could never have grasped from the other side of Easter Day, gathers love and justice together, in a way which satisfies both, beyond the expectation of either.[81]

Although McIntyre does not investigate in detail the matter of God's harmonious attributes, nor return to the subject often, as Forsyth does, the language of drama and dénouement brings out well (and somewhat better than Forsyth, we believe) the reality of both God's holiness and love and the harmony of these attributes in the cross. Perhaps if Forsyth had been more sympathetic to the gospel narratives, and to the *life* of Jesus more generally as conveying theological truth, this sense of drama and dénouement would have aided his cause. McIntyre's description provides a useful way of acknowledging the dynamism and variety revealed in Jesus Christ, without conceding an unacceptable opposition of attributes.

Yet Forsyth is, on the whole, convincing in his view that in Christ's death the holy love of God is operative in a way that reflects the harmony of the divine nature. This drama is not merely a series of scenes played out for the education or encouragement of an audience, as McIntyre indeed points out: "It is only because something is objectively happening that the revelation takes place."[82] That objectivity, however, is precisely the problem. The need for salvation of one sort or another implies that the solution must involve some change. The penal theories of orthodoxy suggest an 'objective' change in God from wrath to grace, while the so-called 'subjective' theories presuppose only a change in humanity. We now turn to see Forsyth's stance on this aspect of the strife or harmony of attributes in Jesus Christ's atoning death.

5.5 AN OBJECTIVE ATONEMENT

The cross was a decisive act in the history of salvation, and Forsyth believes that that work of Christ was an objective atonement. This was true in two senses. The first, which Forsyth often links with the word 'objective,' is that salvation was accomplished by God: "The real meaning of an objective atonement is that God Himself made the complete sacrifice. The real objectivity of the atonement is not that it was made to God but by

---

[81] John McIntyre, *On the Love of God* (London: Collins, 1962), p. 172.
[82] McIntyre, *On the Love of God*, p. 173.

God."[83] The initiative in redemption, therefore, was God's alone. "We know that the satisfaction made by Christ, no less than the sacrifices of the old law, flowed from the grace of God, and did not go to procure it."[84] There was no need for a divine change from anger to acceptance because holiness and love are not equal and opposite, but inseparable aspects of the one God. On this principle, Forsyth can declare, "God never ceased to love us even when He was most angry and severe with us."[85]

There is more to it than that, however. Forsyth maintains that even though God didn't need to be reconciled, a real change took place. The atonement was objective in a second sense, which required an important contrast: "The distinction I ask you to observe is between a change of feeling and a change of treatment. . . . God's feeling toward us never needed to be changed. But God's treatment of us, God's practical relation to us – that had to change."[86] His fundamental point is that propitiation is justification. He says that "the heart [and affection] of God towards us, His gracious disposition towards us, was from His own holy eternity; that grace is of the unchangeable. God in that respect had not to be changed."[87] What was required in the work of Christ, therefore, was not an ingenious solution to pacify what Stott portrays as "a struggle between what Yahweh ought to do because of his righteousness and what he cannot do because of his love,"[88] but a decisive action that would tackle the problem of sin. "It is not a case of altering God's disposition but His relations with man," writes Forsyth, "of enabling Him to treat man as He feels."[89] It was not a change of feeling, because God always loved us, but it was a change of treatment, of personal relations. The attributes of God aren't adjusted, but his relationship with sinners is.

Immediately we must go on to stress that this relationship is a personal one. In Forsyth's thought, the sacrificial language of propitiation and the forensic language of justification are closely yoked to the relational language of adoption:

---

[83] *Work*, p. 92.
[84] *Atonement in Modern Religious Thought*, p. 64.
[85] *Work*, p. 105.
[86] *Work*, p. 105.
[87] *Work*, p. 104.
[88] Stott, p. 130.
[89] *Atonement in Modern Religious Thought*, p. 82.

The Centrality of Holy Love

> You cannot set up a relation between souls [he explains] without affecting and changing both sides, even if on one side the disposition existed before, and led to the act that reconciled. . . .
>
> [Christ's work] set up no new affection in God, but a new and creative relation on both sides of the spiritual world. It gave man a new relation to God, and God, a new relation, though not a new feeling to man. It did not make God our Father, but it made it possible for the Father to treat sinners as sons.[90]

Forsyth's insistence of the unity of "the three-fold cord" of atonement theories is here enlarged to include other images, reminding us that the work of Christ is not an isolated transaction, but a matrix of meaning in which all aspects must be understood together. The cross, Forsyth claims, has not only a retrospective meaning (in which sin is forgiven) but also a prospective aspect (in which sinners become children of God). The objectivity of the atonement extends across these boundaries.

The comparison between John Stott and P. T. Forsyth has yielded a variety of distinctions, and carried our argument into the deepest realities. The essential difference between the two lies in a different approach to the 'attributes and atonement' debate which we have been engaged in throughout this study. While Stott sees God's attributes of holiness and love as in some sense conflicting, and that conflict resolved at the cross, Forsyth affirms that there is no strife of attributes, and that the holy love of God acted in the death of Christ to reconcile and forgive.

When Stott writes, "It would be hard to exaggerate the magnitude of the changes which have taken place as a result of the cross, both in God and in us, especially in God's dealings with us and in our relations with him,"[91] we hear words with which Forsyth would disagree as well as ones that he would assent to. The earlier theologian identified the work of Christ as affecting the God-human relationship, but he would not agree with Stott that God was changed in a fundamental way. According to Forsyth, it would be important not to exaggerate the magnitude of the change; instead, Forsyth's repeated conviction is that God was always gracious to us, even when his wrath was most intense.

---

[90] "Holy Father," in *Father,* pp. 19, 20.
[91] Stott, p. 167.

5.6 THE REAL CONFLICT

There is, as a result, a different focus in the respective soteriological treatments of these two writers. While Stott speaks of the atonement as a solution to the problem of sin (forgiveness, reconciliation), as a change in his relations with us (justification), and as a change in God's own nature, Forsyth takes a different view. As we have seen, he insists that God's nature does not change, but that his attitude and relation to us is adjusted. Any talk of strife or conflict on Forsyth's part is moved to another sphere, namely the impact that the gospel has on humanity. God's holiness and love conflict with our sinful situation.

The strife is not within God's nature, claims Forsyth, but in us when we are confronted by the revelation of Jesus Christ. In a chapter of *The Cruciality of the Cross* with the short title, "The Atonement Central to Christian Experience," Forsyth writes of the inner contradictions of the Christian conscience, including the dramatic contrast between "the damnability of my sin" and "the incredibility of grace."[92] The Lord's demand, "the holiness of His standard," and the seriousness of his judgment impress themselves on the believer. "And so we oscillate between the goodness and the severity of God. . . . And the conscience finds no rest till it find in the cross the one final act in which both are reconciled and inwoven, with the grace uppermost."[93] Here, the strife of attributes is not within God's nature, but a conflict created by the impact of those attributes on human nature. The holiness that speaks of judgment and the love that communicates mercy combine in Christ not only to reconcile the world to the Father, but also to bring home to the believer the good news of righteousness bestowed and sins forgiven.

Forsyth adds that this is not only true for individual consciences, but also for those who consider the wider context, and the judgment of God on a sinful world, a race of individuals. Such people, with their troubled consciences, require "a grace and salvation [that] gathers up the total moral situation in one act, and settles the great strife for good and all."[94] In an imaginative transformation of the categories, Forsyth reiterates the crucial point that the work of Christ was directed toward a problem outside of God's self, namely the jarring separation between God's own righteousness and a

---

[92] *Cruciality*, p. 88.
[93] *Cruciality*, p. 89.
[94] *Cruciality*, pp. 90–91.

rebellious and disobedient humanity. A strife of attributes of sorts is indeed something to be contended with, but it is not a conflict inherent in God's nature but rather a feature of the divine-human situation. As we have seen, according to Forsyth "the moral problem was the adjustment of sin and sanctity, the reconciliation of guilty men and holy God,"[95] not any inner adjustment in the divine nature. And, as we will see in the next section, the solution to that problem was accomplished in a way that entirely satisfied the holy, loving nature of God.

The problem of how God can take both human sin and his own majesty with equal seriousness is not to be defined as essentially a problem within God's own nature. Rather, Forsyth is convinced that the problem is human sinfulness, the principalities and powers that stand behind it, and the concomitant deathly results. There is a conflict in the cross, but it is not between the love and holiness of God, much less between the Father and the Son, but between the holy love of God and the reality of human sin.

We conclude that these two problems, which Stott combines and to some extent confuses, are of very different kinds. Sin's reality is described by the biblical writers as an intrusion into the world God made, and a real problem for humanity, as the anguish of Paul's cry, "Who will deliver me from this body of death?", indicates. And, although we affirm with Stott the duality – indeed the multifaceted nature – of God's character, we take Forsyth's point that there is no scriptural evidence of a strife of attributes, no indication that the redemption accomplished by Christ Jesus was a divine response devised only after considerable difficulty, or a rescue mission hammered out in the heavenly council between Holiness with its demands and Love with its intentions, a skilful compromise to satisfy even the sternest negotiators. Instead of being the reconciliation of conflicting aspects of God's character, Forsyth saw the death of Christ as "the adjustment of sin and sanctity, the reconciliation of guilty men and holy God."[96]

At the close of this discussion and debate between Forsyth and Stott, we admit that there is a point beyond which further exploration becomes difficult and then impossible. Aspects of the doctrine of the atonement remain paradoxical. As Forsyth says, "God's judgment-Grace to sin is His supreme action as righteousness. ... It is the matter and miracle of His revelation, the union in Grace

---

[95] *Authority*, p. 204.
[96] *Authority*, p. 204.

of holy law and holy love, of holy God and evil man." In this whole matter of God's attributes, exact and comprehensive knowledge is denied us. "The precise mode of adjustment, its ultimate moral inwardness, is something He has reserved in His own hands to a large extent."[97] Forsyth's central point remains important, however; God's holy love is harmoniously illustrated and savingly exerted in Christ. In Christ and his cross, there might be complexities beyond our grasp, and paradoxes which test the patience of those who demand a simple word, but there more than anywhere else, God is revealed as the integrated, holy, loving God.

6. TRINITARIAN HOLY LOVE

Although Forsyth's doctrine of the Trinity is neither fully developed nor systematically expounded in his major works, it is my conviction that further light can be shed on his use of the formulation, 'the holy love of God,' by examining it against the backdrop of his views concerning the Trinity. Therefore, the purpose of this section is to examine the relationship between God's attributes (and especially his holy love) and God's trinitarian reality. In the intersection of these two loci of the doctrine of God, the centrality of holy love will be highlighted. Moreover, the unity of these attributes (holiness and love) will be further demonstrated against the background of the unity of Forsyth's doctrine of the triune God.

While references to God's holy love abound in his writing, with distinctive purpose and developed application, Forsyth is more sparing about the triunity of God. J. K. Mozley was right when he observed that "there is something almost incidental in the way in which such a doctrine as that of the Trinity now and then appears" in Forsyth's authorship.[98] That is not to say, however, that he relegated the doctrine to an appendix of dogmatics. While the theological line from Schleiermacher through Ritschl to Harnack, Herrmann, and Häring generally treated the Trinity as either complicated and mysterious or otiose and therefore embarrassing,[99] Forsyth's treatment, though relatively slight, is nevertheless significant. "The doctrine of the Trinity . . . certainly is at the heart

---

[97] *Christian Ethic of War*, pp. 177–178.
[98] J. K. Mozley, *The Heart of the Gospel* (London: SPCK, 1925), p. 72.
[99] See Claude Welch, *The Trinity in Contemporary Theology* (London: SCM, 1953), pp. 3–29.

The Centrality of Holy Love

of Christianity," he says in one place;[100] "The triune God," he insists in another, "is what makes Christianity Christian."[101] More personally, he speaks of "the joy and uplifting that we have in meditating on the revealed depths of the Triune God."[102]

This important, distinctively Christian doctrine is revealed in Christ. Such an assertion, if it were not so often denied, would be an obvious tautology. Forsyth's conviction is that "the historic Jesus, as the kenotic incarnation of the eternal Son by his own act and movement, contained the Godhead in its whole fulness of holy love."[103] The doctrine of God is not a matter of speculation, nor is the doctrine of the Trinity the end result of deduction from first principles, Forsyth believes. These doctrines are not even properly constructed on a theocentric basis, beginning with the one God revealed in the Old Testament. Instead, the reality from which Forsyth proceeds is "the Triune God who is the peculiar revelation of Christ. For the Christian God is not the Father, but the Father of our Lord Jesus Christ in the Spirit."[104] The Father is known in the Son, by the Spirit.

Having begun with the revealed reality of Jesus Christ, Forsyth's doctrine of the Trinity develops consistently along experiential rather than speculative lines. In many of his scattered comments on the Trinity, he makes his familiar distinction between moral reality and metaphysical truth, between Christian experience and what he calls "theological science."[105] While "a scientific theology detached from experience" may begin with discussions of Trinity and incarnation, there is a better way: "The moral method ... is to rise from experience to assent, from experience of the Gospel to assent to the Church theology of it, from life doctrines we can directly verify to thought doctrines we cannot, from experience of Redemption to assent to Incarnation, from personal religion to corporate dogmatic." Similarly, the moral method would begin with "an atoning Redemption" and ascend to "the doctrine of the Trinity."[106] In terms of theological methodology, Forsyth insists on the priority of the moral experience of the gospel.

---

[100] *Justification*, p. 87.
[101] *Freedom*, p. 263.
[102] *Authority*, p. 231.
[103] *Person*, p. 349.
[104] *Authority*, p. 230.
[105] *Justification*, p. 90.
[106] *Justification*, pp. 88–89.

But this contrast between the metaphysical and the moral is not an absolute one. The two are not exclusive categories, as may become starkly apparent as we look at two seemingly opposite statements by Forsyth on the classical formulation of the doctrine. In one place, he rather disparagingly comments that "Athanasianism" is "a [speculative] metaphysic of three transcendental movements of thought."[107] By contrast, in another place he enthuses about the same subject: "The Athanasian doctrine of the Trinity is the truest doctrine of Godhead the world has ever seen."[108] Closer attention to the context of these quotations reveals that Forsyth's intention is neither rejection of, nor subscription to, the Athanasian Creed. His point in both quotations is to assert the Christian experience of redemption in Christ as foundational, and trinitarian dogma as derivative from that dynamic revelation. He neither wants to discount the metaphysical interest, nor to enthrone it. "A doctrine like the Trinity," he writes, is not founded on metaphysic, but must instead be valued as "a foundation, condition, or corollary, of the peculiar quality of the Christian experience, the Christian certainty of holy love, grace, and salvation direct from God."[109] The Christian experience that rises from the work of Christ then (and only then) turns to inquire into the wider truth and the deeper reality revealed in that work. In other words, experience of atonement leads to exposition of Trinity, faith seeking understanding.

Does Forsyth possibly overemphasize the experiential aspect of faith? Does his position represent a turning away from the objective realities of salvation history to a more relativistic concern for what these realities mean for the individual? Far from it! Forsyth's conviction is that theology does not rest on the authority of personal experience, but rather on the One whom faith experiences, and Christian thought must not be separated from that experience. Christ's sacrificial death must be allowed to have its transforming effect even on theology and the methodology of its thinkers. At the same time, however, Forsyth will not swing to the opposite experiential extreme and allow the doctrine of the Trinity to become an optional extra on the latest model of systematics. So the same Forsyth who urges his hearers, "Protest strongly against making salvation depend on assent to the metaphysics of

---

[107] *Theology in Church and State* (1915), p. 36.
[108] "Theosophy and Theology," *Independent,* 6 November 1891, p. 798.
[109] *Theology in Church and State,* pp. 36–37.

Trinity,"[110] can also issue a warning that to neglect that doctrine can lead to serious consequences. Although the doctrine of the Trinity "is not an experimental condition of that personal intercourse between the believer and his Saviour which is the very nerve of Christian religion," nevertheless "the flat, fiery, and deliberate denial of it tends to preclude such communion."[111] In a sense, the doctrine of the Trinity is a secondary one, but it is in no sense less important.

It is particularly important to the church. "A doctrine of the Trinity may be, so far as the crude individual goes, a piece of theological science," writes Forsyth, "but for the church it is a part of its essential faith. It could not renounce it and remain a church." The church's faith is worked out not only in love, says Forsyth, but also in thought, and that includes the church's thinking about the Trinity.[112] Far from discarding trinitarian dogma because it supposedly comes from an outdated metaphysic, he insists on its importance to the church's very existence. For that reason, to follow his argument a step further, it should become even more important to individual Christians, who might then discover that trinitarian thought is much closer to the centre of their faith than they first appreciated. "All the metaphysic of the Trinity, therefore, is at bottom but the church's effort to express in thought the incomparable reality and absolute glory of the Saviour whom faith saw sitting by the Father."[113]

To summarize this point, Forsyth contends that the Trinity is "a *moral* unity rather than a metaphysical. It is a *Holy* Trinity. And the foundation of our belief in it is (as it was for Athanasius) the holy act of redemption."[114] Forsyth's stress on the moral leads him to emphasize the holiness of the Trinity. The holiness of the cross points to the relationship between the Son and his Holy Father, and from there to the Trinity (inclusive of the *Holy* Spirit). Forsyth boldly concludes, "God died for us in a sense which only a Trinitarian doctrine can convey."[115] At this point, Forsyth anticipates a significant tendency within later twentieth century

---

[110] *Cruciality*, p. 49.
[111] "Theosophy and Theology," *Independent*, 30 October 1891, p. 777.
[112] "Faith, Metaphysic, and Incarnation," *Methodist Review* 97 (September 1915): 707.
[113] "Faith, Metaphysic, and Incarnation," p. 707.
[114] *The Church, the Gospel and Society* (1962; orig. pub. as articles, 1905), p. 20.
[115] "Our Experience of a Triune God," *Cambridge Christian Life* 1 (June 1914): 244.

theology; for example, Jürgen Moltmann describes his book *The Trinity and the Kingdom of God* as "an attempt to start with the special Christian tradition of the history of Jesus the Son, and from that to develop a historical doctrine of the Trinity." In more pictorial language he affirms that "the cross of the Son stands from eternity in the centre of the Trinity."[116] Rather than yoking holiness and love, however, Moltmann concentrates on the suffering love of God.

The moral doctrine of the Trinity, based on the holy act of redemption, leads Forsyth (and us) to consider the status of holiness in the triune God. But first, for the sake of comparison, note that Forsyth accepts, indeed embraces, the fundamental concept of God's intra-trinitarian love:

> The Father dwells in the Son of his love. Jesus, in fashion and person as he moved among us, was the eternal object, peer, and polar continuity of God's love. . . . The real personal Father had the real and personal Son who is our life for his love to rest on in the depth and mystery of eternity.[117]

That love, moreover, was an outgoing love, passionately intent on the salvation of humanity. And so the Son, "through his love to both God and man," came into the world "to save God's holy name and purpose by saving man's forfeit soul."[118] The love between Father and Son was expressed as active, outgoing love for humanity. As he explains, "We are loved in the Father's holy love of the Son."[119]

The relation between Father and Son, Forsyth explains, "was not a relation of love simply, but of love holy and yet gracious – which combination is a great miracle. The Father in heaven meant, for Christ, the holy Father. The sonship is the sonship of *holy* love."[120] Besides stressing the intra-trinitarian love, then, Forsyth speaks of the vital place of intra-trinitarian holiness. It is at this point that he makes a distinctive contribution. To speak of God's love without recognizing the holiness of that love is for him a weak assertion, prone to distortion. Love alone is sentimental and ultimately ineffectual. By contrast, holy love is love in its fullness. Trinitarian

---

[116] Jürgen Moltmann, *The Trinity and the Kingdom of God: The Doctrine of God*, trans. Margaret Kohl (London: SCM, 1981), pp. 19, xvi.
[117] "Faith, Metaphysic, and Incarnation," pp. 712–713.
[118] "Faith, Metaphysic, and Incarnation," p. 713.
[119] "Faith, Metaphysic, and Incarnation," p. 706. We introduced Forsyth's view of the trinitarian love in Chapter Five, section 2.2.
[120] *Church and the Sacraments*, pp. 93–94.

love is impressive; trinitarian holy love is God's nature realized in decisive saving action.

Forsyth's contribution, we contend, is to introduce the saving presence of holiness into the very heart of God's intra-trinitarian reality. This he does in three characteristic and closely related ways.

6.1 THE OBEDIENCE OF THE SON

Forsyth's doctrine of the atonement stresses the holiness of Christ the Son, and defines that holiness both negatively in terms of sinlessness and positively in terms of obedience. While he does not discount the perfect purity of Jesus, Forsyth draws our attention particularly to the fact that Christ was more than sinless, perfect, and pure: he was entirely obedient to the Father. As the incarnation of God's holiness, Jesus defines what holiness really is. And on the cross, we see to what lengths the Holy One will go: "he humbled himself and became obedient to death – even death on a cross!" (Philippians 2.8).

Such obedience is not merely the obedience of the Son's human nature, according to Forsyth, who is unwilling to make a distinction between God as he is toward us and God as he is in himself. Instead, Christ's holy obedience reflects the divine holiness. In his masterwork on christology, Forsyth affirms what many would deny, "An incarnation may be possible of that element in Godhead which ... represents absolute obedience, and absolute holiness of response. That element of subordination and sacrifice must be there surely."[121] Further elaboration comes from an unexpected source, in Forsyth's book, *Marriage: Its Ethic and Religion*. With his eyes as always fixed on the cross, Forsyth again considers the obedience of Jesus Christ, and does that specifically in relation to the two concerns which form the matrix of our current discussion: the nature and attributes of God, and the Trinity. As before, his starting-point is the relationship of the Father and the Son.

> But Father and Son [he writes] is a relation inconceivable except the Son be obedient to the Father. The perfection of the Son and the perfecting of His holy work lay, not in His suffering, but in His obedience. And as He was Eternal Son, it meant an eternal obedience....
>
> But obedience is not conceivable without some form of subordination. Yet in His very obedience the Son was co-equal with the Father; the Son's yielding was no less divine than the Father's exigent

---

[121] *Person*, p. 243.

will. Therefore, in the very nature of God, subordination implies no inferiority.... There is an obedience bound up with the supreme dignity of Christian love, so that where most love is, there also is most obedience.[122]

In the equality of the triune persons, obedience and love exist together, not as uneasy partners but as genuinely divine aspects of God's personality. Within a context and framework of love, Jesus is obedient to the Holy Father. The holiness of the Son and the love of the Father harmonize perfectly in the work of the cross.

To paraphrase closely the words of John Thompson, who discusses this quotation from Forsyth in his volume on Karl Barth's christology, Forsyth's ideas about the intra-trinitarian obedience of the Son (in many ways a novelty in the history of dogma) find a significant successor and confirmation in Karl Barth's *Church Dogmatics*.[123] On this topic, their respective ideas have several similarities. Where Forsyth would speak of God's holy love, Barth writes about "the free love of God established in the event of atonement." Forsyth says that "subordination implies no inferiority," while Barth asks rhetorically, "Does subordination in God necessarily involve an inferiority, and therefore a deprivation, a lack?" Forsyth speaks in many places of the pre-eminent holiness of God enacted in Christ's obedience; similarly, Barth refers to "the obedience of Christ as the dominating moment in our conception of God."[124]

Two aspects of this obedience are especially noteworthy in this context. The first is the complementary nature of Christ's freedom and his obedience. Forsyth comments that the Son "was not only sent by the Father but himself came with equal spontaneity into the world to save it, ... through his own free responsive obedience to

---

[122] *Marriage: Its Ethic and Religion* (1912), pp. 70–71.

[123] John Thompson, *Christ in Perspective: Christological Perspectives in the Theology of Karl Barth* (Edinburgh: Saint Andrew Press, 1978), p. 164. Thompson looked at the relationship from the opposite perspective, and the quotation runs: "Barth's views (in many ways a novelty in the history of dogma – a personal remark made to me by Professor E. Jüngel, Tübingen) find a significant anticipation and confirmation in P. T. Forsyth's *Marriage: Its Ethic and Religion*." Thompson's extended note on "Critique of the Idea of the Obedience of the Son" (note 102, pp. 163–165) is a useful discussion. Barth's work on the subject of Christ's obedience is in *Church Dogmatics* 4/1, pp. 192–204.

[124] Barth, *Church Dogmatics* 4/1, pp. 193, 202, 199.

The Centrality of Holy Love

his Father's saving will."[125] Jesus not only did the will of the Father, but his obedience was freely offered. In him, freedom and obedience were entirely compatible.

Secondly, at the end of his life, the obedience of Jesus went to the very limit of human experience, namely to the point of death and judgment. When Jesus was dying on the cross, says Forsyth, "[silent] submission was essential to His complete recognition of the holiness of the judgment He bore. It was part of that perfect obedient praise of the Father's righteousness which rose in human extremity from His faith and love."[126] There is an aspect of the intra-trinitarian holiness that not only obeys the Father's saving will, but also answers in love by praising the Father's righteousness.

In the atonement, the obedient holiness of the Son answered and honoured the holiness of the Father. Jesus was obedient to the divine command, even to the farthest reaches of human experience. In the end, he even recognized and confessed the Father's perfect holiness to judge human sin in his own person. And that dynamic of holiness between Father and Son went hand in hand with the love that also characterizes their relationship. Both holiness and love are marks of the triune God.

6.2 THE SATISFACTION OF THE FATHER

The second way Forsyth stresses the intra-trinitarian holiness is with a singular interpretation of the satisfactionary aspect of the atonement. In the Anselmian theory of atonement, couched largely in terms of the feudal system of the day, sin was seen as infinitely serious because it was sin against God. Rather than giving God the honour he deserved, humans sinned, putting themselves in debt to God and liable to judgment. Simple forgiveness would be dishonourable, but a satisfaction could atone. However, the requirements for such a satisfaction were daunting: it must be made by humanity, because humanity sinned; and it must be of infinite worth, to match the magnitude of the sin. The latter condition was possible only to God, the former was accomplished when God became human in Christ.[127]

---

[125] "Faith, Metaphysic, and Incarnation," p. 713.

[126] "Holy Father," in *Father,* p. 21.

[127] For summaries of Anselm's theory, see, for example, Robert S. Franks, *The Work of Christ: A Historical Study of Christian Doctrine* (London: Thomas Nelson & Sons, 1962; orig. pub. 1918), pp. 126–142.

The objections raised against the theory were great, and Forsyth adds his to the list: the difficulty with quantifying sin, the problematic idea of an equivalent satisfaction, the idea of satisfying a demand rather than a person, and above all the concentration on judicial penalty rather than moral reality. "The Anselmic theory of satisfaction is now out of date," he declared, "and has little more than a historic value. With it and its habit of mind have gone also the various substitutionary schemes and commercial transactions into which it has been degraded. They are all more judicial than moral. They fail to satisfy the modern conscience."[128]

In an attempt to avoid these difficulties, Forsyth employed a distinctive use of the idea of satisfaction. The key to his thought here is that the satisfaction which atones is not of a demand, but of a person. So the obedient holiness of Christ prompts the Father's considered personal judgment, "You are my Son, whom I love; with you I am well pleased" (Mark 1.11). In Forsyth's view, the satisfying thing, the atoning element, is holiness: "A holy God could be satisfied by neither pain nor death, but by holiness alone." In practical terms that means obedience: "Holy obedience alone, unto death, can satisfy the Holy Lord."[129] And that holiness was in the form of perfect obedience within the personal relationship of Father and Son.

Although much more could be said on this point, the significance of this inter-personal obedience for our discussion of the Trinity is that God himself provided the satisfaction. To use Forsyth's word, it was self-satisfaction.

> God is always the author of His own satisfaction: that is to say, His holiness is always equal to its own atonement. God in the Son is the perfect satisfaction and joy of God in the Father; and God holy in the sinful Cross is the perfect satisfaction of God the holy in the sinless heavens.[130]

There were many characteristics of Christ's holiness that pleased the Father – he accepted the judgment of God on sin, which he offered from the side of humanity on their behalf, and his work prompted the answering holiness of a grateful race – but the key thing to note is that in Christ, God's own holiness was expressed within a trinitarian context. The cross is the triune God's holy self-satisfaction.

---

[128] *Religion in Recent Art* (1889), p. 294.
[129] *Work*, pp. 205, 206.
[130] *Work*, p. 205.

6.3 THE TRINITARIAN HOLINESS OF THE SPIRIT

Until now, our examination of God's attributes within a trinitarian context has been limited to the relationship between the Father and the Son. But when we broaden our attention to include the Holy Spirit, we discover a third way in which Forsyth emphasizes the place of holy love within God's nature. Even though he speaks less frequently about the Spirit[131] (a trait reflected in the wider Christian tradition, and one justified to some extent by Jesus's description, in John 16.13–15, of the self-deprecatory nature of the Spirit), Forsyth's treatment of the divine reality in not a binitarian one. As he says, "we believe not only in the Father and in the Son but in the Holy Ghost and the love He sheds abroad in our hearts."[132]

The many references to the Holy Ghost in Forsyth's authorship witness to an impressive breadth of attention to the Spirit's person and work. Regarding the full personhood of the Spirit, Forsyth speaks of the Holy Ghost as an "active subject in the Godhead,"[133] and as "the eternal bond of communion" between the Father and the Son,[134] thus emphasizing both eastern and western conceptions of the Spirit within the Trinity. The Spirit is "a person and a power,"[135] and is at the same time "equally personal with Father and Son" and "a power co-equal with Father and Son in the Christian God."[136]

If Forsyth was convinced of the personhood of the Spirit, he was even more forthright in his wide-ranging treatment of the Spirit's work, which he sees directed toward humanity both personally and corporately. With regard to individuals, Forsyth declares, "We believe in the Holy Ghost. We have in Christ as the Spirit the sanctifier of our single lives, the Reader of our hearts, the Helper of our most private straits, the Inspirer of our most deep and sacred confessions. We must have one to wring from us '*My* Lord and *my* God.'"[137] But the Spirit's work is wider: "It lights the Bible, it leads

---

[131] Forsyth's treatment of the Spirit is largely incidental to other concerns, although substantial exceptions to this generalization can be found in *Freedom*, especially chap. 1; *Authority*, chap. 6; and "Does the Church Prolong the Incarnation?" *London Quarterly Review* 133 (January and April 1920): 1–12, and especially 204–212.

[132] "Our Experience of a Triune God," p.243.

[133] *Positive Preaching*, p. 314.

[134] *Authority*, p. 230.

[135] *Church and the Sacraments*, p. 301.

[136] "Does the Church Prolong the Incarnation?", p. 210.

[137] "The Living Christ" (1897), in *Father*, p. 96.

the Church, it anoints the ministry, and all by a constant rejuvenation of the Gospel and of its power to create, criticize, and create anew."[138] Forsyth's thought spans the Spirit's work, from "the spirit of the Creator uniquely pervading the creation," through his work in "selecting a nation [and] inspiring the prophets," to "His unique and individual action in the Church."[139]

In addition to these and other customary and rather unsurprising aspects, Forsyth chooses two facets of the doctrine of the Spirit for special attention. As we have already noted at the end of the opening paragraph of this section, Forsyth approvingly quotes Romans 5.5 to the effect that part of the Spirit's role is to communicate the divine love to human hearts. But owing to the author's particular context and personal conviction, it was the holiness of that love that occupied more of his attention. In Forsyth's opinion, the holy love of the Spirit is discernible in the cross and resurrection of Jesus Christ.

In Forsyth's theology, with its strong orientation toward salvation history, the cross is the source of the Holy Spirit. Following the Latin consensus about the procession of the Spirit, but colouring it with his own crucicentric emphasis, he sees "the Spirit as coming from the Father through the work of the Son."[140] The foundational work of Christ is the basis of the Spirit's work. As Forsyth says, "It is only the certainty of the Cross that can give us the sanctity of the Spirit. For the fountainhead of the Spirit is the Cross."[141]

Forsyth's thought fits well within the traditional western framework, which is susceptible to a linear and unitary, perhaps even hierarchical, interpretation. Just as the Son was obedient to the Father, the Spirit serves the purposes of the Son. Because the Spirit does no new work which could in some way supersede the atoning death of Christ, Forsyth criticizes those who "keep asking for new pentecosts without going back to the old agony" and the Spirit's accomplishments there.[142] To be sure, Christ is "amplified and glorified in the Spirit," but according to Forsyth it would be going

---

[138] *Church, the Gospel and Society*, p. 91.
[139] *Freedom*, p. 12.
[140] *Freedom*, p. 308.
[141] *Positive Preaching*, p. 179.
[142] *Church, the Gospel and Society*, p. 114.

The Centrality of Holy Love 233

too far to say that the Spirit is "an independent and even corrective power."[143]

One reason that Forsyth wanted to stress the close relationship between the cross and the Spirit is a desire to counter the Hegelian tendency of relativizing the distinctive character of Christ's action in history. "One of the greatest actions of the Spirit in modern thought," Forsyth writes, "is to preserve Christ's influence from being detached from his act and turned into a moral process."[144] Instead, the Spirit interacts with the historical reality, and communicates it to a new generation. Another purpose, and one more important for our present concern, was to make explicit the close connection between the holiness involved in the atonement made by Christ, and the holiness of the Spirit who conveys that reality to the world. We note Forsyth's own stress when he insists that the cross is "the source of the *Holy* Spirit, searching to moral depths, filling a universal church . . . , and renewing all things. . . ."[145] Holiness is not an extraneous or supplementary aspect of God's nature, but the defining characteristic of the Spirit of God. Forsyth finds confirmation of this in a text he often quoted:

> When Paul in Romans 1.4 says that Christ rose by the spirit of holiness, the meaning of holiness there is not merely ethical. For in the Old Testament the Holy Spirit of God is more than that, and means the majesty and sublimity and Godhead of a God that transcends even the ethical world. The spirit of holiness which rose in Christ was the supernatural element which placed Him in the eternal majesty of God.[146]

Therefore, not only the cross but also the resurrection bears witness to the close intra-trinitarian connection between Christ and the Spirit, a relationship marked by holiness as well as love.

With this twofold connection (in both cross and resurrection) between God's holiness and the Holy Spirit in view, Forsyth concluded that the Spirit's presence in the Trinity was an affirmation of the place of holiness in the divine nature. God in his triune fulness was not merely a God of love, but of *holy* love. The divine revelation was of "a God, supremely ethical, as being supremely holy – so supremely holy that, from the Cross onwards, holiness ceased to be an attribute of God, and became, in the Holy

---

[143] *Freedom*, pp. 307–308.
[144] *Positive Preaching*, pp. 24–25; see also p. 214, where Forsyth elaborates this point.
[145] *Christian Ethic of War*, p. 142.
[146] *Freedom*, p. 12.

Spirit, a constituent father and active subject in the Godhead itself."[147] In another place, Forsyth reiterates the point but adds an explicit conclusion about trinitarian thinking: the divine holiness, he writes, is "much more than an attribute of God. In the Holy Spirit it becomes a constituent element in the Godhead, on its way to become at last a coequal person in the Trinity."[148] The vivid hyperbole of 'holiness joining the Trinity' underlines Forsyth's concern to promote the cause of an attribute which much current theology had virtually ignored. Despite his lack of interest in metaphysics, at this juncture Forsyth insisted that God's holiness was not only an important 'active ingredient' in the divine economy, but was also "a constituent element in the Godhead."

Forsyth summarizes this idea by reminding his readers that "a positive Gospel is a revelation of *holy* love. ... If the great revelation of God is in the Cross, and the great gift of the Cross is the Holy Spirit, then the revelation is holiness, holiness working outward as love."[149] God's holy love is revealed to be a trinitarian reality, an aspect of the nature of God as Father, Son, and Holy Spirit.

Forsyth's treatment of the Holy Spirit, though incidental and, not as well integrated into his wider vision as it might be, is nevertheless wide-ranging and suggestive of insights. Particularly in the distinctive aspects which we have noted, namely the close relationship between the cross and the Spirit, and the stress on the holiness of the Holy Spirit, Forsyth's contribution will repay study.[150] At the end of his survey of Forsyth's theology, J. K. Mozley acknowledges the omission in his article of much that ought to be considered, and includes among those aspects "the reality of holiness within the Godhead as Holy Spirit leading on to the doctrine of the Trinity."[151] That idea, we have discovered, is an important one in seeing the holy love of God in trinitarian perspective.

In each of these three concerns – the obedience of the Son, the satisfaction of the Father, and the trinitarian holiness of the Spirit –

---

[147] *Positive Preaching*, pp. 313–314.
[148] *Positive Preaching*, p. 368.
[149] *Positive Preaching*, pp. 212–213.
[150] Thomas A. Smail, *The Giving Gift: The Holy Spirit in Person* (London: Hodder & Stoughton, 1988), p. 159, notes that "the Spirit is also the Spirit of Calvary, the Spirit of the Son's self-giving to the Father. He is the Spirit of whom John 19:30 says that when his work was triumphantly completed Jesus 'bowed his head and handed over the Spirit (*paredoken to pneuma*).'"
[151] Mozley, *Heart of the Gospel*, p. 109.

The Centrality of Holy Love

Forsyth gives a central place to God's holiness. When this emphasis is combined with the prominent place that Forsyth accords to the divine love – as a trait of his own trinitarian life expressed in Christ – the reader can appreciate the richness of his distinctive expression, the 'holy love' of God. Forsyth's conception of the relationships within the Trinity does not only concern hallowing God's name, but also praising "the love beyond all love – God's love of His own holy Self."[152] In a career-long effort to emphasize the combination of these two great attributes, and not to sacrifice one in order to exalt the other, P. T. Forsyth often spoke of God's holy love. As we have seen, it is a concept particularly suited to the trinitarian God.

In addition, Forsyth's rejection of the strife of attributes is a way to maintain an emphasis on God's trinitarian unity. The holy, loving God – the one, indivisible God – atones. This is all the one work of the undivided and holy God who provides the way of salvation by judging sin in his own Self. God provides the atonement. Just as he reacts strongly to any tendency to separate love and holiness in the divine nature, Forsyth will not allow any suggestion of a divided Trinity to linger long in the minds of his readers. The unity of God's attributes is also the unity of the Father and Son, and the unity of the Trinity.

7. THE VICTORY OF HOLY LOVE

This even-handedness with God's attributes, this conviction that both love and holiness are equally real aspects of God's nature, does not, however, result in a deadlocked theology, with these two attributes each claiming supremacy which neither can have. Just as there was no strife of attributes on the cross, there is no conceptual impasse between love and holiness. Once again it is important to recall Forsyth's emphasis on the dynamic quality of God's attributes, which are not static entities to be kept in some sort of theoretical equilibrium, but personal and therefore dynamic characteristics of the living God. "Reality lies in action, and Christ has done the deed of history."[153] In his love and holiness, God has acted in Jesus Christ. Divine love does not prevent his holiness from taking effect, and the holiness of God is no impediment to his love. Both these attributes are revealed and active in the cross. The holy love of God

---

[152] *Preaching of Jesus*, p. 59.
[153] *Church, the Gospel and Society*, p. 95.

is shown to be a dynamic reality there. And, as we have pointed out earlier in this chapter, the cross is a victory for that holy love. The fact that Jesus Christ has taken this central place in the midst of humanity, says Forsyth,

> means that the Eternal conscience is the Eternal love, that judgment is, in the heart of it, grace, that the judge is on our side and is our Redeemer. It is only love that can do justice, it is only grace that can right all wrong. The righteous Lord whom we cannot escape is our Saviour.[154]

The whole point of the cross is the victory of God's holy love, and the result is unexpected mercy and amazing grace. As in the last sentence of this quotation, Forsyth often quotes or alludes to Isaiah 45.21: the Lord is "a just God and a Saviour," and the purpose of such a reference was to stress both the harmony of God's attributes (a major concern in the thesis of a whole) and the reality of the gospel of grace. God in faithfulness carries out justice. In the context of judgment God is merciful. In the very act of condemnation, God forgives. "There needed no adjustment of His justice with His forgiveness. So also in Isaiah, 'A just God and a Saviour.' There can therefore be no strife of attributes."[155] What there is, is atonement, justification, salvation.

John McIntyre, in the continuation of a passage we looked at earlier in this chapter, echoes this point. After speaking dramatically of "the juxtaposition of love and justice in the Christian understanding of the Atonement," McIntyre turns to the result. "The dénouement, which we could never have grasped from the other side of Easter Day, gathers love and justice together, in a way which satisfies both, beyond the expectation of either."[156] Here is a view of God's attributes that refuses to compromise one at the expense of the other, and here, too, is Forsyth's dynamic view of satisfaction, which we have enlarged upon in the previous section on 'trinitarian holiness.' In the act of atonement, both love and justice retain their absoluteness, both are fulfilled, and a new relation with God becomes a reality. In Forsyth's terms, the holy love of God issues in grace.

In this context, however, McIntyre adds a warning: "We must not try to minimise the wonder of that dénouement, by suggesting that out of love and justice a *tertium quid,* holy love, has been magically

---

[154] *Cruciality,* p. 132.
[155] *Work,* p. 118.
[156] John McIntyre, *On the Love of God* (London: Collins, 1962), p. 172.

produced, something out of relation to them."[157] Forsyth's purpose in using the expression (and in this he meets McIntyre's objection) is to relate the outcome of the cross to the characteristics of the God who accomplished it. Reconciliation proceeded from personal unity: "The new thing in Christ's revelation of God was not a new attribute, but the unity in holy love of all His attributes, conflicting before."[158] The Father's holy love that sends Christ and overcomes sin is the same grace that meets sinners with the good news of forgiveness. Holy love is not a magical something, but the triumphant God bringing salvation without compromising the integrity of his justice or lessening the impact of his mercy.

Surveying Forsyth's thinking on this subject of holy love victorious as grace, and attempting to restate it as simply as possible, we find that the language of 'God in himself' and 'God toward us' provides a helpful framework. Three cautionary notes must be stated, however, and all support the view that what God is towards us in Christ, he is in his own inner being. First, given his anti-metaphysical bias, we suspect the contrast would not especially appeal to Forsyth, yet we have seen that nevertheless, and unavoidably, he does employ a tacit ontology. Secondly, Forsyth is convinced that the two are one, and that the reality of God's nature is known definitively in Christ. And thirdly, the distinctions we make here between words are by no means absolute ones; Forsyth feels free to use 'love' and 'grace' to describe both sides of the contrast, and his occasional inconsistency with the terms 'holiness,' 'righteousness,' and 'justice' has already been noted.

With that said, it seems that Forsyth sees the love and holiness of God as aspects of God's nature, with other attributes (omnipotence, faithfulness, omniscience, etc.) as qualities and qualifiers of holy love; words such as these describe, however inadequately, 'God in himself.' When God the Father comes near in Christ the Son, those characteristics are revealed – but more than that, they are exerted. God's holy love is put into saving action in the life, death, and resurrection of Jesus Christ.

The result is salvation for humans, who experience the holy love of God variously as judgment and grace, majesty and mercy, goodness and severity. In a passage which we quoted earlier in another context, Forsyth addresses what we have called this other 'strife of attributes' – ours. "We oscillate between the goodness and

---

[157] McIntyre, *On the Love of God,* p. 172.
[158] *This Life and the Next,* 2nd ed. (1946; orig. pub. 1918), p. 111.

severity of God," he writes. "We are tossed from the one to the other," and the result is a confusion of colliding emotions. "And the conscience finds no rest till it find in the cross the one final act in which both are reconciled and inwoven, with the grace uppermost."[159] When the preaching of the cross meets humanity, when that Word comes home to us, it is "with the grace uppermost." Holy love's harmonious work meets human strife with grace. Or, to put the same assertion in other words, and yet still Forsyth's words:

> If ever you are impressed with the greatness, majesty, and power of God, depend upon it it means that still greater is His mercy. If ever you are caught by the judgment of God, caught by the law of God, and cannot escape, depend upon it, behind the power that holds you there is also the mercy that will not let you go.[160]

---

[159] *Cruciality*, p. 89.
[160] "Majesty and Mercy," *Christian World Pulpit* 79 (17 May 1911): 305.

Chapter Eight

The Future of Holy Love

Theology is thinking in centuries.
P. T. Forsyth

Up to this point in our discussion, it has been our concern to show the important place which Peter Taylor Forsyth gave to the expression, "the holy love of God," and to explicate in some detail the theological usefulness of that distinctive phrase in the doctrines of God's character and Christ's saving death. Now, at the end of our study, we wish to indicate that the 'holy love' formulation, understood in Forsythian terms, has a future. A double meaning is intended in our chapter title: we propose to think about this distinctive expression in two senses – historical progress and theological prospect. In both these areas, historical and systematic, it will be contended, Forsyth's conception of the holy love of God is useful and important. It had, and has, a future. Without endeavouring to offer exhaustive treatments, this chapter will show the enduring usefulness of understanding God in terms of holy love.

1. THE TWENTIETH-CENTURY PROGRESS OF AN IDEA

After Forsyth's death in 1921, the spotlight on individual Christian thinkers moved to other figures. After a flurry of obituary notices in the papers – *The Times* characterized him as "a brilliant theologian dealing with the deepest matters in a massive way"[1] – and

---

[1] "Death of Principal Forsyth: An Original Thinker," *The Times* (London), 12 November 1921, p. 14. Jessie Forsyth Andrews collected many of these – from the long and 'important' assessments of the national press to numerous one-line notices – in a scrapbook, now held at Dr Williams's Library, London.

glowing commemorations in the periodicals, Forsyth's name was only mentioned occasionally in published theological debate. The only significant exception is J. K. Mozley's articles in the *Expositor* in early 1922.[2] Various opinions have been advanced about the reason for that obscurity,[3] but Mozley's verdict before the fact is apt: "His mind and the *Zeitgeist* have never marched in sympathy."[4]

Whatever the reason, it would not be true to say that Forsyth's ideas fell on deaf ears. In particular, his conviction that God's nature was one of holy love was appropriated from him, and from other writers of the time, and used often. Although we do not intend to offer a comprehensive treatment at this stage of our study, in this section enough evidence will be provided to indicate the continuing vitality of the distinctive expression whose content we have previously investigated. In this brief historical survey, we will show the breadth of interest in this formulation. Just as Chapter One introduced the subject of Forsyth's use of the expression 'holy love' by examining its history in nineteenth-century theology, this chapter traces that history after Forsyth's lifetime, until the present day.

1.1 THE FIRST TWO DECADES (1921–1940)

In the two decades following Forsyth's death, several notable British scholars made use of the idea of God's holy love. Some, like A. E. Garvie and Sydney Cave, were Congregational colleagues with Forsyth. Others were younger contemporaries in the established Church of England, including J. K. Mozley, William Temple, and H. Maurice Relton.

1.1.1 Congregational followers

Alfred Garvie (1861–1945), principal of nearby New College for much of the time that Forsyth was principal at Hackney, had as a result much opportunity to be influenced by the man he described as "my beloved and esteemed friend."[5] Leaving to the side the 1943–

---

[2] J. K. Mozley, "The Theology of Dr. Forsyth," *Expositor*, 8th series, 23 (February, March 1923): 81–98, 161–180; reprinted in Mozley, *The Heart of the Gospel* (London: Society for Promoting Christian Knowledge, 1925)
[3] See especially Thomas D. Meadley, "The 'Obscurity' of P. T. Forsyth," *Congregational Quarterly* 24 (October 1946): 308–317.
[4] Mozley, *Heart of the Gospel*, p. 66.
[5] The reference occurs in the autobiographical article, "Alfred Ernest Garvie," in *Die Religionswissenschaft der Gegenwart in Selbstdarstellungen,* ed. Erich

1944 articles devoted specifically to Forsyth's contribution, Garvie employs the term most often in his substantial one-volume systematic theology, published four years after Forsyth's death.[6] Although the accomplishment of the book as a whole is impressive, Garvie's use of the holy love formulation lacks the comprehensive sweep and polemical utility of Forsyth's usage. Indeed, the younger theologian suggests that his former colleague's concern about the sentimental distortion of divine love is overdone: "If we conceive love aright, we need not fear to declare that love alone."[7] Holy love, although possessed of a certain usefulness, might therefore be outgrown as a theological term. Despite this essentially Ritschlian inclination to marginalize God's holiness, Garvie uses Forsyth's term to yoke holiness and love in his exposition of both the cross of Christ and the Fatherhood of God.

Other Congregationalists used the term as well, of whom Sydney Cave is a representative example. In speaking of God's nature, Cave said that the dogmatic category, 'the being and attributes of God,' was a misleading one, because the two cannot be separated. "What we call His attributes are His one nature seen from different aspects," and all these are intermingled. "His holiness is the holiness of love; His love is a love that is holy. His power is the power not of arbitrary force but the power of holy love."[8]

1.1.2 Influence on Anglican theology

John Kenneth Mozley (1883–1946) has accurately been called "Forsyth's finest interpreter."[9] The two corresponded,[10] and Mozley on more than one occasion acknowledged his indebtedness to the

---

Stange (Leipzig: Felix Meiner, 1928), p. 79. Despite the affirmation, one sometimes senses an element of competitiveness in their collegiality.

[6] Alfred E. Garvie, *The Christian Doctrine of the Godhead: or The Apostolic Benediction as the Christian Creed* (London: Hodder & Stoughton, [1925]), see especially pp. 210–212, 227–231.

[7] Garvie, *Christian Doctrine of the Godhead,* p. 227. For other examples of his use of 'holy love,' see Garvie, "Glorying in the Cross," in *If I Had Only One Sermon to Preach,* ed. James Marchant (London: Cassell, 1928), pp. 63–64; and "Fifty Years' Retrospect," *Congregational Quarterly* 7 (January 1929): 22–23.

[8] Sydney Cave, *The Doctrine of the Work of Christ* (London: University of London Press, 1937), pp. 264–265.

[9] A. M. Hunter, "P. T. Forsyth Neutestamentler," *Expository Times* 73 (January 1962), p. 104.

[10] A 4-page letter from Mozley to Forsyth, written on 20 January 1909, is held at Dr Williams's Library, London (New College London MS 536/22).

older theologian.[11] Although his scholarly gifts were used more in the service of the history of dogma than for creative theological construction, J. K. Mozley applied his wide historical grasp to useful and eloquent effect (for example) concerning the work of Christ. The cross, he writes, reveals "God as holy and gracious love, as the Father of His people who forgives their sins, not sparing the cost to Himself of a forgiveness which left no moral claim – the vindication of His holiness and the penalty of sin – unprovided for." Later he adds, "I would emphasise with Dr. Forsyth the truth that God's love is holy love."[12]

William Temple (1881–1944) served as Archbishop of Canterbury for the last two-and-a-half years of his life. For the last seven years of Forsyth's life, Temple was living in London, serving latterly as Canon of Westminster Abbey. Although it seems likely that they met on previous occasions, in early 1920 the two were fellow-participants in a conference in Oxford between Free Church and Church of England leaders on the subject of church reunion.[13] In writing about the doctrine of the atonement, Temple identified the theological danger of "the pendulum-swing of human thought as it sways from one reaction to another"; to slow that swing, he suggested that "no doctrine can be Christian which starts from a conception of God as moved by any motive alien from holy love."[14] Further, in comparing the "idol" of "Aristotle's 'apathetic' God" with the God revealed in Jesus Christ, Temple explains that "His anger and His compassion are but the aspect of His holy love appropriate to varying circumstances."[15] This view is reminiscent of Forsyth's conception of the various attributes of God as modifiers of the divine holiness and love.

In a 1931 article, the Anglican H. Maurice Relton (1882–1971) makes the same point. Speaking of omnipotence, omniscience, and omnipresence, he writes: "It is clear that as attributes of a Personal God, whose nature is Holy Love, they must be considered not in isolation but as governed in their exercise by the character and

---

[11] See for example, J. K. Mozley, *The Doctrine of the Atonement* (London: Gerald Duckworth, 1915), p. 56, and an article that appeared only days before his death, "Forsyth – The Theologian," *British Weekly,* 21 November 1946, p. 110.
[12] Mozley, *Heart of the Gospel*, pp. 42, 51; see also p. 32.
[13] F. A. Iremonger, *William Temple, Archbishop of Canterbury: His Life and Letters* (London: Oxford University Press, 1948), pp. 455–456.
[14] William Temple, *Christus Veritas: An Essay* (London: Macmillan, 1925), pp. 256, 257.
[15] Temple, *Christus Veritas,* p. 261.

purpose of the One whose attributes they are." On the same page he referred, in Forsythian style, to "the Omnipotence of Holy Love."[16] In 1910, when Forsyth was appointed Dean of the Faculty of Theology of the University of London, Relton was a theological student at one of the participant institutions, King's College. Following graduation, he remained in London as both parish minister and lecturer in dogmatic theology. Although Relton refers to Forsyth elsewhere in his writings, in this context concerning God's holy love, he quotes instead Walter Senior's 1880 volume of sermons and G. B. Stevens's New Testament theology.[17]

1.1.3 A Methodist example

A similar contemporary emphasis was made by biblical scholar H. Maldwyn Hughes, a Methodist who was Principal of Wesley House, Cambridge. He sees God's holiness not only as "transcendent majesty and awe-fulness," but also ethically "in terms of the Good." In Forsythian fashion he insists, "It is a misinterpretation of the Christian doctrine of the Fatherhood of God to take it as involving a lessened sense of the transcendent majesty of God.... He is the Holy Father 'in heaven.'" Then, in a concluding paragraph of his survey, Maldwyn Hughes writes, "But God's supreme attribute, that in which all others inhere, is *holy love.*" The adjective is necessary, he explains, to convey the richness of what the New Testament means by God's love: unsentimental, righteous, consistent, and active. "It is a holy love which redeems, and its passion for holiness is one with its passion for redemption.... It is the holy love of God manifested supremely in the incarnation and travail of His eternal Son."[18]

1.1.4 H. R. Mackintosh

More significant than these examples of the use of "holy love" in the first generation after Forsyth's death, however, is the comprehensive employment of the formulation by Hugh Ross Mackintosh (1870–1936), a Scottish theologian who "took over

---

[16] H. Maurice Relton, *Studies in Christian Doctrine* (London: Macmillan, 1960), p. 5. The concept recurs often under the section title, "The Nature of God in Christian Dogma," pp. 3–17. The article was originally published in 1931.
[17] For these writers, see Chapter One, section 2.3.
[18] H. Maldwyn Hughes, *The Christian Idea of God* (London: Duckworth, 1936), pp. 40–43.

much from the singularly arresting writings of P. T. Forsyth."[19] At the age of 34, he was appointed Professor of Systematic Theology at New College, Edinburgh; one of his students later wrote that "his lectures drew us out under the searching light of the holy love of God incarnate in Christ."[20]

His first original, academic theological writing was *The Doctrine of the Person of Jesus Christ* (1912), in which the idea of God's holy love appears only in the context of a discussion of what he described as "Principal Forsyth's rich and living volume, *The Person and Place of Jesus Christ.*" What is needed in the Christological debate, he says in agreement with Forsyth, is "a metaphysic of the conscience, in which not substance but Holy Love is supreme."[21]

In subsequent writings, Mackintosh begins to use the phrase more deliberately. Most memorable among these occasional utterances is his conviction that the cross reveals God's nature, which in our discussion of Forsyth's similar conviction we called his crucicentricity.[22] "Calvary is a window opening into God's heart" writes Mackintosh. "If, then, we take our cue from Jesus Christ we must think of God as redemptive Love, not shallow or good-natured, but passionately righteous and utterly self-denying."[23] On another occasion he states the same conviction, arguing that because God is acting in Christ, the atonement expresses God's character: "If what I see in the dying Saviour is holy judgment of sin and infinite self-abnegating love," that truth can be carried back, as it were, into God's nature – "I can take the central experience of Christ and assert it of God Himself."[24] Then, going a step further than Forsyth, he draws a conclusion about the necessity of Christ's death. If the cross is a true expositor of the nature of God, it reveals the very purposes of God, and so, for Jesus, "the Cross was necessary, not

---

[19] James W. Leitch, *A Theology of Transition: H. R. Mackintosh as an Approach to Barth* (London: Nisbet, 1952), p. 5. See also Robert R. Redman, Jr., "H. R. Mackintosh's Contribution to Christology and Soteriology in the Twentieth Century," *Scottish Journal of Theology* 41 (1988): 517–534.

[20] T. F. Torrance, "H. R. Mackintosh: Theologian of the Cross," *Scottish Bulletin of Evangelical Theology* 5 (1987): 162.

[21] H. R. Mackintosh, *The Doctrine of the Person of Jesus Christ,* International Theological Library (Edinburgh: T. & T. Clark, 1912), pp. 465, 472; see also pp. 472–473 on the immutability of holy love, and p. 478.

[22] See Chapter Three, section 11 above.

[23] H. R. Mackintosh, "Christ and God," *Expository Times* 31 (November 1919), p. 77.

[24] H. R. Mackintosh, *Some Aspects of Christian Belief* (London: Hodder & Stoughton, [1923]), p. 93.

merely that the human heart should be affected by the sight of loving sacrifice, but for deeper reasons based in the nature of the Father – because holy love *must* express itself so, because the last step love can take in condemning sin and resisting it is to bear its malignant assault to the very end."[25]

Although Mackintosh's use of the idea of God's holy love could be illustrated more widely in his books, pamphlets, and articles, such a task is beyond the scope of this chapter. Instead, we move at once to the most developed use of this expression in his writings, in his exploration of *The Christian Apprehension of God*. The book is a prolonged argument for what we noted as one of Mackintosh's early concerns: that God's nature is known "in that holy redeeming Love which has touched and blessed us in Christ."[26] He rejects the speculative deity of idealism and the all-encompassing God of pantheism, and warns against a retreat into mysticism or the rationalistic analysis of ideas. Then in three large chapters, he deals successively with the holiness, love, and sovereign purpose of God. These are not to be seen in a fragmented way, however, but as aspects of the one, personal God revealed in Christ: "When a Christian says 'God,' he does not mean 'Holy Love' simply; he means absolute or almighty holy love; and the term almighty stands for a vital feature apart from which God would not be God. . . . God, then, is both these things in a living unity – holy love and absolute power."[27] As we have seen, Forsyth had made a similar point in speaking of the omnipotence of holy love; Mackintosh adds an emphasis on God as the absolute, learned perhaps from Martin Kähler.

One final observation about the content of Mackintosh's use of God's holy love lies in his concern that holiness be seen as equally an attribute of God. He writes, "Holy love – and holiness as intrinsically as love is constitutive of the Ultimate Reality we name God – is the fount of all salvation."[28] To say that 'God is love' has become a commonplace, but it is the farthest thing from an obvious fact, according to Mackintosh. Instead, this truth derives from the unique revelation of God's love given in Christ's sacrifice. Therefore, it is not surprising that, like Forsyth, Mackintosh warns

---

[25] Mackintosh, *Some Aspects of Christian Belief*, p. 97.
[26] H. R. Mackintosh, *The Christian Apprehension of God* (London: Student Christian Movement, 1929), p. 130.
[27] Mackintosh, *Christian Apprehension of God*, p. 146.
[28] Mackintosh, *Christian Apprehension of God*, p. 156.

about the dangers of "a feeble and shallow sentimentalism," and even suggests that we would be truer to the New Testament to say, "God, the Holy One, is love."[29]

H. R. Mackintosh crowned his career with an analysis of German theology from Schleiermacher to Barth, and in this posthumously published volume he reiterated the central point about God's holy love, and justified his professional concern over God's attributes: "To assert unflinchingly that love and holiness are one in God, despite their seeming antagonism," he wrote, "is as much the business of a true theology as to assert that manhood and deity are one in Christ."[30]

1.1.5 H. H. Farmer

In the writings of the English Presbyterian H. H. Farmer (1892–1981), we again encounter the use of the term holy love.[31] Farmer was the successor to John Oman at Westminster College, Cambridge, and to C. H. Dodd in the University's Norris-Hulse chair of divinity. He is perhaps best-known for his theological personalism. Although the title of his 1935 book, *The World and God: A Study of Prayer, Providence and Miracle in Christian Experience,* is descriptive of the volume's contents, it gives only a hint of Farmer's main thesis, which is instead concisely stated in his first sentence: "The conviction that God is personal, and deals personally with men and women, lies at the heart of Christian experience and thought."[32] After an exploration of general principles about experiential Christianity in the first half of the book, Farmer turns to the specific Christian experience of reconciliation. Because the divine revelation in Jesus Christ "is a revelation of God as holy love," Christians experience God as "utterly loving even in His most austere demands," and at the same time "utterly forgiving in His ceaseless exposure of and judgement upon sin."[33] This comment is typical of Farmer's view in two ways. First, it moves quickly from the reality of Christ to our experience of that reality. Although he often sheds fresh light on Christian experience, Farmer's treatment of the objective realities from which that experience stems are

---
[29] Mackintosh, *Christian Apprehension of God,* pp. 187, 188.
[30] H. R. Mackintosh, *Types of Modern Theology: Schleiermacher to Barth* (London: Nisbet, 1937), p. 159.
[31] My thanks to Christopher Partridge for his helpful references to H. H. Farmer.
[32] Herbert H. Farmer, *The World and God: A Study of Prayer, Providence and Miracle in Christian Experience* (London: Nisbet, 1935), p. 1.
[33] Farmer, *World and God,* pp. 197, 202.

fleeting and only suggestive. Second, there is a strong emphasis on the revelatory value of Jesus Christ. It is the human apprehension rather than the divine revelation that has the priority in his thought. Thus in the realm of ethics, Farmer maintains that God's will is revealed in the cross: "To apprehend God as holy love is to apprehend His absolute demands as demands for love."[34] In both these aspects, Forsyth differs somewhat, preferring to stress the priority of God's act in Christ to our experience of it, and the reality of the revelation more than our apprehension of it. Therefore, in the quotation given just above, where Farmer sees God's holy love as a demand for love, Forsyth by contrast more often highlights the good news that divine holiness has triumphed over sin. While Farmer sees the main influence of God's holy love in the ongoing life of the believer, Forsyth insists on rooting the holy love of God in the finished work of Christ's cross.

Despite the differences, however, there are significant similarities with Forsyth in Farmer's writing about God's attributes, especially in his concern to balance the love and holiness of God. In a volume of sermons whose title page bears the text, "Behold therefore the goodness and severity of God" (Romans 11.22), Farmer sets out to instill in his readers "a true vision of God" by showing them "Christ's vision of God. . . . He saw God as One who is not merely inexorably holy but also infinitely giving."[35] Without using the term 'holy love' even once, Farmer presents this balanced picture of God again and again, but never more memorably than in the pivotal sermon of the collection.[36] Taking one of Forsyth's favourite passages as his text, he begins this sermon on "a just God and a Saviour" (Isaiah 45.21) with the vivid juxtaposition of two London landmarks – the cross atop St Paul's and the figure of Justice on a nearby court-house. The preacher maintains that justice and gospel are separate both in history and in our own experience, but that the separation must not become too wide: the law of the land must include compassion, and the gospel cannot overlook sin. "We do not see the love of God for what it is," insists Farmer, "until we realize that it searches and pursues and tears out and exposes all the evil in us."[37] And then he concludes with this paragraph:

---

[34] Farmer, *World and God*, p. 216; cf. pp. 197, 214, 261. For other references to holy love, see pp. 201, 213, 242–243, 253, 261, 289.
[35] Herbert H. Farmer, *The Healing Cross: Further Studies in the Christian Interpretation of Life* (London: Nisbet, 1938), pp. 53, 54.
[36] "Justice and Gospel," in Farmer, *Healing Cross*, pp. 105–112.
[37] Farmer, *Healing Cross*, p. 111.

Somewhere here surely is the very heart of the Gospel. Somewhere here lies the power of Christ, and supremely of His Cross, to cleanse and redeem the souls of men. Certainly no presentation of the Christian message to-day is likely to be of the least avail which does not hold firmly together both the goodness and the severity of God. A Gospel without the goodness of God, the utterly gracious and undeserved goodness of God to us, would, it is superfluous to say, be no Gospel; but a Gospel without the severity of God, "tearing their evil out of men," would not in these days be credible, if it has ever been. "Behold then the goodness and the severity of God" – severe because it is good, good because it is severe.[38]

In his later books, although he uses the holy love formulation only occasionally,[39] he continues to defines God as "that final reality of righteousness and love."[40] In his Lyman Beecher Lectures on preaching at Yale (which Forsyth had given some forty years earlier), Farmer spoke about God's closely related attributes: "We must keep the truth of the love of God and the truth of the holiness of God, the nearness and the distance of God, in quite inseparable connection with each other."[41] In contrast somewhat to Forsyth's treatment, Farmer explains the wrath of God by saying, "It is part of the continuous outgoing of His agapé towards persons; it is the inevitable and spontaneous recoil of love from lovelessness, the stedfast [sic] setting of itself against it. Wrath is the burning fiery heart of utterly pure love; it is love as 'consuming fire.'"[42]

In 1966, well beyond the period with which this section is concerned, Farmer resumed his use of the distinctive expression 'holy love' in *The Word of Reconciliation*. In the following quotation, we choose the outline of an argument that covers two pages:

> To be deeply and truly penitent for sin and yet at the same time to be at peace about it before God, is only possible through an apprehension of God as holy love. . . . To be *really* reconciled [to God] and not merely reluctantly submissive, only becomes possible as a man is able to apprehend that those requirements are not the demands of an inscrutable and impersonal moral order, nor the exactions of a hard and inexorable lawgiver . . . , but are rather the divine love itself drawing near to him.

---

[38] Farmer, *Healing Cross*, p. 112.
[39] See for example, Herbert H. Farmer, *Towards Belief in God* (London: Student Christian Movement, 1942), pp. 81–85, and Farmer, *God and Men* (London: Nisbet, 1948), pp. 157–158.
[40] Herbert H. Farmer, *God and Men* (London: Nisbet, 1948), p. 20.
[41] Farmer, *God and Men*, p. 124.
[42] Farmer, *God and Men*, p. 140.

The Future of Holy Love 249

... To be reconciled to God in and through the new relation of *agapé* to other persons is only possible ... if a man is brought to see them in a new light, the light of God's own holy will of love.[43]

Here are the familiar words about God's holy love, consistent with Farmer's earlier usage, but different from Forsyth's understanding of their importance. For Farmer, God's attitude toward humanity is one of 'infinite succour' and 'absolute demand,' of holy love, of experienced realities related to God's revelation. The emphasis is not that God is holy and loving, but our "apprehension" of that reality; to be reconciled is to be "brought to see ... in a new light," in order to respond in a godly way.

The key to this moral concern is found in Farmer's doctrine of the atonement, which is framed largely in exemplary terms, as evidenced by the following quotation, once again in terms of God's holy love:

The Christian gospel has from the beginning claimed to rest on God's own active disclosure of Himself in the midst of our world as holy love. The Christian gospel is not, strictly speaking, the simple statement that God is love; it is rather that God Himself discloses, exhibits, commends, makes credible His nature and purpose as love to us through Christ, and very especially through Christ's death on the Cross.[44]

Forsyth's reply to such a view may well have been to query how these realities of love and holiness can be revealed, and how any reconciliation with God is possible, apart from an objective accomplishment at the cross. The problem is not our seeing but our sin, and Christ's sacrifice has triumphed over sin and evil. Forsyth repeatedly made the point that God not only showed but exerted love, that God's holiness was at work to judge and be judged in the cross, that something fundamental in the God-person relation was decisively changed by the death of Jesus, in short, that God's holy love was active to save in Christ's cross. God's nature *was* revealed in the cross, but Forsyth repeatedly urged that the revelation of God's holy love was given in the act of redemption. Further, although our apprehension of that reality is important, the cross emphasizes Christ's accomplishment. As Forsyth might well have said, the work is more done than to do. Considering their differing interpretations of the atonement, therefore, it is perhaps not

---

[43] H. H. Farmer, *The Word of Reconciliation* (Digswell Place, Welwyn, Herts: James Nisbet, 1966), p. 43; other references to holy love occur on pp. 52, 62, 68–72, 77, 95.

[44] Farmer, *God and Men*, p. 157.

surprising that Farmer does not quote Forsyth in support of his use of use of the words 'holy love.'

1.1.6 Summary

As we look back over the preceding paragraphs, with their summary treatment of scholars who wrote of God in terms of holy love, we find that the term flourished during this period, roughly spanning the 1920s and 1930s. Its use was widespread, and as we have illustrated in the previous paragraphs, not limited to Congregational or Free Church theologians. Interest in this way of describing the attributes of God extended across generational as well as denominational lines. Some of the scholars we have discussed, such as Garvie and Mackintosh, were part of the generation who succeeded Forsyth, and their careers overlapped with his. Others, like Mozley, Temple, Relton, and Farmer, were yet another generation removed, and just beginning their writing in the two decades after Forsyth's last book. But all of them employed this way of speaking about God's attributes primarily in the 1920s and 1930s; those who continued to write after this time tended to use the 'holy love' formulation much less often, a tendency which is quite marked, for example, in Garvie and Farmer.

Forsyth's influence on this theological development would seem to be of significant proportions. Several of the theologians whom we have surveyed in this sub-section (1.1) knew Forsyth personally, read and reviewed his books, and/or corresponded with him; included in this category would be Garvie, Cave, Mozley, and Mackintosh. Others have a more direct relationship to one of this latter group than to other sources of the expression: Temple and Relton knew Mozley well, and Mackintosh would be known by Farmer. We conclude, therefore, that Forsyth's influence (both directly and indirectly) was an important reason for the proliferation of interest in discussion of God's attributes in terms of holy love in the period between 1921 and 1940.

1.2 A WANING OF INTEREST

When we turn to the four decades that follow, we find only a sporadic and incidental use of the phrase 'holy love' to refer to God's attributes. In a 1941 article that quotes both Forsyth and H. R. Mackintosh, T. F. Torrance refers to the sinful human effort to snatch redemption from God, "and that," Torrance adds, "God must judge, else He were not Holy Love."[45] Fifteen years later, in a sermon about "the Holy Trinity of Divine Love," the phrase once again comes to Torrance's mind: "What man is there who can look into the face of God and live? His holy Love would only uncover our unloveliness and sin, and we would only come under its utter condemnation." Later in the same sermon he writes:

> Are we not afraid of the Love of God? God is Holy, Pure, True, utterly and only Love. Are you prepared for that God to give Himself to you, for His holy, pure Love to be a living presence in your heart and life? Is that not just what we are afraid of? If God in His love gave Himself to me, His love would burn up my self-love; His purity would attack my impurity; His truth would slay my falsehood and hypocrisy. The Love of God would be my judgment.[46]

This assessment, acutely aware of evangelical and experiential realities, is reminiscent of Forsyth's comment "there is everything in the love of God to be afraid of. Love is not holy without judgment. It is the love of holy God that is the consuming fire."[47]

Two examples have been discovered from the 1950s. In a discussion of "The Attributes of Divine Fatherhood," the Canadian theologian John Mackintosh Shaw avers that "there is much in favour of speaking of one absolute or central attribute of God rather than of two, bringing the two together in the one term 'Holy Love' or 'Holy Father-love.'" He later utilizes the term in discussing Christ's death as a condemnation of sin and a revelation of love.[48]

Another instance of the use of this expression comes from H. F. Lovell Cocks (1894–1983), a student of Forsyth's who later became Principal of Western College in Bristol. He echoed his mentor's way of describing the attributes of God: "Because God is holy love, ... [b]ecause God intends our holiness, and because we are sinners, the revelation of His love to us must come as a word of judgment."[49] The subsequent argument reveals that his concern is the same as

---

[45] T. F. Torrance, "Predestination in Christ," *Evangelical Quarterly* 13 (April 1941): 121.
[46] T. F. Torrance, "A Sermon on the Trinity," *Biblical Theology* 6 (Belfast, 1956): 44, 41, 43. Similarly, see Thomas F. Torrance, *The Mediation of Christ* (Exeter: Paternoster, 1983), p. 50.
[47] *The Work of Christ* (1910), p. 85.
[48] John Mackintosh Shaw, *Christian Doctrine: A One-Volume Outline of Christian Belief* (Toronto: Ryerson, 1953), pp. 47, 207.
[49] H. F. Lovell Cocks, *The Wondrous Cross* (London: Independent Press, 1957), p. 55.

Forsyth's: to show that there is no strife of attributes in God's nature.[50]

Besides H. H. Farmer's usage quoted earlier, examples from the 1960s of those who spoke of God's holy love include John McIntyre. In the context of a discussion of atonement theories, he warns of the danger of treating holy love as an attribute of God in its own right.[51] Interestingly, in his most recent book on soteriology, he refers to Christ's sacrificial death as "the essence of righteous love," using essentially the same expression in a more positive way.[52]

From a very different perspective, Daniel Day Williams looked at God's nature in terms of process theology, and quoted Forsyth on one occasion. In using the words that are the focus of our interest in this thesis, he makes an interesting contrast: "While God's spirit always remains one in the integrity of Holy Love, man's spirit is subject to the distortions, estrangement and perversity of his finite freedom."[53] Although Williams and Forsyth would disagree on several levels, the point the former makes here finds a parallel in Forsyth's conviction that the strife of attributes is not within God's nature, but between God's nature and purpose for humanity and the sinful human situation.[54]

All these examples are slight and sporadic. After much use in the period between the wars, interest in Forsyth's expression waned, and it was not until much later that that interest would revive. Even in the post-World War II years when Forsyth's theology was receiving new attention, theologians did not fasten on this distinctive way of speaking about God's attributes.

1.3 THE CONTINUING USE OF HOLY LOVE IN EUROPEAN THEOLOGY

Before continuing our historical sketch of Forsyth's influence on the future of holy love in English-speaking theology, we look sideways, as it were, to note that this distinctive expression had a

---

[50] For Lovell Cocks, and Forsyth's influence on him, see Alan P. F. Sell, *Commemorations: Studies in Christian Thought and History* (Calgary: University of Calgary Press, 1993), pp. 303–340.
[51] John McIntyre, *On the Love of God* (London: Collins, 1962), p. 172. See our discussion of his point in Chapter Seven, section 7.
[52] John McIntyre, *The Shape of Soteriology: Studies in the Doctrine of the Death of Christ* (Edinburgh: T. & T. Clark, 1992), p. 46.
[53] Daniel Day Williams, *The Spirit and the Forms of Love* (Welwyn, Herts: James Nisbet, 1968), p. 3.
[54] We discussed this concern in Chapter Seven, section 5.6.

parallel history in continental theology. In Chapter One, section 2, we traced the use of 'holy love' as a description of God's nature along a line of nineteenth-century German scholars that included C. I. Nitzsch, Ernest Sartorius, Isaac Dorner, and Martin Kähler. At this point, we pick up the historical thread again, and illustrate its progress in the twentieth century.

Aside from Wilhelm Herrmann, perhaps the most notable German systematic theologian writing contemporaneously with Forsyth was Julius Kaftan (1848–1926). Already well-respected in the 1880s as a result of the publication of two important books, Kaftan's *Dogmatik* was published in 1897, and went through several editions. Although the earlier *Truth of the Christian Religion* (1888) does not mention holy love, the phrase is a common one in the *Dogmatik*.[55] It would seem that Kaftan's experience in this matter may well have been quite similar to Forsyth's. Interestingly, recently discovered materials relating to Forsyth include a notebook in which he had translated substantial passages of Kaftan's *Dogmatik*.[56] Another German writing at the same time with a similar emphasis on God's holy love was Theodore Häring (1848–1928). His one-volume systematic theology, published in 1906, included "God as Holy Love" as a section title.[57]

As in British theology, God's holy love was a vital theme in German theology in the 1920–1940 period. Perhaps the most notable example is Ernst Troeltsch (1865–1923), whose earlier writings Forsyth knew well. His *Glaubenslehre,* although given as lectures in 1912–1913, was not published until 1925. In his discussion of the divine attributes, he uses the 'holy love' formulation in a deliberate and sometimes moving way:

---

[55] Julius Kaftan, *The Truth of the Christian Religion,* 2 vols., trans. George Ferries (Edinburgh: T. & T. Clark, 1894; orig. pub. in German, 1888); J. K. Mozley, *Doctrine of the Atonement,* p. 170, quotes Kaftan's use of 'holy love' in *Dogmatik,* 6th. ed (1909; orig. pub. 1897), pp. 586, 591, and 594f.

[56] The undated notebook, held in Dr Williams's Library, London, covers the Introduction and sections 48, 49, and 52 of Kaftan's work. These sections consider respectively the Biblical teaching on redemption, and on atonement, followed by the church's development of these doctrines. See Julius Kaftan, *Dogmatik* (Freiburg: J. C. B. Mohr, 1897), pp. 446–465, 476–485.

[57] Theodore Häring, *The Christian Faith: A System of Dogmatics,* trans. from the second revised and enlarged German edition, 1912, by John Dickie and George Ferries (London: Hodder & Stoughton, 1915); see especially pp. 337–359. The first edition was published in 1906, and had the same structure for God's attributes; see Karl Barth, *Church Dogmatics* 2/1, p. 344.

The divine holiness is no moralism. God did not give the world his law and then abandon it; instead, he searches for the creature with love and passion, creating the very holiness that he demands. Here we find no cold law, no crushing commandment that seeks fulfilment in human compliance; we find a holy love that embraces us and incorporates us into itself, thereby bringing us to faith.[58]

Another post-1920 scholar with a similar emphasis was Horst Stephan, whose own *Glaubenslehre* is comparable with Troeltsch's.[59] Our purpose here, however, does not extend beyond merely noting the developments concerning 'holy love' in German theology, as a counterpoint to the history of the expression in English.

While the influence of German theology on the English-speaking world has been strong, significant, and often noted, the opposite combination – of German interest and British influence – is worth noting. As the particular instance we have in mind involves P. T. Forsyth and the holiness and love of God, it is especially important. The young Emil Brunner, fresh from doctoral study in Zurich, spent two years in Britain (1913–1914) when Forsyth was at the height of his career. During this time, Forsyth's work impressed the young Swiss theologian, and that high regard endured, so much so that much later, when asked by a television interviewer who he considered the greatest modern British theologian, Brunner mentioned Forsyth.[60] Twice in his *Dogmatics,* Brunner commended Forsyth's contribution, first as proof that in England "the dogmatic spirit was not destroyed by the spirit of the Enlightenment,"[61] and then in reference to Forsyth's "valuable book on *The Work of Christ,* in which he discusses, with genuine biblical understanding, various alternative modern theories [of the atonement]."[62] In light of this

---

[58] Ernst Troeltsch, *The Christian Faith,* trans. Garrett E. Paul, ed. Gertrud von le Fort, Fortress Texts in Modern Theology (Minneapolis: Fortress, 1991; orig. pub. in German 1925), p. 119, see also p. 112, and especially section 14, "God as Love," pp. 174–194.

[59] Horst Stephan, *Glaubenslehre,* 2nd ed. (1928), see especially sections 12–13; the reference is in Karl Barth, *Church Dogmatics* 2/1, p. 341.

[60] Vernon Sproxton, "Emil Brunner on his Faith and Work," *The Listener,* 16 February 1961, pp. 307–308.

[61] Emil Brunner, *The Christian Doctrine of God,* trans. Olive Wyon, *Dogmatics,* vol. 1, Lutterworth Library, vol. 35 (London: Lutterworth, 1949), p. 92.

[62] Emil Brunner, *The Christian Doctrine of Creation and Redemption,* trans. Olive Wyon, *Dogmatics,* vol. 2, Lutterworth Library, vol. 39 (London: Lutterworth, 1952), p. 315. On the connection between Forsyth and Brunner, see Samuel J. Mikolaski, "P. T. Forsyth," in *Creative Minds in Contemporary*

esteem and appreciation, and of the fact that "the dialectic of Holiness and Love" is prominent in his writings,[63] it is disappointing to discover that Brunner uses the holy love formulation only rarely,[64] and although others could have been mentioned, cites only Alexander von Oettingen, a nineteenth-century German Lutheran, as one who used the expression.[65]

Forsyth's influence on Brunner in this matter is an exception, however. For the most part, the occurrences of 'holy love' in modern continental theology can be attributed largely to the influence of the German theologians surveyed in Chapter One. Undoubtedly, there were many, like Karl Barth, who used the term occasionally. Indeed, one is tempted to say that it would be more surprising if this particular combination of 'holy love' did *not* occur within the hundreds of thousands of words of the multi-volume *Church Dogmatics*.[66] More interesting, however, is Barth's distinctive pairing of God's perfections.[67] An interesting study, far

---

[63] *Theology*, ed. P. E. Hughes (Grand Rapids, Michigan: Eerdmans, 1966), pp. 333–337.

Brunner, *Christian Doctrine of God*, p. 163. Later in the same volume, in another context, Brunner makes a similar programmatic statement: "The right understanding of Election is, therefore, only possible where that dialectical relation of Holiness and Mercy is rightly understood, which is the fundamental characteristic in the Biblical Idea of God...." (p. 337). See also Brunner, *The Mediator: A Study of the Central Doctrine of the Christian Faith*, trans. Olive Wyon, Lutterworth Library, vol. 3 (London: Lutterworth, 1934), pp. 279–282, 449–452, 465–468; *Christian Doctrine of God*, pp. 157–240; and *Christian Doctrine of Creation and Redemption*, pp. 295–297.

[64] Brunner, *Mediator*, p. 484; *Christian Doctrine of God*, p. 203. See also Anders Nygren, "Emil Brunner's Doctrine of God," in *The Theology of Emil Brunner*, ed. Charles W. Kegley, The Library of Living Theology, vol. 3, eds. Charles W. Kegley and Robert W. Bretall (New York: Macmillan, 1962), pp. 179–180.

[65] Brunner, *Christian Doctrine of God*, p. 203, indicates that von Oettingen "finds his way back to the truth of the Bible as taught at the Reformation, and teaches the Holiness and the Love of God ('God, the Holy Love') as the Nature of God, which are to be distinguished from His Attributes (*Lutherische Dogmatik*, II, pp. 140ff.)." Von Oettingen's multi-volume work was published from 1897–1902.

[66] See, for example, Karl Barth, *Church Dogmatics* 2/1, pp. 339–341, 368.

[67] Barth, *Church Dogmatics* 2/1, see especially pp. 351–406. One writer vividly described Barth's wider project on "The Reality of God," pp. 257–677, as "a kind of cat's cradle of connected attributes of God, all related to a key pair, God's love and God's freedom," and concludes that this book-length chapter "is of classical significance in modern theological thinking." William Nicholls, *Systematic and Philosophical Theology*, The Pelican Guide to Modern Theology, vol. 1, ed. R. P. C. Hanson (Harmondsworth, Middlesex: Penguin Books, 1969), pp. 119, 149.

beyond the scope of the present work but parallel to it, would be to examine Barth's treatment of the interaction of attributes and atonement in light of Forsyth's convictions. Is Bernard Ramm correct in suggesting that Barth's 'Christomonism' leads him to side with "the liberal tradition of the monism of love," which in turn "makes serious inroads into the concept of the holiness of God"?[68] Or, is Ramm not taking sufficiently into account the holy love of a God who becomes 'the Judge judged in our place'?[69]

The Dutch scholar Hendrikus Berkhof, who acknowledges his inheritance from the same mediating theologians who spoke so often about holy love, discusses the substance of the doctrine of God's attributes in successive chapters entitled, "Holy Love,"[70] "The Defenseless Superior Power," and "The Changeable Faithfulness." His chapter on holy love begins by making the qualification that God and love are not interchangeable: "He is the subject and love the predicate." Therefore, holy love expresses "the uniqueness and divine character of this love," as well as "the unity of his transcendence and condescendence."[71] Further, the holiness of God's love indicates that it is "completely sovereign and free";[72] it would seem that Berkhof's view would treat Forsyth's and Barth's treatment of the attributes as similar. Further still, Berkhof speaks of the biblical theme of God as a jealous God, asserting that God's desire for humanity meets with resistance, and "God's holy love cannot acquiesce in that. It cannot tolerate opposition. It crosses our path to break our resistance."[73] Berkhof, in short, uses the holy love expression in a creative and prominent way. Following such notables as Julius Kaftan, Ernest Troeltsch, and Emil Brunner, Hendrikus Berkhof is the latest in a long line of European theologians to use the formulation.

---

[68] Bernard L. Ramm, *The Evangelical Heritage* (Waco, Texas: Word Books, 1973), p. 119.
[69] See Karl Barth, *Church Dogmatics* 4/1, pp. 211–283.
[70] Hendrikus Berkhof, *Christian Faith: An Introduction to the Study of the Faith,* trans. Sierd Woudstra (Grand Rapids, Michigan: William B. Eerdmans, 1979; orig. pub. in Dutch, 1973), pp. 118–133.
[71] Berkhof, p. 121.
[72] Berkhof, p. 122.
[73] Berkhof, p. 123.

1.4 RENEWED INTEREST IN GOD'S HOLY LOVE (1978–1993)

We have seen that the popularity of 'the holy love of God' as a theological construction has waxed and waned. After its widespread use by Forsyth in the first two decades of the twentieth century, it was used by a variety of theologians in Britain in the 1920s and 1930s. Then it fell into disuse in the middle decades, although this distinctive phrase never entirely disappeared from current theological writing; occasional sightings have been noted in the previous section of this chapter. The last fifteen years, however, have witnessed a reversal of the fortunes of this paradoxical way of referring to God's attributes, and it is our contention that the impetus for this revival is in significant part related to Forsyth's influence.

1.4.1 Donald G. Bloesch

Summarizing P. T. Forsyth's considerable impact upon British theology, Stephen Sykes concluded: "He was an excellent theologian, but his inheritance needed to be developed more fully and rigorously. Though in his day he had numerous admirers, Forsyth had no obvious successor."[74] Even those who followed Forsyth in the matter of attributes and atonement in the two decades after his death could not be considered successors to the wider position Forsyth represented. J. K. Mozley and H. R. Mackintosh would be the most likely candidates for that task, but Mozley (who often referred to Forsyth) was more of an historical theologian, and Mackintosh (who appreciated much of Forsyth's contribution) did not follow Forsyth so much as walk alongside him, developing his own theology in a distinctive way. Of subsequent theologians, however, none has better credentials to succeed Forsyth than Donald Bloesch, who on two significant occasions, has acknowledged his debt to the subject of our study. In the introduction to *Essentials of Evangelical Theology,* he included Forsyth in his "ancestral tree from a theological perspective," while in a more recent volume he identifies his "principal mentors" as Luther, Calvin, Forsyth, and Barth.[75]

---

[74] S. Y. Sykes, "Theology through History," in *The Modern Theologians: An Introduction to Christian Theology in the Twentieth Century,* ed. David. F. Ford (Oxford: Basil Blackwell, 1989), vol. 2, p. 11.

[75] Donald G. Bloesch, *Essentials of Evangelical Theology,* vol. 1: *God, Authority, and Salvation* (San Francisco: Harper & Row, 1978), p. 4; Donald G.

In 1978, Bloesch published the first of two volumes of his *Essentials of Evangelical Theology*. Conceived not as a full-scale systematic theology but rather as a presentation of "the hallmarks of the historic faith from an evangelical perspective,"[76] the book dealt with the conventional loci of systematics by setting out the sometimes controversial evangelical centre of each doctrine. So, for example, christology is dealt with under the title, "The Deity of Jesus Christ," while soteriology is headed "The Substitutionary Atonement." Despite this approach, however, invariably the discussion in each chapter broadens to include a more comprehensive handling of the doctrine. So, while the chapter on the doctrine of God begins with a consideration of divine sovereignty in the light of the Holocaust and Hiroshima, Bloesch widens his purview to discuss God's perfections. Then, before moving to the Trinity and to the glory of God as the crown of divine attributes, he writes a significant section with the title "Holy Love."

"God in his essence is both love and holiness," declares Bloesch, "and therefore it is of a holy love that we must speak when referring to divinity."[77] These two distinct attributes are nevertheless inseparable, and although they sometimes exist in tension, "neither must be emphasized to the detriment of the other."[78] On the one hand, Bloesch sees God's holiness in terms of both the numinous and the moral (indeed, the moral purity God demands is the reason why he must be approached 'in fear and trembling'), while on the other, he conceives God's love as not merely a quality of his nature but as an action expressed in giving, sacrificing, and forgiving.

Envisioning God as holy love enables Bloesch to make some useful distinctions. For example: "The love that comes from God accepts the sinner as he is, in his sins, but because it is also a holy love, it demands that the sinner change his ways." Or again: "Holy love does not cancel the demands of the law but seeks the fulfillment of these demands."[79] With the encouragement of this last quotation,

---

[76] Bloesch, *A Theology of Word and Spirit*, Christian Foundations, vol. 1 (Carlisle: Paternoster, 1992), p. 32.

[77] Bloesch, *Essentials of Evangelical Theology*, vol. 1, p. ix.

Bloesch, *Essentials of Evangelical Theology*, vol. 1, p. 32. Bloesch has elaborated these views in chapter 6 of *God the Almighty: Power, Wisdom, Holiness, Love*; Christian Foundations, vol. 3 (Downers Grove, Illinois: InterVarsity Press, 1995), which appeared after the completion of this thesis.

[78] Bloesch, *Essentials of Evangelical Theology*, vol. 1, p. 32.

[79] Bloesch, *Essentials of Evangelical Theology*, vol. 1, p. 35.

we turn in the same volume to Bloesch's treatment of the atonement, and discover that Forsyth's concept of God's holy love is applied there: "God in the person of his Son experiences the death and hell which humankind deserves, and in this identification his holy love is both demonstrated and satisfied."[80] In the brief but concentrated discussion that follows, Bloesch quotes Forsyth twice. Forsyth's influence is also apparent in the modern theologian's treatment of the wrath of God. While liberalism rejected that concept as unworthy of God and orthodoxy inadvertently allowed it to divide the Godhead, Bloesch says, "The wrath of God must properly be understood as the necessary reaction of his holiness to sin. It is one form of his holy love."[81] That holy love was revealed in Christ, and pre-eminently at the cross: "The agonizing death of Christ on the cross attests to both the wrath of God against sin and his unfailing love for the sinner."[82]

Before we leave Donald Bloesch's discussion of the holy love of God, we note that (like Forsyth) he uses the conception in a variety of contexts extending beyond the doctrines of God and the atonement. In a discussion of ethics, and particularly of love and justice, he introduces God's love and holiness:

> God's love is a holy love concerned about wrongdoing and injustice and demanding social holiness and righteousness. God's holiness is a loving holiness, which forgives and forbears. His holiness is perfected in love just as his love is infused by holiness.[83]

Applying this to the political sphere, he comments: "Love without justice degenerates into anarchy. Justice without love becomes tyranny (as in Marxist regimes)."[84] Among much else, the fertile conception of God's holy love was one of the valuable theological ideas which Bloesch inherited from Forsyth.

1.4.2 Alan P. F. Sell

P. T. Forsyth's influence, not least in the matter of the divine holy love, is markedly evident in a book called *God our Father*, published in 1980 by Alan Sell, whose stated objective here is "to

---

[80] Bloesch, *Essentials of Evangelical Theology*, vol. 1, p. 161.
[81] Bloesch, *Essentials of Evangelical Theology*, vol. 1, p. 34.
[82] Donald G. Bloesch, *The Crisis of Piety: Essays toward a Theology of the Christian Life*, 2nd ed. (Colorado Springs: Helmers & Howard, 1988), pp. 29–30.
[83] Donald G. Bloesch, *Freedom for Obedience: Evangelical Ethics in Contemporary Times* (San Francisco: Harper & Row, 1987), p. 97.
[84] Bloesch, *Freedom for Obedience*, p. 98.

marry the spirit of enquiry with that of devotion."[85] He trawls the scriptures and the Christian centuries for wisdom about God's attributes, quoting widely from hymns and prayers as well as from more academic theology. The opening pages deal with epistemology ("I have begun resolutely with Christ. He is Christianity's distinctive datum."[86]), and with God as the Father of Jesus Christ and of many adopted children. Then, in the longest chapter of the book, Sell quotes the Bible's fundamental conviction that "God is love" (1 John 4.8,16), but immediately adds that love's meaning is sometimes elusive and often misused. For that reason, he claims,

> we need to think of God's love in relation to other qualities he possesses, and to understand them all in relation to Christ, the Son who shows us the Father.
> When we contemplate God's love in Christ, I think we see that it is, above all, holy love with which we have to do. God is the holy loving Father.[87]

Further, if the positive justification for speaking of God's holy love is the Father's revelation in the Son, the negative impetus for doing so is the theological distortions that result when holiness and love are separated:

> If we do not think of God's love as holy love we shall be in danger of driving a wedge between God's justice and his mercy, his wrath and his grace. We shall conjure up inaccurate pictures of Christ the obedient Son pleading with God, the outraged Father, to stay his justice, to sit light to sin, and to resort to benevolence; whereas the Cross reveals a holy love which is satisfied, and which is victorious.[88]

In the course of subsequent examination, God's holy love is shown to encompass holiness (both in terms of "holy dread" and in terms of "his purity, his righteousness, his moral demand"[89]) and righteousness (thus shedding light on God's law that reflects the divine character, and on the wrath of God expressed against sin). In addition, "holy love is victoriously atoning love," expressed as mercy and grace, as "general favour" and also "forgiving love."[90] This last expression of holy love – grace to sinners – results from

---

[85] Alan P. F. Sell, *God Our Father,* Doctrine and Devotion, vol. 1 (Edinburgh: Saint Andrew Press, 1980), p. vii.
[86] Sell, p. 5.
[87] Sell, p. 35.
[88] Sell, pp. 35–36.
[89] Sell, pp. 37, 39.
[90] Sell, p. 45.

Christ's atoning death. Holiness is satisfied, love is victorious, and sinners are forgiven.

In the material briefly surveyed here, Alan Sell's treatment of divine love and holiness is consistently presented in the Forsythian terms of holy love, and he is quoted at three key points within the chapter. Elsewhere in his wide-ranging writings, with their frequent references to Forsyth, Sell reminds his readers that "P. T. Forsyth was prominent in seeking to recall the church to the idea that God's love is *holy* love."[91] In the pages of *God Our Father,* Sell accents some distinctive emphases from Forsyth: the active and outgoing quality of holy love, the strong moral cast to his thought, and most distinctively of all, the fact that God's holy love in Christ's cross issues as grace. Furthermore, as Sell turns to other attributes of God in the succeeding chapters, we find Forsyth's practice of seeing those attributes in the context of holy love developed in a clear and systematic way:

> If we do not begin from the holy love of God made known to us in Christ, we shall find ourselves in difficulties when we come to fill out our understanding of God. We should have no reason to suppose that an omnipresent God who was *not* holy love had our best interests at heart; omniscience divorced from holy love could be threatening in the extreme; and apart from holy love omnipotence could be sheer, and even hostile, power.[92]

1.4.3 John Stott and J. I. Packer

The contribution of John Stott in his 1986 book, *The Cross of Christ,* has already been noted.[93] That this is a significant example of the use of the expression that Forsyth put forward is indicated by

---

[91] Alan P. F. Sell, *A Reformed, Evangelical, Catholic Theology: The Contribution of the World Alliance of Reformed Churches, 1875–1982* (Grand Rapids, Michigan: William B. Eerdmans, 1991), p. 10. According to this author, "it fell to Forsyth," when faced with nineteenth century liberalism's sentimental view of divine love, "to emphasise as few others have done the *holiness* of God's love" (Alan P. F. Sell, "The Heart of the Christian Gospel," *Indian Journal of Theology* 28 (January 1979), p. 26).

[92] Sell, *God Our Father,* p. 55.

[93] See our discussion in Chapter Seven, section 5, of John R. W. Stott, *The Cross of Christ* (Leicester: Inter-Varsity, 1986). For specific references to the holy love formulation, see pp. 88–89, 129–133, 152, 158–159, 161, 214. Interestingly, when Stott replied to David Edwards's critique of his soteriology, the holy love of God featured on nearly every page; see "John Stott's Response," in David L. Edwards and John Stott, *Essentials: A Liberal-Evangelical Dialogue* (London: Hodder & Stoughton, 1988), pp. 158–168.

the large number of references to "God, love of (and holy love of)" in the index to his book. Stott acknowledges Forsyth, Temple, and Brunner as his sources for his emphasis on holy love,[94] but it is Forsyth who dominates the discussion, and justly so, as the latter two used the expression only occasionally.

J. I. Packer, a theologian in the same evangelical tradition as Stott, uses the phrase "holy love" in two circumstances, both in the context of the characteristic nature of God, though on neither occasion does he elaborate or explain its use. In the popular presentation of the doctrine in *Knowing God,* Packer writes of God as love (1 John 4.8,16) and light (1 John 2.7–11, 1.6–7). He concludes, "So the God who is love is first and foremost light, and sentimental ideas of His love as an indulgent, benevolent softness, divorced from moral standards and concerns, must therefore be ruled out from the start. God's love is holy love."[95] In a later dictionary article, Packer says that God's attributes include his being and his character. The former is a lengthy list which includes self-existence, immutability, infinity, omnipotence, and impassability; the second consists of two assertions: "God is holy love," and "God is moral perfection."[96] The picture of God which results is not first of all personal, but rather bears the mark of an over-reliance on speculative thinking.[97] Consequently, Packer's use of the holy love construction lacks the vitality and prominence displayed by Forsyth.

1.4.4 Thomas Oden

Thomas Oden represents a very different theological tradition – American, Methodist, Arminian, and ecumenical. In the earlier part of his career, Oden was preoccupied with the cutting edge of American pastoral theology, including psychotherapy, transactional analysis, and group experiences, but a significant reversal in his priorities led him to the conviction that theological truth was

---

[94] Stott, *Cross of Christ,* p. 88, note 5.
[95] J. I. Packer, *Knowing God* (London: Hodder & Stoughton, 1973), p. 134.
[96] J. I. Packer, "God," in *New Dictionary of Theology,* eds. Sinclair B. Ferguson and David F. Wright (Downers Grove, Illinois: Inter-Varsity Press, 1988), p. 277. In the same dictionary, see also J. P. Baker, "Love of God" p. 400.
[97] This conclusion is borne out by an examination of Packer's critique of the role of natural theology, the *analogia entis,* and the scholastic 'ways' of negation and eminence, a critique which in the end affirms all three; see James I. Packer, "Theism for Our Time," in *God Who is Rich in Mercy: Essays Presented to D. B. Knox,* eds. Peter T. O'Brien and David G. Peterson (Homebush West, Australia: Lancer Books, 1986), pp. 10–14.

contained in revealed scripture and conveyed by centuries of Christian thinking. So, in writing a three-volume systematics, he says, "My concern is not primarily with knocking down beliefs but with upbuilding, not with polemics but with peacemaking, not with differences but with consensus, not with development of doctrine but with the unity of the Christian tradition, which has so astutely and imaginatively addressed so many different cultural environments."[98] In the first volume, the attributes of God are the first major topic under discussion, and Oden considers them under four headings: the "Transcendent Nature," "Outreaching Majesty," and "Free Personal Spirit" of God are the first three; the fourth is encapsulated in the sentence: "The Moral Character of God – is holy love."[99] This concept is an important one for Oden: his fundamental conviction is that "God is holy love. Holiness and love point directly to the center of the character of God."[100]

Beyond this central assertion, Oden also construes various other attributes in the light of God's holy love. Immutability, for example, is seen not "in wooden, Aristotelian terms;" rather, it should be understood to mean that "the deeper intentionality of the will of God – *chesed,* God's unfailing holy love – is sure and unchanging."[101] More interestingly, Oden considers the self-sufficiency of God in the context of his holiness. It is true to say that God is accountable only to himself, and that his holiness is the standard by which all others are measured, but such a statement is insufficient on its own, and potentially misleading. It is important to add, Oden claims, that "God's holiness expresses itself in the form of holy love. To affirm that the holy God is the God of love suggests that God is not centered in himself but reaches out toward others with ease and pleasure."[102]

We see "the coalescence of holiness and love," Oden says, "in the atoning work of God the Son." "Holy love is most radically beheld in God's treatment of sin, especially in the cross of Christ."[103] And although "holy love is attested by Scripture of God from the beginning," "it is especially through beholding and responding to this salvation event, Jesus Christ, that Christians have come to

---

[98] Thomas C. Oden, *The Living God,* Systematic Theology, vol. 1 (San Francisco: Harper & Row, 1987), p. xii.
[99] Oden, p. 31. His treatment of this fourth aspect is on pp. 97–130.
[100] Oden, p. 123.
[101] Oden, p. 113.
[102] Oden, p. 105.
[103] Oden, p. 123.

understand the holy love of God and the relation between God's holiness and God's love. As it was the *love* of God that sent the only Son (John 3.16), it was the *holiness* of God that required the satisfaction of divine justice through the sacrifice of the Son."[104] But Forsyth is unwilling to make such an exclusive distinction. It was God's holiness that sent Jesus, and his love that sacrificed. God's holy love is not divisible; it is God himself. Oden goes on to make a similar point, reviewing the scriptural evidence that brings these two themes together: 1 John 4.10, Romans 3.21-22 and 5.8, John 3.16 and 19, and (in an ethical context) Ephesians 5.2.[105]

1.4.5 Paul K. Jewett

Our final example of modern theologians who use the holy love formulation takes us into the current decade. The first volume of Paul Jewett's systematic theology appeared in 1991, and in some 500 pages covered the traditional dogmatic categories of prolegomena, revelation and scripture, God's nature and attributes, and creation.[106] The organization of this volume is relevant to our concern here because Jewett, without quoting Forsyth, makes several decisions in a decidedly Forsythian way. The first is that in the unit entitled "Who God Is: The Divine Nature," Jewett considers four topics, all of which Forsyth (especially if he were as neatly systematic as Jewett) would affirm: God is (1) Personal Being, (2) the Holy One, (3) Love, and (4) a Trinity of Holy Love. The second organizational decision also reminds us of Forsyth. In the next major unit, about God's attributes, Jewett distinguishes between nature and attributes, including holy love in the former category and God's will, power, wisdom, knowledge, etc. in the latter.

Jewett begins his first main section on these two attributes of holiness and love with the assertion: "Believing that he is who he has revealed himself to be, the church has taught that God is the God whose very nature is Holy Love."[107] He explains that his concern is for "balance of treatment," and that he wishes "to maintain the unity (not identity) of the divine holiness and love."[108] Therefore,

---

[104] Oden, pp. 123, 124.
[105] Oden, pp. 124-125.
[106] Paul K. Jewett, *God, Creation, and Revelation: A Neo-Evangelical Theology* (Grand Rapids, Michigan: William B. Eerdmans, 1991). Jewett studied under Brunner at Zurich, and subsequently taught at Fuller Theological Seminary.
[107] Jewett, p. 189; for other uses of this distinctive combination, see, for example, pp. 197, 239, 246, 250, 262, 324.
[108] Jewett, p. 190.

he writes, "The God who is the Holy One is the God who is in our midst as Love." God's holiness and love are "mutually inclusive" but not "ultimately synonymous." "His holiness and love encompass each other, contain and comprise each other in a mysterious embrace."[109] Later, he usefully suggests that these attributes be understood in a 'reciprocal' way, not dualistically, and that the wrath of God be considered as the manifestation of God's love, and not of his holiness alone.[110] All this is quite Forsythian.

There is a significant difference in the treatments of the two theologians, however. Jewett separates two senses of God's holiness: identifying as of God's essential nature that he is "essentially other," while designating as an attribute the fact that God "is in no way morally compromised."[111] For his part, Forsyth would hold the numinous and the ethical together, recognizing that God's awesome greatness is in part due to his exquisite purity. In practice, Jewett fails to maintain the distinction, admitting later that God's reality is "just too complex to fit neatly into the classification of 'nature' and 'attributes.' The lines of demarcation become blurred."[112] Overall, however, Jewett's use of this term is lucid and helpful.

In addition, as the last in a rather distinguished list of theologians who use the term, Jewett's treatment of God's nature and attributes illustrates that the interest in speaking of God in terms of holy love has been a lively one on the theological scene of the last fifteen years. Although the history of its use since Forsyth's time has been broken in places, enough evidence has been presented to show that theological discourse about the holy, loving God is likely to continue into the future. If the foregoing historical evidence is anything to go by, interest in the expression is growing, and 'holy love' would seem to have a profitable future.

2. A THEOLOGICAL FUTURE

In considering 'the future of holy love,' our intention in this chapter is not only to present the historical evidence which shows that this distinctive formulation had a future and a history following its considerable use by Forsyth, but in addition, to illustrate that the idea of God's holy love has a continuing usefulness and importance.

---

[109] Jewett, p. 228.
[110] Jewett, p. 244.
[111] Jewett, p. 196.
[112] Jewett, pp. 343–344.

Just as he used his conception of God's holy love to critique and correct both orthodoxy and liberalism, the insights gained from the study of his thought can usefully be applied to contemporary versions of those views.

We have already seen the usefulness of 'holy love' in critiquing the modern version of Protestant orthodoxy represented by John Stott.[113] Now, in the remaining pages of this chapter, a very different current proposal concerning the attributes of God will be examined, and its contribution evaluated in terms of Forsyth's understanding of God's holy love. It is our conviction that the lessons learned from this study are useful in at least these two directions, in critical examination of the successors of both Protestant orthodoxy and nineteenth-century liberalism.

2.1 SALLIE MCFAGUE'S MODELS OF GOD

Sallie McFague is professor of theology at Vanderbilt Divinity School, Nashville, Tennessee. During a sabbatical year in Cambridge, one focus of her attention was the manuscript for the 1987 work, *Models of God: Theology for an Ecological, Nuclear Age*.[114] In a challenge to what she describes as "the monarchical model" of God, with its emphasis on "the redemption of rebellious humanity,"[115] and its "metaphors of God as king, ruler, lord, master, and governor,"[116] McFague advocates alternative models: God as mother, lover, and friend. While incorporating many aspects of the tradition she criticizes, McFague opens many interesting new perspectives. Hers is a lucidly-argued theology that is tentative and minimalist, whose agenda is dominated by urgent ecological and nuclear threats. It is a monistic theology, "presuming the basic oneness of all of reality, including the unity of God and the world."[117] On this basis, she conceives of that world as God's body, and sees "the creation as bodied forth from the divine being."[118]

---

[113] See Chapter Seven, section 5.
[114] Sallie McFague, *Models of God: Theology for an Ecological, Nuclear Age* (London: SCM, 1987).
[115] McFague, p. 93.
[116] McFague, p. 19.
[117] McFague, p. 93.
[118] McFague, p. 106; on the general conception, see especially pp. 69–78.

All of this is background to McFague's discussion of three particular metaphors or models for God.[119] On the face of it, not much is being claimed. Standing in the experiential tradition of Schleiermacher, McFague states that the attributes and names for God refer only to our religious perceptions: "Models of God are not definitions of God but likely accounts of experiences of relating to God with the help of relationships we know and understand."[120] That has direct implications not only for the various names we use for God, but also for any discussion of divine attributes: "Predicates such as omniscience, infinity, omnipotence, and omnipresence do not properly apply to God either, for the meaning of all such language – knowledge, finitude, power, presence – applies properly only to our own existence, not God's."[121]

If human experience of 'our own existence' is the basis of theological thinking, then it is entirely consistent to frame one's doctrine of God primarily in response to current social problems. If, however, the names and attributes of God are revealed and in some sense directly related to the one who reveals them (as Forsyth would claim), a certain authoritative priority attaches to such names and characteristics. From this it follows that the given reality – God in Christ, rather than modern social conditions, is the starting-point for theological reflection on God's nature. Forsyth therefore would disagree with McFague on a fundamental level, giving first place not to the religious experience but to the reality experienced. This means that comparisons between the two theologians is hampered; when Forsyth refers to God's love, for example, he is speaking of a quality revealed in God's passionate concern to redeem the world, while McFague understands that love to stem from human love, which can then "serve as a metaphor for God's love."[122]

Nevertheless, a comparison is appropriate and indeed invited for two reasons. First, in practice McFague does not consistently maintain the distinction between perception and reality. For example, she often states that God is *like* a mother, lover, or friend, but sometimes declares simply that God *is* our mother, lover, or friend. To choose examples from the third category, McFague suggests that one may choose "to join with God the friend in a

---

[119] McFague, pp. 91–180. The distinction between the two terms – "A model is a metaphor with 'staying power'" (p. 34) – is not rigorously maintained.
[120] McFague, p. 39.
[121] McFague, p. 39.
[122] McFague, pp. 108–109.

mutual project of great interest to both," asserts that "God is the friend of the world," and claims that "God is with us, immanent in the world as our friend."[123] Even if we accept at face value her claim that what appears to be an ontological claim as a metaphorical construction, and that "to say that 'God is mother' is not to identify God with mother, but to understand God in light of some of the characteristics associated with mothering,"[124] we are left wondering about the ontological reality of the God to which so many metaphors apply. In an endnote, McFague answers our question: "To be a Christian is to be persuaded that there is a personal, gracious power who is on the side of life and its fulfillment." God is an unknowable mystery, and the available clues yield no more than "a hypothesis, a guess, a projection of a possibility that . . . may not be true." "At the most," concludes McFague, "I find I can make what Philip Wheelwright calls a 'shy ontological claim' with the metaphors and models we use to speak of divine reality."[125]

This admission confirms our conviction that it is difficult to maintain consistently that the names and attributes of God refer only to one's own religious experience. It is far easier to deny that God is an ontological reality, and then to describe one's religious experiences solely in terms of their human causes. To adopt a facade of religious language merely confuses the issue. However, as we have shown in our exposition above, McFague does want to make a 'shy ontological claim,' and to build on that a minimalist theology of metaphors or models of God. Even though the reality of God is an unknowable mystery, and the clues to that reality are uncertain, and the theologian's faith in such a God is so small as to be considered 'a projection of a possibility,' and the connection between the metaphors she proposes and reality only slight and suggestive, Sallie McFague still wants to redefine in considerable detail our picture of God.

Second, despite the methodological differences, McFague intends that the models she proposes will replace, or at least relativize, the ones Forsyth (to say nothing of the Christian tradition more generally) cherishes. *Models of God* is a sustained polemic against traditional Christian thinking about the trinity, names, and attributes

---

[123] McFague, pp. 193, 195, 197.
[124] McFague, pp. 22–23.
[125] McFague, pp. 192–193 n. 37, citing Philip Wheelwright, *Metaphor and Reality* (Bloomington: Indiana University Press, 1971), p. 162.

of God, "a deliberate attempt," McFague avers in the book's closing pages, "to unseat those names [Father, Son, and Holy Spirit] as descriptions of God which will allow no supplements or alternatives."[126] She opposes those who "tend to identify the trinity with revelation and to see it focused on God's nature," preferring to understand it as "a form of dialectic that underscores both the relational quality of divine existence and human experience of divine transcendence and immanence."[127] As in the previous point, what is at stake here is the objectivity of revelation and the consequent authority of the names, attributes, and person of the one revealed. While McFague's stated intentions are modest ones – "We are not making pronouncements but experimenting, not dealing with all possible models but only one, not suggesting our model comprises a complete doctrine of God but only certain aspects, not claiming the model is for all time but only for our time"[128] – the resulting pronouncements, if proven, would have the effect of seriously eroding the trinitarian view of God.

Turning from this general introduction and critique of McFague's position to a specific consideration of her treatment of God's holiness and love, we note first her use of the terms *agape, eros,* and *philia* to describe the divine love. Contradicting Anders Nygren's conclusion that God's love is characterized by self-giving, McFague examines the traits of *human* love and concludes that divine love could be better imagined as (respectively) creative and life-giving, passionate attraction and valuing the other, and solidarity.

Nygren's book, of course, appeared more than a decade after Forsyth's death, and so he was not compelled to honour the greatness of the book by thinking in its categories! However, one of Forsyth's main convictions about God's love makes a telling point about McFague's usage. As we have seen in a previous chapter, Forsyth sees the love of God in the closest possible relation to the person of Jesus Christ.[129] He identifies the Father's love with the Son's person and work, and is convinced that not only did Jesus reveal the divine love throughout his life and supremely in the cross, but as the Son, he exerted that love uniquely:

> For that sonship there was an inner condition in his nature, a native and unique unity with God. . . . He knew the Father's love, and he was

---

[126] McFague, p. 181.
[127] McFague, p. 223 n. 2.
[128] McFague, p. 131.
[129] See Chapter Five, especially section 1.1.

himself pure love. . . . For the peculiar revelation of his Father's love there was in Christ a peculiar being.[130]

In contrast, for McFague, the love of Christ is paradigmatic but not unique. She writes that "Jesus' response as beloved to God as lover was so open and thorough that his life and death were revelatory of God's great love for the world." Jesus Christ is not ontologically different, but "he is special to us as our foundational figure: he is our historical choice as the premier paradigm of God's love."[131] This is the Socinian view of Christ as prophet which Forsyth described as "the individual saintliness and moral supereminence of Christ."[132] By his own testimony, insists Forsyth, we are convinced that Christ is not "*a* revelation of God but *the* revelation, the final revelation. . . . His love was not an echo of God's love; or a declaration of it by one who might have exaggerated by temperament. . . . 'God only knows the love of God.'"[133] Forsyth's critique makes it clear that by refusing to see Christ as the unique revelation of the divine love, McFague's position misses the dynamic fulness of that love.

These contrasting positions widen even more in practice. Because McFague sees Christ as only one illustration of God's love, she quickly turns away from that picture to the real authority in her theology, namely the experienced world of an ecological, nuclear age. For her, the foundation of these models of God is not some aspect of what God has revealed, but rather the human context. For example, in seeing God as mother, "the base of the model [is] the physical act of giving birth," and "it is from this base that the model derives its power."[134] From such a perspective, a Christ-centred approach like Forsyth's is actually a problem, because (McFague believes) it leads to a preoccupation with redemption and a failure to appreciate creation.[135] These two theologians, then, differ widely in their perception of God's love.

What then about the holiness of God? It is almost entirely absent from McFague's suggested models of God. And, although she repeatedly claims that her proposal is modest and her results tentative, the intention of the project as a whole is to renovate the doctrine of God in a comprehensive way. There is a threefold comprehensiveness in her presentation of God as creating mother,

---

[130] Forsyth, *The Person and Place of Jesus Christ* (1909), p. 41.
[131] McFague, p. 136.
[132] *Person*, p. 76.
[133] *Person*, pp. 92, 93.
[134] McFague, p. 105.
[135] McFague, p. 206 n. 21.

saving lover, and sustaining friend. As she points out, this is no coincidence, because her intention in advancing these models is to supplant the traditional trinitarian imagery and language.[136] These skilfully constructed models of God, she asserts, form "a habitable house in which to live for a while," although she assures the reader that "additions and renovations" may well be made.[137] An interim assessment of the building project, however, reveals that substantial alterations have been made to the ancient dwelling of faith. Most importantly from Forsyth's point of view is the renovation almost beyond recognition of the doctrine of the attributes of God, and specifically the almost complete absence of the holiness of God. He was convinced that to speak of God's love without a prominent concern for his holiness is to misrepresent that love. It is a critique of fundamental importance. God's love is holy love. To virtually eliminate all trace of God's holy otherness, his thoroughgoing opposition to human sin, and Christ's divine and human obedience that overcomes the world's dilemma, is to seriously distort the gospel and misunderstand God's nature.

In fairness, on two occasions McFague does connect love with justice, but it is our contention that these references do not go far towards softening the above critique. In the first, just two sentences long, she uses an expression reminiscent of God's 'holy love.' She states that the love of God as mother "nurtures all creatures," and so "divine agapic love impartially fulfilling all of creation is a model of inclusive justice. ... The parental model of God is especially pertinent as a way of talking about God's 'just' love, the love that attends to the most basic needs of all creatures."[138] Here is the biblical image of the heavenly parent who sends rain on the just and the unjust, and the theological conception of the universal love of God. With such a view Forsyth would have no objection, but it is a far cry from what he would understand by 'just' or holy love. One suspects that to use these meaning-laden words only in this way would be, in his view, to devalue their currency. In Forsyth's own words, the fatherhood of God "is more than natural paternity spiritualised. ... The soul of divine fatherhood is forgiveness by holiness."[139]

---

[136] McFague, p. 181.
[137] McFague, p. 182.
[138] McFague, pp. 106, 107.
[139] "The Holy Father" (1896), in *God the Holy Father* (1957), p. 5.

On the other occasion, again in the context of God as a metaphorical mother, McFague says that the maternal instinct is often aggressively protective. God as mother not only gives birth but also defends her young, and in this "we see the toughness in the model." "The mother-God as creator is necessarily judge, at the very basic level of condemning as the primary (though not the only) sin the inequitable distribution of basic necessities for the continuation of life in its many forms."[140] Forsyth, whom Claude Welch called "a strong proponent of social theology,"[141] would have no objection to that principle, having himself sided with the workers in the great dock strike of 1889 and taken a number of other similar stands.[142] But to say that selfishness is the 'primary sin,' and to give as little importance to sin as McFague does in her theology, is to take God's holiness much less seriously than Forsyth thinks imperative.

One possible response to this criticism is that McFague does not intend to present a complete picture of God, or a comprehensive system of complementary models of the divine nature. Perhaps a more convincing and wide-ranging presentation of her theology of sin would reveal a more prominent place for God's holy, loving severity. However, McFague herself does not leave this possibility open, but specifically asserts that to imagine God as holy is part of the problem with classical Christian thought. A theology that views God as "the supreme and holy being who rules and saves the world," she says, is "untenable" and "incredible."[143] Her theology opposes every suggestion of transcendence in favour of a God so closely identified with the world that it can be conceived of as 'God's body.' The dominance of love and the near-disappearance of holiness in McFague's stylized picture of God is a deliberate construction. As such, Forsyth would proclaim, it is worthy of double criticism.

We conclude, therefore, that P. T. Forsyth's balanced emphasis on God's love and holiness is a useful standard by which to judge

---

[140] McFague, pp. 113–114.
[141] Claude Welch, *Protestant Thought in the Nineteenth Century*, vol. 2, *1870–1914* (New Haven: Yale University Press, 1985), p. 255, n. 47. On p. 238, Welch concludes a review of the distinctive themes in Forsyth's theology in this way: "For Forsyth, all this had to issue in the social struggle, in which Christianity might seek a reordering of the social machine to give all the blessings and none of the dangers of socialism."
[142] Regarding the miners, Forsyth explained later: "They had no union, were only struggling on to their feet, [and] were receiving so much less than a living wage." See *Socialism, the Church and the Poor* (1908), p. 44.
[143] McFague, pp. 17–18.

various theological positions, whether they emphasize holiness and tend to a dualistic strife of attributes (as John Stott's doctrine of the atonement tends to do), or whether they champion a monistic view that devalues holiness while concentrating on the divine love (as Sallie McFague's 'models' of God do).

Looking back on the chapter as a whole, we have shown that the 'holy love' of God is an expression with a future, both historically and theologically. Historians of dogma will note that not only was this distinctive phrase used often and profitably in the decades following Forsyth's usage, but in recent years there has been a renewed interest in God's holy love as a vital construction in systematic theology. Theologians themselves, we believe, will find the idea a useful and indeed important one, both in critiquing some current trends in theology, and in constructing the doctrines of God and of the atonement in a way that takes the harmony of those perfections seriously.

Conclusion

Theology is taking rational trouble over the mystery.
Karl Barth

The true and competent theology is one disiplined to think in proportion, to think together the various aspects of the Cross, and make them enrich and not exclude one another.
P. T. Forsyth

At the end of our study, we look back to summarize and gather together the various findings made in these chapters, and to state the cumulative force of the argument presented there. The context of our discussion has been the intersection of two dogmatic categories – God's attributes and the atonement effected through Jesus Christ – in the writings of the distinguished British theologian Peter Taylor Forsyth. The distinctive phrase 'holy love,' referring to the integral relation of love and holiness in God's nature, has provided the specific focus of our study.

Holy love – these are words that frequently recur in Forsyth's authorship, and find a personal context in his own life. They are not without their own history, however, and we have illustrated (in Chapter One) that they had an important place in the mediating theology of nineteenth-century German theology. It seems likely that Forsyth took over the expression from these continental theologians, and introduced (or at least played a large part in introducing) the use of this word-combination to English-speaking theology. After studying in Göttingen, Forsyth maintained his interest in continental theology throughout his life, subscribing to journals and reading German theology to the extent that about one-third of his library consisted of German-language material. Specifically, his interest in the writings of Julius Kaftan and Martin Kähler has been indicated; these two writers used the expression in a significant way. It is important to add that although Forsyth's use of the term 'holy love' was deeply influenced by German theology, it may well have also been prompted by the use of the term by the Scottish lay theologian Thomas Erskine. Forsyth quotes several of the German theologians we have named; the connection with Erskine is harder to substantiate and therefore less certain.

Forsyth's frequent and distinctive employment of the idea of God's holy love also found an important context within his own spiritual experience. In the early 1890s, his writings began to reveal the effects of an important personal transformation, one he later described as being turned "from a lover of love to an object of grace." The revelation of God's holiness in Jesus Christ gave Forsyth a keen sense of his own sin, but even more importantly, it launched him on a career of forceful advocacy of the gospel of God's holy love. In sermons, addresses, and lectures, and in the books and articles that they later became, Forsyth preached the necessity of a similar conversion in western theological thought. What was needed was a sense and knowledge of God's love that included an awareness of the strength of God's holiness. In tracing the emergence of this theme in Forsyth's writing from 1891 to 1896, we discovered that the words and (more importantly) the message of God's holy love were asserted with growing confidence and power.

'The early Forsyth,' by contrast, was a Ritschlian in his theological emphasis during his years as a young minister (roughly 1876–1885). An examination of his thought in the mid-1880s revealed this as a time of transition, when the liberal themes were still present, but during which a new concern for the moral nature of reality began to emerge. We concluded that Forsyth's 'theological conversion' occurred during this time, around 1886, and that the process of change was not sudden, but one that extended over several months. This sea-change in Forsyth's thinking led to vital theological insights about God's attributes and Christ's atonement, expressed a short time later in terms of God's holy love. Forsyth's thought, the primary focus of this thesis, had an integral connection with his own religious experience.

In the literature survey that formed the next component of this work (Chapter Two), we found that there has been considerable study of Forsyth's doctrine of the atonement, but that his doctrine of God's attributes was virtually unexplored territory, and his frequent use of the term 'holy love,' although noted, had not yet been investigated in any detail. We have therefore built on the work of others regarding soteriology, but broken new ground in our study of God's holy love. Our survey of previous scholarship also revealed that previous writers differed over the relationship between holiness and love in Forsyth's authorship. Some portrayed Forsyth as preaching the pre-eminence of holiness, others interpreted him as saying that holiness was an aspect of God's love, while a third group of scholars took a mediating position, pointing to the distinctive phrase which is the focus of this thesis as an indication that neither holiness nor love play a dominant role in the atonement. Even within this last position, there was some debate: should these divine attributes be understood as holy *love,* or *holy* love?

With the contexts thus described and the questions thus asked, we turned (in Chapter Three) to examine how Forsyth thinks of the knowledge of God, in order better to understand his thought concerning the knowledge of God's attributes. His view is that God cannot be found in human experience, rational argumentation, or philosophical idealism, but only in the one in whom God has revealed his unique nature, Jesus Christ. In exploring in some detail Forsyth's view of conscience, we discovered his unwillingness to speculate about what might have been had humanity not sinned, and his insistence that we take seriously the situation of turn-of-the-century western persons, for whom the Christian message has accentuated a sense of sin. It is Christ in the conscience who is the inner judge. Forsyth's position is carefully nuanced, and presented with the concerns of his hearers in mind. From our perspective at the other end of the twentieth century, however, Forsyth's view of a culture suffused by the Christian message, and thus aware in conscience of God's judgment, seems less convincing, because it is less applicable to the largely secular society of the 1990s.

Another issue relating to the knowledge of God concerns Forsyth's understanding of the conscience as a point of contact. Is not such a view an admission that there is some human contribution to that knowledge (and therefore to the accomplishment of salvation)? No, we concluded, Forsyth's view of humanity's ability to be addressed is not an assertion of an independent human prerogative, but only of receptivity. Although God has revealed something of his nature in a general way, human sinfulness prevents the conscience from taking in the truth. The sure knowledge of the divine nature is instead decisively revealed in Christ, and especially in his cross. Perhaps a general revelation can convey what Forsyth called "mere impressions," but *real* revelation comes through Jesus Christ alone.

This discussion highlighted the fact that P. T. Forsyth's starting-point and centre-point – for theology generally, for the knowledge of God, and specifically for a study of God's attributes – is a Christological one. In Christ, we know God and what God is like. Our examination (in Chapter Four) of that second concern, God's attributes, led to a number of wide-ranging conclusions. Like God's nature generally, his perfections are revealed rather than discovered. They are personal instead of what might be called 'material,' governed by God's freedom to act rather than by any outside constraint, and explicated above all in Christ's cross.

Further, Forsyth does not isolate particular attributes, but considers them as interrelated aspects of a unitive personality. He believed that the paradox of "the majesty and the mercy of God," of "the immanence of the transcendent," and of "the infinite mobility of the changeless God" (to choose only three of Forsyth's characteristic phrases) were revealed by God's personal action in Christ. These phrases were not neatly crafted expressions designed to obscure an essential contradiction, but ways of expressing the truth revealed in Christ that God's nature was multifaceted and complex. The same dynamic is operative in Forsyth's use of the holy love construction to wed together what others separated, namely God's love and holiness.

Another aspect of Forsyth's doctrine of God's attributes is his conviction that the divine perfections are dynamic rather than static. This overly disjunctive statement illustrates Forsyth's anti-ontological bias, which arises out of his concentration on the moral nature of reality, and the purposive will of God. At the risk of reproof for following Forsyth in his fondness for alliteration, attributes are acted out in atonement. Especially in the cross, the incredible love and overwhelming holiness of God is evidenced. If it was required, here is sufficient justification for our attention to the intersection of these two concerns.

Although much of Forsyth's understanding of God's attributes both generally and specifically is instructive, it is not beyond criticism. His distinction between attributes and functions of attributes raises more problems than it solves, tending to obscure the ontological reality of some of the perfections. This stress on *doing* and a corresponding devaluation of *being* results in the *person* of Jesus Christ receiving less attention than the *work,* with a consequent loss to the doctrine of God. Forsyth's view of God's holy love could only have been strengthened, we believe, by more balanced attention being given to Christ's person, and also more broadly to his ministry of interpersonal relationships and authoritative teaching. These, it could be argued, reflected the same combination of love and holiness, goodness and severity, justice and mercy, judgment and grace, as was exerted in the cross.

When we turned to look more particularly at God's love (in Chapter Five), our key assertion was included in the chapter title: God's love is a prominent concern on Forsyth's theological agenda. After gathering together the many references to the divine love in Forsyth's writings, we showed that he considered God's love as an important component in every aspect of Christ's career, in the varied experiences of the believer, and in the successive doctrines of systematic theology. Furthermore, when we looked at the characteristics of that love according to Forsyth, we appreciated his view of its multifaceted reality. In addition, we established that Forsyth's view of divine love was understood in the broad, though lightly-sketched, context of the Trinity. In a section that explored an aspect of Forsyth's theology to which little attention had previously been drawn, we saw that the relationship between the Father and the Son is Forsyth's key to understanding God's trinitarian nature as a communion of love.

Regarding Forsyth's treatment of God's love, criticism most naturally applies to the *degree* of prominence he gives to that attribute. While his theology is comprehensive at this point, it is not entirely compelling. It lacks the verve he employed when speaking of God's holiness. Forsyth might well have gone further in his praise of the divine love, without compromising his message that such love is holy love. Nevertheless, it is our contention that this judgment is lessened when two further considerations are taken into account. First, in the theological context of Forsyth's day, a variety of influences – mysticism, romanticism, humanism, as well as a merely exemplary doctrine of the atonement – combined to exalt divine love without a corresponding emphasis on God's holiness. Liberalism had majored on love, often to the near-exclusion of holiness. In prophetic style, and to our mind, in a convincing way, Forsyth insisted that love alone was not enough for either a doctrine of the atonement or a doctrine of God. Secondly, it must not be forgotten that the constant repetition of this theme – the holy love of God – in the most significant contexts serves to keep God's *love* in a prominent theological place. Forsyth was not reverting to the opposite position, but insisting that it be qualified and deepened by what it lacked. A wider conception of God's nature was required, one that would take into account the full reality of God's nature revealed in Christ.

What was lacking, Forsyth came to realize, was an accent on the holiness of God, neglected by some, overemphasized by others (and considered in Chapter Six of this thesis). The neglect, he decided, should be remedied by an insistence that in the cross, the *holy* love of God was operative. Without neglecting the importance of God's love, a strong stress on the divine holiness was necessary. Regarding the disproportionate stress on holiness by some popular versions of Protestant orthodoxy, Forsyth was critical of an impersonal, rationalistic, legal, and penal doctrine of the atonement, which in a paradoxical way did less justice to holiness by making it less personal and more abstract. But Forsyth believed that despite its distortions, orthodoxy had a true sense of what was most important in the gospel, and so the appropriate theological task was not to destroy the edifice of Protestant orthodoxy, but to adapt and build on its accomplishments.

If a corrective to orthodoxy's misinterpretation of holiness was called for, Forsyth turns once more to Jesus Christ and his atoning work in order to provide it. Following his lead, our attention at this point focused more closely on the atonement, after being concerned in greater detail in the previous chapters with the attributes of God. Even though both concerns were in view throughout our argument, a shift occurred at this stage to a deeper engagement with the cross of Christ. This dynamic is noticeable in Forsyth's theology: the attributes of God and the atonement accomplished by Christ are developed together. The more deeply we investigate God's attributes, the closer we must attend to the cross which reveals them. Conversely, it is only with a clear understanding of the atonement that we will have a correct picture of God's nature.

The cross, according to a key phrase of Forsyth's, was "the offering of a holy self to a holy God from sin's side."[1] In an exposition of that assertion, we looked successively at the cross as an atoning sacrifice within a broader theological framework, at the sinlessness and obedience of Jesus, at the Son's acknowledgment of the Father's holiness, and at the human context for this decisive action by God in Christ. Forsyth considers the cross as a fact with many interlocking interpretations, and makes a convincing case for holiness as the common theme. His theory of the atonement is an eclectic one, and not limited to one particular way of thinking, but the atoning element, the decisive thing in the death of Christ, was "the perfect obedience of holy love which he offered amidst the conditions of sin, death, and judgment."[2]

The personal holiness of Christ, Forsyth maintains, is not only (and not even primarily) sinlessness, but obedience. Such a position is congruent with Forsyth's emphasis on the work and activity more than the person of Christ, yet he doesn't separate the two: the obedience is a sinless obedience. Moreover, Christ's obedience is directed to the Father, confessing the Father's holiness, and therefore acknowledging the seriousness of sin, not only in its debilitating effects on the individual, but also concerning its affront to God and to the relationship between God and humanity.

All this – Christ's obedient sacrifice that acknowledged God's holiness – took place within the human context, and can only be properly understood as an act which involved humanity. Jesus Christ lovingly identified with us, and our sin was judged in his sacrifice. Although here we see Forsyth taking the incarnation with renewed seriousness, and sturdily defending the full humanity of Christ, we sense a deficiency in his doctrine of Christ's identification with humanity. He puts so much emphasis on what Christ has done for us that he sometimes undervalues the solidarity with us that forms it's basis. At the same time, as we examined Forsyth's idea of "the Son

---

[1] *The Cruciality of the Cross,* 1st ed. (1909), p. 182; see Chapter Five, section 1.5.
[2] *The Work of Christ* (1910), p. 201.

made sin," we realized that he presses on to a deep understanding of what Christ has done for humanity from within the human context. The key word in this regard is judgment: God's victorious judgment on sin and evil, the Son's sinless obedience in offering a perfect sacrifice judged acceptable by God, his acknowledgment of the Father's perfect holiness in judging sin on him, within the human context. Forsyth's conviction is clear:

> The Cross, I keep saying, is God's final judgment on the world. ... He is eternal Judge in His great work as the Crucified, a work historic yet timeless and final. In Him the prince of this world has been finally and effectually judged, and the absolute condemnation passed. ... The absolute and irreversible judgment was passed upon evil. There, too, the judgment of our sins fell once for all on the Holy One and the Just.[3]

Accentuated by Christ's sense of Godforsakeness, Forsyth's discussion of God's judgment continues with important qualifications: God's wrath is not hate, the cross was a sacrifice willingly undertaken, and the relationship between Father and Son was paramount.

That theme of judgment introduced the possibility of a strife of attributes in God's own nature (the topic of Chapter Seven above). Forsyth tackles this problem in terms of the holy love of God. God in the unity of his attributes was at work in Christ to reconcile the world to himself. It was not a situation in which God's holiness demanded a sacrifice and God's love provided it, but rather the one God – and no schizophrenic deity – who willed, sent, and sacrificed. There can be no question of a loving God with one intention for some, and a holy God with another plan for others, but one holy, loving God whose plan for humanity is expressed in Jesus Christ's cross.

Therefore, the cross is not to be understood in any sense as the reconciliation of God's conflicting attributes. The 'problem of forgiveness' is not due to any hesitation on God's part, but is to be found in the sinful, rebellious humanity who reject God's holy love. Furthermore, God did not change; he always loved us, as Forsyth reminds us, even when he was most angry with us. What did change in the cross was God's relationship with us: sin no longer stands in the way of communion with God, having been decisively defeated. Now God's treatment of sinners as sons and daughters is possible.

Forsyth's view of God's love and holiness acting in harmony in Christ's cross is a substantial achievement, we believe. While

---

[3] *Missions in State and Church* (1908), p. 73.

steering clear of the dangers to both sides of the debate – whether it be orthodoxy's transactional and dualistic approach that gives priority to divine holiness, or liberal theology's sentimental and monistic overemphasis on God's love – Forsyth maintains a soteriological position that takes full account of the various atonement motifs in scripture. Allowing for the reservations expressed earlier, we consider that he gives full value to both God's love and holiness without maintaining an uncomfortable existence straddling two opinions. This is accomplished by the frequent, deliberate, and sophisticated use of an expression to refer to God's nature and attributes – the holy love of God.

Having seen the importance to Forsyth of God's holy love active in the atoning death of Christ, we turned in a lengthy section (Chapter Seven, section 6) to look at the conjunction of attributes and atonement in specifically trinitarian terms. As with other items on the theological agenda, Forsyth's doctrine of the Trinity is not speculative but revealed in Christ, and driven by moral reality instead of defined in metaphysical categories. For our purposes in this study, the distinctive feature of that doctrine, however, is that Forsyth extends the traditional idea of intra-trinitarian love to include holiness as well. He says not only that "the Father dwells in the Son of his love," but speaks, too, of "the Father's holy love of the Son."[4] The atonement, Forsyth asserts, can be understood in terms of intra-trinitarian holy love. This yields specific insights about God's holiness, which we summarized under three headings. Regarding the obedience of the Son, Forsyth accents the Son's "subordination and sacrifice" to the Father, freely given to praise the Father's holiness. Speaking of the satisfaction of the Father, Forsyth's emphasis is on the personal pleasure of a God who was always well-pleased with his Son. That was especially true in death, when Christ's perfect holiness atoned for human sin. Finally, in relation to the trinitarian holiness of the Spirit, Forsyth suggests that the distinctive New Testament name for the Spirit indicates the importance of holiness within God's nature. In all three persons, trinitarian holiness is an important factor. Combined with an acknowledgment that God is a Trinity of love, this doctrinal construction adds another way in which Forsyth uses the expression 'holy love' in an original, thought-provoking, and useful way.

---

[4] "Faith, Metaphysic, and Incarnation," *Methodist Review* 97 (September 1915): 712, 706.

Before leaving the doctrinal significance of holy love, we asserted that the victory of God's holy love in the cross resulted in grace to sinners. This distinctive expression is not meant to indicate a deadlock in God's nature, but a reciprocity and balance within God's attributes. By means of the cross, in which God's holy love is passionately at work to defeat every enemy and rescue humanity, the grace of God becomes a present reality.

Our final substantial concern in the present study was to indicate the future of holy love (in Chapter Eight). Historically speaking, the expression flourished in the 1920s and 1930s, influenced significantly by Forsyth, although other, especially German, influences would have been important as well. The popularity of this way of referring to God's nature extended across denominational, generational, and (less often) theological boundaries. In the middle decades of this century, interest in this theological formulation waned, but the last fifteen years has witnessed renewed interest in 'holy love,' perhaps even more impressively than in the earlier period. Several modern theologians have expressed their indebtedness to P. T. Forsyth for their use of the term.

We concluded, finally, that 'holy love' has a future theologically as well as historically. With our findings about Forsyth's view of God's holy love in mind, we applied a critique to two very different contemporary writers. Because the tendencies which Forsyth sought to correct with his use of the term are still represented in modern dogmatics, a theology which takes God's love and God's holiness with equal seriousness still can raise important questions for the representatives of strict Calvinism and modern liberalism alike.

In short, the theology of God's holy love has not only an interesting pre-history and a promising future, it also has an accomplished advocate in the person of Peter Taylor Forsyth, whom J. K. Mozley called "[English Christianity's] most powerful, its most challenging, and, perhaps, its actually greatest theologian in the sphere of dogmatics, ... one as scientifically competent as Ritschl, as spiritually proficient as Dale."[5] Within the matrix of attributes and atonement, Forsyth speaks of the holy love of God to serve several important theological assertions, which we have outlined in the preceding pages. The most important of these concerns is Forsyth's conclusion that there is no strife of attributes in the cross of Jesus Christ. In him, God is revealed as a holy, loving God who has acted decisively for the salvation of the world.

---

[5] J. K. Mozley, *The Heart of the Gospel* (London: SPCK, 1925), pp. 66, 109.

Bibliography

Bibliography

Please note that an asterisk (*) indicates a correction or addition to the previous version of this bibliography, published in *Justice the True and Only Mercy: Essays on the Life and Theology of Peter Taylor Forsyth*, ed. Trevor Hart (Edinburgh: T&T Clark, 1995), pp. 256–330.

Abbreviations for periodicals:

AmJTh	*American Journal of Theology*
BCong	*British Congregationalist*
BW	*British Weekly*
ChrW	*Christian World*
ChrWP	*Christian World Pulpit*
CongM	*Congregational Monthly*
CongQ	*Congregational Quarterly*
ConR	*Contemporary Review*
EvMag	*Evangelical Magazine*
EvQ	*Evangelical Quarterly*
Ex	*Examiner*
Exp	*Expositor*
HibJ	*Hibbert Journal*
Ind	*Independent*
IndNon	*Independent and Nonconformist*
LQR	*London Quarterly Review*
ManExT	*Manchester Examiner and Times*
RExp	*Review and Expositor*
SJTh	*Scottish Journal of Theology*
TLS	*Times Literary Supplement*
WestGaz	*Westminster Gazette*

1. BOOKS BY P. T. FORSYTH

The Charter of the Church: Six Lectures on the Spiritual Principle of Nonconformity. London: Alexander & Shepheard, 1896. Latest impression. London: Alexander & Shepheard, 1905.

The Church and the Sacraments. See: *Lectures on the Church and the Sacraments.*

The Cruciality of the Cross. Expositor's Library. London, New York, and Toronto: Hodder & Stoughton, n.d. [1909]. Second edition. London: Independent Press, 1948. New edition, with an Introduction by John E. Steely. Wake Forest, North Carolina: Chanticleer, 1983. *Latest impression: Biblical Classics Library, no. 31. Carlisle, U.K.: Paternoster, 1997. *Second Japanese translation: *Jujika no Kettei-sei.* Trans. Goki Saito and Hiroshi Omiya. Tokyo: Yorudan-sha, 1989.

Christ on Parnassus: Lectures on Art, Ethic, and Theology. London: Hodder & Stoughton, n.d. [1911]. Latest impression: Eugene, Oregon: Wipf and Stock, 1996.
The Christian Ethic of War. London: Longmans, Green, 1916.
Christian Perfection. Little Books on Religion. Edited by W. Robertson Nicoll. London: Hodder & Stoughton, 1899. *Japanese translation: *Kirisuto-sha no Kanzen.* Translated by Saburo Ishijima. Tokyo: Shinkyo-shuppan-sha, 1960.
Faith, Freedom and the Future. London: Hodder & Stoughton, 1912. New edition, with a Foreword by Jessie Forsyth Andrews and an Appendix, "Declaration of the Faith, Church Order, and Discipline of the Congregational, or Independent Dissenters" from 1833. London: Independent Press, 1955. *Latest impression: Eugene, Oregon: Wipf and Stock, 1996.
The Holy Father and the Living Christ. Little Books on Religion. Edited by W. Robertson Nicoll. London: Hodder & Stoughton, 1897.
Intercessory Services for Aid in Public Worship. Manchester: John Heywood, n.d. [1897].
The Justification of God: Lectures for War-Time on a Christian Theodicy. Studies in Theology. London: Duckworth, 1916. New edition, omitting the Preface, with a Foreword by D. R. Davies. London: Latimer House, 1948. Latest impression, with a Foreword by Dean J. Carter. Blackwood, South Australia: New Creation Publications, 1988.
Lectures on the Church and the Sacraments. With a chapter by H. T. Andrews. London: Longmans, Green, 1917. Second edition titled *The Church and the Sacraments*, with a Note by Jessie Forsyth Andrews, and a Preface by J. K. Mozley. London: Independent Press, 1947. *Latest impression: Eugene, Oregon: Wipf and Stock, 1996.
Marriage: Its Ethic and Religion. London: Hodder & Stoughton, n.d. [1912]. *Latest impression: Eugene, Oregon: Wipf and Stock, 1996.
Missions in State and Church: Sermons and Addresses. London: Hodder & Stoughton, 1908.
The Person and Place of Jesus Christ. The Congregational Union Lecture for 1909. London: Congregational Union of England and Wales, and Hodder & Stoughton, 1909. *Latest impression: Eugene, Oregon: Wipf and Stock, 1996.
Positive Preaching and Modern Mind: The Lyman Beecher Lecture on Preaching, Yale University, 1907. London: Hodder & Stoughton, 1907. Second edition titled *Positive Preaching and the Modern Mind.* London: Hodder & Stoughton, 1909. Third edition. London: Independent Press, 1949. New impression, with Foreword by Ralph G. Turnbull. Grand Rapids, Michigan: Baker Book House, 1980. New impression in Donald G. Miller, Browne Barr, and Robert S. Paul, *P. T. Forsyth: The Man, The Preachers' Theologian, Prophet for the 20th Century: A Contemporary Assessment.* Pittsburgh, Pennsylvania: Pickwick Press, 1981. New impression, with a Foreword by Geoffrey Bingham and a Biographical Introduction [by Noel Due]. Blackwood, South Australia: New Creation Publications, 1993.
The Power of Prayer. With Dora Greenwell. Little Books on Religion. Edited by W. Robertson Nicoll. London: Hodder & Stoughton, n.d. [1910].
The Principle of Authority in Relation to Certainty, Sanctity and Society: An Essay in the Philosophy of Experimental Religion. London: Hodder & Stoughton, n.d. [*1913]. Second edition, with a Note by Jessie Forsyth Andrews, additional footnotes, and an Index compiled by Robert McAfee

Brown. London: Independent Press, 1952. Latest impression: Eugene, Oregon: Wipf and Stock, 1996.
Pulpit Parables for Young Hearers. With J. A. Hamilton. Manchester: Brook & Chrystal; London: Simpkin, Marshall; London: Hamilton, Adams, n.d. [1886].
Religion in Recent Art: Being Expository Lectures on Rossetti, Burne Jones, Watts, Holman Hunt, & Wagner. Manchester: Abel Heywood & Son; London: Simpkin, Marshall; London: Hamilton, Adams, 1889. Second edition, with eight illustrations. London: Hodder & Stoughton, 1901. Third edition, with an additional chapter on "Art, Ethic, and Christianity." London: Hodder & Stoughton, 1911. Latest impression: New York: AMS Press, 1972.
Rome, Reform and Reaction: Four Lectures on the Religious Situation. London: Hodder & Stoughton, 1899.
Socialism, the Church and the Poor. London: Hodder & Stoughton, 1908.
The Soul of Prayer. London: Charles H. Kelly, 1916. Second edition. London: Independent Press, 1949. *Latest impression, with an Introduction by Eugene H. Peterson. Vancouver: Regent College, 1995. *Japanese translation: *Kito no Seishin.* Translated by Hachiro Tobara. Nagoya: Ichiryu-sha, 1934. *Second Japanese translation: *Inori no Seishin.* Translated by Goki Saito. Tokyo: Yorudan-sha, 1969, 1986.
The Taste of Death and the Life of Grace. Small Books on Great Subjects, no. 21. London: James Clarke, 1901. Second edition. London: James Clark, 1906.
Theology in Church and State. London: Hodder & Stoughton, 1915.
This Life and the Next: The Effect on This Life of Faith in Another. London: Macmillan, 1918. Second edition, with a Preface by Jessie Forsyth Andrews. London: Independent Press, 1946.
The Work of Christ. Expositor's Library. London and New York: Hodder & Stoughton, 1910. New edition. Foreword by John S. Whale. Memoir of the author by Jessie Forsyth Andrews. London: Independent Press, 1938. *Japanese translation: *Shokuzai-ron.* Translated by Hachiro Tobara. Tokyo: Nagasaki-shoten, 1939. *Second Japanese translation: *Kirisuto no Hataraki.* Translated by Hiroshi Omiya. Gendai Kirisuto-kyo Shiso-sosho [Great Christian Thought Series]. Tokyo: Hakusui-sha, 1974. *Latest impression: Eugene, Oregon: Wipf and Stock, 1996.

2. ANTHOLOGIES AND COLLECTIONS OF FORSYTH'S WRITING

The Church, the Gospel and Society. Foreword by Jessie Forsyth Andrews. London: Independent Press, 1962.
Congregationalism and Reunion: Two Lectures. London: Independent Press, 1952.
The Creative Theology of P.T. Forsyth: Selections from His Works. Edited by Samuel J. Mikolaski. Grand Rapids: Wm. B. Eerdmans, 1969.
God the Holy Father. London: Independent Press, 1957. New edition with a Publisher's Foreword by Geoffrey Bingham. Blackwood, South Australia: New Creation Publications, 1987.
The Gospel and Authority: A P.T. Forsyth Reader: Eight Essays Previously Published in Journals. Edited by Marvin W. Anderson. Minneapolis: Augsburg, 1971.
P.T. Forsyth and the Cure of Souls. See following entry.

Peter Taylor Forsyth (1848–1921), Director of Souls: Selections from His Practical Writings. Compiled and edited by Harry Escott. Preface by W. F. Rowlands. London: Epworth Press, 1948. New edition titled *P. T. Forsyth and the Cure of Souls: An Appraisement and Anthology of His Practical Writings.* London: George Allen and Unwin, 1970.
The Preaching of Jesus and the Gospel of Christ. Foreword, Biographical Sketch, and Theological Introduction by Noel Due. Blackwood, South Australia: New Creation Publications, 1987.
Revelation Old and New: Sermons and Addresses. Edited with a Preface by John Huxtable. London: Independent Press, 1962.
**A Sense of the Holy: An Introduction to the Thought of P. T. Forsyth through His Writings.* Eugene, Oregon: Wipf and Stock, 1996. Comprising *God the Holy Father*, *The Soul of Prayer*, and *This Life and the Next*.

3. ARTICLES, PAMPHLETS, REVIEWS, AND LETTERS TO THE EDITOR BY FORSYTH

"About Giving." *Ex*, 26 Dec 1901, p. 756.
"The Address from the Chair." *BCong*, 16 May 1907, p. 489.
Address. In *The Story of the Scottish Congregational Theological Hall, 1811–1911*, pp. 20–22. Edinburgh: Morrison & Gibb, 1911.
Address to out-going students, Stockwell College for Women Teachers. From an annual report, pp. 106–112. Included with the Forsyth papers, Dr. Williams's Library, London.
"After Graduation What? New Series – No. V. The Congregational Church." *Alma Mater. Aberdeen University Magazine* 25 (Aberdeen: Student's Representative Council, 18 Dec 1907): 110–112.
"An Allegory of the Resurrection." *ChrWP* 61 (14 May 1902): 312–319.
"An Open Letter to a Young Minister on Certain Questions of the Hour." *ChrW*, 27 May 1909, p. 11; 3 June, p. 14.
Annotations on a paper written in 1906 by Robert Mackintosh, "The Authority of the Cross," in *CongQ* 21 (July 1943): 209–218.
"Annual Sermon." ["The Holy Father."] *IndNon*, 1 Oct 1896, pp. 219–221.
The Antiquity of Dissent. Leicester & Birmingham: Midland Educational; Manchester: Brooke & Chrystal, n.d. [1889].
"The Apostolate of Negation." *BCong*, 21 Mar 1907, p. 271.
"Appeal to the Primate." *ChrW*, 19 Oct 1905, pp. 21–22.
"Appreciations and Tributes." *BCong*, 15 Feb 1912, p. 116.
"The Argument for Immortality Drawn from the Nature of Love: A Lecture on Lord Tennyson's 'Vastness'." *ChrWP* 28 (2 Dec 1885): 360–364.
"Art Wrestling with Death." *IndNon*, 3 June 1892, p. 381.
Article. *Daily Chronicle*, 16 Jan 1907.
"'The Ascent through Christ.'" Review of *The Ascent through Christ*, by E. Griffith-Jones. *Puritan* 1 (1899): 151–154.
"The Atonement in Modern Religious Thought: Persistence of the Doctrine." *ChrW*, 9 Nov 1899, p. 11. Reprinted in *The Atonement in Modern Religious Thought: A Theological Symposium*, pp. 59–88. By Frederick Godet and 16 others. London: James Clarke, 1900.
"The Attacks on the Churches." Letter. *BW*, 23 and 30 Mar 1905, pp. 614, 638.

"The Attitude of the Church to the Present Unrest." *BCong,* 17 Mar 1910, pp. 214–215.
"Authority and Theology." *HibJ* 4 (Oct 1905): 63–78.
"Authority and Theology." *Living Age,* 6 Jan 1906, pp. 18–27.
"Authority in Religion." Review of *Authority in Religion,* by J. H. Leckie. *BCong,* 23 Dec 1909, p. 538.
"Baldwin Brown: A Tribute, a Reminiscence, and a Study." In *In Memoriam: James Baldwin Brown,* pp. 133–142. Edited by Elizabeth Baldwin Brown. London: James Clarke, 1884. Reprinted as a pamphlet. London: James Clarke, 1884.
"Bribery and Legislation." Signed, "Publicola." *ManExT,* 11 Feb 1887, p. 5.
"The Call of the New Century: I. – The Century's First Need." *Sunday at Home* (London, 1900–1901): 96–102.
"Calvinism and Capitalism." *ConR* 97 (June 1910): 728–741, and 98 (July 1910): 74–87.
"The Catholic Threat of Passive Resistance." *ConR* 89 (Apr 1906): 562–567.
"The Chairman's Address: A Holy Church the Moral Guide of Society." *Ex,* 11 May 1905, pp. 441–449.
"The Chairman's Address: The Grace of the Gospel as the Moral Authority in the Church." *Ex,* 12 Oct 1905, pp. 319–325.
"Chairman's Autumnal Address [etc.]" in *The Congregational Year Book 1905,* pp. 57–97. London: Congregational Union of England and Wales, 1906.
"The Chairman's Mantle. Dr. Forsyth to Mr. Jowett." Poem. *Ex,* 11 Jan 1906, p. 28.
"Chairman's Spring Address [etc.]" in *The Congregational Year Book, 1905,* pp. 15–56. London: Congregational Union of England and Wales, 1906.
"The Charter of Missions." *ChrWP* 63 (20 May 1903): 305–312.
"Chinese Labour in the Transvaal." Letters. *Times* (London), 18 Jan 1906, p. 4; 20 Jan, p. 12; 25 Jan, p. 11; 26 Jan, p. 7; 29 Jan, p. 7.
"Christ – King or Genius?" *Methodist Review* 65 (Nashville, July 1916): 433–447.
"Christ and the Christian Principle." In *London Theological Studies,* pp. 133–166. By members of the Faculty of Theology in the University of London. London: University of London Press, 1911.
"Christ at the Gate." *ChrWP* 73 (18 Mar 1908): 177–182.
"Christ our Sanctification." *Wesleyan Methodist Magazine* 134 (1911): 732–734.
"Christ's Person and His Cross." *Methodist Review* 66 (Nashville, Jan 1917): 3–22.
"The Christening of Christmas." Poem. *BW,* 16 Dec 1897, p. 188.
Christian Aspects of Evolution. London: Epworth Press, 1950.
"Christianity and Nationality." *BW,* 9 July 1914, pp. 385–386.
"Christianity and Society." *Methodist Review Quarterly* 63 (Nashville, Jan 1914): 3–21.
"The Christianity of Christ and Christ our Christianity." *RExp* 15 (July 1918): 249–265.
"The Church and Divorce. Principal Forsyth's Memorandum." *BCong,* 30 Oct 1913, p. 885.
"Church and Nation: A Nonconformist on the Enabling Bill." Letters on the Church of England National Assembly Bill. *Times* (London), 28 May 1919, p. 8; corrected 29 May, p. 8; 6 June, p. 8; 16 June, p. 8.
"The Church and Society – Alien or Allied?" *BW,* 9 Oct 1913, p. 43.

"The Church and Society." *WestGaz,* 6 Sept 1913, p. 3; 13 Sept, p. 13; 20 Sept, p. 2.
"The Church and the Children." Letter. *BW,* 15 May 1913, p. 169.
"The Church and the Nation – In Education, for Instance." *WestGaz,* 6 July 1914, pp. 1–2.
"The Church and the Nation." *BCong,* 14 May 1914, p. 383.
"The Church and the Nation." *WestGaz,* 12 May 1914, pp. 1–2.
"Church and University." *BCong,* 27 Sept 1906, pp. 201–202.
"Church Statistics." *BW,* 15 June 1911, p. 284.
"Church, Ministry and Sacraments." In *The Validity of the Congregational Ministry,* pp. 33–52. With J. Vernon Bartlett and J. D. Jones. London: Congregational Union of England and Wales, n.d. [1916].
"Church, State, Dogma and Education." *ConR* 90 (Dec 1906): 827–836.
"The Church, the State, the Priest, and the Future." *Ex,* 9 and 16 July 1903, pp. 27, 54.
"Churches, Sects and Wars." *ConR* 107 (May 1915): 618–626.
"The Churches and Bible Study: Present-Day Needs." *ChrW,* 18 Feb 1909, p. 5.
"The Church's One Foundation." *Living Age,* 10 Nov 1906, pp. 351–356.
"The Church's One Foundation." *LQR* 106 (Oct 1906): 193–202.
Coleridge's "Ancient Mariner": An Exposition and Sermon from a Modern Text. Bradford: William Byles and Sons, n.d. [c. 1880–1883].
"The Colleges and Recruiting." Letter from Forsyth, A. E. Garvie, W. B. Selbie and W. H. Bennett. *BW,* 18 Nov 1915, p. 134.
"Comments on a Paper at the Congregational Union." *BCong,* 19 Oct 1917, pp. 297–298.
"The Condition of Evangelicalism." From a correspondent. *ChrW,* 13 Dec 1917, p. 11.
"Congregational Union Chairmanship." Letter. *BW,* 2 Apr 1896, p. 390.
Congregationalism and Reunion. London, Congregational Union of England and Wales, n.d. [1918]. Pamphlet.
"Congregationalism and the Principle of Liberty." *Constructive Quarterly* 1 (Sept 1913): 498–521.
"Congregationalism at Cambridge." Letter. *BW,* 24 Sept 1896, p. 356.
"The Conquest of Time by Eternity." *ChrWP* 87 (17 Feb 1915): 104–108.
"The Conversion of Faith by Love." *BW,* 28 Oct 1897, p. 22.
"The Conversion of the 'Good.'" *ConR* 109 (June 1916): 760–771.
Corruption and Bribery: A Sermon. Preached at the Anniversary of the Congregational Church, Shipley, Yorkshire, on Sunday, Nov. 27, 1881. Bradford, T. Brear, n.d. [1882].
"The Courage of Faith." *Ex,* 11 July 1901, pp. 270–271.
The Courage of Faith. Glasgow: William Asher, 1903.
"The Courage of Faith." Letter. *Ex,* 1 Aug 1901, p. 320.
"The Cross as the Final Seat of Authority." *ConR* 76 (Oct 1899): 589–608.
"The Cross as the Final Seat of Authority." *Living Age,* 16 Dec 1899, pp. 671–687.
"The Cross of Christ as the Moral Principle of Society." *Methodist Review* 99 (New York, Jan 1917): 9–21.
"'The Cruciality of the Cross.'" Letter. *BW,* 12 July 1906, p. 344.
"The Dead Heart." *EvMag* 107 (Sept 1899): 435–440.
"The Depletion from the Ministry." *Ex,* 19 and 26 June 1902, pp. 555–556, 586–587.

Different Conceptions of Priesthood and Sacrifice. Report of a conference held at Oxford, Dec 13 and 14, 1899. [Contributions by Forsyth.] Edited by William Sanday. London: Longmans, Green, 1900.
"The Disappointment of the Cross." *Puritan* 3 (1900): 135–139.
"Discourses by Professor Bouvier." With M. Forsyth. Review of *Le Divin d'après les apôtres* and *Paroles de Foi et de Liberté*, by Auguste Bouvier. *Modern Review* 4 (1883): 410–413.
"Dissent: Mr Lyulph Stanley's Address." Signed, "Publicola." *ManExT*, 23 Dec 1886, p. 5.
"The Distinctive Thing in Christian Experience." *HibJ* 6 (Apr 1908): 481–499.
"The Divine Self-Emptying." *ChrWP* 47 (1 May 1895): 276–280.
"The Divorce Commission Report. Opinions of Prominent Congregationalists." *BCong*, 21 Nov 1912, p. 847.
"Does the Church Prolong the Incarnation?" *LQR* 133 (Jan and Apr 1920): 1–12, 204–212.
"Dr. Barrett and 'Higher Criticism.'" Letters. *Ex*, 30 Aug 1900, p. 580, and 20 Sept 1900, pp. 650–651.
"Dr. Berry: II. – A Tribute by Rev. Dr. Forsyth, Cambridge." *BW*, 2 Feb 1899, p. 310.
"Dr. Dale." Review of *The Life of R. W. Dale*, by A. W. W. Dale. *LQR* 91 (Apr 1899): 193–222.
"Dr. Dale." *Sunday Magazine* (May 1895): 331–337.
"Dr. Forsyth and Mr. Campbell." Letter. *BW*, 19 May 1910, p. 172.
"Dr. Forsyth and Mr. Campbell." Letter. *BW*, 4 Nov 1915, p. 93.
"Dr. Forsyth and Mysticism." Letter. *Ex*, 9 Nov 1905, p. 434.
"Dr. Forsyth and the 'Delegate.'" Letter. *Ex*, 12 Nov 1903, p. 476.
"Dr. Forsyth and the Rev. R. J. Campbell." Letter. *BCong*, 19 May 1910, p. 418.
"Dr. Forsyth on Modernism." Abstract of a speech. *ChrW*, 14 Oct 1909, pp. 22–23.
"Dr. Forsyth's Address." Letter. *BW*, 18 May 1905, p. 143.
"Dr. Forsyth's Appeal to the Archbishop of Canterbury." Letter. *Ex*, 19 Oct 1905, pp. 358–359.
"Dr. G. A. Smith's Yale Lecture." *BW*, 25 Apr 1901, pp. 51, 53.
"Dr. Martineau." *LQR* 93 (Apr 1900): 214–250.
"Dr. Wendt's Picture of Christ." Letters. *BW*, 28 May and 4 June 1896, pp. 82–83, 100.
"Dumb Creatures & Christmas: A Little Sermon to Little Folk." *ChrW*, 24 Dec 1903, p. 13.
"The Duty of the Christian Ministry." *BCong*, 13 July 1911, p. 27.
"The Effectiveness of the Ministry." *BCong*, 12 Mar 1914, pp. 198–199.
"The Effectiveness of the Ministry." *LQR* 122 (July 1914): 1–20.
"The Efficiency and Sufficiency of the Bible." *Biblical Review* 2 (Jan 1917): 10–30.
"Egypt: A Sermon for Young Men." *ChrWP* 22 (1 Nov 1882): 275–278.
"The Empire for Christ." *ChrWP* 57 (16 May 1900): 303–311.
"The Evangelical Basis of Free Churchism." *ConR* 81 (May 1902): 680–695.
"The Evangelical Churches and the Higher Criticism." *ConR* 88 (Oct 1905): 574–599.
"Evangelical Experience." *Ex*, 17 Apr 1902, pp. 320–321.
"The Evangelical Principle of Authority." In Volume of Proceedings of the Second International Congregational Council Held in Tremont Temple, Boston, Mass. September 20–29, 1899, pp. 57–63. Edited by Eugene C. Webster. Boston:

Bibliography 291

Samuel Usher, 1900.
"Evangelicals and Home Reunion." *Churchman* 32 (Sept 1918): 528–536.
"The Evidential Value of Miracles." *LQR* 112 (July 1909): 1–7.
"Faith and Charity." *CongM* 5 (Jan 1892): 13–17.
"Faith and Experience." *Wesleyan Methodist Quarterly* 123 (1900): 415–417.
"Faith and Mind." *Methodist Review Quarterly* 61 (Nashville, Oct 1912): 627–643.
"The Faith of Congregationalism. 'Our Unwritten Belief as Progressive Evangelical Churches.'" With A. E. Garvie. *BCong*, 18 June 1908, p. 593.
"The Faith of Jesus." *ExpT* 21 (Oct 1909): 8–9.
"Faith, Metaphysic, and Incarnation." *Methodist Review* 97 (New York, Sept 1915): 696–719.
"Faith, Timidity, and Superstition." *EvMag* 108 (March 1900): 111–116.
"A Fancy: Concerning the Critic's Inversion of Old Testament History." Poem. *IndNon*, 27 May 1892, p. 365.
"Farewell Counsels to Students." *BW*, 14 June 1900, pp. 179–180.
"Federate on the Gospel of Grace." *ChrW*, 30 Nov 1905, p. 21.
*"A Few Hints about Reading the Bible." *Biblical Review* 3 (Oct 1918): 530–544. Japanese translation: *Seisho to Dendo*. Trans. Hichiro Tobara. Nagoya: Ichiryu-sha, 1939.
A Few Hints about Reading the Bible. Pamphlet. New York: Association Press, 1919. *Japanese translation: *Seisho to Dendo*. Trans. Hachiro Tobara. Nagoya: Ichiryu-sha, 1939.
"The First and Second Adam." *Methodist Review* 98 (New York, May 1916): 347–351.
"A First Primer of Apologetics." Review of *A Primer of Apologetics*, by Robert Mackintosh. *Ex*, 10 Jan 1901, p. 222.
"The flash of arms he sees no more" [first line]. Poem. *Ind.*[1898]. Reprinted in *Poetical Tributes to the Memory of the Rt. Hon. W. E. Gladstone*, p. 167. Eds. Samuel Jacob and Charles F. Forshaw. London: Elliot Stock, 1898.
"The Foolishness of Preaching." *ExpT* 30 (Jan 1919): 153–154.
*"Forgiveness Through Atonement the Essential of Evangelical Christianity." Abstract. In *BCong*, 2 July 1908, p. 8.
"Forgiveness Through Atonement the Essential of Evangelical Christianity." In *Proceedings of the Third International Congregational Council*, Edinburgh, 1908, pp. 28–53. Edited by J. Brown. London: Congregational Union of England and Wales, 1908.
"Freedom." Choral ode. Concert program, n.d., pp. 13–16.
"The Fund and the Faith." *BW*, 29 May 1913, p. 219.
"Gain and Godliness." In *Emmanuel Congregational Church, Cambridge: Past and Present: 1691–1895*. No publication data. And in *EvMag* 105 (1897): 482–484.
The Glorious Gospel. 1795–1945 Triple Jubilee Papers, no. 3. London: Livingstone Press, n.d. [1943].
"God as Holy Father." Abstract of "The Holy Father." *Homiletic Review* 33 (Mar 1897): 234–236.
"God send you health, and bless your wealth." Poem. Privately printed. Cheetham Hill Congregational Church, Manchester, 1 Jan 1887.
"'God Takes a Text and Preaches.'" *BW*, 14 Apr 1910, p. 36.
"The Goodness of God." *BCong*, 10 Aug 1911, p. 97.

The Grace of the Gospel as the Moral Authority in the Church. Pamphlet. London: Congregational Union of England and Wales, n.d. [1905].
The Happy Warrior: A Sermon on the Death of Mr. Gladstone, May 22nd, 1898. London: H. R. Allenson, 1898.
"The Healing of the Paralytic." Signed, "F." Poem. *BW,* 25 Oct 1894, p. 4. Reprinted in Norah Waddington, *The First Ninety Years: Clarendon Park Congregational Church, Leicester,* p. 9. No publication data.
"The Historian of Rationalism as Poet." Review of *Poems,* by W. E. H. Lecky. *IndNon,* literary supplement, 20 Nov 1891, p. 2.
"History and Judgment." *ConR* 108 (Oct 1915): 457–470.
Holy Christian Empire. London: James Clarke, n.d.
"A Holy Church the Moral Guide of Society." Excerpt in *BW,* 11 May 1905, pp. 129–131.
A Holy Church the Moral Guide of Society. Pamphlet. London, Congregational Union of England and Wales, 1905.
"Holy Father." *BW,* 19 and 26 Nov 1896, pp. 74, 94–95.
"The Holy Father." *ChrWP* 50 (7 Oct 1896): 225–229.
"The Holy Father." *ChrWP* 100 (30 Nov 1921): 254–259.
"The Home Rule Bill. Some Representative Opinions." *BCong,* 18 Apr 1912, p. 259.
"How to Help Your Minister." *ChrW,* 24 Aug 1950, p. 5.
"How to Help Your Minister." *Irish Christian Advocate* (Belfast), 8 Sept 1950), p. 1.
"How You Can Help Your Minister." *Congregational Magazine,* n.d. [c. 1900–1905], pp. 200–201.
"A Hymn to Christ." Poem. *BW,* 1 June 1899, p. 133.
"Ibsen's Treatment of Guilt." *HibJ* 14 (Oct 1915): 105–122.
"The Ideal Ministry of the Church." *ChrW,* 18 Oct 1906, p. 22.
"The Ideal Ministry." *BCong,* 18 Oct 1906, pp. 283–285.
"Immanence and Incarnation." In *The Old Faith and the New Theology,* pp. 47–61. Edited by C. H. Vine. London: Sampson Low Marston, 1907.
In Memoriam: Andrew Baden, Esq., F.I.A. (Died February 9th.). [A sermon preached at] St Thomas Square Chapel, Hackney, February 19th, 1882. For private circulation. Bradford: William Byles and Sons, 1882.
"The Inner Life of Christ." *Constructive Quarterly* 7 (Mar 1919): 149–162.
"The Insufficiency of Social Righteousness as a Moral Ideal." *HibJ* 7 (Apr 1909): 596–613.
"The Insufficiency of Social Righteousness as a Moral Ideal." *Living Age,* 26 June 1909, pp. 779–789.
"Intellectual Difficulties to Faith." *Record* (London), 22 and 29 July 1910, pp. 708–710, 744–745.
"Intellectualism and Faith." *HibJ* 11 (Jan 1913): 311–328.
"The Interest and Duty of Congregationalists in the Present Crisis. (A Symposium.)" By Forsyth and others. *BCong,* 23 Dec 1909, p. 539.
Introduction to *The Inspiration and Authority of Holy Scripture,* by John Monro Gibson, pp. vii–xviii. Christian Faith and Doctrine Series, vol. 1. London: Thomas Law, 1908. New York: Fleming H. Revell, 1912.
"Is Anything Wrong with Our Churches? A Symposium." *BCong,* 19 Jan 1911, pp. 46–48.
"Is Christianity Played Out?" Leaflet. Privately printed. Clarendon Park

Congregational Church, Leicester, Feb 1893.
"John Norris, of Bemerton." Review of *A Dissertation on John Norris, of Bemerton,* by Fred. J. Powicke. *IndNon,* 14 Dec 1893, pp. 498–499.
"Judgment unto Salvation." *Ex,* 2 Oct 1902, pp. 332–335.
"Judgment." *ChrWP* 62 (1 Oct 1902): 209.
"Land Laws of the Bible." *ConR* 104 (Oct 1913): 496–504.
"A Larger Comprehension the Remedy for the Decay of Theology." In *Public Conference on the Terms of Religious Communion,* pp. 18–24. London: Judd, n.d. [1878].
"The Late Rev. C. S. Horne – A Tribute." *BW,* 7 May 1914, p. 140. Quoted in full in W. B. Selbie, *The Life of Charles Silvester Horne* (London: Hodder & Stoughton, 1920), pp. 302–305.
"The Late Silvester Horne. Memorial Service at the City Temple. Dr. Forsyth's Address." *BCong,* 21 May 1914, pp. 420–422.
"Law and Atonement." Letter. *ChrW,* 24 Sept 1908, p. 9.
"Lay Religion." *BCong,* 29 Apr and 6 May 1909, pp. 337–338, 357–358.
"Lay Religion." *Constructive Quarterly* 3 (Dec 1915): 767–789.
Letter to Albert Peel. In *Transactions of the Congregational Historical Society* 14 (Nov 1941): 67–68.
Letter to *English Independent,* 8 Nov 1877, pp. 1231–1232. Reprinted in the Appendix to W. L. Bradley, *P. T. Forsyth: The Man and His Work,* pp. 279–284.
Letter. *BW,* 14 Oct 1897, p. 435.
Letter. *BW,* 26 Oct 1911, p. 100.
Letter. *ChrW,* 10 Sept 1908, p. 3.
Letter. *ChrW,* 26 Mar 1908, p. 11.
Letter. *CongM* 5 (Jan 1892): 2–3.
Letter. From Forsyth and others to Adolf Harnack. *BW,* 3 Sept 1914, p. 557.
"Liberal Education." Signed, "Publicola." *ManExT,* 15 Dec 1885, p. 8.
"Liberal Education." Signed, "Publicola." *ManExT,* 18 Dec 1885, p. 8.
"Liberal Imperialism." Signed, "Publicola." *ManExT,* 30 June 1886, p. 5.
"Liberty and Its Limits in the Church." *ConR* 101 (Apr 1912): 502–512.
"The Living Christ." *BW,* 22 July 1897, pp. 228–229.
"The Love of Liberty and the Love of Truth." *ConR* 93 (Feb 1908): 158–170.
"The Love of Liberty and the Love of Truth." *Living Age,* 28 Mar 1908, pp. 771–789.
"Mackintosh on the Person of Christ." Review of *The Doctrine of the Person of Jesus Christ,* by H. R. Mackintosh. In *BW,* 28 Nov 1912, pp. 281–282.
"Maid, Arise:" A Sermon to School Girls. Preached in Shipley Congregational Church, Sunday July 28, 1878. Bradford: T. Brear, n.d. [1878].
"Majesty and Mercy." *ChrWP* 79 (17 May 1911): 305–307.
"The Majesty and the Mercy of God." *BCong,* 4 May 1911, p. 367.
"The Man and the Message." *LQR* 121 (Jan 1914): 1–11.
"A Manual of Devotion, Theological and Critical." Review of *The Communion of the Christian with God,* by Willibald Herrmann. *IndNon,* 16 and 23 July 1896, pp. 36, 54.
"Marriage: Its Ethic and Religion." *BCong,* 30 Nov 1911, p. 403.
Mercy the True and Only Justice. A Sermon Preached in Shipley Congregational Church, on the Missionary Sunday, September 30, 1877. Bradford, T. Brear, n.d. [1877 or 1878].

"Message for the Times." *British Missionary*, Jan 1906.
"Message from Principal Forsyth, D.D." *CongM*, new series, 6 (July 1905): 74–75.
"Messages from the Progressive Leaders: Principal Forsyth." *BW*, 6 Jan 1910, p. 421.
"Milton's God and Milton's Satan." *ConR* 95 (Apr 1909): 450–465.
"Milton's God and Milton's Satan." *Living Age*, 29 May 1909, pp. 519–530.
"The Minister's Prayer." *BCong*, 6 June 1907, p. 561.
The Minister's Prayer. Pamphlet. London: National Council of Evangelical Free Churches, n.d.
"Miraculous Healing, Then and Now." *BCong*, 11 Mar 1909, p. 194.
"Miss Overtheway." Poem. Christian World, 20 Dec 1900, p. 14.
"Missions as the True Imperial and Apostolic Succession." *Methodist Recorder*, 8 May 1902, pp. 14–16.
"Missions the Soul of Civilisation." *ChrWP* 77 (4 May 1910): 273–277.
"Modernism: Home and Foreign." *BCong*, 14 Oct 1909, pp. 303, 323–326.
Monism. London Society for the Study of Religion. Letchworth: Garden City Press, n.d. [1909].
"Moral Manhood." *Young Man* (Cambridge), n.d. [after 1901], pp. 151–153.
"The Moralization of Religion." *LQR* 128 (Oct 1917): 161–174.
"Motherhood." *BCong*, 26 Sept 1907, pp. 255–256.
"Mr Balfour as a Theologian." Signed, "Publicola." *ManExT*, 8 Oct 1888, p. 8.
"Mr. Campbell's Book: Dr. Forsyth on the Status of the Free Churches." *ChrW*, 2 Nov 1916.
"Mr. Horton's New Book." Review of *Revelation and the Bible*, by R. F. Horton. *Ind*, 28 Oct 1892, p. 127.
"Music and Worship." *CongQ* 33 (Oct 1955): 339–344.
"Music and Worship." *Homiletic Review* 67 (Jan 1914): 18–22.
"Mystics and Saints." *ExpT* 5 (June 1894): 401–404.
"The Need for a Positive Gospel." *LQR* 101 (Jan 1904): 64–99.
"The Need for a Revival of Personal Religion." *Ex*, 26 Mar 1903, pp. 291–292.
"The Need of a Church Theory for Church Union." *ConR* 111 (Mar 1917): 357–365.
"The New Congregationalism and the New-Testament Congregationalism." *Ex*, 4 and 11 June 1903, pp. 551–552, 575–576. Also published as a pamphlet. Introduction by W. Cunliffe-Jones and J. Mullens, pp. iii–iv. Sydney [Australia]: William Brooks, 1903.
"The New Theology. I. – Immanence and Incarnation." *BCong*, 24 Jan 1907, pp. 77–78.
"The New Year." *CongM* 1 (Jan 1888): 13.
"A New Year Meditation." *EvMag* 103 (1895): 29–35.
"A New Year Message to the Churches." *Ex*, 5 Jan 1905, pp. 7–8.
"New Year's Messages. How Congregationalists Should Meet 1912." *BCong*, 4 Jan 1912, pp. 3–4.
"The Newest Theology." *BW*, 7 Mar 1907, pp. 581–582.
"Nonconformists and the Education Bill." Letter from Forsyth and 15 others. *BW*, 11 July 1901, p. 309.
"Nonconformity and Home Rule." Signed, "Publicola." *ManExT*, 28 Nov 1887, p. 6, and 2 Dec 1887, p. 6.
"'Nonconformity and Politics.'" Review of *Nonconformity and Politics*, "by a Nonconformist minister." *BCong*, 4 Feb 1909, pp. 85–86.

"Notes from Pisgah." *BW*, 3 Oct 1901, p. 551.
"Nouvelles Paroles de Foi et de Liberté." Review of *Nouvelles Paroles de Foi et de Liberté*, by Auguste Bouvier. *Modern Review* 5 (1884): 379–381.
"O sweet the song that in the deep, grey shade." Poem. *Manchester Evening Gazette*, 11 Dec 1885. Privately reprinted on a small card.
"The Obligations of Doctrinal Subscription: A Discussion. – II," pp. 273–281. In *Modern Review* 2 (Apr 1881): 252–281.
The Old Faith and the New. Leicester, Birmingham, and Leamington: Midland Educational Company; Manchester: Brook & Chrystal, n.d. [1891].
"Old Testament Theology." Review of *Old Testament Theology: The Religion of Revelation in its Pre-Christian Stage of Development*, by Hermann Schultz. *IndNon*, 9 Feb 1893, pp. 107–108.
"One Step to Reunion: Interchange of Pulpits." Letter. From Forsyth and others. *Times* (London), 30 Aug 1919, p. 6.
Ordination statement. *Shipley and Saltaire Times*, 25 Nov 1876.
"Origin of the Conception of God." Review of *Lectures on the Origin and Growth of the Conception of God, as illustrated by Anthropology and History: The Hibbert Lecture for 1891*, by Count Goblet d'Alviella. *IndNon*, 19 and 26 Aug 1892, pp. 554 and 571.
"Orthodoxy, Heterodoxy, Heresy and Freedom." *HibJ* 8 (Jan 1910): 321–329.
"Our Colleges." Letter. *Ex*, 29 June 1905, p. 620.
"Our Experience of a Triune God." *Cambridge Christian Life* 1 (June 1914): 240–246.
"Our Need of a Positive Gospel." *Ex*, 5 and 12 Nov 1903, pp. 462–463, 486–487.
"The Paradox of Christ." *LQR* 102 (June 1904): 111–138.
"The Pastoral Duty of the Preacher." *BCong*, 28 Mar 1907, pp. 297–298.
"The Peers or the People." Symposium. *ChrW*, 16 Dec 1909, p. 4.
"Pessimism." *ChrWP* 25 (16 Jan 1884): 42–44.
"The Pessimism of Mr. Thomas Hardy." *Living Age*, 23 Nov 1912, pp. 458–473.
"The Pessimism of Mr. Thomas Hardy." *LQR* 118 (Oct 1912): 193–219.
"Pfleiderer's View of St. Paul's Doctrine." Review of *Paulinism: A Contribution to the History of Primitive Christian Theology*, by Otto Pfleiderer. *Modern Review* 4 (Jan 1883): 81–96. Reprinted as a pamphlet. London: W. Speaght, n.d. [possibly 1883].
"The Place of Spiritual Experience in the Making of Theology." *ChrW*, 15 Mar 1906, p. 12.
"The Place of Spiritual Experience in the Making of Theology." *ChrWP* 69 (21 Mar 1906): 184–187.
"Plebiscite and Gospel." *ConR* 100 (July 1911): 60–76.
"A Pocket of Gold." Review of *The Way, the Truth, and the Life*, by F. A. J. [sic] Hort. *IndNon*, 8 Mar 1894, p. 187.
"A Point in Christian Ethics." *ChrW*, n.d. [c. 1895–1901], p. 11.
"The Power of the Resurrection." *Ex*, 11 Apr 1901, p. 26.
Prayer and its Importunity. Also titled "The Preacher in Prayer." Pamphlet (privately printed by the Minister's Prayer Union of the United Free Church of Scotland, 1907).
"Prayer and its Importunity." *LQR* 110 (July 1908): 1–22.
"Prayer." *BW*, 22 Feb 1900, p. 424.
"Prayer." *LQR* 124 (Oct 1915): 214–231.
"The Preacher and the Publicist." *LQR* 127 (Jan 1917): 1–18.

"Preachers and Politics." *Ex,* 6 and 13 Feb 1902, pp. 107, 129.
"Preachers and Politics." Signed, "Publicola." *ManExT,* 29 Dec 1887, p. 5.
"Preaching and Poetry." *ExpT* 1 (Sept 1890): 269–272.
"Preaching Christ and Preaching for Christ." *Ex,* 21 Dec 1905, p. 574.
"The Preaching of Jesus and the Gospel of Christ: I." *Exp,* 8th series, 9 (Apr 1915): 325–335.
"The Preaching of Jesus and the Gospel of Christ: II." *Exp,* 8th series, 9 (May 1915): 404–421.
"The Preaching of Jesus and the Gospel of Christ: III. The Mind of Christ on His Death." *Exp,* 8th series, 10 (July 1915): 66–89.
"The Preaching of Jesus and the Gospel of Christ: IV. Christ's Offering of His Soul for Sin." *Exp,* 8th series, 10 (Aug 1915): 117–138.
"The Preaching of Jesus and the Gospel of Christ: V. Moral Finality and Certainty in the Holiness of the Cross." *Exp,* 8th series, 10 (Oct 1915): 340–364.
"The Preaching of Jesus and the Gospel of Christ: VI. In What Sense Did Jesus Preach the Gospel?" *Exp,* 8th series, 10 (Nov 1915): 445–465.
"The Preaching of Jesus and the Gospel of Christ. [VII:] The Meaning of a Sinless Christ." *Exp,* 8th series, vol. 25 (Apr 1923): 288–312.
The Priesthood and Its Theological Assumptions. Free Church Tracts for the Times, no. 3. London: Thomas Law, n.d. [c. 1898–1890].
"A Prince of Critics on English Literature." Review of *Essays on English Literature,* by Edmund Scherer. *IndNon,* literary supplement, 20 Nov 1891, p. 2.
"Principal Forsyth on 'Church and State.'" *BCong,* 9 July 1914, p. 40.
"Principal Forsyth on Church and University: A Striking Address." *Aberdeen Free Press,* 24 Sept 1906, p. 11.
"Principal Forsyth on Preaching." *BW,* 31 Oct 1907, p. 83.
"The Problem of Forgiveness in the Lord's Prayer." In *The Sermon on the Mount: A Practical Exposition of the Lord's Prayer,* pp. 181–192, 193–207. By E. Griffith-Jones and 5 others. Manchester: James Robinson, 1903.
"The Public Importance of Religion." *WestGaz,* 21 Feb 1919, pp. 1–2.
The Pulpit and the Age. Manchester: Brook & Chrystal, 1885.
A Radiant Life: In Memory of Charles Silvester Horne. Privately printed pamphlet (1914).
"A Rallying Ground for the Free Churches: The Reality of Grace." *HibJ* 4 (July 1906): 824–844.
"The Reality of God: A War-time Question." *HibJ* 16 (July 1918): 608–619.
"Reconstruction and Religion." *WestGaz,* date and page numbers not known. In *Problems of Tomorrow: Social, Moral and Religious,* pp. 15–23. Edited by Fred A. Rees. London: James Clark, 1918.
"Regeneration, Creation, and Miracle." *Methodist Review Quarterly* 63 (Nashville, Oct 1914): 627–643, and 64 (Jan 1915): 89–103.
"The Relation of the Church to the Poor." *CongM* 1 (Mar 1888): 64.
"Religion and Reality." *ConR* 115 (May 1919): 548–554.
"Religion, Private and Public." *LQR* 131 (Jan 1919): 19–32.
"Religious Communism." Letter to *English Independent,* 1 Nov 1877, pp. 1202–1203. Reprinted in the Appendix to W. L. Bradley, *P. T. Forsyth: The Man and His Work,* pp. 276–279.
"The Religious Strength of Theological Reserve." *BW,* 13 Feb 1913, pp. 576–578.
"Reminiscences of the School-days of Two Distinguished F. P.'s [Former Pupils]." [Aberdeen] *Grammar School Magazine* 8 (March 1905): 48–50. With the

exception of the first sentence, reprinted as "When We Were Boys." In *Bon Record: Records and Reminiscences of Aberdeen Grammar School from the Earliest Times by many Writers,* pp. 259–261. Edited by H. F. Morland Simpson. Aberdeen, D. Wyllie & Son, 1906.

Reunion and Recognition. London: Congregational Union of England & Wales, n.d.

"The Rev. R. J. Campbell." Letter. *BW,* 6 Jan 1916, p. 284.

"Revelation and Bible." *HibJ* 10 (Oct 1911): 235–252.

"Revelation and Inspiration." *Sunday Magazine* (1902): 178. Brief excerpt from a sermon called "How to Read the Bible."

"Revelation and the Person of Christ." In *Faith and Criticism: Essays by Congregationalists,* pp. 95–144. London: Sampson Low Marston, 1893.

Revelation Old and New. Edinburgh: William Blackwood & Sons, 1911.

"Ritschl on Justification." Review of *The Christian Doctrine of Justification and Reconciliation,* vol. 3, by Albrecht Ritschl, translated by H. R. Mackintosh and A. B. Macaulay. In *Speaker* (London), 16 Feb and 9 Mar 1901, pp. 549–551, 629–631.

"The Roman Road of Rationalism. What Do the Advanced Critics Ask Us to Give Up?" *ChrW,* 26 Aug 1909, p. 6; 2 Sept, p. 3.

The Roots of a World-Commonwealth. London: Hodder & Stoughton, 1918. New York: George H. Doran Co., 1918. Reprinted. London: Independent Press, 1952.

"Sacramentalism the True Remedy for Sacerdotalism." *Exp,* 5th series, 8 (Sept, Oct 1898): 221–233, 262–275.

"Sanctity and Certainty." Letter. *Ex,* 23 July 1903, p. 86.

"The School at the End of the Century: A Symposium on the Alleged Decline in Sunday School Attendance: Some Opinions and Suggestions." *Sunday School Chronicle,* 13 Dec 1900, pp. 849–852. Forsyth's contribution, subtitled "As to the causes of decline," is on p. 850.

"The Scotch Church Case: 'How It Strikes a Contemporary.'" *Ex,* 18 Aug 1904, pp. 144–145.

"The Second Victory." *WestGaz,* n.d. [c. 1918], pp. 1–2.

"The Sects and the Public." *Ex,* 23 Mar 1905, p. 262.

"Self-Denial and Self-Committal." *Exp,* 8th series, 4 (July 1912): 32–43.

"Self-Sacrifice." Letter. *Ex,* 7 Jan 1904, p. 5.

*"Sentiment and Sentimentalism." *BCong,* 11 July 1907, pp. 22, 32.

Sermon on Matthew 23.39, quoted in full in Arthur Porritt, "Leading Churches and Preachers: VI. – Emmanuel Church, Cambridge, and Dr. P. T. Forsyth," pp. 715–719. *Puritan* 1 (1899): 713–719.

"Service in the University Chapel." In *Record of the Celebration of the Quartercentenary of the University of Aberdeen,* pp. 315–325. Edited by P. J. Anderson. Aberdeen: Aberdeen University Press, 1907.

"Shelley." *IndNon,* 5 Aug 1892, p. 523.

"The Significance of the Church Fabric." *ChrWP* 59 (26 June 1901): 415–418.

"A Simple Gospel." *BW,* 11 Oct 1900, p. 504.

"Sir Joseph Compton-Rickett's New Book." Review of *Origins and Faith,* by Sir Joseph Compton-Rickett. *BW,* 13 May 1909, p. 122.

"The Slowness of God." *ExpT* 11 (Feb 1900): 218–222.

Socialism and Christianity in Some of their Deeper Aspects. Manchester: Brook & Chrystal, 1886.

*"Sociality, Socialism and the Church." *BCong*, 28 Nov 1907, pp. 487–488; 5 Dec, pp. 509–510; 12 Dec, pp. 534–535; 19 Dec, pp. 561–562.
"Society, Church and Dissent." Signed, "Publicola." *ManExT*, 13 Dec 1886, p. 5.
"The Solitude of Christ." *EvMag* 106 (Oct 1898): 485–491.
"Some Christian Aspects of Evolution." *Living Age*, 11 Nov 1905, pp. 323–341.
"Some Christian Aspects of Evolution." *LQR* 104 (Oct 1905): 209–239.
"Some Christmas Thoughts." *BCong*, 24 Dec 1908, p. 553.
"Some Effects of the War on Belief." *Holborn Review* 9 (Jan 1918): 16–26.
"The Soul of Christ and the Cross of Christ." *LQR* 116 (Oct 1911): 193–212.
"The Spiritual Needs in the Churches." *ChrWP* 89 (3 May 1916): 251–255.
"The Spiritual Reason for Passive Resistance." *Ex*, 8 Oct 1903, p. 338.
"The Strength of Weakness." *ChrWP* 13 (6 Feb 1878): 85–87.
"A Study of Dr. Martineau." Review of *James Martineau: A Biography and Study*, by A. W. Jackson. *Ex*, 6 Dec 1900, p. 129.
"Sunday Schools and Modern Theology." *ChrWP* 31 (23 Feb 1887): 123–127.
"The Taste of Death and the Life of Grace." *ChrWP* 58 (28 Nov 1900): 296–302.
"Teachers of the Century: Robert Browning." *Modern Church*, 15 Oct 1891, pp. 451–452.
"Testamentary Ethics." *LQR* 129 (Apr 1918): 169–179.
"Theological Liberalism v. Liberal Theology." *BW*, 17 Feb 1910, pp. 557–558.
"A Theological Pathfinder: Dr. Fairbairn's New Book." Review of *Christ in Modern Theology*, by A. M. Fairbairn. *EvMag* 101 (London, May 1893): 247–256.
"Theological Reaction." *BW*, 13 May 1909, p. 150.
"Theology in the Future." *IndNon*, 10 June 1897, pp. 450–452, 454.
"Theosophy and Theology." *Ind*, 30 Oct and 6 Nov 1891, pp. 777–778 and 798.
"Things New and Old in Heresy." *Ex*, 12 July 1900, p. 399.
"Things New and Old." *ChrWP* 84 (29 Oct 1913): 273–276.
"Thos. Campbell Finlayson, D.D." Review of *Essays, Addresses, and Lyrical Translations*, by Thos. Campbell Finlayson. *IndNon*, 26 Oct 1893, p. 348. Subsequently, "A Correction" by Forsyth was published. *IndNon*, 2 Nov 1893, p. 380.
"To the Congregational Churches of England and Wales." *BW*, 27 Feb 1908, p. 556.
"Treating the Bible Like Any Other Book." *BW*, 15 Aug 1901, pp. 401–402.
"A Tribute to the Rev. Dr. John Hunter." Leaflet [1922]. Forsyth papers, Dr. Williams's Library, London.
"A Tribute." In Leslie S. Hunter, *John Hunter, D.D.: A Life*, pp. 289–291. London, Hodder and Stoughton, 1922.
"Tributes to Andrew Martin Fairbairn." *WestGaz*, 12 Feb 1912.
"Tributes to Principal Fairbairn: II." *BW*, 15 Feb 1912, pp. 568, 574.
"The Truncated Mind." Signed, "F." *Manchester Guardian*, 4 Nov 1916, p. 5.
"The Truncated Mind." Letter. *Manchester Guardian*, 16 Nov 1916, p. 7.
"The Unborn, the Once Born, the Twice Born and the First-Born." *ChrW*, 14 Feb 1918, p. 9.
"The Union and the Railway Dispute." *BCong*, 24 Oct 1907, p. 361.
"The United States – of the Church." In *A United Free Church of England*, pp. 15–47. With J. H. Shakespeare. London: National Council of Evangelical Free Churches, n.d.
"Unity and Theology. A Liberal Evangelicalism the True Catholicism." In

Towards Reunion: Being Contributions to Mutual Understanding by Church of England and Free Church Writers, pp. 51–81. By J. Scott Lidgett and 13 others. London: Macmillan, 1919.
"The Unity Beneath Reunion." *Challenge*, 15 and 22 Feb 1918.
"The Unrest in the Churches: Dr. Forsyth's Statement." *Tribune* (London), 22 Jan 1907, pp. 7–8.
"Veracity, Reality, and Regeneration." *LQR* 123 (Apr 1915): 193–216.
"The Village Churches and the War." Letter. *BW*, 29 Mar 1917, p. 496.
"The Way of Life." *Wesleyan Methodist Magazine* 120 (London, Feb 1897): 83–88.
The Weariness in Modern Life. No publication data. [possibly 1879].
"Welding the Churches: A World Congress for Christian Unity." *Daily Chronicle* (London), 19 Feb 1914, p. 6.
"Welfare and Charity." Letter. *BCong*, 24 Nov 1910, pp. 439–440.
"What Is Meant by the Blood of Christ?" *Exp*, 7th series, 6 (Sept 1908): 207–225.
"What is the Evangelical Faith?" *BCong*, 10, 17, and 24 Sept 1908, pp. 217–218, 239–240, 257–258.
"The wind from the heath." Poem.
"The Word and the World." *BW*, 10 Feb 1910, pp. 533–534.
"The Work of Christ." Abstract of five lectures given at the Mundesley Bible Conference, 1909. In *Verbatim Report of Sermons and Lectures*. London: Westminster Chapel and Morgan and Scott, [1909].

4. UNPUBLISHED MANUSCRIPTS AND LETTERS

Unless otherwise indicated in square brackets, these items are held at Dr. Williams's Library, London. NCL indicates the New College London materials at Dr. Williams's Library.

"Be ye reconciled to God." Sermon manuscript. Text: 2 Corinthians 5.20.
"A Dramatic Lyric." Poem.
"Freedom our vocation; freedom our temptation; freedom our education." Sermon manuscript. Text: Galatians 5.13. c. 6 Nov 1898.
"Glory in Cross." Sermon manuscript. Text: Galatians 6.14.
"God was in Christ reconciling." Sermon manuscript. Text: 2 Corinthians 5.19. Christmas 1896.
"The Joy that was before him." Sermon manuscript. Text: Hebrews 2.12. 2 July 1899.
"Martyrdom not come yet but threatened." Sermon manuscript. Text: Hebrews 12.4–11. Hackney College, Jan 1913.
"Prayer and its Answer: An Apologue." Poem.
"Spring." Sermon manuscript. Text: Hebrews 5.12–14.
"Thy kingdom come." Poem.
Lecture notes on Christology, 1901ff. NCL ms.
Letter to H. F. Lovell Cocks, 14 Aug 1915 [Alan Lamb, Fort Augustus].
Letter to James Shepheard, 23 July 1913. NCL ms 536/22.
Letter to M. Auchterlonie, 8 July 1904 [James Gordon, Aberdeen].
Letter to Matthew Stanley, 27 July 1908.
Letter to R. Morton Stanley, 19 June 1916.
Letter to R. Morton Stanley, 28 Apr 1916.

Letter to R. Morton Stanley, 6 Dec 1919.
Midsummer examination in apologetics, set by Forsyth, 1902. NCL ms 244/2.
Notes of addresses by Forsyth for Wednesday evening devotional services at Hackney College; valedictory address, June 1909; and ordination address, 20 Oct 1909.
Sermon manuscript. Text: 1 Corinthians 1.24. June 1909.
Sermon manuscript. Text: Genesis 3.9–10.
"'Shall I from the Christmas mart?'" Poem. Christmas 1886.

5. BOOKS ABOUT P. T. FORSYTH

Benedetto, Robert. *P. T. Forsyth Bibliography and Index*. Foreword by Donald G. Miller. Bibliographies and Indexes in Religious Studies, no. 27. Westport, Connecticut: Greenwood Press, 1993.
Bradley, W. L. *P. T. Forsyth: The Man and His Work*. London: Independent Press, 1952.
Brake, George Thompson. *Peter Taylor Forsyth: An Introduction*. Theology Starters, no. 2. Ilford, Essex: Robert Odcombe, [1990].
Brown, Robert McAfee. *P. T. Forsyth: Prophet for Today*. Philadelphia: Westminster, 1952.
Griffith, Gwilym O. *The Theology of P. T. Forsyth*. London: Lutterworth, 1948.
*Hart, Trevor, ed. *Justice the True and Only Mercy: Essays on the Life and Theology of Peter Taylor Forsyth*. Edinburgh: T&T Clark, 1995.
Hunter, A. M. *P. T. Forsyth: Per Crucem ad Lucem*. SCM Book Club, no. 217. London: SCM, 1974.
*McCurdy, Leslie. *Attributes and Atonement: The Holy Love of God in the Theology of P. T. Forsyth*. Paternoster Biblical and Theological Monographs. Carlisle, UK: Paternoster, 1998.
Miller, Donald G., Browne Barr, and Robert S. Paul, *P. T. Forsyth – The Man, The Preacher's Theologian, Prophet for the Twentieth Century: A Contemporary Assessment*. Pittsburgh Theological Monograph series, vol. 36. Pittsburgh: Pickwick Press, 1981.
Ohmiya, Hiroshi. *Fosaisu*. [The Life and Work of P. T. Forsyth. Series of Man and Thought.] Tokyo: Nippon Kirisuto Kyodan Shuppanbu, 1965.
Pitt, Clifford S. *Church, Ministry and Sacraments: A Critical Evaluation of the Thought of Peter Taylor Forsyth*. Washington, D. C.: University Press of America, 1983.
Rodgers, John H. *The Theology of P. T. Forsyth: The Cross of Christ and the Revelation of God*. London: Independent Press, 1965.

6. THESES AND DISSERTATIONS

This section includes PhD, ThD, DPhil, and MPhil theses and dissertations.

Allen, Ray Maxwell. "The Christology of P. T. Forsyth." Duke University, Durham, North Carolina, 1953.
Bosse, Walter. "Theologie und Kirche bei Peter Taylor Forsyth." Munster, 1967.
Bradley, W. L. "The Theology of P. T. Forsyth, 1848–1921." University of Edinburgh, 1949. Published as *P. T. Forsyth: The Man and His Work* (1952).
Brown, Robert McAfee. "P. T. Forsyth and the Gospel of Grace." Columbia Univer-

sity, New York, 1951. Revised and condensed as *P. T. Forsyth: Prophet for Today* (1952).
*Fleming, Deryl. "Towards a Theology of Worship from a Free Church Perspective." Wesley Theological Seminary, 1982.
Gardner, Harry M. "The Doctrine of the Person and Work of Jesus Christ in the Thought of Peter Taylor Forsyth and Emil Brunner." Boston University, 1962.
Gardom, James T. D. "The Cross in Time and the Hidden Hand of God: Theology and the Problem of Evil with Reference to the Work of Peter Forsyth and Austin Farrer." University of London, 1992.
Hsü, John Dao-Luong. "Peter Taylor Forsyth's Concept of Spirituality." Aquinas Institute of Theology, Dubuque, Iowa, 1974.
Jackson, George D. "The Biblical Basis of the Theology of P. T. Forsyth." Princeton Theological Seminary, Princeton, New Jersey, 1952.
Jones, Frank F. "The Christological Thought of Peter Taylor Forsyth and Emil Brunner: A Comparative Study." University of St. Andrew's, 1970.
McCurdy, Leslie. "Attributes and Atonement: The Holy Love of God in the Theology of P. T. Forsyth." University of Aberdeen, 1994. Published under the same title (1998).
McKay, Clifford Anderson. "The Moral Structure of Reality in the Theology of Peter Taylor Forsyth." Vanderbilt University, Nashville, Tennessee, 1970.
Mikolaski, Samuel J. "The Nature and Place of Human Response to the Work of Christ in the Objective Theories of the Atonement Advanced in Recent British Theology by R. W. Dale, James Denney and P. T. Forsyth." Oxford University, 1958.
Newman, Guy Douglas. "The Theology of P. T. Forsyth with Special Reference to his Christology." Southwestern Baptist Theological Seminary, Fort Worth, Texas, 1952.
Norwood, D. W. "The Case for Democracy in Church Government: A Study in the Reformed Tradition, with Special Reference to the Congregationalism of Robert William Dale, Peter Taylor Forsyth, Albert Peel and Nathaniel Micklem." King's College, London, 1983.
Parker, Gary Edmund. "A Comparison of the Concept of Proclamation in the Writings of Peter Taylor Forsyth and Rudolf Bultmann." Baylor University, Waco, Texas, 1984.
Pitt, Clifford S. "Church, Ministry and Sacraments: A Critical Evaluation of the Thought of Peter Taylor Forsyth." New College, London, 1977. Published under the same title (1983).
Rodgers, John H. "The Theology of P. T. Forsyth: The Cross of Christ and the Revelation of God." University of Basle, 1963. Published under the same title (1965).
Rosenthal, Klaus. "Die Stellung des Kreuzes in der Theologie von Forsyth." Heidelberg, 1956.
Rosser, William Ray. "The Cross as the Hermeneutical Norm for Scriptural Interpretation in the Thought of Peter Taylor Forsyth." Southern Baptist Theological Seminary, Louisville, Kentucky, 1990.
Simpson, A. F. "Certainty Through Faith: An Examination of the Religious Philosophy of Peter Taylor Forsyth." New College, London, 1949.
*Smith, Stephen McCray. "Dogma and History: The Creative Ferment in British Christology, 1890–1920." Claremont Graduate School, Claremont, California, 1980.

Stewart, Winthrop R. "The Biblical Foundations and Insights of P. T. Forsyth's Theology." University of Aberdeen, 1965.

Sturm, William A. "The Self-Authenticating Character of Revelation: Authority and Certitude Studied in Twentieth Century English Nonconformist Thought, with Special Reference to the Works of P. T. Forsyth, John Oman and H. Wheeler Robinson." Oxford University, 1959.

Thompson, Robert Franklin. "Peter Taylor Forsyth: A Pre-Barthian." Drew University, Madison, New Jersey, 1940.

*Vicchio, Stephen J. "The Problem of Evil with Special Reference to P. T. Forsyth, John Wisdom and Ludwig Wittgenstein." University of St. Andrew's, 1985. Published as *The Voice from the Whirlwind: The Problem of Evil and the Modern World*. Westminster, Maryland: Christian Classics, 1989.

*Wilkinson, D. A. "'We Preach Jesus Christ and Him Crucified': A Comparison and Contrast of P. T. Forsyth and James Denney's Understanding of the Atonement and How They Preached it." King's College, London, 1995.

Wilson, Reginald A. "The Problem of Religious Authority in Contemporary Theological Thought with Particular Reference to the Interpretations of John Oman, P. T. Forsyth, and A. E. J. Rawlinson." Columbia University, New York, 1960.

Wismar, Don Ray. "A Sacramental View of Preaching as Seen in the Writings of John Calvin and P. T. Forsyth and Applied to the Mid-Twentieth Century." Pacific School of Religion, Berkeley, California, 1963.

5. ARTICLES AND PAMPHLETS ABOUT FORSYTH

This section includes articles which focus specifically on P. T. Forsyth, but does not include short items of an historical nature.

Anderson, K. C. "Dr. Forsyth and Reaction." *Message Extra*, no. 1. [Bristol, c. 1905.]
    Available at Mansfield College, Oxford.

Anderson, Marvin W. "P. T. Forsyth: Prophet of the Cross." *EvQ* 47 (July-Sept 1975): 146–161.

Andrews, Jessie Forsyth. "Memoir." In *The Work of Christ*, by P. T. Forsyth, pp. vii–xxviii. London: Independent Press, 1938.

Anonymous. "Dr. Forsyth's Newest Theology." Signed, "By a Man in the Street." *Christian Commonwealth* (London), 31 Jan 1907, p. 331.

—. "Dr. Forsyth Again." Signed, "By a Man in the Street." *Christian Commonwealth*, 7 Feb 1907, p. 338.

—. "A Lost Leader: Principal Forsyth, M.A., D.D." *Christian Commonwealth*, 14 Feb 1907, p. 362.

Barr, Browne. "P. T. Forsyth: The Preachers' Theologian – A Witness and Confession." In Donald G. Miller, Browne Barr, and Robert S. Paul, *P. T. Forsyth: The Man, The Preachers' Theologian, Prophet for the Twentieth Century: A Contemporary Assessment*, pp. 31–42. Pittsburgh Theological Monograph series, vol. 36. Pittsburgh: Pickwick Press, 1981.

Barth, Markus. "P. T. Forsyth: The Theologian for the Practical Man." *CongQ* 17 (Oct 1939): 436–442.

Bergh, O., ed. "The Missiological Legacy of P. T. Forsyth." [Quotations from *Missions in State and Church.*] *Japan Christian Quarterly* 51 (Spring 1985):

69–74.
Binfield, Clyde. "Principal when Pastor: P. T. Forsyth, 1876–1901." In *The Ministry: Clerical and Lay,* pp. 397–414. Edited by W. J. Sheils and Diana Wood. Studies in Church History, vol. 26. Oxford: Basil Blackwell, 1989.
Bishop, John. "P. T. Forsyth: 'Preaching and the Modern Mind.'" *Religion in Life* 48 (Autumn 1979): 303–308.
Bradley, W. L. "Forsyth's Contributions to Pastoral Theology." *Religion in Life* 28 (Autumn 1959): 546–556.
Brown, Robert McAfee. "The 'Conversion' of P. T. Forsyth." *CongQ* 30 (July 1952): 236–244.
—. "P. T. Forsyth." In *A Handbook of Christian Theologians,* pp. 144–165. Edited by Martin E. Marty and Dean G. Peerman. Cleveland: World Publishing, 1965. Enlarged edition. Nashville: Abingdon, 1984.
Camfield, F. W. "Peter Taylor Forsyth." *Presbyter* 6, no. 2 (1948): 3–10.
Cave, Sydney. "Dr. P. T. Forsyth: The Man and His Writings." *CongQ* 26 (Apr 1948): 107–119.
Child, R. L. "P. T. Forsyth: Some Aspects of His Thought." *Baptist Times,* 20 May 1948, p. 9; 27 May, p. 7; 3 June, p. 9.
Cocks, H. F. Lovell. "The Message of P. T. Forsyth." *CongQ* 26 (July 1948): 214–221.
—. Radio program. BBC Third Program, 20 July 1948.
—. Address delivered at Commemoration. In *New College London Report for Session, 1976–1977,* pp. 8–11. Excerpt in Donald G. Miller, Browne Barr, and Robert S. Paul, *P. T. Forsyth: The Man, The Preachers' Theologian, Prophet for the Twentieth Century: A Contemporary Assessment,* pp. 71–72. Pittsburgh Theological Monograph series, vol. 36. Pittsburgh: Pickwick Press, 1981.
Connelly, William. "P. T. Forsyth and Dora Greenwell: A Brief Encounter." [Unknown British Congregational journal]: 14–16.
Craston, R. C. "The Grace of a Holy God: P. T. Forsyth and the Contemporary Church." In *Authority in the Anglican Communion: Essays Presented to Bishop John Howe,* pp. 47–64. Edited by Stephen S. Sykes. Toronto: Anglican Book Centre, 1987.
Cunliffe-Jones, H. "P. T. Forsyth: Reactionary or Prophet?" *CongQ* 27 (Oct 1950): 344–356.
Davies, D. R. "The Watch Tower." Signed, "Agro." *Record,* 1 December 1944, p. 479.
Douglas, Crerar. "The Cost of Mediation: A Study of Augustus Hopkins Strong and P. T. Forsyth." *CongQ* 3 (1978): 28–35.
Duthie, Charles S. "The Faith of P. T. Forsyth," "Fireworks in a Fog?" *BW,* 17 Dec 1964, p. 9.
Forster, John. "Dr. Forsyth on the Authority of Grace." *Holborn Review* (Apr 1907): 286–300.
Garrett, John. "Forsyth, Forsooth." In *Studies of the Church in History: Essays Honoring Robert S. Paul on His Sixty-fifth Birthday,* pp. 243–252. Edited by Horton Davies. Pittsburgh Theological Monographs, new series, vol. 5. Allison Park, Pennsylvania: Pickwick Publications, 1983.
Garvie, A. E. "Placarding the Cross. The Theology of P. T. Forsyth." *CongQ* 21 (Oct 1943): 343–352.
—. "A Cross-Centred Theology." *CongQ* 22 (1944): 324–330.

—. "P. T. Forsyth and Reunion." Letter to the Editor. *CongQ* 23 (1945): 96.
Griffith-Jones, E. "Dr. Forsyth on the Atonement." *Exp*, 7th series, 9 (1910): 307–319.
Gummer, Selwyn. "Peter Taylor Forsyth: A Contemporary Theologian." *London Quarterly and Holborn Review* 173 (Oct 1948): 349–353.
Hamilton, Kenneth. "Love or Holy Love? Nels Ferré versus P. T. Forsyth." *Canadian Journal of Theology* 8 (Oct 1962): 229–236.
Hermann, E. "Studies of Representative British Theologians: VI. – Peter Taylor Forsyth, D.D." *Homiletic Review* 66 (New York, July-Dec 1913): 178–185. Includes a portrait on p. 178.
Higginson, R. E. "The Authentic Word: A Study in Forsyth's Attitude to the Bible." *Churchman* 50 (London, June 1946): 82–86.
Hughes, Philip Edgcumbe. "Forsyth: Theologian of the Cross." *Christianity Today*, 23 Dec 1957, pp. 5–7.
Hughes, T. Hywel. "A Barthian Before Barth?" *CongQ* 12 (July 1934): 308–315.
—. "Dr. Forsyth's View of the Atonement." *CongQ* 18 (Jan 1940): 30–37.
Hunt, George L. "Interpreters of our Faith: P. T. Forsyth." *A.D.* 4 (Philadelphia, May 1975): 39–41.
Hunter, A. M. "P. T. Forsyth Neutestamentler." *ExpT* 73 (Jan 1962): 100–106.
—. "The Theology of P. T. Forsyth." In *Teaching and Preaching the New Testament*, pp. 129–187. London: SCM, 1963.
Huxtable, W. J. F. "P. T. Forsyth: 1848–1921." *Journal of the United Reformed Church History Society* 4 (Oct 1987): 72–78.
Jackson, George D. "The Interpreter at Work: XIV. P. T. Forsyth's Use of the Bible." *Interpretation* 7 (July 1953): 323–337.
Justice and Mercy: A Review of a Sermon Published by Rev. P. T. Forsyth, M.A. By a Curious Reader. Bradford: M. Field, n.d. [likely 1878].
Kellogg, Edwin H. "A Theologian for the Hour: Peter Taylor Forsyth." *Bulletin of Western Theological Seminary* 6 (Apr 1914): 204–233.
Lambert, D. W. "A Great Theologian and His Greatest Book: *The Work of Christ*." *LQR* 173 (1948): 244–247.
—. "The Missionary Message of P. T. Forsyth." *EvQ* 21 (July 1949): 203–208.
—. "The Theology of Missions: The Contribution of P. T. Forsyth." *London Quarterly and Holborn Review* 176 (Apr 1951): 114–117.
Leembruggen, W. H. "The Witness of P. T. Forsyth – A Theologian of the Cross." *Reformed Theological Review* (1945): 18–46. Also published as a pamphlet, *P. T. Forsyth: A Theologian of the Cross*. With a Foreword by John Gillies. Melbourne: S. John Bacon, n.d.
Mackintosh, R. "The Authority of the Cross." *CongQ* 21 (1943): 209–218. Annotated by Forsyth.
Meadley, Thomas D. "The 'Obscurity' of P. T. Forsyth." *CongQ* 24 (Oct 1946): 308–317.
—. "A Preacher's Theologian: P. T. Forsyth." *Preacher's and Class-leader's Magazine* 22 (Jan-Feb 1949): 149–153, 157.
—. "The Great Church, P. T. Forsyth, and Christian Unity." *London Quarterly and Holborn Review* 190 (July 1965): 225–233.
—. "The Forsyth Saga: Fifty Years On." *Methodist Recorder*, 11 Nov 1971, p. 17.
Mews, Stuart. "Neo-Orthodoxy, Liberalism and War: Karl Barth, P. T. Forsyth and John Oman 1914–1918." In *Renaissance and Renewal in Christian History,*

pp. 361–375. Edited by Derek Baker. Studies in Church History, vol. 14. Oxford: Basil Blackwell, 1977.
Mikolaski, Samuel J. "The Theology of P. T. Forsyth." *EvQ* 36 (Jan-Mar 1964): 27–41.
—. "P. T. Forsyth on the Atonement." *EvQ* 36 (Apr-June 1964): 78–91.
—. "P. T. Forsyth." In *Creative Minds in Contemporary Theology*, pp. 307–339. Edited by P. E. Hughes. Grand Rapids: Wm. B. Eerdmanns, 1966. 2nd ed., 1969.
Miller, Donald G. "P. T. Forsyth: The Man." In Donald G. Miller, Browne Barr, and Robert S. Paul, *P. T. Forsyth: The Man, The Preachers' Theologian, Prophet for the 20th Century: A Contemporary Assessment*, pp. 1–29. Pittsburgh Theological Monograph series, vol. 36. Pittsburgh: Pickwick Press, 1981.
"Ministerial Libraries: V. Principal Forsyth's Library at Hackney College." *British Monthly* 4 (May 1904): 267–270.
Mozley, J. K. "The Theology of Dr. Forsyth." *Exp*, 8th series, 23 (Feb, Mar 1922): 81–98, 161–180. Reprinted in *The Heart of the Gospel*, pp. 66–109. London: SPCK, 1925.
—. "Forsyth – The Theologian." *BW*, 21 Nov 1946, p. 110.
*Omiya, Hiroshi. "P. T. Forsyth no Shingaku-tek: Ken'i-ron." [A Theological Teaching about Authority in P. T. Forsyth.] *Shingaku* [Journal of Theology] 24 (1966): pages unknown.
*—. "P. T. Forsyth no Shokuzai-ron." [The Doctrine of Atonement of P. T. Forsyth.] *Shingaku* [Journal of Theology] 16 (1959): 26–67; and 18 (1960): 119–144.
Paul, Robert S. "P. T. Forsyth: Prophet for the 20th Century." In Donald G. Miller, Browne Barr, and Robert S. Paul, *P. T. Forsyth: The Man, The Preachers' Theologian, Prophet for the 20th Century: A Contemporary Assessment*, pp. 43–70. Pittsburgh Theological Monograph series, vol. 36. Pittsburgh: Pickwick Press, 1981.
Porritt, Arthur. "Leading Churches and Preachers: VI. – Emmanuel Church, Cambridge, and Dr. P. T. Forsyth." *Puritan* 1 (1899): 713–719.
Robinson, N. H. G. "The Importance of P. T. Forsyth." *ExpT* 64 (Dec 1952): 76–79.
Rosenthal, Klaus. "Die Bedeutung des Kreuzesgeschehens für Lehre und Bekenntnis nach Peter Taylor Forsyth." *Kerygma und Dogma Zeitschrift fur Theologische Forschung und kirchliche Lehre* 7 (Göttingen, July 1961): 237–259.
Shaw, J. M. "The Theology of P. T. Forsyth." *Theology Today* 3 (Oct 1946): 358–370.
Simpson, A. F. "P. T. Forsyth: The Prophet of Judgment." *SJTh* 4 (1951): 148–156.
Turner, John Munsey. "Theologian of Righteousness: Peter Taylor Forsyth (1848–1921)." *Methodist Sacramental Fellowship Bulletin*, no. 119 (1990): 1–14.
Waddell, H. C. "Is P. T. Forsyth Coming to His Own?" *Biblical Theology* 7 (Jan 1957): 35–39.
Warschauer, J. "'Liberty, Limited': A Rejoinder to Dr. Forsyth." *ConR* 101 (June 1912): 831–839.
Webster, Douglas. "P. T. Forsyth's Theology of Missions." *International Review of Missions* 44 (Apr 1955): 175–181.
Wiersbe, W. W. "Theologian For Pastors." *Moody Monthly*, May 1975, pp. 97–101.
Wood, Ralph C. "Christ on Parnassus: P. T. Forsyth Among the Liberals." *Literature and Theology* 2 (Mar 1988): 83–95.

Worrall, B. G. "The Authority of Grace in the Theology of P. T. Forsyth." *SJTh* 25 (Feb 1972): 58–74.
Ziegler, Robert E. "P. T. Forsyth and His Theology." *Methodist Quarterly Review* 62 (Nashville, July 1913): 455–463.

8. EXCERPTS FROM BOOKS AND ARTICLES

This section is comprised of books and articles which discuss Forsyth's life or thought within a larger work than the articles specifically devoted to him, listed in Section 7. Not included here are materials which only mention his contribution or cite his works. Page references indicate major consideration of Forsyth, but are sometimes not exhaustive.

Bloesch, Donald G. *Essentials of Evangelical Theology*, 2 vols., passim. San Francisco: Harper & Row, 1978 and 1979.
—. *Jesus Is Victor! Karl Barth's Doctrine of Salvation*, pp. 53–58. Nashville: Abingdon, 1976.
Carpenter, James. *Gore: A Study in Liberal Catholic Thought*, pp. 226–227. London: The Faith Press, 1960.
Cave, Sydney. *The Doctrine of the Person of Christ*, pp. 222–224. London: Duckworth, 1925.
Clements, Keith W. "An Indefinable Something: R. J. Campbell and the 'New Theology,'" pp. 39–41. In *Lovers of Discord: Twentieth-Century Theological Controversies in England*, pp. 19–48. London: SPCK, 1988.
*—. *What Freedom? The Persistent Challenge of Dietrich Bonhoeffer*, pp. 108–111. Bristol: Bristol Baptist College, 1990.
Corner, Mark A. "'The Umbilical Cord': A View of Man and Nature in the Light of Darwin," pp. 128–132. *Scottish Journal of Religious Studies* 4 (Autumn 1983): 121–137.
Davie, Donald. *A Gathered Church: The Literature of the English Dissenting Interest, 1700–1930*, pp. 141–143. Clark Lectures, 1976. London: Routledge & Kegan Paul, 1978.
Davies, Rupert E. *Religious Authority in an Age of Doubt*, pp. 166–183. London: Epworth Press, 1968.
Dawe, Donald. "Kenosis and the Moralizing of Dogma." In *The Form of a Servant: A Historical Analysis of the Kenotic Motif*, pp. 131–141. Philadelphia: Westminster, 1963.
Essex, E. C. "The Atonement in Post-Reformation Writers," pp. 252–256. In *The Atonement in History and in Life: A Volume of Essays*, pp. 236–263. Edited by L. W. Grensted. London: Society for Promoting Christian Knowledge, 1929.
Ferré, Nels. *The Christian Understanding of God*, pp. 116–117. New York: Harper, 1951.
The Fourth Lesson in the Daily Office, pp. 165–172. Edited by Christopher Campling. London: Darton Longman Todd, 1974. Excerpts from *The Work of Christ*.
Fuller, Peter. *Theoria: Art, and the Absence of Grace*, pp. 144–146. London: Chatto & Windus, 1988.
Garvie, Alfred E. *The Christian Certainty amid the Modern Perplexity: Essays, Constructive and Critical, towards the Solution of Some Current Theological Problems*, pp. 460–474. London: Hodder & Stoughton, 1910.

Glover, Willis B. *Evangelical Nonconformists and Higher Criticism in the Nineteenth Century,* pp. 272–282. London: Independent Press, 1954.
Gordon, James W. *Evangelical Spirituality [:From the Wesleys to John Stott],* pp. 229–254. London: SPCK, 1991.
Grant, John. W. *Free Churchmanship in England 1870–1940: With Special Reference to Congregationalism,* pp. 227–253. London: Independent Press, n.d. [pre–1957].
Greeves, Frederic. *Theology and the Cure of Souls: An Introduction to Pastoral Theology,* pp. 161–167. The Cato Lecture of 1960. London: Epworth Press, 1960.
Gunton, Colin E. *The Actuality of Atonement: A Study of Metaphor, Rationality and the Christian Tradition,* pp. 106–109. Edinburgh: T. & T. Clark, 1988.
—. *Yesterday and Today: A Study of Continuities in Christology,* pp. 169–173. London: Darton, Longman & Todd, 1983.
Hamilton, Kenneth. "Created Soul – Eternal Spirit: A Continuing Theological Thorn," pp. 27–28. *SJTh* 19 (1966): 23–34
Hanshell, Deryck. "Christian Worship: Catholic and Evangelical," pp. 266–267. *Downside Review* 90 (1972): 260–267.
Hanson, Anthony Tyrrell. *The Wrath of the Lamb,* pp. 187–188. London: SPCK, 1957.
Hardy, Daniel W. "Created and Redeemed Sociality," pp. 38–41. In *On Being the Church: Essays on the Christian Community,* pp. 21–47. Edited by Colin E. Gunton and Daniel W. Hardy. Edinburgh: T. & T. Clark, 1989.
*Hart, Trevor A. "Sinlessness and Moral Responsibility: A Problem in Christology." *SJTh* 48 (1995): 37–54.
Hendry, George S. *The Gospel of the Incarnation,* pp. 92–98. Philadelphia: Westminster, 1958.
Hick, John. *Evil and the God of Love,* pp. 246–250. London: Macmillan, 1966. Forsyth is not mentioned in the second edition of 1977.
Hinchliff, Peter. "Off with the New and On with the Old: R. J. Campbell and the New Theology," pp. 212–217. In *God and History: Aspects of British Theology 1875–1914,* pp. 198–222. Oxford: Clarendon, 1992.
Hughes, Thomas Hywel. *The Atonement: Modern Theories of the Doctrine,* pp. 38–46. London: George Allen & Unwin, 1949.
Huxtable, John. *The Bible Says,* pp. 82–87. London: SCM, 1962.
—. "National Recognition of Religion," pp. 304–310. In *CongQ* 35 (1957): 297–310.
Jenkins, Daniel. *Congregationalism: A Restatement,* pp. 48–50. London: Faber & Faber, 1954.
Johnson, Robert Clyde. *Authority in Protestant Theology,* pp. 100–107. Philadelphia: Westminster, 1959.
Jones, Edgar DeWitt. *The Royalty of the Pulpit: A Survey and Appreciation of the Lyman Beecher Lectures on Preaching [etc.],* pp. 128–134. New York: Harper & Bros., 1951. Reprinted. Freeport, N.Y.: Books for Libraries Press, 1970.
Jones, J. D. *Three Score Years and Ten,* pp. 279–282. London: The Book Club, 1940.
Jones, Peter d'A. *The Christian Socialist Revival 1877–1914: Religion, Class, and Social Concern in Late-Victorian England,* pp. 419–421. Princeton, New Jersey: Princeton University Press, 1968.
Kiek, Edward S. *The Modern Religious Situation,* pp. 151–160. Edinburgh: T. &

T. Clark, 1926.
Langford, T. A. *In Search of Foundations: English Theology 1900–1920*, pp. 170–175. Nashville: Abingdon, 1969.
*Lischer, Richard, ed. *Theories of Preaching: Selected Readings in the Homiletical Tradition*, pp. 74–79, 333–337. Durham, North Carolina: Labyrinth Press, 1987.
MacKinnon, Donald M. "Aspects of Kant's Influence on British Theology," pp. 354–358. In *Kant and His Influence*, pp. 348–366. Edited by George MacDonald Ross and Tony McWalter. Bristol: Thoemmes, 1990.
—. "Philosophy and Christology," pp. 285–287. In *Essays in Christology for Karl Barth*, pp. 269–297. Edited by T. H. L. Parker. London: Lutterworth, 1956. Reprinted as "Philosophy and Christology," pp. 70–71. In *Borderlands of Theology and Other Essays*, pp. 55–81. Edited and introduced by George W. Roberts and Donovan E. Smucker. London: Lutterworth, 1968.
Mackintosh, H. R. *The Doctrine of the Person of Jesus Christ*, pp. 465–466, 472–475. Edinburgh: T. & T. Clark, 1912.
Maxwell, Jack M. "A Conversation with Robert Paul," pp. 4–6, 8–10. In *Studies of the Church in History: Essays Honoring Robert S. Paul on His Sixty-fifth Birthday*, pp. 3–26. Edited by Horton Davies. Pittsburgh Theological Monographs, new series, vol. 5. Allison Park, Pennsylvania: Pickwick Publications, 1983.
*McClendon, James William. *Doctrine*, pp. 460–462. Systematic Theology, vol. 2. Nashville: Abingdon, 1994.
McDonald, H. D. *The Atonement of the Death of Christ: In Faith, Revelation, and History*, pp. 250–257. Grand Rapids, Michigan: Baker Book House, 1985.
—. *Theories of Revelation: An Historical Study 1860–1960*, pp. 87–89, 304–305. London: George Allen & Unwin, 1963.
Mozley, J. K. "Christology and Soteriology," pp. 182–184. In *Mysterium Christi: Christological Studies by British and German Theologians*, pp. 167–190. Edited by G. K. A. Bell and D. Adolf Deissmann. London: Longmans, Green, 1930.
—. *The Doctrine of the Atonement*, pp. 182–189. London: Gerald Duckworth, 1915.
—. *The Doctrine of the Incarnation*, pp. 93–94, 105–109. London: Geoffrey Bles, 1936.
—. *The Gospel Sacraments*, pp. 98–100. London: Hodder & Stoughton, 1933.
—. *Some Tendencies in British Theology: From the Publication of* Lux Mundi *to the Present Day*, pp. 45–46. London: SPCK, 1951.
*Packer, James I. "British Theology in the Twentieth Century," pp. 29–30, 37–39. In *Christian Faith and Modern Theology: Contemporary Evangelical Thought*, pp. 23–43. Ed. Carl F. H. Henry. New York: Channel Press, 1964.
Pattison, George. *Art, Modernity and Faith: Towards a Theology of Art*, pp. 78–99. London: Macmillan, 1991.
Paul, R. S. *The Atonement and the Sacraments*, pp. 227–240. London: Hodder & Stoughton, 1961.
Porritt, Arthur. *The Best I Remember*, pp. 128–132. London: Cassell, 1922.
Robinson, N. H. G. *Christ and Conscience*, pp. 132–143. London: James Nisbet, 1956.
Rogers, Jack B., and Donald K. McKim. *The Authority and Interpretation of the Bible: An Historical Approach*, pp. 393–398. San Francisco: Harper & Row,

1979.
Sell, Alan P. F. "Anabaptist-Congregational Relations and Current Mennonite-Reformed Dialogue," pp. 321–329. *Mennonite Quarterly Review* 61 (July 1987): 321–334. Also published in Sell, *Dissenting Thought and the Life of the Churches: Studies in an English Tradition*, pp. 578–599. San Francisco: Mellen Research University Press, 1990.
—. *Aspects of Christian Integrity*, pp. 46–47 and passim. Louisville, Kentucky: Westminster/John Knox, 1990.
—. *A Reformed, Evangelical, Catholic Theology: The Contribution of the World Alliance of Reformed Churches, 1875–1982*, pp. 33–36. Grand Rapids, Michigan: William B. Eerdmans, 1991.
—. *Theology in Turmoil: The Roots, Course and Significance of the Conservative-Liberal Debate in Modern Theology*, passim. Grand Rapids, Michigan: Baker, 1986.
Stott, John R. W. *The Cross of Christ*, pp. 129–132. Downers Grove, Illinois: InterVarsity, 1986.
Sturch, Richard. *The Word and the Christ: An Essay in Analytic Christology*, pp. 37–39, 182–184, 199–200, 254–255. Oxford: Clarendon, 1991.
Surin, K. *Theology and the Problem of Evil*, pp. 132–136. Signposts in Theology. Oxford: Basil Blackwell, 1986.
*Suzuki, Mitsutake. "Kiristo-ron josetsu" [An Introduction to Christology]. *St. Paul University Bulletin of Theology* 2 (Tokyo, 1954).
—. "Kiristo-ron no ichi-kosatsu" [A Reflection on Christology]. Shukyo-kenkyu [Religious Studies] 143 (1955).
—. "Kiristo-ron kara Kyokai-ron-e" [From Christology to Ecclesiology]. *St. Paul University Bulletin of Theology* 3 (Tokyo, 1955).
Swanton, R. "Scottish Theology and Karl Barth," pp. 23–25. In *Reformed Theological Review* (1974): 17–25.
Sykes, S. W. "Theology through History," pp. 6–11. In *The Modern Theologians: An Introduction to Christian Theology in the Twentieth Century*, vol. 2, pp. 3–29. Edited by David F. Ford. Oxford: Basil Blackwell, 1989.
Thomas, J. Heywood. "Influence on English Thought," pp. 167–171. In *The Legacy and Interpretation of Kierkegaard*, pp. 160–177. Edited by Niels Thulstrup and M. Mikulová Thulstrup. Bibliotheca Kierkegaardiana Edenda Curaaverunt, vol. 8. Copenhagen: C. A. Reitzels Boghandel, 1981.
Thompson, John. *Christ in Perspective: Christological Perspectives in the Theology of Karl Barth*, pp. 164–165 and passim. Edinburgh: Saint Andrew Press, 1978.
Turnbull, Ralph G. *A History of Preaching*, vol. 3, *From the Close of the Nineteenth Century to the Middle of the Twentieth Century*, pp. 474–477. Grand Rapids, Michigan: Baker Book House, 1974.
Tuttle, George M. *John McLeod Campbell on Christian Atonement: So Rich a Soil*, pp. 115–116. Edinburgh: Handsel, 1986.
*Wacker, Grant. "The Dilemmas of Historical Consciousness: The Case of Augustus H. Strong." In *In the Great Tradition: Essays on Pluralism, Voluntarism, and Revivalism in Honor of Winthrop S. Hudson*, ed. Joseph D Ban and Paul R. Dekar. Valley Forge, Penn.: Judson Press, 1982.
Wallace, Ronald S. *The Atoning Death of Christ*, chaps. 7–9 passim. Foundations for Faith. Edited by Peter Toon. Westchester, Illinois: Crossway Books, 1981.
Welch, Claude. *Protestant Thought in the Nineteenth Century*, vol. 2, 1870–1914,

pp. 236–238. New Haven: Yale University Press, 1985.
Wickham, E. R. *Church and People in an Industrial City,* pp. 200–209. London: Lutterworth Press, 1957.
Williams, R. R. *Authority in the Apostolic Age: With Two Essays on the Modern Problem of Authority,* pp. 119–122. London: SCM, 1950.
*Worrall, B. G. "R. J. Campbell and his New Theology," p. 347. *Theology* 81 (1978): 342–348.

9. DICTIONARY AND ENCYCLOPEDIA ARTICLES

Signed articles:
Albright, Raymond W. In *New Twentieth-Century Encyclopedia of Religious Knowledge.* 2nd ed. Ed. J. D. Douglas. Grand Rapids, Michigan: Baker Book House, 1991.
—. In *New Twentieth Century Enclopedia of Religious Knowledge.* Second edition. Ed. J. D. Douglas. Grand Rapids, Michigan: Baker Book House, 1991.
Anderson, Andrew F. In *Dictionary of Scottish Church History and Theology.* Ed. Nigel M. de S. Cameron. Edinburgh: T. & T. Clark, 1993.
Bloesch, D. G. In *Evangelical Dictionary of Theology.* Ed. Walter A. Elwell. Grand Rapids, Michigan: Baker Book House, 1984.
Bowden, John. In *Who's Who in Theology.* London: SCM, 1990.
Brown, R. In *New Dictionary of Theology.* Eds. Sinclair B. Ferguson and David F. Wright. Downers Grove, Illinois: InterVarsity, 1988.
*Childers, Jana. In *Concise Encyclopedia of Preaching.* Eds. William H. Willimon and Richard Lischer. Louisville, Kentucky: Westminster John Knox, 1995.
Hannah, W. In *New Catholic Encyclopedia.* New York: McGraw-Hill, 1967.
Huxtable, John. In *Dictionary of National Biography: Missing Persons.* Ed. C. S. Nicholls. Oxford: Oxford University Press, 1993.
Lane, Tony. In *The Lion Book of Christian Thought,* pp. 190–192. Oxford: Lion, 1992.
*McCurdy, Leslie. In *Dictionary of Historical Theology.* Ed. Trevor A. Hart. Carlisle, U. K.: Paternoster, forthcoming.
Miller, Donald G. In *Encyclopedia of the Reformed Faith.* Ed. Donald K. McKim. Louisville, Kentucky: Westminster/John Knox, 1992.
Rodgers, John H. In *Encyclopedia of Christianity.* Ed. Philip E. Hughes. Marshallton, Delaware: National Foundation for Christian Education, 1972.
Schrey, H.-H. In *Religion in Geschichte und Gegenwart: Handwörterbuch für Theologie und Religionswissenschaft.* 3rd ed. Eds. Hans Frhr. v. Campenhausen et al. Tübingen: J. C. B. Mohr (Paul Siebeck), 1958.
Sell, Alan P. F. In *Dictionary of Biblical Interpretation.* Nashville: Abingdon, forthcoming.
Toon, Peter. *Who's Who in Christian History.* Eds. J. D. Douglas and Philip W. Comfort. Wheaton, Illinois: Tyndale House, 1992.
Willmer, Haddon. In *New International Dictionary of the Christian Church.* 2nd ed. Gen. ed. J. D. Douglas. Exeter: Paternoster, 1978.

Unsigned articles:
Blackwell Encyclopedia of Modern Religious Thought. Ed. Alister E. McGrath. Oxford: Blackwell, 1993.

Chambers Biographical Dictionary (1990). 5th ed. Gen. ed. Magnus Magnusson. Edinburgh: Chambers, 1990.
Chambers Dictionary of Beliefs and Religion. Ed. Rosemary Goring. Edinburgh: Chambers, 1992.
Concise Dictionary of the Christian Tradition. Eds. J. D. Douglas, Walter A. Elwell, and Peter Toon. London: Marshall Pickering, 1989.
Concise Oxford Dictionary of the Christian Church. Ed. Elizabeth A. Livingstone. Oxford: Oxford University Press, 1977.
Corpus Dictionary of Western Churches. Ed. T. C. O'Brien. Washington, D. C.: Corpus Publications, 1970.
Dictionary of Bible and Religion. Ed. William H. Gentz. Nashville: Abingdon, 1986.
Encyclopaedia Britannica. 11th ed. Cambridge University Press, 1910. Updated in 12th ed., 1922, and 13th ed., 1926.
Encyclopedic Dictionary of Religion. Eds. Paul K. Meagher, Thomas C. O'Brien, and Consuelo Maria Ahernee. Washington, D. C.: Corpus Publications, 1979.
New Encyclopaedia Britannica. 15th ed., 1989.
New Schaff-Herzog Encyclopedia of Religious Knowledge. Ed. Samuel Macauley Jackson et al. New York: Funk & Wagnalls, 1909.
Oxford Dictionary of the Christian Church. 2nd ed. Eds. F. L. Cross and E. A. Livingstone. London: Oxford University Press, 1974.
Westminster Dictionary of Church History. Ed. Jerald C. Brauer. Philadelphia: Westminster, 1971.
Who Was Who 1916–1928. 4th ed. London: Adam & Charles Black, 1967.
Wycliffe Biographical Dictionary of the Church. Ed. Elgin Moyer. Revised and enlarged by Earle E. Cairns. Chicago: Moody, 1982.

10. REVIEWS OF PRIMARY LITERATURE

Forsyth's books are listed alphabetically. Under each title, the reviews are listed in chronological order. Titles of the review articles are only occasionally included. Items with incomplete references can be found in Jessie Forsyth Andrews' scrapbooks in Dr. Williams's Library, London.

The Atonement in Modern Religious Thought (contribution to)
*Garvie, Alfred E. In *Ex*, 23 and 30 Aug 1900, pp. 555, 578–579.
Duff, Prof. Arch. In *ChrW*, 3 Jan 1901, pp. 16, 18.

The Charter of the Church
[Denney, James.] "I Will Build My Church." *BW*, 21 May 1896, p. 65.
Russell, F. A. "For Christ and His Church." *IndNon*, 4 June 1896, p. 400.
Expository Times 7 (July 1896): 447.
Presbyterian and Reformed Review 7 (Oct 1896): 757.
Primitive Methodist Quarterly Review 18 (Oct 1896): 774–777.
In "The Problem of Christian Unity," p. 205. *LQR* 87 (Jan 1897): 205–229.

The Christian Ethic of War
TLS, 24 August 1916, p. 408.
"Cromwellian Religion." In *TLS*, 7 Sept 1916, p. 426.
Holborn Review (London, Oct 1916): 593.

LQR 126 (Oct 1916): 300.
Expository Times 28 (Nov 1916): 55–56.
Lyman, Eugene W. "Discussions of War and Christianity," pp. 469–470. In AmJTh 21 (July 1917): 467–470.
Farmer, J. H. In RExp 14 (Apr 1917): 264–265.
Ethics 27 (Chicago, 1916–1917): 399.

Christian Perfection
LQR 92 (Apr 1899): 383.
Puritan 3 (1900): 420.
Wesleyan Methodist Magazine 123 (1900): 878.

Christ on Parnassus
Art Journal, n.s. [no volume number] (1899): 128.
Church Quarterly Review 75 (Oct 1912): 226–227.
Expository Times 23 (Nov 1916): 74.
LQR 117 (Apr 1912): 362.
TLS, 5 Oct 1911, p. 371.
Robertson, A. T. In RExp 9 (Jan 1912): 130.
Wheaton, David. In Church of England Newspaper, 10 Feb 1961, p. 12.
Cope, G. In Church Quarterly Review 162 (July 1961): 387–388.
*Aberdeen Press and Journal, 4 March 1967.

The Church and the Sacraments [Lectures on]
TLS, 24 May 1917, p. 251.
LQR 128 (July 1917): 131–132.
Expository Times 28 (Aug 1917): 497–498.
Hamilton, Harold. In Journal of Theological Studies 19 (Oct 1917): 91–94.
Wilson, Charles. In Churchman 31 (1917): 632–634.
Griffith-Thomas, W. H. In Bibliotheca Sacra 74 (1917): 638–639.
Christie, Francis A. In AmJTh 22 (Jan 1918): 143–145.
Methodist Review 101 (New York, May 1918): 462–464.
McConnachie, John. "His Work was a Bell Heard Ringing in the Night." BW, 22 July 1949, p. 4.
Smith, C. Ryder. In London Quarterly and Holborn Review 173 (Oct 1948): 377.
Expository Times 60 (Dec 1948): 63.

The Church, the Gospel and Society
Preston, R. In Modern Churchman n.s., 6 (Apr 1963): 245–246.
TLS, 10 May 1963, p. 346.

Congregationalism and Reunion
TLS, 28 Nov 1952, p. 783.
Hughes, G. W. In Baptist Quarterly 15 (Jan 1953): 46–47.

The Cruciality of the Cross
Expository Times 21 (Nov 1909): 84.
Glasgow Herald, Nov 1909.
LQR 113 (Jan 1910): 145.
Child, R. L. In Baptist Quarterly 13 (Jan 1949): 44–45.
Gossip, A. J. In Expository Times 60 (Mar 1949): 149.
Smith, C. Ryder. In London Quarterly and Holborn Review 174 (1949): 92.

Smith, L. B. In *Faith and Mission* 1 (Spring 1984): 86–87.

Faith and Criticism (contribution to)
"Modern Congregational Theology," pp. 12–18. In *LQR* 81 (Oct 1893): 1–24.
Somerville, D. In *Critical Review of Theological and Philosophical Literature* 3 (Edinburgh, 1893): 418–424; see esp. pp. 420–421.
Warfield, B. B. In *Presbyterian and Reformed Review* 5 (Apr 1894): 354–356.

Faith, Freedom and the Future
TLS, 21 Mar 1912, p. 119.
Expository Times 23 (June 1912): 411–412.
Mozley, J. K. In *Journal of Theological Studies* 14 (Oct 1912): 132–133.
Whitley, W. T. In *RExp* 9 (Oct 1912): 573–574.
Church of England Newspaper, 23 Dec 1955.
Joyful News, 5 Jan 1956. Signed, "R. P."
Huxtable, John. In *BW*, 5 Jan 1956.
Towlson, Clifford W. In *Yorkshire Observer*, 14 Jan 1956.
Duthie, Charles. S. In *Expository Times* 67 (Apr 1956): 202–203.
Smith, C. Ryder. In *London Quarterly and Holborn Review* 181 (1956): 157.
Bradley, William L. In *Religion in Life* 26 (Spring 1957): 310–312.
Huxtable, John. In *CongQ* 36 (Oct 1958): 270.

God the Holy Father
Cocks, H. F. Lovell. In *CongQ* 36 (June 1958): 169–170.
Flew, R. Newton. In *London Quarterly and Holborn Review* 183 (1958): 78.
ChrW, 14 Dec 1978.
Cumbers, Frank. In *Methodist Recorder*, 18 January 1979, p. 6.

Holy Christian Empire (n.d.)
Wesleyan Methodist Magazine 125 (1902): 800.

The Holy Father and the Living Christ
Expository Times 8 (Nov 1896): 53–55.
Expository Times 9 (Apr 1898): 269–270.
LQR 90 (Apr 1898): 179.

Intercessory Services for Aid in Public Worship
IndNon, 10 Dec 1896, p. 443.

The Justification of God
TLS, 23 Nov 1916, p. 564.
Expository Times 28 (Jan 1917): 177.
Methodist Review 99 (New York, July 1917): 650–653.
Boston Transcript, 12 Sept 1917, p. 6.
New York Times, 25 Nov 1917, p. 500.
Cook, E. Albert. "The Defense of God and Other Problems." *AmJTh* 22 (Apr 1918): 303–305.
Davies, D. A. "On Re-Reading T. P. [sic] Forsyth's *Justification of God*." *BW*, 19 Oct 1939, p. 31.
LQR 173 (July 1948): 280.Gardner, J. In *Journal of Bible and Religion* 20 (Jan 1952): 44–45.
Dillistone, F. W. In *Anglican Theological Review* 35 (Jan 1953): 63–64.

*Brown, Robert McAfee. In *Union Seminary Quarterly Review* 6, no. 4, p. 47.

Marriage: Its Ethic and Religion
Expository Times 24 (Nov 1912): 79.
Eager, George B. In *RExp* 10 (Jan 1913): 146–147.
Helm, Mary. In *Methodist Quarterly Review* 62 (Nashville, July 1913): 609.
Greene, William Brenton, Jr. In *Princeton Theological Review* 11 (1913): 546–548.
Strange, E. H. In *Ethics* 24 (1913–1914): 115.

Missions in State and Church
Denney, James. In *BW*, 15 Oct 1908, p. 50.
Expository Times 20 (Nov 1908): 86.
WestGaz, 23 Jan 1909, p. 6.
Primitive Methodist Quarterly Review 51 (Jan 1909): 166–167.
LQR 111 (Apr 1909): 355–356.
Church Quarterly Review 70 (Apr 1910): 208.

The Old Faith and the New
"The Cross and the Kingdom." *IndNon*, 2 Oct 1891, p. 682.
CongM 4 (Dec 1891): 320–324.

The Person and Place of Jesus Christ
Mackintosh, H. R. In *BW*, 21 Oct 1909, pp. 57–58.
Glasgow Herald, Nov 1909.
Expository Times 21 (Apr 1910): 320.
Exley, C. A. "The Person and Place of Christ." *AmJTh* 14 (Apr 1910): 313.
Boutwood, Arthur. In *HibJ* 8 (May 1910): 686–690.
New York Times: Saturday Review of Books 15 (16 July 1910): 400.
Ind 69 (28 July 1910): 197.
Eager, George B. In *RExp* 7 (July 1910): 435–436.
Lamar, A. J. *Methodist Quarterly Review* (Nashville, July 1910): 618–621.
Nation 91 (US, 20 Oct 1910): 367.
Hodge, C. W. In *Princeton Theological Review* 8 (Oct 1910): 688–693.
Hodge, Charles W. In *Bibliotheca Sacra* 67 (1910): 363–364.
Mozley, J. K. "The Person and Place of Jesus Christ." *Journal of Theological Studies* 12 (Jan 1911): 298–300.
Mozley, J. K. In *Theology* 42 (Apr 1941): 229–235.
Lawton, J. S. "Salute to Forsyth." *Guardian*, 18 July 1947, p. 318.
Stewart, R. W. "Old Soldiers Never Die." *Expository Times* 58 (Aug 1947), p. 289.
Lambert, D. W. In *London Quarterly and Holborn Review* 173 (1948): 246.
Cocks, H. F. Lovell. "Books on the Person of Christ: P. T. Forsyth's *The Person and Place of Jesus Christ*." *Expository Times* 64 (Apr 1953): 195–198.

Positive Preaching and [the] Modern Mind
Denney, James. "Principal Forsyth on Preaching." In *BW*, 24 Oct 1907, pp. 57–58.
TLS, 19 Dec 1907: 387.
Expository Times 19 (Dec 1907): 98–99.
Davison, W. T. "The Changeless Gospel and the Modern Mind," pp. 11–17. In *LQR* 109 (Jan 1908): 1–20.
Outlook 88 (7 Mar 1908): 560.
Nation 86 (26 Mar 1908): 284.

New York Times: Saturday Review of Books 13 (9 May 1908): 267.
Methodist Review 90 (New York, May 1908): 491–492.
Biblical World 31 (May 1908): 400.
Saturday Review 106 (4 July 1908): 24, 400.
Ind 65 (20 Aug 1908): 436.
Bibliotheca Sacra 65 (1908): 596–597.
Smith, Gerald Birney. In "The Modern-Positive Movement in Theology." *AmJTh* 13 (Jan 1909): 92–99.
Erdman, Charles P. "Practical Theology." *Princeton Theological Review* 7 (1909): 519–521.
Public Opinion (May 1949): 333.
Barnes, I. J. In *Baptist Quarterly* 13 (Oct 1949): 190–191.
Harris, S. B. In *Presbyter* 7 (1949): 27–28.
Fallows, W. G. In *Modern Churchman* 40 (June 1950): 166–167.
Coggan, F. D. In *Expository Times* 72 (Aug 1961): 324–326.
Aho, G. In *Springfielder* 30 (1966): 67–69.
Rossow, F. C. In *Concordia Journal* 7 (Nov 1981): 260–261.
Ind (U. S.), no date.

The Principle of Authority
"Theology and the Church." *Expository Times* 24 (Feb 1913): 213.
LQR 119 (Apr 1913): 340–341.
Grover, Delo C. In *Methodist Quarterly Review* (Nashville, July 1913): 587–588.
Mullins, E. Y. In *RExp* 10 (Oct 1913): 584–587.
Whateley, A. R. In *HibJ* 12 (July 1914): 936–941.
Johnson, George. In *Princeton Theological Review* 12 (1914): 125–127.
Cunliffe-Jones, Hubert. In *London Quarterly and Holborn Review* 172 (Oct 1947): 316.
Argyle, A. W. In *Baptist Quarterly* 14 (Oct 1952): 378–379.
Stewart, R. W. "Unrusted Claymore." In *Expository Times* 63 (Aug 1952): 329–330.
Cocks, H. F. Lovell. In *CongQ* 31 (Jan 1953): 75–76.

Religion in Recent Art
Scotsman, 11 Feb 1889.
ManExT, 16 Feb 1889, p. 5.
Liverpool *Daily Post*, 28 Feb 1889.
Bradford Observer, 1 Mar 1889.
BW, 9 Mar 1889.
Manchester Guardian, 14 Aug 1889.
Art Journal (London, 1889): 128.
Spectator 62 (1889): 639.
LQR 97 (Jan 1902): 201.
New York Times: Saturday Review of Books, 7 June 1902, p. 379.
Nation 74 (US, 1902): 472.
Outlook 72 (1902): 463–464.
ChrW, n.d.

Rome, Reform and Reaction
Bennett, J. H. In *BW*, 11 Jan 1900, p. 306.
Banks, J. S. In *LQR* 93 (Apr 1900): 352–355.

Socialism, the Church and the Poor
LQR 110 (July 1908): 171.
Garvie, Alfred E. In *Review of Theology and Philosophy* 4 (Edinburgh, 1908–1909): 421–422.

The Soul of Prayer
LQR 127 (Jan 1917): 130–131.

The Taste of Death and the Life of Grace
Expository Times 12 (June 1901): 367.

Theology in Church and State
"The Charter of the Church." *TLS*, 30 Dec 1915, p. 495.
Springfield Republican, 5 Mar 1916, p. 15.
Expository Times 27 (Mar 1916): 276–277.
Kellogg, Edwin H. In *Biblical World* 47 (May 1916): 341–342.
Boston Transcript, 17 June 1916, p. 6.
New York Times: Saturday Review of Books, 6 Aug 1916, p. 312.
Methodist Review 98 (New York, Sept 1916): 816–818.
Starratt, Frank Aubrey. "Dogma and Theology." *AmJTh* 20 (Oct 1916): 615–616.
DuBose, H. M. In *Methodist Quarterly Review* 65 (Nashville, Oct 1916): 782–785.
Hodge, C. W. In *Princeton Theological Review* 14 (1916): 674–676.
Murray, R. H. In *Quarterly Review of Literature* 266 (Princeton, 1944): 205.

This Life and the Next
LQR 130 (Apr 1918): 121.
American Library Association Booklist 14 (18 July 1918): 313.
Van Dyke, Tertius. In *Boston Transcript*, 24 Aug 1918, p. 3.
*Keith, Khodadad E. In *Churchman* 32 (Sept 1918): 575.
Springfield Republican, 27 Aug 1918, p. 6.
Van Dyke, Tertius. In *Bookman* 47 (Aug 1918): 653.
Methodist Review 101 (New York, Sept 1918): 807–810.
TLS 17 (Sept 1918): 175.
Griffith-Thomas, W. H. In *Bibliotheca Sacra* 75 (1918): 604–607.
Griffith-Thomas, W. H. In *Biblical World* 53 (1919): 204.
Lawton, J. S. "Salute to Forsyth." *Guardian*, 18 July 1947, p. 318.
Stewart, R. W. "Old Soldiers Never Die." *Expository Times* 58 (Aug 1947): 289.
Child, R. L. In *Baptist Quarterly* 13 (Jan 1949): 44–45.

Towards Reunion (1919)
Holborn Review 11 (Jan 1920): 1–12

The Work of Christ
Denney, James. *BW*, 10 Nov 1910.
Expository Times 22 (Nov 1910): 84.
Carver, W. O. In *RExp* 8 (Jan 1911): 122–123.
LQR 115 (Jan 1911): 151.
London Quarterly and Holborn Review 164 (1939): 111.
Stewart, R. W. *Expository Times* 59 (Jan 1948): 92.
Smith, C. Ryder. In *London Quarterly and Holborn Review* 173 (July 1948): 185.

11. REVIEWS OF SECONDARY LITERATURE

Reviews are arranged chronologically for each title.

Anderson, Marvin W., *The Gospel and Authority: A P. T. Forsyth Reader.*
Pfatteicher, P. H. In *Lutheran Quarterly* 24 (May 1972): 210–212.
Galloway, Allan. In *Expository Times* 84 (Nov 1972): 57–58.
Choice 9 (1972): 660.

Benedetto, Robert, *P. T. Forsyth Bibliography and Index.*
*Steece, Arvel M. In *Church History* 63 (1994): 511–512.
*Heiser, W. Charles. In Theology Digest 41 (Summer 1994): 156.
*McCurdy, Leslie C. In *EvQ* 68 (Jan 1996): 83–84.

Bradley, W. L., *P. T. Forsyth: The Man and His Work.*
Lofthouse, W. F. "A Great Theologian." *Church Quarterly Review* 153, no. 309 (London, Oct 1952): 516–520.
Jenkins, Daniel. "Forsyth and Our Time." *Christian Century*, 3 Dec 1952, p. 1409.
Cave, S. In *CongQ* 31 (Jan 1953): 73–74.
Hough, Lynn Harold. In *Religion in Life* 22 (Summer 1953): 469–470.
Gamble, C. In *Interpretation* 8 (Oct 1954): 490–491.

Brown, Robert McAfee, *P. T. Forsyth: Prophet for Today.*
Kirkus 20 (15 Sept 1952): 633.
Lawson, O. G. In *Library Journal* 77 (15 Oct 1952): 1804.
Jenkins, Daniel. "Forsyth and Our Time." *Christian Century*, 3 Dec 1952, p. 1409.
Saturday Review 36 (21 Feb 1953): 58. [By K. D. M.]
Hough, Lynn Harold. In *Religion in Life* 22 (Summer 1953): 469–470.
Shaw, J. M. In *Theology Today* 10 (Oct 1953): 429–431.
Cully, K. B. In *Interpretation* 8 (Jan 1954): 99–100.
Bromiley, G. W. In *SJTh* 9 (Dec 1956): 447.

Escott, Harry., *P. T. Forsyth: Director of Souls.*
Gossip, A. J. In *Expository Times* 60 (Mar 1949): 149.
Church, Leslie F. In *London Quarterly and Holborn Review* 174 (1949): 2–4.

Griffith, Gwilym O., *The Theology of P. T. Forsyth.*
Cocks, H. F. Lovell. "P. T. Forsyth, 'A Voice from a Better Future.'" *BW*, 6 May 1948, p. 7.
LQR 173 (July 1948): 280
Thomas, John Newton. In *Theology Today* 7 (July 1950): 268–269.

Hart, Trevor, ed., *Justice the True and Only Mercy: Essays on the Life and Theology of Peter Taylor Forsyth*
Chapman, Mark D. In *Modern Believing* 36 (Oct 1995): 57–58.
Logan, Alastair H. B. In *ExpT* 107 (Jan 1996): 115–116.
Turner, John Munsey. In *Epworth Review* 23 (Jan 1996): 123–124.
Heslam, Peter Somers. In *Theology* 99 (Jan-Feb 1996): 66–67.
Gordon, James. In *EvQ* 69 (1997): 181–183.

Hunter, A. M., *P. T. Forsyth: Per Crucem ad Lucem*.
Worrall, B. G. In *Theology* 77 (Oct 1974): 544–545.
Gillespie, Neal C. In *Church History* 44 (June 1975): 274–275.
Scott, Geoffrey D. In *Perkins School of Theology Journal* 29 (Winter 1976): 45–46.
McClain, Frank M. In *Anglican Theological Review* 59 (July 1977): 349–350.

A. M. Hunter, *Teaching and Preaching the New Testament*.
Cunliffe-Jones, H. In *SJTh* 16 (1963): 435–438.

Mikolaski, Samuel J., *The Creative Theology of P. T. Forsyth*.
Robinson, William Childs. "A Movable Feast." *Christianity Today*, 1 Aug 1969, p. 16.
Bos, W. H. In *Reformed Review* 23 (Fall 1969): 29–30.
McKay, C. A., Jr. In *Journal of the American Academy of Religion* 38 (Sept 1970): 342–343.
Harman, A. M. In *Westminster Theological Journal* 33 (Nov 1970): 111–112.
Wood, A. Skevington. In *EvQ* 42 (Oct 1970): 247–248.

Miller, Donald G., Browne Barr, and Robert S. Paul, *P. T. Forsyth: The Man, the Preacher's Theologian, Prophet for the Twentieth Century: A Contemporary Assessment*.
Ford, D. W. C. In *Expository Times* 94 (Mar 1983): 184.

Rodgers, John H., *The Theology of P. T. Forsyth*.
Daane, James. "Apostle of Grace." *Christianity Today*, 24 Sept 1965, pp. 20–21.
Woodyard, D. O. In *Christian Century*, 6 Oct 1965, pp. 1230–1231.
Baker, J. P. In *Churchman* 80 (Mar 1966): 49–50.
Aldwinckle, R. F. In *Canadian Journal of Theology* 12 (Apr 1966): 141–142.
Greeves, Frederic. In *London Quarterly and Holborn Review* 191 (Apr 1966): 164–165.
Coggan, Donald. In *Expository Times* 77 (June 1966): 268–269. [signed, Donald Ebor]
Roberts, J. D. In *Journal of Religious Thought* 23 (1966–1967): 187–188.
Robinson, N. H. G. In *Journal of Theological Studies*, n.s., 18 (Apr 1967): 288–289.

Vicchio, Stephen J. *The Voice from the Whirlwind: The Problem of Evil and the Modern World*.
*Tripole, Martin R. In *Theological Studies* 51 (Dec 1990): 763–764.
*Bube, Richard H. In *Perspectives on Science and Christian Faith* 43 (June 1991): 133–134.
*Johnson, Timothy G. M. In *CTNS Bulletin* 13 (Summer 1993): 26–27.

12. ITEMS OF HISTORICAL INTEREST

While the bibliography as a whole intends to present a comprehensive picture of the theological writings by and about Forsyth, this section is an eclectic selection of shorter items of mainly historical interest: news reports, accounts of unpublished sermons, interviews, obituaries, reminiscences, etc.

Bibliography 319

They are listed in chronological order of their connection with Forsyth's life.

Records of the Arts Class, 1864–68, University of Aberdeen, pp. 66–67. Edited by W. S. Bruce. Aberdeen: Central Press, 1912.
Record of the Arts Class, 1865–69, University of Aberdeen, pp. 25–26. Edited by James B. Duncan and William Smith. Aberdeen: Milne and Hutchison, 1913.
Wicks, Sidney F. "He Loved the Children in Cheetham Hill." *Manchester City News*, 23 Sept 1949.
*"Ministers and the Sunday Question." *ManExT*, 23 Jan 1888, p. 7.
"Manchester Free Library Lectures: Rev. P. T. Forsyth on Popular Religious Literature." *ManExT*, 26 Jan 1888, p. 6.
Waddington, Norah. "The Rev. P. T. Forsyth 1888–1894," and "Appendix I." In *The First Ninety Years: Clarendon Park Congregational Church, Leicester*, pp. 4–9, 55–56. No publication data, [c. 1976].
"First Impressions: Dr. P. T. Forsyth at Cambridge." Signed, "A Country Cousin." *ChrW*, 15 Dec 1898.
Manning, B. L. *This Latter House: The Life of Emmanuel Congregational Church, Cambridge, from 1874–1924*, pp. 10–13. Cambridge: W. Heffer & Sons, 1924.
"Dr. P. T. Forsyth on 'The Supreme Evidence of God's Love.'" *Ex*, 20 Dec 1900, p. 167.
[Stoddart, Jane]. "Dr. P. T. Forsyth, of Cambridge: A Special Biography." Signed, "Lorna." *BW*, 7 Mar 1901, pp. 530–531.
"Cambridge Character Sketches: The Rev. Dr. P. T. Forsyth." *Cambridge Graphic*, 23 Mar 1901, pp. 1, 4.
"How to Read the Bible." *Ex*, 21 Nov 1901, p. 647.
[Stoddart, Jane]. "Principal Forsyth's Impressions of America." Signed, "L[orna]." *BW*, 27 April 1907, p. 59.
"The Modern Ministry: Its Duties and Perils." Interview. Signed, "E. C." *BCong*, 30 Dec 1909, pp. 559–560.
Sell, Alan P. F. "Theology for All: The Contribution of H. F. Lovell Cocks," pp. 304–305. In *Commemorations: Studies in Christian Thought and History*, pp. 303–340. Calgary: University of Calgary Press, 1993.
"Roosevelt of Modern Theology." Editorial. *Literary Digest* 47 (23 Aug 1913), p. 289. And in "Principal Forsyth: The Roosevelt of Modern Theology." *BW*, 4 Sept 1913, p. 549. These articles are largely composed of quotations from Ziegler's article – see Section 7.
*"The Future of the Ministry: A Talk with Dr. Forsyth." *ChrW*, 23 Aug 1917, p. 4.
"Death of Principal Forsyth, an Original Thinker." *Times* (London), 12 Nov 1921, p. 14.
Report of Forsyth's funeral. *Times* (London), 16 Nov 1921, p. 13.
Nicoll, W. R. "Principal Forsyth: A Memoir." *BW*, 17 Nov 1921, pp. 145–146.
Mozley, J. K. "A Personal Tribute." *BW*, 17 Nov 1921, p. 146.
D[arlow], T. H. "A Cedar Has Fallen." *BW*, 17 Nov 1921, p. 146.
Jowett, J. H. "Dr. P. T. Forsyth." *BW*, 17 Nov 1921, p. 146.
Glegg, A. J. Tribute to Forsyth. *ChrW*, 17 Nov 1921, p. 4.
"Dr. Forsyth." *Australian Christian Commonwealth* (Adelaide), 18 Nov 1921, p. 1.
Ruhu, H. Vincent. Letter. *BW*, 24 Nov 1921.
Cave, Sydney. "Dr. P. T. Forsyth: His Influence in Congregationalism." *ChrW*, 24 Nov 1921.

Aberdeen Grammar School Magazine 25 (Nov 1921): 25–26.
Bruce, [W. S.] "Leading Minds in Modern Times: Principal Forsyth." *Aberdeen Daily Journal*, 2 Dec 1921.
Correspondence on Forsyth's style. Manchester *Guardian*, 12 and 13 Dec 1921.
Cave, Sydney. "Dr. Forsyth: 'A Student Tribute.'" Letter. *ChrW*, no date, Dec 1921.
Rowe, Gilbert T. "The Passing of Peter Taylor Forsyth." *Methodist Quarterly Review* 71 (Jan 1922): 104–106.
Scullard, H. H. "Principal Forsyth." *LQR* 137 (Jan 1922): 104–106.
Peake, A. S. "Peter Taylor Forsyth." *Holborn Review* (Jan 1922). Reprinted in *Recollections and Appreciations*, pp. 192–195. Edited by W. F. Howard. London: Epworth Press, 1938.
Hackney College: The Addresses delivered at the Unveiling of the Tablet, May 11th, 1922, erected in the College Library, to the memory of Rev. Peter Taylor Forsyth. Addresses by James Carmichael, Alex Glegg, T. Yates, R. Macleod, and R. J. Campbell.
Aberdeen University Review 9 (March 1922): 186.
A[ndrews], H. T. Obituary. *Congregational Year Book 1922*, pp. 104–105.
Thomas, H. Arnold. "Preachers I Have Known," p. 60. *CongQ* (Jan 1923): 51–62.
B[inns], J. B. "Peter Taylor Forsyth." *New College London: Report for Session 1945–1946*, pp. 14–18. London: Independent Press, 1946.
Green, Alan. "Personal Memories of P. T. Forsyth." *BW*, 13 May 1948, p. 11.
McMurray Adams, R. H. "Postman's Son Who Became Church Leader." Aberdeen *Press and Journal*, 21 May 1948, p. 11.
*Church, Leslie F. "Editorial Comments: Principal P. T. Forsyth." *London Quarterly and Holborn Review* 174 (1949): 2–4.

13. UNPUBLISHED MANUSCRIPTS

Binfield, Clyde. "In Celebration of Peter Taylor Forsyth 1848–1921, Minister of Emmanuel Church, Cambridge, 1894–1901." Sermon preached at Emmanuel Church, Cambridge, 15 November 1981.
"Dr. Peter Taylor Forsyth." Coward Trust ms 16, pp. 142–145, including p. 142a. Dr. Williams's Library, London.
Garvie, Alfred E. "Placarding Jesus Christ the Crucified: The Theology of the Late Dr. Peter Taylor Forsyth." Essay (97 pages). New College London (NCL) ms 537/1, in Dr. Williams's Library, London.
McKim, Donald K. "The Authority of Scripture in P. T. Forsyth." Pittsburgh, 1973.
Mozley, J. K. Letter to Forsyth, 20 January 1909. NCL ms 536/22.
Price, Charles P. "Notes for Lectures on P. T. Forsyth." Virginia Seminary, Alexandria, 1960–1963.

14. GENERAL BIBLIOGRAPHY

Baillie, D. M. *God Was in Christ: An Essay on Incarnation and Atonement.* London: Faber & Faber, 1948.
Baillie, John. *The Interpretation of Religion: An Introductory Study of Theological Principles.* Edinburgh: T. & T. Clark, 1929.

Bibliography

Baker, J. P. "Love of God." In *New Dictionary of Theology*. Edited by Sinclair B. Ferguson and David F. Wright. Downers Grove, Illinois: Inter-Varsity Press, 1988.
Balthasar, Hans Urs von. *Mysterium Paschale: The Mystery of Easter*. Translated by Aiden Nichols, O.P. Edinburgh: T. & T. Clark, 1990.
Barth, Karl. *Church Dogmatics*. Vol. 2: *The Doctrine of God*, first half-volume. Edited by G. W. Bromiley and T. F. Torrance. Edinburgh: T. & T. Clark, 1957.
—. *Church Dogmatics*. Vol. 4: *The Doctrine of Reconciliation*, first half-volume. Edited by G. W. Bromiley and T. F. Torrance. Edinburgh: T. & T. Clark, 1956.
—. "An Introductory Report." In Alexander J. McKelway, *The Systematic Theology of Paul Tillich: A Review and Analysis*. Richmond, Virginia: John Knox, 1964.
Barth, Karl and Emil Brunner. *Natural Theology*. Translated by Peter Fraenkel. London: Geoffrey Bles, The Centenary Press, 1946.
Bavinck, Hermann. *The Doctrine of God*. Translated and edited by William Hendriksen. Edinburgh: Banner of Truth Trust, 1977.
Berkhof, Hendrikus. *Christian Faith: An Introduction to the Study of the Faith*. Translated by Sierd Woudstra. Grand Rapids, Michigan: William B. Eerdmans, 1979.
—. Personal letter, 23 February 1992.
—. *Two Hundred Years of Theology: Report of a Personal Journey*. Translated by John Vriend. Grand Rapids, Michigan: Wm. B. Eerdmans, 1989.
Berkhof, Louis. *Systematic Theology*. London: Banner of Truth Trust, 1958.
Berkouwer, G. C. *General Revelation*. Studies in Dogmatics. Grand Rapids, Michigan: Wm. B. Eerdmans, 1955.
—. *The Work of Christ*. Studies in Dogmatics. Grand Rapids, Michigan: Wm. B. Eerdmans, 1965.
Bertrand, Ernest. *Une Nouvelle Conception de la Redemption: La Doctrine de la Justification et de la Réconciliation dans le Système Théologique de Ritschl*. Paris: Librairie Fischbacher, 1891.
Bloesch, Donald G. *Essentials of Evangelical Theology*. Vol. 1: *God, Authority, and Salvation*. San Francisco: Harper & Row, 1978.
—. *Freedom for Obedience: Evangelical Ethics in Contemporary Times*. San Francisco: Harper & Row, 1987.
—. *The Crisis of Piety: Essays toward a Theology of the Christian Life*. 2nd ed. Colorado Springs: Helmers & Howard, 1988.
—. *A Theology of Word and Spirit*. Christian Foundations, vol. 1. Carlisle: Paternoster, 1992.
—. *God the Almighty: Power, Wisdom, Holiness, Love*. Christian Foundations, vol. 3. Downers Grove, Illinois: InterVarsity Press, 1995.
Braaten, Carl E. "Revelation, History, and Faith in Martin Kähler." In Martin Kähler, *The So-Called Historical Jesus and the Historic, Biblical Christ*, pp. 1–38. Philadelphia: Fortress, 1964.
Brown, William Adams. *Christian Theology in Outline*. Edinburgh: T. & T. Clark, 1907.
Brunner, Emil. "Emil Brunner on his Faith and Work." Interview by Vernon Sproxton, 8 February 1961. In *Listener*, 16 February 1961, pp. 307–308.
—. *The Christian Doctrine of God*. Translated by Olive Wyon. Dogmatics, vol. 1. Lutterworth Library, vol. 35. London: Lutterworth, 1949.

—. *The Christian Doctrine of Creation and Redemption.* Translated by Olive Wyon. Dogmatics, vol. 2. Lutterworth Library, vol. 39. London: Lutterworth, 1952.
—. *The Mediator: A Study of the Central Doctrine of the Christian Faith.* Translated by Olive Wyon. Lutterworth Library, vol. 3. London: Lutterworth, 1934.
Butler, Joseph. *The Analogy of Religion.* Everyman's Library. Edited by Ernest Rhys. London: J. M. Dent & Sons, 1906.
Calvin, John. *Institutes of the Christian Religion.* 2 vols. Edited by John T. McNeill. Translated by Ford Lewis Battles. Library of Christian Classics. General editors: John Baillie, John T. McNeill, and Henry P. Van Dusen. Philadelphia: Westminster, 1960.
Campbell, John McLeod. *The Nature of the Atonement and its Relation to Remission of Sins and Eternal Life.* 4th ed. London: Macmillan, 1873.
Campbell, R. J. "The Foundation of the Christian Doctrine of God." *Christian Commonwealth,* 29 August 1907, pp. 845–846.
—. *A Spiritual Pilgrimage.* London: Williams and Norgate, 1916.
Cave, Sydney. *The Doctrine of the Work of Christ.* London Theological Library. Edited by Eric S. Waterhouse. London: University of London Press, 1937.
Clarke, William Newton. *The Christian Doctrine of God.* International Theological Library. Edited by Charles A. Briggs and Stewart D. F. Salmond. Edinburgh: T. & T. Clark, 1909.
Clayton, John Powell. *The Concept of Correlation: Paul Tillich and the Possibility of a Mediating Theology.* Theologische Bibliothek Töpelmann, Bd. 37. Berlin: Walter de Gruyter, 1980.
Clements, Keith W. *Lovers of Discord: Twentieth-Century Theological Controversies in England.* London, SPCK, 1988.
Cocks, H. F. Lovell. *The Wondrous Cross.* London: Independent Press, 1957.
Coleridge, Samuel Taylor. *Aids to Reflection.* Vol. 1. Edited by Henry Nelson Coleridge. London: William Pickering, 1848.
—. *Confessions of an Inquiring Spirit, and Some Miscellaneous Pieces.* Edited by Henry Nelson Coleridge. London: William Pickering, 1849.
CongM [Manchester], April 1901.
Cook, Harold E. *Shaker Music: A Manifestation of American Folk Culture.* Lewisburg: Bucknell University Press, 1973.
Dale, A. W. W. *The Life of R. W. Dale of Birmingham.* 2nd ed. London: Hodder & Stoughton, 1899.
Dale, R. W. *The Atonement.* The Congregational Lecture for 1875. 12th ed. London: Congregational Union of England and Wales, 1890.
—. "Dr. Dale at Home Again: Sermon on the Meaning of Grace." In *Ind,* 23 Sept 1892, p. 633.
—. *The Old Evangelicalism and the New.* London: Hodder & Stoughton, 1889.
Denney, James. *The Death of Christ.* London: Hodder & Stoughton, 1902.
—. *The Christian Doctrine of Reconciliation.* London: Hodder & Stoughton, 1917.
Darlow, T. H. *William Robertson Nicoll: Life and Letters.* London: Hodder & Stoughton, 1925.
Dickie, John. *Fifty Years of British Theology.* Edinburgh: T. & T. Clark, 1937.

Bibliography 323

Dorner, I. A. *A System of Christian Doctrine.* Translated by Alfred Cave and J. S. Banks. Clark's Theological Library. 4 vols. Edinburgh: T. & T. Clark, 1880–1882.
—. *System of Christian Ethics.* Edited by A. Dorner. Translated by C. M. Mead and R. T. Cunningham. Edinburgh: T. & T. Clark, 1880–1887.
Engen, J. Van. "Natural Theology." In *Evangelical Dictionary of Theology.* Edited by Walter A. Elwell. Grand Rapids, Michigan: Baker, 1984.
Fairbairn, A. M. *The Place of Christ in Modern Theology.* London: Hodder & Stoughton, 1893.
Farmer, Herbert H. *The World and God: A Study of Prayer, Providence and Miracle in Christian Experience.* London: Nisbet, 1935.
—. *The Healing Cross: Further Studies in the Christian Interpretation of Life.* London: Nisbet, 1938.
—. *Towards Belief in God.* Part 1. London: Student Christian Movement, 1942.
—. *God and Men.* London: Nisbet, 1948.
—. *The Word of Reconciliation.* Digswell Place, Welwyn, Herts: James Nisbet, 1966.
Farrar, F. W. In *The Atonement in Modern Religious Thought: A Theological Symposium,* pp. 31–57. London: James Clarke, 1900.
Ferré, Nels F. S. *The Christian Understanding of God.* London: SCM, 1951.
—. *Searchlights on Contemporary Theology.* New York: Harper & Brothers, 1961.
Flewelling, R. T. "Personalism." In *Encyclopedia of Religion and Ethics.* Edited by James Hastings. Edinburgh: T. & T. Clark, 1917.
Flint, Robert. *Agnosticism.* Edinburgh: William Blackwood & Son, 1903.
Franks, Robert S. *The Work of Christ: A Historical Study of Christian Doctrine.* London: Thomas Nelson & Sons, 1962; orig. pub. 1918.
Garvie, A. E. "Alfred Ernest Garvie," in *Die Religionswissenschaft der Gegenwart in Selbstdarstellungen,* pp. 63–113. Edited by Erich Stange. Leipzig: Felix Meiner, 1928.
—. *The Christian Doctrine of the Godhead, or The Apostolic Benediction as the Christian Creed.* London: Hodder & Stoughton, [1925].
—. "Fifty Years' Retrospect." In *CongQ* 7 (Jan 1929): 18–25.
—. "Glorying in the Cross." In *If I Had Only One Sermon to Preach,* pp. 55–68. Edited by James Marchant. London: Cassell, 1928.
Goodwin, Thomas. *Works.* Nichol's Series of Standard Divines: Puritan Period. Edinburgh, 1861–1866.
Grenz, Stanley J. and Roger E. Olson. *Twentieth Century Theology: God and the World in a Transitional Age.* [Carlisle]: Paternoster Press, 1992.
Häring, Theodore. *The Christian Faith: A System of Dogmatics.* Translated from the second revised and enlarged German edition, 1912, by John Dickie and George Ferries. London: Hodder & Stoughton, 1915.
Hart, Trevor. "A Capacity for Ambiguity?: The Barth-Brunner Debate Revisited." In *Tyndale Bulletin* 44 (Nov 1993): 289–305.
—. *The Teaching Father: An Introduction to the Theology of Thomas Erskine of Linlathen.* Devotional Library. Edited by James B. Torrance and Michael Jinkins. Edinburgh: Saint Andrew Press, 1993.
Hebblethwaite, Brian. "Butler on Conscience and Virtue." In *Joseph Butler's Moral and Religious Thought: Tercentenary Essays,* pp. 197–207. Edited by Christopher Cunliffe. Oxford: Clarendon, 1992.

Heron, Alasdair I. C. *A Century of Protestant Theology*. Cambridge: Lutterworth, 1980.
Herrmann, Wilhelm. *The Communion of the Christian with God: Described on the Basis of Luther's Statements*. 2nd English ed. Translated by J. Sandys Stanyon. Revised by R. W. Stewart. London: Williams & Norgate, 1906.
Hodge, Charles. *Systematic Theology*. Vol. 1. London: Thomas Nelson & Sons, 1871.
Holmes, Richard. *Coleridge: Early Visions*. London: Hodder & Stoughton, 1989.
—. Personal letter, 5 January 1992.
Hughes, H. Maldwyn. *The Christian Idea of God*. London: Duckworth, 1936.
Iremonger, F. A. *William Temple, Archbishop of Canterbury: His Life and Letters*. London: Oxford University Press, 1948.
Jewett, Paul K. *God, Creation, and Revelation: A Neo-Evangelical Theology*. Grand Rapids, Michigan: William B. Eerdmans, 1991.
Johnson, Mark D. *The Dissolution of Dissent, 1850–1918*. Modern European History: A Garland Series of Outstanding Dissertations. General editor: William H. McNeill. New York: Garland Publishing, 1987.
Jones, R. Tudor. *Congregationalism in England 1662–1962*. London: Independent Press, 1962.
Kaftan, *Dogmatik*. Freiburg: J. C. B. Mohr, 1897.
Kaftan, Julius. *The Truth of the Christian Religion*. 2 vols. Translated by George Ferries. Edinburgh: T. & T. Clark, 1894; orig. pub. in German, 1888.
Kähler, Martin. *Die Wissenschaft der christlichen Lehre von dem evangelischen Grundartikel aus im Abrisse dargestellt*. Neukirchen: Neukirchener, 1966. First German ed. 1883.
Kaiser, Christopher B. *The Doctrine of God: An Historical Survey*. Foundations for Faith. General Editor: Peter Toon. London: Marshall Morgan & Scott, 1982.
Kant, Immanuel. *Religion within the Limits of Reason Alone*. Translated by Theodore M. Greene and Hoyt H. Hudson. Harper Torchbooks. New York: Harper & Brothers, 1960.
Langford, Thomas A. *In Search of Foundations: English Theology 1900–1920*. Nashville: Abingdon, 1969.
Leitch, James W. *A Theology of Transition: H. R. Mackintosh as an Approach to Barth*. London: Nisbet, 1952.
Lidgett, J. Scott. *The Fatherhood of God: In Christian Truth and Life*. Edinburgh: T. & T. Clark, 1902.
Mackintosh, H. R. "Christ and God." In *ExpT* 31 (Nov 1919): 74–78.
—. *The Christian Apprehension of God*. London: Student Christian Movement, 1929.
—. *The Doctrine of the Person of Jesus Christ*. International Theological Library. Edinburgh: T. & T. Clark, 1912.
—. "Recent Thought on the Atonement." In *RExp* 12 (1915): 348–359.
—. *Some Aspects of Christian Belief*. London: Hodder & Stoughton, [1923].
—. *Types of Modern Theology: Schleiermacher to Barth*. London: Nisbet, 1937.
Mackintosh, Robert. "The Fact of the Atonement." In *ExpT* 14 (May 1903): 344–350.
Martineau, James. *Essays, Reviews, and Addresses*. Vol. 2: *Ecclesiastical: Historical*. London: Longmans, Green, 1891.
Maurice, F. D. *The Doctrine of Sacrifice Deduced from the Scriptures: A Series of Sermons*. New edition. London: Macmillan, 1879.

Mays, James Luther. *Hosea: A Commentary*. Old Testament Library. London: SCM, 1969.
McConnachie, John. Foreword to F. W. Camfield, *Revelation and the Holy Spirit: An Essay in Barthian Theology*. London: Elliot Stock, 1933.
McDonald, H. D. *The Atonement of the Death of Christ: In Faith, Revelation, and History*. Grand Rapids, Michigan: Baker Book House, 1985.
McFague, Sallie. *Models of God: Theology for an Ecological, Nuclear Age*. London: SCM, 1987.
McGrath, Alister. *Bridge-Building: Effective Christian Apologetics*. Leicester: Inter-Varsity, 1992.
McIntyre, John. *On the Love of God*. London: Collins, 1962.
—. *The Shape of Soteriology: Studies in the Doctrine of the Death of Christ*. Edinburgh: T. & T. Clark, 1992.
Melanchthon, Philip. *Loci Communes Theologici* (1521). In *Melanchthon and Bucer*, pp. 1–152. Edited by Wilhelm Pauck. Library of Christian Classics, vol. 19. London, SCM Press, 1969.
Migliore, Daniel L. *The Power of God*. Library of Living Faith, vol. 8. General editor: John M. Mulder. Philadelphia: Westminster, 1983.
Moberly, R. C. "The Incarnation as the Basis of Dogma." In *Lux Mundi: A Series of Studies in the Religion of the Incarnation*, pp. 217–272. Edited by Charles Gore. London: John Murray, 1890.
Moberly, W. H. "The Atonement." In *Foundations: A Statement of Christian Belief in Terms of Modern Thought*, pp. 265–335. London: Macmillan, 1912.
Moffatt, James. *Love in the New Testament*. London: Hodder & Stoughton, 1929.
Moltmann, Jürgen. *The Trinity and the Kingdom of God: The Doctrine of God*. Translated by Margaret Kohl. London: SCM, 1981.
Mozley, J. K. "Christology and Soteriology." In *Mysterium Christi: Christological Studies by British and German Theologians*, pp. 167–190. Edited by G. K. A. Bell and D. Adolf Deissmann. London: Longmans, Green, 1930.
—. *The Doctrine of God*. London: SPCK, 1928.
—. *The Doctrine of the Atonement*. London: Gerald Duckworth, 1915.
—. *Some Tendencies in British Theology: From the Publication of "Lux Mundi" to the Present Day*. London: SPCK, 1951.
Neill, Stephen. *Christian Holiness*. The Carnahan Lectures for 1958. London: Lutterworth, 1960.
Nicholls, William. *Systematic and Philosophical Theology*. The Pelican Guide to Modern Theology, vol. 1. Edited by R. P. C. Hanson. Harmondsworth, Middlesex: Penguin Books, 1969.
Nitzsch, C. I. *System of Christian Doctrine*. Translated by R. Montgomery and J. Hennen from the German ed. of 1844. Edinburgh: T. & T. Clark, 1849.
Nygren, Anders. *Agape and Eros*. Translated by Philip S. Watson. London: SPCK, 1957.
—. "Emil Brunner's Doctrine of God." In *The Theology of Emil Brunner, pp. 177–186. Edited by Charles W. Kegley. The Library of Living Theology, vol. 3. Edited by Charles W. Kegley and Robert W. Bretall. New York: Macmillan, 1962*.
Oden, Thomas C. *The Living God*. Systematic Theology, vol. 1. San Francisco: Harper & Row, 1987.

Orr, James. *The Ritschlian Theology and the Evangelical Faith.* 3rd ed. London: Hodder & Stoughton, 1905; orig. pub. 1897.
—. *The Progress of Dogma.* London: Hodder & Stoughton, 1901.
—. *The Virgin Birth of Christ.* London: Hodder & Stoughton, 1907.
Otto, Rudolf. *The Idea of the Holy: An Inquiry into the Non-rational Factor in the Idea of the Divine and its Relation to the Rational.* Translated by John W. Harvey. London: Oxford University Press, 1923.
Packer, James I. "God" In *New Dictionary of Theology.* Edited by Sinclair B. Ferguson and David F. Wright. Downers Grove, Illinois: Inter-Varsity, 1988.
—. *Knowing God.* London: Hodder & Stoughton, 1973.
—. "Theism for Our Time." In *God Who is Rich in Mercy: Essays Presented to D. B. Knox,* pp. 1–23. Edited by P. T. O'Brien and D. G. Peterson. Homebush West, Australia: Lancer Books, 1986.
Pfleiderer, Otto. *The Development of Theology in Germany since Kant and its Progress in Great Britain since 1825.* Translated by J. Frederick Smith. 2nd ed. London: Swan Sonnenschein, 1893.
Pope, William Burt. *Compendium of Christian Theology: Being Analytical Outlines of a Course of Theological Study, Biblical, Dogmatic, Historical.* Vol. 1, 2nd ed. London: Wesleyan Conference Office, 1880.
Prenter, Regin. *Creation and Redemption.* Translated by Theodor I. Jensen. Philadelphia: Fortress, 1967.
Ramm, Bernard L. *The Evangelical Heritage.* Waco, Texas: Word Books, 1973.
Ramsey, Arthur Michael. *F. D. Maurice and the Conflicts of Modern Theology.* The Maurice Lectures, 1948. Cambridge: University Press, 1951.
Redman, Robert R., Jr. "H. R. Mackintosh's Contribution to Christology and Soteriology in the Twentieth Century." In *SJTh* 41 (1988): 517–534.
Relton, H. Maurice. *Studies in Christian Doctrine.* London: Macmillan, 1960.
Ritschl, Albrecht. *The Christian Doctrine of Justification and Reconciliation.* Vol. 3: *The Positive Development of the Doctrine.* Translated by H. R. Mackintosh and A. B. MacAuley. Edinburgh: T. & T. Clark, 1900.
—. "Instruction in the Christian Religion." In *Three Essays,* pp. 219–291. Translated and edited by Philip Hefner. Philadelphia: Fortress Press, 1972.
Sanders, Charles R. *Coleridge and the Broad Church Movement.* New York: Octagon Books, 1972; 1st ed., 1942.
Sartorius, Ernest. *The Doctrine of Divine Love; or, Outlines of the Moral Theology of the Evangelical Church.* Translated by Sophia Taylor. Clark's Foreign Theological Library, n.s. vol. 18. Edinburgh: T. & T. Clark, 1884.
Schleiermacher, Friedrich. *The Christian Faith.* Edited by H. R. Mackintosh and J. S. Stewart. Edinburgh: T. & T. Clark, n.d. [1928].
Sell, Alan P. F. *God Our Father.* Doctrine and Devotion, vol. 1. Edinburgh: Saint Andrew Press, 1980.
—. "The Heart of the Christian Gospel." In *Indian Journal of Theology* 28 (January 1979): 15–32.
—. *The Philosophy of Religion 1875–1980.* London: Croom Helm, 1988.
Senior, Walter. *God's "Ten Words": A Course of Lectures on the Decalogue.* London: Richard D. Dickenson, 1880.
Shaw, D. W. D. *Who is God?* SCM Centrebooks. London: SCM, 1968.
Shaw, John Mackintosh. *Christian Doctrine: A One-Volume Outline of Christian Belief.* Toronto: Ryerson, 1953.

Smail, Thomas A. *The Giving Gift: The Holy Spirit in Person*. London: Hodder & Stoughton, 1988.
Stevens, George Barker. *The Christian Doctrine of Salvation*. International Theological Library. Edited by Charles A. Briggs and Stewart D. F. Salmond. Edinburgh: T. & T. Clark, 1905.
Stott, John R. W. *The Cross of Christ*. Leicester: Inter-Varsity, 1986.
—. In David L. Edwards and John Stott, *Essentials: A Liberal-Evangelical Dialogue*. London: Hodder & Stoughton, 1988.
Temple, William. *Christus Veritas: An Essay*. London: Macmillan, 1925.
Thomasius, Gottfried. *Christi Person und Werk: Darstellung der evangelischlutherischen Dogmatik vom Mittelpunkte der Christologie aus*. 2nd ed. Erlangen: Verlag von Andreas Diechert, 1888.
Thompson, John. *Christ in Perspective: Christological Perspectives in the Theology of Karl Barth*. Edinburgh: Saint Andrew Press, 1978.
Tillich, Paul. *Systematic Theology*. 3 vols. Digswell Place, Welwyn, Herts.: James Nisbet, 1953–1964.
Torrance, T. F. "H. R. Mackintosh: Theologian of the Cross." *Scottish Bulletin of Evangelical Theology* 5 (1987): 160–173.
—. "Predestination in Christ." In *EvQ* 13 (1941): 108–141.
—. "A Sermon on the Trinity." In *Biblical Theology* 6 (Belfast, 1956): 40–44.
Troeltsch, Ernst. *The Christian Faith*. Translated by Garrett E. Paul. Edited by Gertrud von le Fort. Fortress Texts in Modern Theology. Minneapolis: Fortress, 1991.
Tuttle, George M. *So Rich a Soil: John McLeod Campbell on Christian Atonement*. Edinburgh: Handsel Press, 1986.
Vidler, Alec R. *Twentieth-Century Defenders of the Faith*. London: SCM, 1965.
—. *The Theology of F. D. Maurice*. London: SCM, 1948.
Wallace, Ronald S. *The Atoning Death of Christ*. Foundations for Faith. Edited by Peter Toon. Westchester, Illinois: Crossway Books, 1981.
Welch, Claude. *The Trinity in Contemporary Theology*. London: SCM, 1953.
—. *Protestant Thought in the Nineteenth Century*. Vol. 2, 1870–1914. New Haven: Yale University Press, 1985.
Widdicombe, David. Thesis in preparation for Oxford University.
Williams, Daniel Day. *The Spirit and the Forms of Love*. Welwyn, Herts: James Nisbet, 1968.
Worrall, B. G. *The Making of the Modern Church: Christianity in England since 1800*. London: SPCK, 1988.